DATE DUE			

THE
COHERENCE
THEORY
OF TRUTH

Nicholas Rescher

UNIVERSITY
PRESS OF
AMERICA

Library of Congress Catalog Card Number: 81-43904

FOR DOROTHY
who helped to make it possible

PREFACE

THE task of this book is ambitious. It seeks to transform a defunct and discredited philosophical theory into a significant instrument of epistemology. Its purpose is to articulate a coherence theory of truth at once faithful to the historical spirit of British idealism and adequate to present-day standards of philosophical rigour in all matters relating to logic and the theory of knowledge. The central task is to develop a workable formal theory of coherence, free from the objections which have traditionally been advanced against the earlier versions of the theory. A viable coherence theory that is exact and *formalized* is the prime objective. Unfortunately, the idealistic coherence theorists themselves have generally eschewed formalization—and for this paid the price of imprecision and obscurity. Even A. C. Ewing, that most acute and sympathetic of critical expositors of idealism, has endorsed this approach: 'The coherence theory provides a wider and, I think, sounder view of logic than one which restricts this subject to inferences capable of being put in definite symbolic form.'[1] Just this attitude to formalization has forced the coherence theory into a mould where the latter-day generation of philosophers accustomed to higher demands of exactness and precision have been disinclined to accord this theory that respectful hearing which is its due.

I was myself trained in philosophy in the hey-day of logical positivism in America during the period immediately after World War II. None of my teachers manifested the slightest interest in idealism or sympathy for it—with one important exception. A few sessions of a graduate seminar on recent philosophy given by Walter Terence Stace at Princeton were devoted to the first chapters of Bradley's *Appearance and Reality*. At the time my convictions led me to feel that Bradley was headed in altogether the wrong direction, that he was badly misguided and terribly wrong about fundamental issues. But none the less, Stace's discussions did manage to impress on me the idea that Bradley was an important philosopher, a determined exponent of a tendency of thought which, however wrong it might seem to me, was nevertheless significant.

The purpose of this examination of the coherence theory is not exegetical. It does not seek to present the coherence theory in the

[1] *Idealism: A Critical Survey* (London, 1934), p. 249.

particular form that this or that author has given it. Rather, its objective is to *construct* a coherence theory of truth that is at every major point within the spirit of the historical enterprise, however much it might depart from the letter of this or that philosopher's declarations. The book endeavours to transform a miscellaneous collection of dark hints regarding the workings of coherence into a formal theory. The theory itself is what concerns us, not some particular author's generally imperfect formulation of it. Consequently, it need cause no dismay to have it pointed out that the coherence theory presented here departs in this or that detail from its treatment by some eminent coherence theorist.

The coherence theory of truth derives its substantial philosophical significance from two sources. In part it is of interest in its own right, thanks to its prominent role in the history of philosophy as one of the few major theories of truth—along with the correspondence theory of truth, the intuitionistic theory of truth, and the pragmatic theory of truth. But as my thoughts on the subject developed, I became convinced that the major source of philosophical value of the coherence theory derives from the variety and fertility of its applications in many areas, ranging from the methodology of the use of historical sources to the analysis of counterfactual conditionals. Above all, the coherence theory of truth provides the framework for an alternative approach to problems of inductive logic that is capable of resolving various fundamental difficulties (such as the problem of probabilistic acceptance rules) encountered on the orthodox Carnapian approach. Indeed, my own path into the territory of the coherence theory came from the side of its applications. The starting-point was the theory of inference from inconsistent premisses constructed for the analysis of counterfactual conditionals as presented in my book on *Hypothetical Reasoning* (Amsterdam, 1964).

In writing this work I have profited from the help of several of my colleagues and students. In particular Ruth (Mrs. David) Manor deserves prime mention. Serving as my research assistant during the latter part of 1969, she helped me to work out the considerations of Chapters IV and V, parts of which were included in a paper we wrote in collaboration ('On Inference From Inconsistent Premisses', *Theory and Decision*, vol. 1 (1970)). Mr. Zane Parks read all of the book and enabled me to profit from his comments and criticisms. Professors Myles Brand and Alex Michalos and Messrs. Arnold vander Nat, Joseph Buijs, and Igal Kvart also read parts of the work and made some useful suggestions for improvement. During the fall of 1970, I presented this material in some lectures for graduate students at the University of Western Ontario and the ensuing discussions were helpful in sharpening the exposition of certain ideas. Finally, I should like also to thank Miss Kathy Walsh for patiently and competently producing the final typescript through a sequence of revisions, and Mr. Brian Baker for his help in checking the proofs.

CONTENTS

I

THE CRITERIOLOGY OF TRUTH

1. *Definitional versus Criterial Theories of Truth*

PHILOSOPHICAL theories of truth in general deal exclusively with the truth of statements or propositions—or, derivatively, such complexes thereof as accounts, narrations, and stories. Other uses of 'true' in ordinary language (such as its adjectival use in contexts like 'a true friend' or 'a true line' or 'a true artist') are beside the point of concern. The basic aim is to clarify the meaning and application of expressions of the form '*P* is true' or 'it is true that *P*', with *P* representing a statement or proposition.

There are two basic alternatives for explicating propositional truth. One is the *definitional* route: the attempt to provide a definition of the conception 'is true' as a characteristic of propositions. The second is the *criterial* route: the attempt to specify the test-conditions for determining whether or not there is warrant for applying the characterization 'is true' to given propositions. A cogent discussion of a given theory of truth becomes possible only after one becomes clear as to which of these questions the theory is designed to answer. Is its aim to explain the *meaning* of truth, and so to give a *definition* of this concept? Or is its aim to present conditions for the appropriate *application* of the concept, and so to give a *criterion* of truth?[1]

The two issues are obviously different, as some examples suffice to show. By means of litmus paper we can determine whether or not a certain liquid is an acid, but the litmus paper test does not tell us what it *means* to be an acid. Intelligence tests can be used to determine if a person is highly intelligent, but the *meaning* of 'highly intelligent' has little to do with the test responses. To have a criterion for determining the presence or absence of some factor (be it acidity, intelligence, or truth) is one thing, and to have a definition or specification of meaning is another. The situation is analogous to that of other, more familiar cases. The chemist's definition of gold as the metallic

[1] 'Der Begriff der Wahrheit bestimmt deren Wesen, und dieses ist vom einzelnen Kennzeichen (Kriterium) der Wahrheit (wahrer Urteile) wohl zu unterscheiden.' Eisler's *Handwörterbuch der Philosophie* (2nd edn., Berlin, 1922), s.v. *Wahrheit*.

element of such-and-such atomic weight and structure does not in general help in determining whether a certain nugget is or is not gold. The assayer's procedures for testing—with reference to such factors as, for example, solubility in *aqua regia*—provide criteria for such a determination, but do not furnish a definition.

This distinction between definition and test-criterion, established in and familiar from other contexts, is also operative with respect to truth. The criterial approach to truth is decision-oriented: its aim is not to specify in the abstract what 'is true' *means*, but rather to put us into a position to implement and apply the concept by instructing us as to the circumstances under which there is rational warrant to characterize or class something (i.e. some proposition) as true.

Why bother with a criterion once a definition is at hand? The answer is implicit in the preceding examples. To know the meaning of a word or concept is only half the battle: we want to be able to *apply* it too. The courtier knows perfectly well what 'pleasing to the king' *means*; what he strives to know is where it applies. Whenever the meaning-specification of a concept-word is ineffectual for determining its rules of application, the criterial problem remains an important issue—perhaps even for the issue of 'meaning' itself, though in a broader sense. It does us little good to know how terms like 'speed limit' or 'misdemeanour' are defined in the abstract if we are left in the dark as to the conditions of their application.

This line of thought applies to 'is true' as well. Rudolf Carnap has put the matter with characteristic clarity:

> We must not expect the definition of truth to furnish a criterion of confirmation [of propositions as truths] such as is sought in epistemological analyses. On the basis of this [i.e. Tarski's] definition, the question regarding the criterion of truth can be given only a trivial answer, which consists in the statement itself. Thus from the [Tarskian] definition of truth we can conclude only, e.g.: The statement 'Snow is white' is true if and only if snow is white. This conclusion is surely correct. . . . But the question of the criterion of confirmation is thereby left unanswered.[2]

Thus even if a certain conception of truth does not qualify as a definition, and so does not answer the question of meaning, there remains the significant task of examining its prospects from the criterial angle of approach.

An astonishing variety of writers have in fact seen the relationship of the correspondence and coherence theories of truth in

---

[2] 'Truth and Confirmation' in H. Feigl and W. Sellars (eds.), *Readings in Philosophical Analysis* (New York, 1949), p. 120.

just this light: correspondence for a definition, coherence as fundamentally criterial. Arthur Pap, for example, writes:

> It is quite conceivable that the coherence theory is a description of how the truth or falsehood of statements comes to be known rather than an analysis of the meaning of 'true'. . . . One might agree that a given statement is accepted as true in virtue of standing in certain logical relations to other statements; still it would not follow that in calling it true one *means* to ascribe to it those relations.[3]

Pap in fact endorses A. Tarski's semantic theory of truth as explicating the *meaning* of this concept, but opts, at any rate in the case of empirical hypotheses and laws, for what he terms 'coherence' or 'reciprocal confirmation' as the *test* of truth.[4] Again, A. N. Whitehead distinguishes between propositional statements of fact and judgmental endorsements of propositions. At the former, ontological level, correspondence to fact is the governing conception; at the latter, epistemological level, the coherence criterion reigns supreme: 'We shall say that a proposition can be *true* or *false*, and that a judgment can be *correct*, or *incorrect*, or *suspended*. With this distinction we see that there is a "correspondence" theory of the truth and falsehood of propositions, and a "coherence" theory of the correctness, incorrectness and suspension of judgments.'[5] Thus philosophers of very diverse positions have joined together in the view that the correspondence theory of truth should be thought of as essentially definitional, the coherence theory as essentially criterial.

And yet if we do take a criterial perspective upon truth, a critic might object: 'You are not really grappling with the core issue of *what it is to be true* but with the merely peripheral question of what *is thought or taken to be true*.' To this we reply: Our concern is *not* simply with the factual question of what 'is thought or taken' to be true, but with the logico-epistemological question what is *reasonably and warrantedly* to be so thought or taken.[6]

3 A. Pap, *Elements of Analytic Philosophy* (New York, 1949), p. 356.
4 Ibid., pp. 361–2.
5 *Process and Reality* (London, 1929), p. 291. In a similar vein, E. W. Hall in *Our Knowledge of Fact and Value* (Chapel Hill, N.C., 1961) combines a *correspondence theory of truth* with a *coherence theory of verification*. It should be noted, however, that none of these latter-day advocates of a coherence criterion at the epistemological level espouses a conception of coherence that is continuous with that of the idealistic pioneers. Indeed for the most part they seem to envisage merely a somewhat shadowy *mutual support* along deductive or probabilistic lines, without offering any explicitly articulated theory whatsoever as to the nature of the 'coherence' at issue.
6 This *normative* aspect of the matter serves to set the *epistemological* question of truth-criteria entirely apart from the *psychological* question of the conditions of the acceptance of propositions by a certain person or group. The epistemological issues of *adequate* warrant are perfectly interpersonal and objective: they are not subjective

In this area the themes of definition and criteria draw close to one another. With some things there is virtually no difference at all (What is a chair? What is reasonably to be thought to be a chair?); with others a gap does open up (What is an insoluble problem? What is reasonably to be regarded as an insoluble problem?). The criterial question can be important in its own right, and can even be a significant aspect of the question of 'meaning' in a sense broader than the strictly definitional.

One further important distinction must be recognized: the difference between a *guaranteeing* criterion and an *authorizing* criterion. The issue is posed by the question: 'What is the relationship between *passing-the-criterion-for-being-an-X* and *actually-being-an-X*?' When criterion-satisfaction *logically precludes* the failure of feature-possession—when the criterion is *absolutely decisive* for the feature—then we have a guaranteeing criterion. (Among plane figures, triangularity, for example, provides a guaranteeing criterion for trilaterality.) On the other hand, if criterion-satisfaction at best provides a *rational warrant* for the claim of feature-possession—without giving a logically air-tight guarantee—then we have an authorizing criterion. Satisfaction of an authorizing criterion provides a *presumptive* assurance of feature-possession, and constitutes a reasonable basis for claiming the feature: but it is not tantamount to giving a logically binding set of necessary and sufficient conditions.[7] Now a *guaranteeing* criterion is certainly very closely linked to the issue of definition; indeed it might be viewed as simply an aspect of the question of definition in its larger sense. With an *authorizing* criterion, however, we leave the logico-semantical issues of definition sufficiently far to enter a distinct, genuinely criterial realm, a realm where definitional considerations blend with substantially epistemic ones.

and psychological but objective and methodological. This point would seem almost too obvious for special emphasis did not one recent philosopher of the first rank insist upon classing *all* criterial theories of truth as subjective. (See K. R. Popper, *Conjectures and Refutations* [London, 1963], p. 225.) On our view, the epistemic criterion of acceptability-qualifications poses no question of a route to truth through 'a special kind of mental state, or as a disposition, or as a special kind of belief'. A criterial approach to *acceptability* need make no reference to any psychological convictions or other such subjective conditions of *acceptance* (any more than the test of calculations by 'casting out nines' hinges on questions of the psychological mechanisms for making calculations).

[7] Philosophers who have discussed the question of truth-criteria have generally tended to concern themselves with criteria of the guaranteeing type alone. Here the following passage affords but one example among many: 'This distinction between the *nature* of truth and a *criterion* of truth is important, and has not always been sufficiently emphasised by philosophers. A criterion is a sort of trade-mark, i.e. some comparatively obvious characteristic which is a guarantee of genuineness' (B. Russell, *Philosophical Essays* [London, 1910], p. 172).

2. *Strengths and Weaknesses of the Correspondence Theory of Truth*

Perhaps the most ancient and certainly in all eras the most widely accepted theory of truth is the *correspondence theory*, according to which truth is *correspondence to fact*. The theory stipulates that a proposition is true if the results of a confrontation between it and the objective situation with which it deals show that the facts actually are as it represents them. Aristotle formulated the principle as follows: 'To say that what is is not, or that what is not is, is false, while to say that what is is, or that what is not is not, is true' (*Metaphysics* 1011ᵇ26). According to the correspondence theory, the truth of a proposition lies in its agreement with—and so its correspondence to—the facts of the case: 'agreement of knowledge with its object' in the traditional terminology, or, as Leibniz puts it, 'correspondence of the proposition in the mind with the things in question'.⁸ The truth of a proposition thus becomes akin to the faithfulness of a portrait: we effect a confrontation of the purported facts with the objective situation and carry out a comparison to determine whether the two are in agreement.

In this somewhat loose and metaphorical characterization, the formulation of the theory is undoubtedly deficient. However, one modern attempt to put the correspondence theory of truth upon a systematic and precise footing is Tarski's well-known contextual condition upon truth:

'P' is true if and only if P.

Viewed as a definition, the Tarski condition is not actually an *explicit* but rather a *contextual* definition: it does not say by a defining formula what 'being true' means, but only indicates the circumstances under which attributions of truth qualify as correct. To affirm that 'P'-is-true, we are told, is tantamount to affirming P. Thus, although this condition does indeed bring to the fore and clarify the correspondence at issue—and so provides a more solid footing for a correspondence *theory* of truth—it gains these successes at the cost of a failure to implement the idea of a correspondence *definition* of truth. Indeed Tarski himself is emphatic in his insistence that the condition does not afford a

---

⁸ *New Essays*, Bk. IV, ch. V, *ad fin.* (tr. A. G. Langley). Cp. Thomas Aquinas's characterization of truth as *adaequatio intellectus et rei*. Locke has put the matter in a seemingly more definite but actually more problematic way: 'Truth, then, seems to me, in the proper import of the word, to signify nothing but *the joining or separating of signs, as the things signified by them do agree or disagree one with another*' (*Essay*, Bk. IV, ch. 5).

definition of truth at all, but is rather a criterion-of-adequacy to be imposed upon proposed definitions:

Let us consider an arbitrary sentence; we shall replace it by the letter '*p*'. We form the name of this sentence and we replace it by another letter, say '*X*'. We ask now what is the logical relation between the two sentences '*X is true*' and '*p*'. It is clear that from the point of view of our basic conception of truth these sentences are equivalent. In other words, the following equivalence holds:

$$(T) \qquad X \text{ is true if, and only if, } p.$$

We shall call any such equivalence (with '*p*' replaced by any sentence of the language to which the word '*true*' refers, and '*X*' replaced by a name of this sentence) an '*equivalence of the form* (*T*)'.

Now at last we are able to put into a precise form the conditions under which we will consider the usage and the definition of the term '*true*' as adequate from the material point of view: we wish to use the term '*true*' in such a way that all equivalences of the form (*T*) can be asserted, and we shall call a definition of truth 'adequate' if all these equivalences follow from it. It should be emphasized that neither the expression (*T*) itself (which is not a sentence, but only a schema of a sentence) nor any particular instance of the form (*T*) can be regarded as a definition of truth.[9]

It is thus clear that Tarski regards the formula at issue not as presenting a *definition*,[10] but as affording an at least partial *standard* by which the adequacy of proposed definitions can be assessed.

Indeed, where (as here) analyticity is taken to be a necessary condition for the adequacy of a definition, Tarski's schema *cannot* be regarded as providing a definition of truth. As Quine[11] points out, the same method Church[12] used to show that the statements '*X* believes that there are unicorns' and '*X* believes the proposition meant by "There are unicorns" in English' are not analytically equivalent 'can be used to show that "There are

[9] A. Tarski, 'The Semantic Conception of Truth', *Philosophy and Phenomenological Research*, 4 (1944), 341–75; reprinted in H. Feigl and W. Sellars (eds.), *Readings in Philosophical Analysis* (New York, 1944), pp. 52–84 (see p. 55). This paper is a shortened and popularized version of Tarski's ground-breaking essay 'Der Wahrheitsbegriff in den formalisierten Sprachen', *Studia Philosophica*, 1 (1936), 261–405. (A Polish version had appeared some three years earlier.)
[10] Tarski despairs on logical grounds of giving a definition for natural languages —and for all languages that are 'semantically closed'—but offers a definition for formalized languages in terms of the abstract concept of 'satisfaction'. ('The Semantic Conception of Truth', loc. cit., especially pp. 57–63.)
[11] W. V. Quine, 'Quantifiers and Propositional Attitudes', *The Ways of Paradox* (New York, 1966), pp. 183–94.
[12] A. Church, 'On Carnap's Analysis of Statements of Assertion and Belief', *Analysis*, 10 (1950), 97–9.

unicorns" is not strictly or analytically equivalent to "'There are unicorns' is true in English." Nor, indeed, was Tarski's truth paradigm intended to assert analytic equivalence. . . . [A] systematic agreement in truth value can be claimed, and no more.'[13] Presumably, the following analogue of (T) is analytically true:

(T') That-P is true if and only if P.

Hereafter, when we speak of a Tarskian *definition* of truth, we shall have (T') in mind, rather than (T).

However adequate or inadequate this Tarskian approach may be on definitional grounds, it clearly fails to provide any workable *criterion* of truth. To be sure, what is said (correctly) to be true must be the case, but such a truism neither provides nor claims to provide any criteriological mechanism to aid in deciding what is and what is not to be counted as true.[14]

The point just made can be generalized. Any correspondence theory of truth can be construed in two modes: (1) in the *definitional* mode it maintains the thesis that the truth of a proposition consists in a certain relationship to reality—namely that of 'correspondence'; (2) in the *criterial* mode it maintains that the best (or only) way to test the truth of a proposition is to check its 'correspondence' with reality. Now in attempting to apply the correspondence concept of truth *as a criterion* we encounter drastic difficulties because the theory is seriously limited on the side of *application*. The correspondence theory explicates 'true proposition' along the lines of 'true copy' of a text: on the one hand we have the original (the 'facts of the matter') and we compare these with the copy (the proposition) to check if they correspond with one another. Its paradigm is checking the truth of 'The cat is on the mat' by going to *see* whether the cat is on the mat. Criterially this version of the theory would have us proceed by *confrontation* with the situation at issue: the theory is most comfortably at home in the sphere of observation reports

---

[13] Quine, op. cit., 194.
[14] The seemingly truistic character of the thesis has led various writers (pre-eminently F. B. Ramsey and A. J. Ayer) to espouse the view that 'true' has no independent statement-making role and should be regarded as assertively redundant; it being impossible to distinguish the assertive content of the more fulsome 'It is true that it is raining' from 'It is raining'. (See G. Ezorsky, 'Truth in Context', *The Journal of Philosophy*, 60 (1963), 113–35.) But the thesis that 'is true' is *assertively redundant* because '*P* is true' provides the same information as the mere assertion of '*P*' itself cuts both ways. It argues also that declarations are *assertively expansive* with respect to 'is true', because the mere declaration of '*P*' amounts to the declaration of '*P* is true'. Thus assertive redundancy, rather than showing 'is true' to be inane and dispensable, can be construed to show that it is important because ubiquitous, and represents an omnipresent—if tacit—feature of assertions in general.

and their consequences. But this procedure of an observational 'confrontation of the facts' is unworkable in various respects:

(1) it will not be workable for genuinely universal propositions: how can one possibly check by means of some more than fragmentarily operative procedure the 'correspondence with the facts' of a universal proposition with its potential infinity of instances? ('Lions—i.e. *all* lions, past, present, and future—are carnivorous.')

(2) it will not be workable for propositions regarding the past where the 'facts of the matter' are simply not available for comparison.

(3) it will not be workable for propositions that assert probabilities (other than 'logical probabilities').

(4) it will not be workable for modalized propositions of necessity and possibility. With regard to the necessary truths of logic and mathematics we cannot say where to turn to get a view of the actual facts. And true statements of (*unactualized*) possibility are in even worse shape in this regard.

(5) it is not readily workable for hypothetical and conditional propositions—and certainly not for those with unactualized antecedents.[15]

More serious yet is the crucial problem of giving an adequate account of *what sort* of 'correspondence' is in question—a task that no correspondence theorist has discharged in anything like a satisfactory manner. As one recent writer rightly complains: '[The correspondence theory] encourages a natural tendency to think of truth in terms of mirroring our faithful reproduction; and we have a slight shock whenever we happen to notice the obvious fact that the sentence "it is raining" is about as different as possible from the rainstorm.'[16] But it is possible to make too much of this last point—it is a *difficulty*, not an *impossibility* that is at issue. Maps are very different from terrains, musical performances from music-scores. And yet perfectly definite and intelligible correspondences are at issue, although it may not be easy to formulate at the theoretical level the precise nature of such a 'correspondence'.[17]

[15] For an elaboration of these points see A. C. Ewing, 'The Correspondence Theory of Truth' in idem (ed.) *Non-Linguistic Philosophy* (London, 1968), pp. 193–204 (see especially pp. 196–7).

[16] N. Goodman, 'The Way The World Is', *The Review of Metaphysics*, 14 (1960), 48–56 (see p. 53).

[17] 'But it is often said . . . that the Correspondence Theory will not do even as a ground for appraising a statement as true. For, it is said, that theory presupposes that there is a simple relationship between language and the world; it presupposes

Difficulties of this sort debar the correspondence theory—whatever else it merits—from serving a criteriologically effective role.[18] The correspondence theory is doubtless best construed as attempting to answer the question of the definition of truth: as a criterion of truth it suffers from difficulties of the sort just enumerated. Because of this, the other theories—coherence, pragmatic, and intuitionist—are capable, potentially, of playing an important logico-epistemic role. The incapacity of the correspondence theory to solve the problem of a workable criterion of truth suggests the approach of seeing what the traditional rivals of the correspondence theory can do for us along these lines.[19]

3. Rivals of the Correspondence Theory

In view of the dark shadow cast over the conception of *adaequatio intellectus et rei* by Kant's sceptical critique of the *Ding an sich* it is not surprising that the post-Kantian philosophical tradition sought its theory of truth elsewhere than in correspondence. Thus the coherence theory of truth—perhaps the major traditional rival to the correspondence theory—sees the truthfulness of a proposition as somehow implicit in its 'coherence' with others. Now, however 'coherence' is to be explicated here (and this problem is to constitute a central topic of the present work), it is not difficult to see that, when some proposition is claimed to be true, the *meaning* of this characterization of the proposition

that statements mirror or copy the world. Language is not really like that; hence the theory must be wrong.' (D. W. Hamlyn, 'The Correspondence Theory of Truth', *The Philosophical Quarterly*, 12 (1962), 193–205; see p. 193.) But, of course, it is in no way incumbent upon a correspondence theorist to view the relationship of 'language and the world' as *simple*, any more than the relationship between musical notation and musical performance is simple. Thus when Hamlyn goes on to say that 'If propositions and facts are different kinds of entity, there seems no possibility of one being compared with the other in order to find out for certain what is the truth' (p. 198), this despair seems exaggerated in the absence of further and different arguments.

Philosophers of science nowadays generally follow the lead of Pierre Duhem in holding that theoretical claims can never be tested as to their truth-status in isolation, without bringing in others. And present-day epistemologists generally hold that *all* empirical theses involve theoretical claims. When one conjoins *these* views, the immediate upshot is to rule out any attempt to articulate a *criterion* of factual truth along correspondentist lines.

[18] The criticisms adduced score against the correspondence theory when this is construed as an all-embracing criterion that is to apply to truths of all types and categories. A limited articulation claiming criterial applicability to only one sort of truth—such as the atomic proposition of Wittgenstein's *Tractatus*—would need to be scrutinized in *ad hoc* detail.

[19] The recent philosophical literature affords a good deal of controversy regarding the merits and demerits of the correspondence theory, focusing especially upon its claims to afford a fully satisfactory definition of truth. Some of the principal papers in the discussion have been brought together in George Pitcher's anthology *Truth* (Englewood Cliffs, N.J., 1964), which has an extensive bibliography.

cannot be located in its being somehow coherent with other propositions. The discussion to follow will try to show that the coherence theory—rather than competing with the correspondence theory on its own ground—is designed to give (or at any rate is best construed as providing) an answer to the problem of a criterion for truth.

Two other theories of truth beside those based on coherence and correspondence have also been prominent in the history of the subject: the *pragmatic* theory of truth and what might be characterized as the *intuitionistic* theory.

According to the pragmatic theory of truth, the factor determinative of the truthfulness of propositions is their *utility*. A proposition is to count as true if the practical consequences of its acceptance outweigh those of its non-acceptance or perhaps rather (and better) those of its rejection (i.e. acceptance of the contradictory denial). The rationale of the pragmatic theory seems to reside in the (perhaps over-optimistic) view that one cannot 'profit from error' in faring better by rejecting a true proposition than by accepting it, or by accepting a false proposition than by rejecting it. Being right is the most advantageous policy, and so maximal utility is a safe indicator of truth. As William James's pragmatic theory of truth has it, 'ideas become true in so far as they help us to get into satisfactory relation with other parts of our experience'. On the pragmatic theory we are thus to determine whether or not a proposition qualifies as true by assessing the utility of endorsing this proposition as compared with its possible alternatives. The truth, to put it crudely, is that whose acceptance 'proves for the best'. Of course, the possibility of *a lucky mistake* cannot be wholly excluded, but this just underscores the fact that one must construe the pragmatic theory as criterial rather than definitional.

According to the intuitionistic theory there are two sorts of truths: (1) basic or primitive truths whose truthfulness is given immediately by some nondiscursive process or processes that may be characterized as intuitive, and (2) inferred truths that can be established by appropriative processes—be they deductive or inductive—from those of the former group.[20] The primitive truths include (i) primitive judgments that provide the premisses of demonstrations, and (ii) primitive inference-procedures that provide the needed inferential machinery. A

---

[20] It should be remarked that deductive proof is not the only possibility here, but also material or inductive inference that provides merely a *de facto* warrant for the conclusion, rather than establishing it in a definitive way. There can be an *inductive* as well as a *deductive* intuitionism.

truth is then any proposition that is either a primitive datum or else is derivative from these by steps corresponding to primitive inferences. The realm of truth is—according to this theory— a structure constructed by rationally intuited inferences, and erected on the foundation of a starter-set of factually intuited truths. In its insistence upon a secure basis the intuitionistic theory of truth is a descendant of Aristotle's rationalization of Euclidean geometry as the ideal paradigm of man's knowledge of truth.

The characteristic mark of the intuitionist theory is its insistence on an intuitive process ('observation', 'immediate confirmation', 'nondiscursive warrant') for the validation of truths in a manner congenial to the correspondence theory—viz. 'direct confrontation with the facts'. The position is fundamentally antithetical to the stance of the coherence theory that truth-determinations ensue from inter-propositional comparisons. Thus Moritz Schlick argued against Otto Neurath that scientific knowledge cannot be built upon a structure of mere coherence: there can be no known truths whatever—and so no science—if there is nothing of which we are absolutely certain.[21] For then, so Schlick contended, science—i.e. our claims to knowledge of the world—must lack the requisite relationship to reality:

> If attention is directed upon the relation of science to reality, the system of its statements is seen to be what it really is, namely a means of finding one's way among the facts. . . . The problem of the 'basis' changes automatically into that of the unshakable point of contact between knowledge and reality. We have come to know these absolutely fixed points of contact, the confirmations, in their individuality: they are the only synthetic statements that are not *hypotheses.*[22]

It is in this linkage with the unshakable 'fixed points' of reality represented by observation statements that the aim of scientific inquiry is to be located: 'In them [observation statements, confirmation statements] science as it were achieves its goal: it is for their sake that it exists. . . . Science does not rest upon them but leads to them, and they indicate that it has led correctly. They are really the absolute fixed points; it gives us joy to reach them, even if we cannot stand upon them.'[23] Schlick's theory is a model of the intuitionist approach in its insistence on a category of absolutely certain fixed points by reference to which alone the

---

[21] The insistence on absolute certainty is Schlick's own. See his 'The Foundations of Knowledge' in A. J. Ayer (ed.), *Logical Positivism* (Glencoe, Minn., 1959), pp. 209–27 (see p. 223). For a vivid account of the Schlick–Neurath controversy see ch. 5 ('Epistemology of Objectivity') of I. Scheffler's *Science and Subjectivity* (New York, 1967).

[22] Ibid., pp. 226–7.   [23] Ibid., p. 223.

truth of other sectors of our factual knowledge can be determined.

The pragmatic and intuitionist theories have both been described in rather general terms and we shall later have to examine in greater detail how the intuitionistic and pragmatic theories can be explicated in a rigorous and systematic way. But enough has been said to make what is the main point for present purposes, namely that both of these theories of truth take the criteriological rather than the definitional approach. Clearly, neither 'validation with reference to basic propositions' nor 'optimal utility of consequences' can qualify as formulas that present the *meaning* of truth. At most, the determination of provability or the assessment of utility could in principle be looked upon as providing a mechanism for finding an answer to the question of whether or not some given proposition qualifies as a truth. Both theories represent criterial rather than definitional constructions of truthfulness.

Overlooking this fact has led some of its critics to be grotesquely unfair to the pragmatic theory of truth. Bertrand Russell, for example, regarded William James's theory of truth as hopelessly inadequate because James's pragmatic formula does not fit the ordinary meaning of true. If James were right, Russell argued, 'It is true that other people exist' and 'It is useful to believe that other people exist' would have to have an identical meaning and would express one and the same proposition.[24] This objection, however, could be met—as Russell himself emphasized—by recognizing the decisive difference between a definition and a criterion. This difference will be crucial for our approach to the coherence theory of truth. The position we shall defend supposes that coherence is not the *meaning* of truth in the context of factual claims, but its *arbiter* (to use F. H. Bradley's well-chosen word).

4. *The Criteriology of Truth*

The quest for a criterion of truth that has preoccupied philosophers and logicians throughout the ages has not gone uncriticized. The Stoic school of classical antiquity was largely concerned to establish and the sceptical school to invalidate the enterprise. The sceptics' principal line of argument against the concept of a truth-criterion in general was formulated by Sextus Empiricus as follows:

> Besides, in order to decide the dispute which has arisen about the criterion [of truth], we must possess an accepted criterion by which

---

[24] B. Russell, *Philosophical Essays* (London, 1910), p. 136.

we shall be able to judge the dispute; and in order to possess an accepted criterion, the dispute about the criterion must first be decided. And when the argument thus reduces itself to a form of circular reasoning the discovery of the criterion becomes impracticable, since we do not allow them to adopt a criterion by assumption, while if they offer to judge the criterion by a criterion we force them to a regress *ad infinitum*.[25]

Let us attempt to recast this argument according to current standards of detail and precision. Basic to the line of argument at issue are four fundamental assumptions—or perhaps it would be better to say *definitions*:

(I) To warrant *rational assent* to a claim that the thesis p is true, this fact of the truth of p must be established with reference to a criterion of truth.

(II) A *criterion of truth* must take the form: Whenever the thesis p satisfies the requirement R, then p is true:

$$(C) \qquad (\forall p)[R(p) \to T(p)].$$

(III) To *establish* the truth of a thesis p with reference to a criterion of truth is to give a sound deductive argument of the form:

$$\frac{\begin{array}{c} C \\ R(p) \end{array}}{\therefore T(p)}.$$

(IV) A *sound* deductive argument is one that is formally conclusive (valid) and has true premises. Correspondingly, a deductive argument can never qualify as sound unless the truth of its premises has first been established.

The sceptical critique now proceeds as follows: Consider the claim that rational assent is to be given to some proposition p as true. Then by (I)–(III) there must be a sound argument of the form:

$$\frac{\begin{array}{c} C \\ R(p) \end{array}}{\therefore T(p)}.$$

But by (IV) such an argument cannot qualify as sound unless the truth of its premises—and specifically of its first premise C— is established. Consequently, it is a prime requisite to establish $T(C)$. But just how is one to proceed in this?

[25] *Outlines of Pyrrhonism*, II, 20; tr. R. G. Bury in the Loeb series. In his rejection of 'the criterion' Sextus is arguing against the position of the Stoics for which see J. M. Rist, *Stoic Philosophy* (Cambridge, 1969); see especially ch. 8, pp. 133–51.

Case (i): *C is to be self-applicable.*

Then $T(C)$ is to be established by an argument of the form

$$\frac{\begin{array}{c}C\\R(C)\end{array}}{\therefore T(C)}.$$

But before an argument of *this* form can be sound for establishing $T(C)$ we must already have established $T(C)$ to validate our use of the first premiss. Hence we enter into a vicious circle.

Case (ii): *C is not to be self-applicable.*

Then $T(C)$ is to be established with resort to *another* criterion C_1, according to which

$$\frac{\begin{array}{c}C_1\\R_1(C)\end{array}}{\therefore T(C)}.$$

But now whence C_1? Either it is to be self-applicable (in which case we are back in Case (i)) or it is to be established by a further criterion

$$\frac{\begin{array}{c}C_2\\R_2(C_1)\end{array}}{\therefore T(C_1)}.$$

But now whence C_2? With this question we continue our course into an infinite regress.

This line of argument brings to light what must—from any point of view—be regarded as a fundamental problem in any theory of criteria of truth. But just exactly what lesson is to be drawn from the argument?

First there are, of course, the possible lessons the sceptics themselves drew. Some construed the argument as a *reductio ad absurdum* of the concept of rational assent. Others viewed it as refuting the prospect of finding a criterion of truth. Thinkers outside the sceptical tradition regarded the argument as a reinforcement of Aristotle's argument for the need for ultimate, indemonstrable premisses in any deductive systematization—as showing the need for intuitive and immediate truths not validated through any criterion. Perhaps the best lesson to draw is that the domain of the true is not homogeneous and monocriterial. For it seems in any case advisable to distinguish between definitional (conventional), logical, and conceptual truths on the one hand and factual truths on the other.[26] Here at least there is a prospect of breaking outside the Hobson's choice which the sceptical argument offers us between circularity and infinite regress. If logical and conceptual truths can be revealed as ultimately *sui generis* in contrast with factual truths, in such a way that their validation does not require an external criterion—i.e. if they can be 'vindicated' without criterial justification—and if factual truths hinge on criteria whose legitimation rests on considerations that are themselves ultimately conceptual in character, then the argument will not be applicable. Here, of course, we have a long series of *ifs*, but they at least indicate a direction of resolution. We shall have to return to these issues to explore them in greater detail.

One other initial difficulty regarding a criterion of truth must be faced. How is a criterion of factual truth possible in the face of Tarski's demonstration in the semantical theory of truth that a self-sufficient ('semantically closed') language containing a mode of truth-characterization (i.e. a truth-predicate 'is true') must be inconsistent.[27] The answer, put in briefest form, is that Tarski's argument hinges critically on the assumption that the ordinary laws of logic hold, and in particular that the truth-structure of the language is two-valued (Law of Bivalence) and that the Law of Excluded Middle holds (i.e. if the contradictory of a proposition is not true, then this proposition must itself be true). As will be seen in detail in Chapter VI, the logic of the criterial theory of truth central to our discussion will *not* be classical (two-valued), so that the inconsistency at issue in the Tarskian argument cannot arise here.

Criteriological theories of truth share an important common feature that sets them apart from a definitional theory of truth. To bring this out some abbreviative symbolism is helpful. Let us write:

$D(P)$ for 'P conforms to a definition of truth'
$C(P)$ for 'P conforms to a certain criterion of truth (One that may be merely an authorizing criterion according to some now unspecified theory)'
$T(P)$ for 'P is true (in actual fact)'.

[26] Some recent authors rally around the standard of W. V. Quine in calling into question altogether the traditional distinction between factual and logical truth which we regard as basic here. See Appendix I for a discussion of these issues and a defence of the present line of procedure.

[27] See A. Tarski, 'The Semantic Conception of Truth' in H. Feigl and W. Sellars (eds.), *Readings in Philosophical Analysis* (New York, 1949), pp. 52–84 (see pp. 58–61).

Then not-$T(P)$ will be *logically incompatible* with $D(P)$; the failure of $T(P)$ in the face of $D(P)$ would simply reveal that the definition at issue is improper and incorrect. There can be no logical gap between $D(P)$ and $T(P)$. *It must be a point of logical necessity that:*

$$D(P) \text{ iff } T(P).$$

With the entrance of a criterion, however, one that need not necessarily be a guaranteeing criterion, a logical gap does open up. Precisely because the criterion C need not be tied to a definition (in the manner typical of a guaranteeing criterion), there will be a potential gap between criterial and definitional conformity. The logical link is now loosened: it is no longer necessary and inevitable that

$$C(P) \text{ iff } T(P)$$

once C can be an authorizing rather than a strictly guaranteeing criterion. Definitional conformity is an *unfailing guarantee* of truth; criterial conformity may well at best provide a *rational warrant* to justify the claim of truth, and not yield a certainty beyond the possibility of mistake.

Yet it is important to realize that we are dealing with a criterion of truth and *not* a criterion of rational acceptability or acceptance. The criterion at issue aims to answer the question 'Is P true?' and not the question 'Is P rationally acceptable?' Though the issue of rational warrant cannot be expelled from the picture, it applies to the criterion at issue, rather than pertaining in any *direct* way to the propositions governed by that criterion, through an argument of the form

> There is rational warrant for accepting the truth-criterion C
> The truth-criterion C indicates that P is true
> _____
> There is rational warrant for accepting P.

But such a *derivative* warranted acceptability of P does not transform what is basically a criterion of truth into one of rational acceptability as such.

With any genuine criterion, however, we must be prepared to recognize that, at least in principle, our assertions may be wrong —even our rationally well-warranted assertions. Whereas $D(P)$ must logically entail that $T(P)$—and so have it as a *deductive* consequence that P—$C(P)$ does no more than to *commit* us, subject to an acceptance of the criterion C, to endorsing $T(P)$ and thus to asserting (maintaining, claiming) that P. The inference from $D(P)$ to P is one of deductive logic, that from $C(P)$ to P one merely of logico-epistemic policy. Given $D(P)$, it is *impossible* that

$T(P)$ should fail to be so; but given $C(P)$, it is certainly *possible* that $T(P)$ should fail to do so, though an adoption of C puts it—*ex hypothesi*—beyond our power to *claim* that $T(P)$ does fail.

A real definition—one that purports to capture the meaning of a term possessing a definite pre-established usage—is either correct or incorrect and that's the end of the matter: its correctness may need to be pointed out, but it does not need argument or justification. A criterion of truth on the other hand—above all an authorizing criterion—definitely requires justification. In closing the logical gap between $C(P)$ and P it takes a step that can be made well or badly, wisely or foolishly. It represents the adoption of one among alternative procedures, and here—as in all such cases—the question of the rational justification for adopting one specific alternative is in order. This is a question to which extensive attention must and eventually will be given.

The criterial approach to truth addresses itself to the conceptual mechanisms for showing a proposition to be true (or false). It is none the less prepared to recognize the difference between $T(P)$, i.e. 'being true', and $C(P)$, i.e. 'being shown to be true in the light of the criterion C'. By virtue of its very nature as a criterial approach it is not inclined to acknowledge the principle:

It is irrational ever to accept as true a proposition that is false.

But it is perfectly prepared to endorse its variant:

It is irrational ever to accept as true a proposition that *has been shown* to be false.

To reject the first thesis while yet retaining the second is a feasible, indeed a sensible step.[28]

[28] Compare the position of A. Tarski who writes: 'We ask whether the following postulate is a reasonable one: *An acceptable theory cannot contain (or imply) any false statements.* The answer to the last question is clearly negative. For, first of all, we are practically sure, on the basis of our historical experience, that every empirical theory which is accepted today will sooner or later be rejected and replaced by another theory. It is also very probable that the new theory will be incompatible with the old one; i.e., will imply a sentence which is contradictory to one of the sentences contained in the old theory. Hence, at least one of the two theories must include false sentences, in spite of the fact that each of them is accepted at a certain time. Secondly, the postulate in question could hardly ever be satisfied in practice; for we do not know, and are very unlikely to find, any criteria of truth which enable us to show that no sentence of an empirical theory is false.

'The postulate in question could be at most regarded as the expression of an ideal limit for successively more adequate theories in a given field of research; but this hardly can be given any precise meaning.

'Nevertheless, it seems to me that there is an important postulate which can be reasonably imposed on acceptable empirical theories and which involves the notion

One of the tasks of the theory of statistics is that of devising 'acceptance rules' for hypotheses. In employing such a rule it sometimes happens that false hypotheses are accepted (according to the rule), and sometimes that true hypotheses are rejected. Adopting a usage proposed by the statisticians Jerzy Neyman and Egon Pearson, the rejection of a true hypothesis is generally designated as a *type II error* and the acceptance of a false hypothesis a *type I error.* This usage is readily extended to our context. Given the existence of a logical gap between $C(P)$ and $T(P)$, a criterion of truth can commit errors of two corresponding kinds:

(1) A *type I error* arises when $T(P)$ obtains—i.e. when P is in fact true—but not-$C(P)$, i.e. P fails to satisfy the criterion.

(2) A *type II error* arises when $C(P)$ obtains, so that P is acceptable according to the criterion, but not-$T(P)$, i.e. P fails to be true.

Or look at the matter from another perspective. The criteriological rule

$$T(P) \text{ iff } C(P)$$

has two components:

(i) If $T(P)$, then $C(P)$
(ii) If $C(P)$, then $T(P)$.

When (i) leads us into trouble because $T(P)$ and not-$C(P)$, the error is of type I. When (ii) is the source of difficulty because $C(P)$ but not-$T(P)$, the error is of type II. With criteria of truth of the authorizing variety—quite unlike definitions—the prospect of both of these types of errors arises.

The possible presence of these two types of error is not fatal for the criterion as such, so long as the errors occur only sporadically and not in a systematic way. However, if errors were to arise systematically with respect to a well-defined class of propositions, that would be quite another matter. The result here is asymmetric: a systematic type II error establishes merely the *incompleteness* of the criterion, whereas a systematic type I error would mean that it is incorrect and altogether *unacceptable.*

In developing a criteriological theory of truth, one does not want to have it be a matter of *logical* validity that the inferences

From $C(P)$ infer P
From P infer $C(P)$

of truth. It is closely related to the one just discussed, but is essentially weaker. Remembering that the notion of acceptability is provided with a time coefficient, we can give this postulate the following form: *As soon as we succeed in showing that an empirical theory contains (or implies) false sentences, it cannot be any longer considered acceptable*' ('The Semantic Conception of Truth' in H. Feigl and W. Sellars (eds.), *Readings in Philosophical Analysis* (New York, 1949), pp. 52–84 (see pp. 76–7)).

must be warranted. This requisite would be far too confining. A criterion C conforming to it might be adequate as definition but would be too restrictive to serve as a viable criterion. It would mean that in the order of demonstration we would be called upon to settle the question of the truth of the proposition in order to bring our criterion of truth to bear upon it.

One reason why the Tarskian condition regarding truth

$$(T') \quad T(P) \text{ iff } P$$

is best looked upon as definitional rather than criteriological in nature is that it leaves no room for any looseness of fit. Here there cannot be a type I error where $T(P)$ & $\sim P$ or a type II error where P & $\sim T(P)$ (or, equivalently?, P & $T(\sim P)$). It is improper (senseless) to affirm the truth of something in conjunction with an assertion of its contradictory. When $C(P)$ is simply P itself—that is when we have $C(P) =_{\text{Df}} P$—then the tightness of fit between $T(P)$ and $C(P)$ is complete (logical). In stressing this distinction, between a definitional theory of truth and a criteriological theory our aim is not to make a virtue of a defect but to recognize that a criteriological theory has a job to do fundamentally different from that of a definitional one.

And yet the Tarski condition, while in a way 'definitional', is certainly not in any standard sense a *definition* of truth (or 'is true'). Tarski himself rightly inclines to the view that it is best regarded as one among other *conditions of adequacy* for definitional theories of truth. For a *definitional* theory that did not yield this relationship would, so we might contend, be *eo ipso* inadequate.[29] Accordingly, given $D(P)$ iff $T(P)$, we have it that

$$D(P) \text{ iff } P$$

is indeed inevitable, but that

$$C(P) \text{ iff } P$$

is not. The criteriological truth at issue with $C(P)$ at best *approximates* to $T(P)$: with any genuinely criterial theory a potential gap remains between $C(P)$ on the one hand and $T(P)$ or $D(P)$ on the other.

---

[29] From this standpoint, it is clear that *any* theory of truth—correspondentist or otherwise—can accept the Tarski condition. Many writers have insisted on this point. 'Most of us have ringing in our ears Tarski's statement that "it is raining" is true if and only if it is raining, as well as his remark (I think erroneous, but that is beside the point here) that acceptance of this formula constitutes acceptance of a correspondence theory of truth' (N. Goodman, 'The Way the World Is', *The Review of Metaphysics*, 14 (1960), 46–56 (see p. 53)). 'As has often been noted, the [Tarskian] formula " 'snow is white' (in our language) is true ≡ snow is white" is viewed with the greatest equanimity by pragmatist and coherentist alike' (W. Sellars, *Science, Perception, and Reality* [London, 1963], p. 197).

To adopt C as at least an *authorizing* criterion of truth is essentially an adherence to the policy that *we are never to claim* $T(P)$ when $C(P)$ fails, and that *we will always claim* that $T(P)$ when $C(P)$ holds. In short, we subscribe to the *regulative precept*:

$$\text{to-assert-that-}T(P) \text{ iff } C(P).$$

With a criteriological theory of truth we espouse the regulative principle:

> Whenever $C(P)$ has been determined to obtain, then *in any substantive context* maintain that P—and therefore maintain $T(P)$ (via the Tarski relationship).

Accordingly, in *substantive contexts* we can treat $C(P)$ and $T(P)$ as interchangeable, though not in the context of a theoretical meta-principle like $C(P)$ iff $T(P)$—whence, by Tarski's condition one would obtain the unfortunate result: $C(P)$ iff P.

In accepting the possibility of errors of types I and II one thus maintains *on the meta-substantive level* the viability of the two theses:

> It is possible that: $(\exists p)[T(p) \ \& \sim C(p)]$
>
> It is possible that: $(\exists p)[C(p) \ \& \sim T(p)]$.

But it is obvious that we must not regard the *substantive* replaceability of $C(P)$ by $T(P)$ as warrant for maintaining that possibly $(\exists p)[T(p) \ \& \sim T(p)]$. Our insistence that the regulative replacement principle in view is an epistemically warranted policy does not drive *ad absurdum* a recognition of occasional errors of the two types.

The point is this: $C(P)$ is to *approximate* to $T(P)$, and in *substantive* contexts there is to be a rational authorization for treating the approximation as 'the real thing'. But this regulative procedure must never blind us to the essential fact of a logical gap between $C(P)$ and $T(P)$, a gap which must be carefully maintained in higher-level, meta-substantive contexts.

As this discussion shows, there is no reason of principle why any criteriological theory of truth—such as the coherence theory or the pragmatic theory—need pick any quarrels with the Tarski condition (T'). At the *abstract*, meta-substantive level any such theory can endorse this principle in full. But at the *applied*, substantive level, where the regulative precept to treat $C(P)$ as amounting to $T(P)$ enters in, the case is different. For this precept, if applied to (T'), entails the fatal result:

$$C(P) \text{ iff } P.$$

But this conclusion must—and can—successfully be resisted, with the justification that (T') itself is not a substantive context in which the precept can be applied. A recognition of C as an authorizing criterion blocks any such *meta-substantive* application of the regulative precept at issue.

The operative point here is, after all, applicable in any situation where approximations come into play. Whenever Q' is introduced as approximation for Q, the range of effective equivalence of these quantities must be restricted. For example, we shall generally know perfectly well that $Q' \neq Q$, but we should not be prepared to substitute Q' for Q in *this* thesis. The criteriological approach to truth simply proposes to apply this universal truism about approximations to the special circumstance of $T(P)$ and $C(P)$.

One further crucial reservation must be made about the implementation of the regulative precept in question. This principle is to be deployed in an unqualified way only in the setting of *epistemic* or *theoretical* situations outside the sphere of practical action—contexts where the only 'stake' in question is *the purely cognitive stake of being right (rather than being wrong) over as wide a range as possible*.[30] All that matters in such theoretical settings is the cognitive factor of 'getting as much truth as we can'. In *practical* contexts, however, where a genuine stake is at issue (one's time, one's money, or even one's life), application of the principle must be qualified with reference to the proposition between (i) the amount of the stake, and (ii) the magnitude of the potential gap between $C(P)$ and $T(P)$. To say that there is adequate rational warrant for classing P as true (i.e. to say that $C(P)$) is not to say that P is true beyond any shadow of doubt and absolutely certain (i.e. to say that $T(P)$). Accordingly, it would be irrational to 'stake one's life' on P when only $C(P)$ is in hand.

To claim that P is true is to *claim* that P is certain (i.e. that P is certainly true), but this claim—that P is true, and so certain—*can itself be warranted in cases where it is not certain (in a stake-your-life sense) that P is true*. One can be warranted in holding that P is certain without its being certain that P.[31] It is only in this second case—when P is in fact certain rather than merely warranted, however firmly—that taking an all-out or stake-one's-life stance would be appropriate.

[30] The 'purely cognitive' sanctions include (in order of increasing seriousness) 'failing to maintain something true', 'maintaining something that is false', and—worst of all—'maintaining a logical contradiction'.

[31] This is, after all, the whole point of the distinction between an 'adequate warrant' for something and the thing itself.

Any criteriological theory of truth that admits a potential gap between $C(P)$ and $T(P)$ must accordingly recognize this possibility of 'a slip between the cup and the lip', a consideration that has implications which cannot be ignored when the *practical* matter of acting on what we accept as true is in question. Once the possibility of a type II error is admitted, the only rational course in the realm of practice is to compare the likelihood of such an error with the magnitude of the stake at issue.[32]

This line of thought points in the general direction of the precept that the rationality of actions of all sorts—acts of 'acceptance as true' not excluded—is governed by pragmatic considerations of presumptive effectiveness. Only when we put the issue of actual practice aside, confining our attention to the strictly cognitive side of the matter, do we move on ground appropriate to the strictly theoretical mode of acceptance-as-true as a purely intellectual matter. The position of Carnap's opponents who hold that the scientist *qua* scientist is entitled to accept or reject hypotheses can also be vindicated through the regulative principle that practical risks are to be treated as immaterial in theoretical contexts. Acceptance here is a matter of acceptance for *cognitive* purposes alone: the possibility of practical risk is *ex hypothesi* to be discounted in 'pure' science. To say this is not to deny that the scientist can in certain circumstances abstain *without irrationality* from practical implementation of a hypothesis of which he feels quite assured *in foro interno*. One has no doubt that this lead soldier will melt when heated to 350 °F. One knows this perfectly well. All the same, is it *irrational* or *inconsistent* of me to refuse a bet on this issue with a one cent gain if I win as against the destruction of everything that is near and dear to me if I lose? I rather think not. The essential point is that its criteriological acceptability-as-true is by no means a basis for 'acting in *all* circumstances as though' the proposition at issue were certain beyond possibility of error. In truth-sifting, as in assaying, a working criterion must not be treated as an absolutely foolproof guarantee.

[32] In the preceding discussion of criteria, our main concern has been to distinguish between 'P is actually true' and 'There is adequate rational justification for classing P as true'. But now we come upon the concept, different from both the preceding, 'P is to be *acted* on as true'. In this practical realm of (non-cognitive) actions and effects a recourse to pragmatic (or utilitarian) considerations of potential loss or gain is indeed necessary.

II

FUNDAMENTAL ASPECTS OF THE COHERENCE THEORY OF TRUTH

1. *Coherence as a Criterion of Truth*

IT is generally recognized that 'the coherence theory of truth' has historically not been a single monolithic doctrine but has taken significantly different forms—three in particular:

(i) a metaphysical doctrine regarding the *nature of reality* (viz. that it is a coherent system).

(ii) a logical doctrine regarding the *definition of truth* (viz. that truth is to be defined in terms of the coherence of propositions).

(iii) a logico-epistemological doctrine as regarding the prime (or ultimate) *criterion of truth* (viz. that the canonical *test* of truth is to consist in assessing the mutual coherence of [suitably qualified] propositions).[1]

Our present interest lies in the last two items. We propose to deal with the coherence theory solely in its logical and epistemological ramifications, leaving metaphysical issues aside in so far as is possible. The metaphysics of idealism is an issue outside the central concerns of present purpose.

No profound analysis is required to see that the coherence theory as we have outlined it does not purport to give a *definition* of 'truth'. Coherence is certainly not the *meaning* of truth. Idealistic adherents of the theory—F. H. Bradley prominently included—have generally been prepared to grant the merits of the correspondence approach to the intrinsic nature of truth: 'Truth to be true must be true of something, and this something itself is not truth. This obvious view I endorse.'[2] Rather, the aim

---

[1] The doctrinal indeterminacy of the traditional coherence theory has often been stressed. Cf. A. C. Ewing, *Idealism: A Critical Survey* (London, 1934), p. 195.

[2] F. H. Bradley, *Essays on Truth and Reality* (Oxford, 1914), p. 325. A. C. Ewing, a most sympathetic expositor of idealist thought, stresses 'the impossibility of dispensing with the relation described, perhaps very inadequately, as correspondence if we are to give any account of truth that applies to the truths known by us. The strength of the correspondence theory lies in the fact that a judgment is at once different from and yet dependent for its correctness on the object judged about. Whatever metaphysical view we adopt as to the ultimate nature of knowledge and

of the coherence theory is—or should be—to afford a *test* or criterion of truth. As A. C. Ewing rightly insists, 'correspondence might well constitute the nature of truth without constituting its criterion'.[3] Thus construed, the two doctrines are fitted to very different work. The matter of 'correspondence to facts' tells us a great deal about *what truth is*, but can fail badly as a guide to *what is true*. On the other hand, the factor of 'coherence with other (suitably determined) propositions' does not really provide a *definition* of truth, but is most helpful as a tool in the process of deciding whether given propositions qualify as truths.

The workable articulation of a coherence criterion of truth will clearly be a matter of importance in any case, quite apart from its role in anything so grandiose as a 'theory of truth'. For on anyone's approach to the matter—be he of coherentist sympathies or not—there will clearly be *some* cases in which the potential truth of a proposition is best assessed in terms of its coherence with other established or presumed truths. Coherence must be accorded some role, however partial or subsidiary, on *any* approach to the criteria of rational acceptance. It is therefore eminently desirable—quite separately from any penchant towards a coherence theory of truth—to be clear as to the nature and workings of coherence considerations.

2. *The Revival of Coherence Theory among the Logical Positivists*

Some coherentists outside the idealist school have, however, gone so far as to maintain that adoption of a coherence theory of truth calls for a complete rejection of the relationship of truth to correspondence to fact. Substantiation of this point calls for a brief historical excursus.

Idealism had died out as a widely accepted philosophical position by the 1920s. Only a handful of isolated sympathizers carried on the tradition—by 1930, A. C. Ewing in England, C. A. Campbell in Scotland, and Brand Blanshard in the U.S.A. virtually had the field to themselves in the Anglo-American

---

reality we are forced to admit this fact . . .' (Ewing, op. cit., p. 201). For a fuller discussion of Bradley's position in the quoted passage see pp. 201–2 of Ewing's book.

[3] Ewing, op. cit., p. 198. Ewing takes great pains to show that an idealist—even one strongly inclined to a coherentist approach—need not reject the correspondence theory of truth: 'It is true that, when we know, we know real facts, not merely ideas or propositions, but there is no difficulty in reconciling this with the other circumstance emphasized by the correspondence theory, namely that when we do know anything there is a special relation between the fact known and a certain factor in our cognitive process, which relation differentiates the latter from error. Whatever else it is, knowing must involve bringing our minds *into accordance with* reality, and this is also the case with right opinion. It is this that the correspondence theory rightly emphasises as the essential purpose of cognition' (ibid., p. 204).

domain.[4] Yet in the early 1930s new devotees of the coherence theory of truth were to spring up in an unexpected quarter: the Vienna School of logical positivism.[5] During the early 1930s some of the most influential members of the logical positivist school advocated a version of the coherence theory of truth. In a widely discussed paper of 1932,[6] Rudolf Carnap had maintained that all of scientific knowledge can be built up from a certain class of basic statements characterized as *protocol sentences*, i.e. sentences that describe in an exact and incorrigibly correct manner the sensory observations of trained observers. Such sentences provide the evidential base of all factual knowledge, but 'require no verification' themselves. Carnap's position was sharply criticized by Otto Neurath who wrote:

There is no way of taking conclusively established pure protocol sentences as the starting point of the sciences. No *tabula rasa* exists. We are like sailors who must rebuild their ship on the open sea, never able to dismantle it in dry-dock and to reconstruct it there out of the best materials.

In unified science we try to construct a non-contradictory system of protocol sentences and non-protocol sentences (including laws).[7] When a new sentence is presented to us we compare it with the system at our disposal, and determine whether or not it conflicts with that system. If the sentence does conflict with the system, we may discard it as useless (or false). . . . One may, on the other hand, *accept* the sentence and so change the system that it remains consistent even after the adjunction of the new sentence. The sentence would then be called 'true'. The fate of being discarded may befall even a protocol sentence. No sentence enjoys the *noli me tangere* which Carnap ordains for protocol sentences.

Two conflicting protocol sentences cannot both be used in the system of unified science. Though we may not be able to tell which of the two is to be excluded, or whether both are not to be excluded, it is clear that not both are verifiable, that is, that both do not fit into the system.

If a protocol sentence must in such cases be discarded, may not the same occasionally be called for when the contradiction between protocol sentences on the one hand and a system comprising protocol sentences and non-protocol sentences (laws, etc.) on the other is such

---

[4] On the Continent there were rather more idealists, Carlo Gentile perhaps the most prominent among them. In his review of Blanshard's *The Nature of Thought* (London, 1939), published in *Mind* in 1944 (53, 75–85), Ewing wrote: 'It is a generation since any such sympathetic large-scale defence of what, for want of a better name, I shall call idealistic epistemology has been published' (pp. 75–6).

[5] Some idealists had already given up the coherence theory. J. M. E. McTaggart, one of the central figures of later British idealism, rejected the coherence in favour of the correspondence theory of truth.

[6] 'Die physikalische Sprache als Universalsprache der Wissenschaft', *Erkenntnis*, 2 (1931/2), 432–65. Tr. by M. Black in R. Carnap, *The Unity of Science* (London, 1934).

[7] Cf. Carnap, op. cit., pp. 439 ff. (*Unity of Science*, pp. 47 ff.).

that an extended argument is required to disclose it? On Carnap's view, one could be obliged to alter only non-protocol sentences and laws. *We also allow for the possibility of discarding protocol sentences. A defining condition of a sentence is that it be subject to verification, that is to say, that it may be discarded.*[8]

Neurath's position is that (1) *all* factual statements are vulnerable to rejection—observation statements of the protocol type specifically included: 'The fate of being discarded may befall even a protocol sentence',[9] and (2) that the standard by which any such statement is to be evaluated is that we are to 'compare it with the system at our disposal'. In effect, Neurath opposes to the intuitionist/constructivist approach of Carnap a theory of factual truth that is essentially of the coherentist variety.[10] Coherence theorists have always insisted that empirical knowledge 'is not the direct awareness of an independent fact; of a solid constituent of reality, presenting itself, entire and complete, to the passively accepting observer'.[11]

According to Neurath, scientific knowledge is

. . . a sorting-machine into which protocol sentences are thrown. The laws and other factual sentences (including protocol sentences) serving to mesh the machine's gears sort the protocol sentences which are thrown into the machine and cause a bell to ring if a contradiction ensues. At this point one must either replace the protocol sentence whose introduction into the machine has led to the contradiction by some other protocol sentence, or rebuild the entire machine.[12]

Neurath rejected all talk of truth as correspondence with reality. Indeed he rejects this entire conception as ultimately meaningless:

[8] 'Protokollsätze', *Erkenntnis*, 3 (1932/3). Tr. by F. Schick as 'Protocol Sentences' in A. J. Ayer (ed.), *Logical Positivism* (Glencoe, Ill., 1959), pp. 201–4.
[9] Ibid., p. 203.
[10] Neurath's position was discussed critically by M. Schlick in a paper 'Über das Fundament der Erkenntnis', *Erkenntnis*, 4 (1933/4), 79 ff. Neurath answered Schlick in 'Radikaler Physikalismus und "wirkliche Welt"', ibid., 346 ff. Carnap himself was won over to Neurath's position. For a detailed survey of the entire controversy see C. G. Hempel, 'On the Logical Positivists' Theory of Truth', *Analysis*, 2 (1935), 49–59. The background of the controversy is sketched in J. Joergensen, *The Development of Logical Empiricism* (Chicago, Ill., 1951; *Encyclopedia of Unified Science*, vol. 2, no. 9). A retrospective analysis from his own doctrinal standpoint is given in K. R. Popper's *Conjectures and Refutations* (London, 1963), pp. 267–9. See also R. W. Ashby, 'Basic Statements' in P. Edwards (ed.), *Encyclopedia of Philosophy*, vol. 1 (New York, 1968), pp. 251–4.
[11] H. H. Joachim, *Logical Studies* (London, 1906), p. 80.
[12] 'Protokollsätze', op. cit., p. 207. And again, 'Ignoring all meaningless statements, the unified science proper to a given historical period proceeds from proposition to proposition, blending them into a self-consistent system which is an instrument for successful prediction, and, consequently, for life' ('Sociology and Physicalism', op. cit., p. 286).

A social scientist who, after careful analysis, rejects certain reports and hypotheses, reaches a state, finally, in which he has to face comprehensive sets of statements which compete with other comprehensive sets of statements. All these sets may be composed of statements which seem to him plausible and acceptable. There is no place for an empiricist question: Which is the 'true' set? but only whether the social scientist has sufficient time and energy to try more than one set or to decide that he, in regard to his lack of time and energy—and this is the important point—should work with one of these comprehensive sets only.[13]

Thus Neurath not only restored the coherence theory to a place of prominence, he went so far as to invoke coherence as a basis for maintaining the invalidity of the whole concept of 'correspondence with fact'. For him—unlike idealistic coherentists such as Bradley—adoption of the coherence theory calls for rejection of the whole concept of truth as correspondence to fact. On our own view of the matter as set forth in the preceding section, this position that the coherence conception of truth *excludes* the very meaningfulness of correspondence is neither necessary nor desirable.

3. *Does Coherence Pre-empt Correspondence?*

Certain writers maintain that a coherence approach to truth *precludes* a correspondentist view of the nature of truth. They argue that if coherence is to be the *test* of truth then it must also be its *nature*, pre-empting all claims of correspondence in this regard. Brand Blanshard is pre-eminent among those who espouse this line of thought.[14]

The earlier coherence theorists tended to view coherence as a characteristic mark of the truth without any very specific and definite commitment as to the exact nature of the 'mark' at issue. Is coherence a somehow necessary feature of the truth, is it a test of truth, is it a part of the definition of truth or even the whole of it? Such questions did not generally receive close attention. After F. H. Bradley, however, the issue could not readily be avoided, and Brand Blanshard faced it squarely in his characteristically hard-headed fashion. His answer is clear and emphatic—truth *consists* in coherence; coherence is not just a feature of truth, but its very nature.

The critical defect of this approach to the definition of truth in terms of coherence is that it leaves the link from truth to factuality not just unrationalized but unrationalizable. The

---

[13] *Foundations of the Social Sciences*, (Chicago, Ill., 1944), p. 13.
[14] B. Blanshard, *The Nature of Thought* (2 vols., London, 1939); see esp. ch.'s 25–7 of vol. II.

linkage surely cannot be of *contingent* character. But yet how can the step from coherence to factuality possibly be a necessary one? Upon what sort of logical basis could one possibly erect an airtight demonstration that whatever satisfies conditions of maximal or optimal coherence must indeed be the case in actual fact. Surely this poses an insuperable difficulty.

Blanshard himself is, seemingly, perfectly ready to grant this. He writes:

> Suppose that we construe experience into the most coherent picture possible, remembering that among the elements included will be such secondary qualities as colours, odours, and sounds. Would the mere fact that such elements as these are coherently arranged prove that anything precisely corresponding to them exists 'out there' [i.e. less eccentrically formulated, *is actually the case*]? I cannot see that it would, even if we knew that the two arrangements had closely corresponding patterns. . . . It is therefore impossible to argue from a high degree of coherence within experience to its correspondence in the same degree with anything outside [i.e. with what is in fact the case]. . . . In the end, the only test of truth that is not misleading is the special nature or character that is itself constitutive of truth [viz. coherence].[15]

Given my (perhaps somewhat tendentious) reading of this argument against a correspondence theory, it would seem that Blanshard is fully prepared to regard the step from 'coherence' to 'correspondence with the facts of the matter' as problematic and potentially fallible.

Yet even if one utterly rejects the core thesis of the correspondence theory that truth *means* 'correspondence to fact' (*adaequatio ad rem* in the old formula), one is still left—in any event—with the impregnable thesis that a true proposition is one that states what is in fact the case. The link from truth to factuality is not to be broken, regardless of one's preferred conception of the definitional nature of truth. Even the most ardent coherence theorist must grant, certainly not the premiss of the coherence theory that truth *means* correspondence to the facts, but merely its consequence, that truths must correspond to the facts. Even if we follow the coherentist in rejecting the definitional route from the former to the latter, we must still be able to link them mediately, via coherence. But how can coherence of itself ever guarantee factuality? Cannot the clever novelist make his tale every bit as coherent as that of the most accurate historian? Given the (relatively clear) fact that the products of creative invention and imagination can be perfectly coherent, and given

---

[15] B. Blanshard, op. cit., p. 268; cf. B. Russell, *The Problems of Philosophy* (London, 1912), p. 191.

that alternate coherent structures can always be erected from given elements (as scientists frame different hypotheses to account for the same body of data), how can coherence possibly furnish a logical guarantee of fact? So runs one of the standard objections to the coherence theory of truth, one which—to all appearances—tells also against Blanshard's formulation of the theory. In seeking to impugn the correspondence theory by insisting that there is no infallible linkage between coherence and correspondence-to-fact, Blanshard succeeds less in invalidating correspondence as a standard of truth than in highlighting a fundamental difficulty of the coherence theory of the type he espouses, one according to which coherence represents the very *nature* of truth.

Blanshard emphatically recognizes and stresses the critical difference between a criterion or *test* of truth and a *definition* thereof:

It has been contended in the last chapter that coherence is in the end our sole criterion of truth. We have now to face the question whether it also gives us the nature of truth. We should be clear at the beginning that these are different questions, and that one may reject coherence as the definition of truth while accepting it as the test. It is conceivable that one thing should be an accurate index of another and still be extremely different from it. There have been philosophers who held that pleasure was an accurate gauge of the amount of good in experience, but that to confuse good with pleasure was a gross blunder. There have been a great many philosophers who held that for every change in consciousness there was a change in the nervous system and that the two correspond so closely that if we knew the laws connecting them we could infallibly predict one from the other; yet it takes all the hardihood of a behaviourist to say that the two are the same. Similarly it has been held that though coherence supplies an infallible measure of truth, it would be a very grave mistake to identify it with truth.[16]

Recognizing in general the potential difference between a criterion and a definition, Blanshard argues that in the special case of truth this difference cannot be maintained: here definition must collapse into criterion once coherence is recognized as the criterion of truth.

The structure of his argument can be presented as follows:[17]

(1) A coherence theory of truth cannot do less than take coherence as one, nay *the prime*, test of truth.

[16] B. Blanshard, op. cit., p. 260.
[17] Blanshard sets out the argument in the following terms: 'As we saw at the beginning of the chapter, there have been some highly reputable philosophers who have held that the answer to "What is the test of truth?" is "Coherence", while the

(2) Now if the definition of truth finds the nature of truth to reside in something other than coherence, something which—like correspondence—is not logically tantamount to coherence but can potentially diverge from it, then coherence cannot qualify as a foolproof guarantee of truth.

(3) But since a coherence theory of truth must take coherence to be the prime test of truth (Premiss 1), it must see in coherence a foolproof guarantee of truth.

(4) But then it follows (from Premiss 2) that a coherence theory of truth must take coherence to represent the nature of truth, and not merely to provide a test-criterion thereof. For only what is essential to its very nature can provide a conceptually foolproof guarantee for a thing, and not any mere test-criterion.

The upshot of Blanshard's argument is this: that a recognition of coherence as the test-criterion of truth forces the conclusion that coherence must represent the definitional nature of truth.

This argument seems to be perfectly unexceptionable: Given its premisses, the conclusion must be granted. But what is to be said about its premisses? Of the essential premisses (1)–(3) of this Blanshardesque argument, it seems clear that (1) and (2) are effectively beyond cavil. Only (3) is potentially vulnerable—and indeed actually so. For why must the coherence test be seen as providing a *foolproof guarantee* of truth? We are led back once more to the critical distinction between a *guaranteeing* criterion and an *authorizing* criterion. Recognizing this distinction, we may note that, on Blanshard's approach as enshrined in premiss (2),

answer to "What is the nature or meaning of truth?" is "Correspondence". These questions are plainly distinct. Nor does there seem to be any direct path from the acceptance of coherence as the test of truth to its acceptance as the nature of truth. Nevertheless there is an indirect path. If we accept coherence as our test, we must use it everywhere. We must therefore use it to test the suggestion that truth *is* other than coherence. But if we do, we shall find that we must reject the suggestion as leading to *in*coherence. Suppose that, accepting coherence as the test, one rejects it as the nature of truth in favour of some alternative; and let us assume, for example, that this alternative is correspondence. This, we have said, is incoherent, one cannot intelligibly hold either that it is tested by coherence or that there is any dependable test at all. Consider the first point. Suppose that we construe experience into the most coherent picture possible. . . . Would the mere fact that such elements as there are coherently arranged prove that anything precisely corresponding to them exists "out there"? I cannot see that it would, even if we knew that the two arrangements had closely corresponding patterns. . . . It is therefore impossible to argue from a high degree of coherence within experience to its correspondence in the same degree with anything outside. And this difficulty is typical. If you place the nature of truth in one sort of character and its test is something quite different, you are pretty certain, sooner or later, to find the two falling apart. In the end, the only test of truth that is not misleading is the special nature or character that is itself constitutive of truth' (ibid., pp. 267–8).

the partisan of coherence as the criterion of truth is committed to regarding coherence as a *guaranteeing* criterion. He is committed to regarding the link from coherence to truth as inevitable and necessary. Now subject to this presupposition, Blanshard's position is unquestionably a strong one. But why need this presupposition be made? Why could or should not the coherence theorist intent on taking coherence as a criterion of truth regard it as an authorizing rather than a guaranteeing criterion? Why, in short, should coherence not be accepted as *a generally effective test* of truth rather than *an inescapable aspect of its nature*?

From this perspective, Blanshard's version of the coherence theory of truth is faulty because it gets off to a bad start. It goes amiss at a very fundamental point, by insisting on seeing in coherence the *very nature* of truth, and is not content with having coherence play simply the part of a restricted test-criterion for truth-determinations. This deprives Blanshard of the prospect of making sense of the ancient thesis that it is necessary that a true proposition should agree with the facts of the case, a thesis not abrogated by abandoning a definitional correspondence theory of truth, but rather one that must survive any such abandonment.

Blanshard is inexorably forced to this insistence that coherence represents the definitional nature of truth by two considerations: (1) the (essentially unproblematic) premiss that coherence is a key criterion of truth, and (2) the argument that the necessary linkage of truth-criterion to truth-definition cannot be preserved unless the criterial factor (viz. coherence) is taken over as definitional. Blanshard's *argument* here is perfectly correct, but his position is not. For it is neither necessary nor desirable for the adoption of coherence as a (or even *the*) criterion of truth to construe coherence as a *necessitating* or *logically guaranteeing* criterion rather than one that is *presumptive* and *epistemically authorizing*. And once such insistence upon a linkage of necessity is abandoned, the argument that coherence-as-criterion entails coherence-as-definition becomes abortive.

4. *What is Coherence?*

The groundwork of the coherence theory has its roots in the idea of *system*. Its basic insight is formulated by F. H. Bradley as follows: 'Truth is an ideal expression of the Universe, at once coherent and comprehensive. It must not conflict with itself, and there must be no suggestion which fails to fall inside it. Perfect truth, in short, must realize the idea of a systematic whole.'[18] The coherence theory implements the fundamental idealistic conception that truth—and with it the reality of which it is characteristic—represents an inclusive and appropriately connected systematic whole.

According to this doctrine, the truth of a statement or proposition is somehow to be located in its 'coherence'. But 'to cohere' is a transitive verb: all coherence must be coherence *with something*. Clearly this will be a matter of coherence with other statements or propositions. As one recent writer puts it: 'According to the coherence theory, to say that a statement is true or false is to say that it coheres or fails to cohere with a system of other statements; that it is a member of a system whose elements are related to each other by ties of logical implication. . . .'[19] The 'coherence' at issue in the coherence theory is a matter of a proposition's relation to other propositions—not its 'coherence' with *reality* or with *the facts of the matter*. For to proceed thus is to attempt a surreptitious change of the coherence theory into a correspondence theory; and accordingly one recent writer quite properly objects that 'Any attempt to change the meaning of "coherence" from coherence with other statements to coherence with fact (or reality of experience) is to abandon the theory.'[20]

Coherence is thus a feature that propositions cannot have in isolation but only in *groups* containing several—i.e. at least two—propositions. Just wherein does this feature lie? Coherentists have standardly regarded two factors as primary: consistency and connectedness. One recent expositor puts the matter thus:

> But they [the Idealist coherence theorists] did in general follow him [F. H. Bradley] in holding that the real was coherent in a double sense, first in being consistent throughout in spite of apparent incongruities, secondly in being interdependent throughout, that is, so ordered that every fact was connected necessarily with others and ultimately with all.[21]

The 'coherence' of a propositional set is accordingly to be understood as requiring not simply (1) the obvious minimum of *consistency*,[22] but also (2) the feature of being *connected* in some

---

[18] F. H. Bradley, op. cit., p. 223.
[19] A. R. White, art. 'Coherence Theory of Truth' in P. Edwards (ed.), *The Encyclopedia of Philosophy*, vol. 2 (New York, 1967), pp. 130–3 (see p. 130).
[20] Ibid., pp. 132–3.
[21] B. Blanshard, *Reason and Analysis* (La Salle, Ill., 1962).
[22] The consistency of the totality of truths is, of course, an essential aspect of truth from any reasonable point of view: here the coherentist is not in any special position. The following remarks of A. Tarski are illuminating in this regard: 'I believe everybody agrees that one of the reasons which may compel us to reject an empirical theory is the proof of its inconsistency: a theory becomes untenable if we succeed in deriving from it two contradictory sentences. Now we can ask what are the usual

special way. The next and major task is clearly to clarify what sort of connectedness is to be at issue.

The coherence theorists themselves have not always been too successful in explicating the nature of coherence.[23] Bernard Bosanquet's position is neatly summarized by one recent expositor as follows:

> Particularly notorious in Bosanquet's logic was his insistence upon reciprocity. This appears most clearly in his analysis of hypotheticals. The typical hypothetical, for him, is the assertion that if *A is B*, *A is C*. Now, he argues, if *A's being B* really necessitates its being *C*, this is simply to say that there is some system in which *A, B, C* cohere. Since coherence is symmetrical it will follow that *A's being C* must also necessitate *A's being B*. This conclusion, of course, cuts directly across the traditional view that hypothetical assertions are irreversible. But it is naturally connected both with the coherence theory of truth and with the Lotzean presumption that every proposition expresses an identity. Bosanquet admits that 'if he is drowned, he is dead', for example, does not seem to affirm reciprocal connexions. [But he insists that we must treat this as shorthand for 'if he is drowned, he is dead by drowning'.] Only by means of such an interpretation, he argues, can we satisfy logic's demand for coherence. All 'giving of grounds', in fact, is reciprocal—'it is only because the "grounds" alleged in everyday life are burdened with irrelevant matter or confused with causation in time', Bosanquet writes, 'that we consider the hypothetical judgement to be in its nature not reversible'. [See his 'Cause and Ground', *Journal of Philosophy* (1910).][24]

motives for rejecting a theory on such grounds. Persons who are acquainted with modern logic are inclined to answer this question in the following way: A well-known logical law shows that a theory which enables us to derive two contradictory sentences enables us also to derive every sentence; therefore, such a theory is trivial and deprived of any scientific interest.

'I have some doubts whether this answer contains an adequate analysis of the situation. I think that people who do not know modern logic are as little inclined to accept an inconsistent theory as those who are thoroughly familiar with it; and probably this applies even to those who regard (as some still do) the logical law on which the argument is based as a highly controversial issue, and almost as a paradox. I do not think that our attitude toward an inconsistent theory would change even if we decided for some reasons to weaken our system of logic so as to deprive ourselves of the possibility of deriving every sentence from any two contradictory sentences.

'It seems to me that the real reason of our attitude is a different one: We know (if only intuitively) that an inconsistent theory must contain false sentences; and we are not inclined to regard as acceptable any theory which has been shown to contain such sentences' (*The Semantic Conception of Truth* in H. Feigl and W. Sellars (eds.), *Readings in Philosophical Analysis* [New York, 1949], pp. 52–84 (see p. 77)).

[23] Thus H. H. Price says flatly that 'believers in the Coherence Theory do not themselves define this term' (*Perception* (New York, 1933), p. 183). This judgment, as we shall see, is much too harsh, though the case would be otherwise if 'satisfactorily' were appended to Price's sentence.

[24] J. Passmore, *A Hundred Years of Philosophy* (England, 1966), pp. 167–78.

The point of reciprocity-coherence is this: that if we have, seemingly independently, a coherent group of propositions *A*, *B*, *C*, then what we *actually* have is

1. *A*-in-the-context-of-*B*-and-*C*
2. *B*-in-the-context-of-*A*-and-*C*
3. *C*-in-the-context-of-*A*-and-*B*.

The only really coherent statement—and the only really true one—is one that carries its context implicitly along with itself, and so, in effect, is one that affirms everything else that is true. Fully coherent statements—and so fully true statements—are equivalent because they all assert *all* the relevant facts, and this accounts for the reciprocal equivalences at issue.[25] Bosanquet's contention thus effectively justifies his reciprocity thesis, but does so only at the price of accepting two absurdities: (1) that only those declarations are *genuinely* true that state not merely 'nothing but the truth' but actually state 'the *whole* truth',[26] and (2) that only those propositional sets are fully coherent each of whose members entails all the rest—and so all of whose members are actually equivalent and thus completely redundant with the others. Strange though it may seem, this second thesis represents a doctrine widely espoused among the idealists. 'Fully coherent knowledge', Brand Blanshard tells us, 'would be knowledge in which every judgment entailed, and was entailed by, the rest of the system.'[27] This conception of coherence as assertive redundancy, and of a coherent system of propositions as one

---

[25] Compare H. H. Joachim's thesis that 'a system possesses self-coherence (a) in proportion as every constituent of it logically involves and is involved by every other; and (b) in so far as the reciprocal implications of the constituent elements, or rather the constituent elements in their reciprocal implications, constitute alone and completely the significance of the system' ('"Absolute" and "Relative" Truth', *Mind*, 14 (1905), 9).

[26] To grant the perfectly sound point that 'the whole truth' can never be formulated in any single statement, is not to maintain the paradoxical thesis that something that is wholly true cannot be so encapsulated.

[27] *The Nature of Thought*, p. 264. Blanshard goes on to observe: 'It is perhaps in such systems as Euclidean geometry that we get the most perfect examples of coherence that have been constructed. If any proposition were lacking, it could be supplied from the rest; if any were altered, the repercussions would be felt through the length and breadth of the system. Yet even such a system as this falls short of ideal system. Its postulates are unproved; they are independent of each other, in the sense that none of them could be derived from any other or even from all the others together; its clear necessity is brought by an abstractness so extreme as to have left out nearly everything that belongs to the character of actual things. A completely satisfactory system would have none of these defects. No proposition would be arbitrary, every proposition would be entailed by the others jointly and even singly, no proposition would stand outside the system' (ibid., pp. 265–6). (I have omitted Blanshard's text of a footnote citing H. H. Joachim [*Logical Studies* (Oxford, 1948)] as another adherent of this view.)

whose members simply repeat the same thing is not a very useful construction of the idea.

In his excellent book *Idealism: A Critical Survey*,[28] A. C. Ewing criticizes this Bosanquet–Joachim–Blanshard construction of coherence, arguing along the following lines:

> Again, to say that no one proposition in a coherent system could be false if all the other propositions were *true* is not to say that no one could be false without all the other propositions being *false*. It is true that, given a really coherent system of propositions such as that which constitutes arithmetic, we could by a process of correct inference pass from the falsity of any one proposition in the system to the falsity of any other. Using $\neq$ to represent 'is not equal to', we could if we assumed that $7+5 \neq 12$ infer, e.g. multiplying by 20, that $140+100 \neq 240$, or, subtracting 6 from both, that $1-1 \neq 0$, and could by similar processes reach conclusions contradicting the true result of every arithmetical operation; but this, carried to the extreme, would be a self-contradictory procedure, since we can only prove from this premiss that any accepted proposition in arithmetic is false by assuming as true another accepted proposition of arithmetic, e.g. $7 \times 20 = 140$, and so we could only infer from this premiss that all other accepted arithmetical propositions were false by assuming that they were all true. Similarly, I suppose, with any other coherent system of propositions. So we cannot argue that one of the coherent propositions could not be false without their being all false, but only that it could not be false without some of them being so. Thus we need not, as far as I can see, accept coherence in the sense defined by Professor Joachim. . . .[29]

As long as the propositions of a coherent system are not merely redundant with one another, they cannot stand and fall together in the lock-step fashion envisioned by the coherentists whom Ewing is criticizing.

Ewing himself explicates the connectedness-coherence of a set of propositions in the following terms:

A set of (two or more) propositions is coherent if

(i) 'Any one proposition in the set follows with logical necessity if all the other propositions in the set are true' (p. 229)

and moreover

(ii) 'No set of propositions within the whole set is logically independent of all propositions in the remainder of the set' (pp. 229–30)[30]

[28] London, 1934.

[29] A. C. Ewing, op. cit., pp. 233–4.

[30] The motivation for this definition, and in particular of its second clause, is presented by Ewing as follows: 'The easiest way of understanding what coherence means is to consider those cases where the ideal of coherence is admittedly

According to these stipulations, a propositional set **S** (with two or more members) is coherent if:

(i) For every $P \in$ **S**, P is always derivable from the remaining **S**-elements:

$$\text{If } P \in \textbf{S}, \text{ then } \textbf{S} - \{P\} \vdash P$$

(ii) There is no proper subset **S'** of **S** such that every $P \in$ **S'** can be derived from **S'** $- \{P\}$—that is, can be derived from **S**-elements without using elements outside of **S'**.[31]
Or equivalently—once (i) is given:
Every proper subset **S'** of **S** is such that there is some $P \in$ **S'** for whose derivation from **S** $- \{P\}$ some element of **S** $-$ **S'** is required.[32]

Condition (ii) can be reformulated somewhat more simply as:

(ii') There is no proper subset of **S** that fulfills condition (i).

This reformulation shows that 'coherence' in the sense at issue calls for a certain completeness or better *saturation*. The addition of *any* proposition whatever to a coherent propositional set immediately renders it incoherent.

With the reformulation at issue, it becomes quite clear that conditions (i) and (ii) do not entail the consistency of the set at issue: the set $\{p \,\&\, {\sim}p, \,{\sim}p \,\&\, p\}$ conforms to both (i) and (ii). One would certainly want to add the condition

(iii) The set **S** is consistent.

realised or almost realised, though only within a limited sphere. Such cases are provided by the mathematical sciences and perhaps by certain well-knit theories or bodies of doctrine outside mathematics. What are the characteristics of such sets of propositions? In the first place, in so far as they fulfill the coherence ideal, they are so related that any one proposition in the set follows with logical necessity if all the other propositions in the set are true, or, to put it negatively, so that, granted the truth of all the rest, it would be logically impossible for any one of them to be false; and I was first tempted to take this as a definition of coherence. But it is not sufficient without supplementation. For imagine a set of propositions A B C D E F where, writing ent. for entail, we have the relations A+B ent. C, A+C ent. B, B+C ent. A, D+E ent. F, D+F ent. E, E+F ent. D. In such a set every single proposition would be entailed by the remainder, but unless there were some further connection between A B C on the one hand and D E F on the other, it would certainly fall short of the demands of the coherence theory, for it is universally agreed that the latter is incompatible with any admission of the possibility that there might be several different systems of true propositions altogether logically independent of each other. We must therefore enlarge our definition . . .' (ibid., p. 229).

[31] Note that this condition precludes a coherent set from including logically necessary elements, i.e. propositions derivable even when there are no premisses whatsoever.

[32] Actually, condition (ii) as given by Ewing differs somewhat from this formulation, but its effect is the same. The details are set forth in Appendix A.

Let p, q, r be independent propositions. Requirement (i) suffices to block not only $\{p, q, r\}$ as a coherent set, but also $\{p \,\&\, q, q, r \,\&\, p\}$—since $r \,\&\, p$ is not derivable from the remaining elements. However, the set $\{p \,\&\, q, q \,\&\, r, r \,\&\, p\}$ does qualify under the first criterion—each of its elements is derivable from the rest. These examples show that this first condition amounts to a *requirement of (inferential) redundancy*: given *all* the others, any element can be dropped without any loss in inferential content.

The inferential redundancy requirement assures a certain *minimal* connectedness among the elements of a coherent set. The aim of stipulation (ii) is, as Ewing explains (op. cit., p. 229), to assure a yet greater degree of connection. Let A, B, C be three propositions any two of which yield the third as deductive consequence. And let D, E, F be another such set—but wholly independent of A, B, C. Then $\mathbf{S} = \{A, B, C, D, E, F\}$ satisfies requirement (i), but is not fully 'coherent' (now = connected) because it falls into two logically disjointed parts. Stipulation (ii) is designed to block this case. This condition might be called *the requirement of (deductive) interlinkage*. Note that it follows from condition (ii) that a coherent set $\mathbf{S}$ cannot contain any two equivalent propositions A and B. If there were such propositions, then the set $\mathbf{S'} = \{A, B\}$ would lead to a violation of (ii). Coherent sets must be redundant, but not too redundant.

We thus see that these two requirements amount to the following two more generically formulated requirements:

(1) If $\mathbf{S}$ is a coherent set, then if all-but-one of the $\mathbf{S}$-elements are to be classed as true, then the truth of the remaining element is thereby determined and *all* must be classed as true.

(2) If $\mathbf{S}$ is a coherent set, then there is no subset $\mathbf{S'}$ of $\mathbf{S}$ all of whose elements can be classed as false without the presence of falsity among the *other* $\mathbf{S}$-elements (outside $\mathbf{S'}$) thereby being necessitated.

Together, these requirements assure that a coherent set of propositions forms an interrelation-family in point of truth status. With any such set, a specification of the truth status of certain elements must have repercussions for the truth-status of others.

One serious drawback of this definition is that a coherent set can always be made incoherent through the addition of nothing more than its own logical consequences. Thus suppose that the set

$$\mathbf{S} = \{P_1, P_2, \ldots, P_n\}$$

is coherent, and consider

$$S^+ = \{P_1, P_2, \ldots, P_n, P_1 \& P_2 \& \ldots \& P_n\}.$$

S^+—which simply adds to S one of its logical consequences—is not coherent, since it violates condition (ii). For now there is (by the hypothesized coherence of S) no proposition P within the subset S of S^+ for whose derivation from S^+ some element of $S^+ - S = \{P_1 \& P_2 \& \ldots \& P_n\}$ is needed. Thus the indicated procedure has destroyed the coherence initially present, and yet done so simply by making a coherent set 'yet more complete'.

Ewing's definition of 'coherence' has other serious shortcomings from the aspect of a coherence theory of truth. Such a theory must provide *some* basis for two implication-claims:

   I. If the members of a set of propositions are true then they are coherent.
  II. If the members of a set of propositions are coherent then they are true.

Now thesis I is, or rather can be, accommodated to the given concept of coherence, but, alas, in such a way as to trivialize the issue.

Let us assume—to face the 'worst' prospect—a set S of *entirely* independent propositions $P_1, P_2, \ldots, P_n$. Consider now the set

$$S^+ = \{P_1, P_2, \ldots, P_n, P_1 \& P_2 \& \ldots \& P_n\}.$$

Clearly (1) S^+ will have no proper subset *each* of whose elements can be derived from all the rest, although (2) S^+ is such that each of its own elements can be derived from the rest. It is thus readily verified that S^+ is a coherent set in the sense of the definition. And yet in forming S^+ from the incoherent set S we have done no more than to add to S one of its own logical consequences. Accordingly, *any* group of (contingent) propositions —even completely independent ones—can be presented as a coherent set.

But the still more serious difficulty lies with thesis II. Given a set of propositions that is *coherent* in the sense of a definition like that of Bosanquet or Ewing we are entitled to make claims solely about the hypothetical truth-relations that obtain in the set. We can only make claims of the form: 'If such-and-such elements are true (false) then these-and-those elements are true (false).' That is, we have articulated coherence solely with regard to *the strictly internal relationships of implication that obtain within* S. It is problematic, to say the least, to show that a relationship obtains between *this* feature of S-elements and their actual truth status.

Moreover, there will be sets that are internally 'coherent' in the sense of the definition, and yet include externally incompatible elements. The following pair afford an example:

$$\mathbf{S}_1 = \{p, q, p \ \& \ q\}$$
$$\mathbf{S}_2 = \{\sim p, r, \sim p \ \& \ r\}.$$

If—in the manner of thesis II—the step from mere coherence as such to truth could be taken, this would lead to the paradoxical result that a proposition and its contradictory would in some cases both count as true. It thus appears that Ewingesque coherence, of and by itself, cannot be enough to establish any linkage with truth.

5. *The Strategy of Coherence*

A coherence theory of truth may be seen in an essentially regulative role governing the considerations relating to the classification of empirical propositions as true, rather than claiming to present the *constitutive* essence of truth as such. In this regulative guise the central thesis of the theory is to be articulated in terms somewhat as follows:

For beings such as men, whose equipment for the acquisition and processing of data is imperfect, the truth is in general not the starting-point of inquiry but its terminus. To begin with, all that we generally have is a body of *prima facie* truths, i.e., propositions that qualify as potential—perhaps even as promising—*candidates* for truths. The epistemic realities being as they are, these candidate-truths will, in general, form a mutually inconsistent set, and so exclude one another so as to destroy the prospects of their being accorded *in toto* recognition as truths pure and simple. We are accordingly well advised to endorse those as truths that best 'cohere' with the others so as to 'make the most' of the data as a whole. Coherence thus becomes the critical *test* of the qualifications of truth-candidates for being classed as genuine truths.

In accordance with this line of thought our problem may be structured as follows. We begin with a set

$$\mathbf{S} = \{P_1, P_2, P_3, \ldots\}$$

of suitably 'given' propositions—that is, of *data*. These data are *not* given as true (then our criteriological problem would be solved), but rather given merely as *truth-candidates*—and in general competing (i.e. mutually inconsistent) ones. The problem to which the coherence theory addresses itself is to bring order into $\mathbf{S}$ by separating the sheep from the goats, distinguishing what qualifies as true from what does not. A truth-candidate comes to qualify for acceptance as a truth through its consistency with as much as possible from among the rest of the data. The criterion thus assumes an entirely *inward* orientation: it does not seek to compare the truth-candidate directly with other facts *outside* the given epistemic context; rather, having gathered as much information (and this, alas, will include misinformation) about the facts as is possible, it seeks to sift the true from the false *within* this body. The situation arising here resembles the solving of a jigsaw puzzle with superfluous pieces that cannot possibly be fitted into the orderly picture in whose construction the 'correct solution' lies.

The conformity of its approach with the general pattern of the process of deriving significant and consistent results from an inconsistent body of information is a key feature of the coherence theory of truth. To implement the idea of coherence as a pivotal criterion of truth is to face the question of the inferences appropriately to be drawn from an inconsistent set of premises. The initial mass of inconsistent information are the data for applying the concept of coherence as a criterion of truth, and its product is a consistent system of acceptable truths. On this approach, the coherence theory of truth views the problem of truth-determination as a matter of bringing order into a chaos comprised of initial data mingling secure evidence with shaky hypotheses. It sees the problem in transformational terms: incoherence into coherence, disorder into system, candidate-truths into qualified truths. From this perspective, the key task comes to be seen as that of devising the tactical means by which this strategy can be implemented.

III

PROGRAMMATIC CONSIDERATIONS GOVERNING A COHERENCE ACCOUNT OF TRUTH

1. *The Coherence Screening of Truths*

THE chapters to follow will endeavour to reconstruct a coherence theory of truth adequate to the historical views of the matter, and to do so in a manner consonant with modern standards of rigour and precision. They will attempt to develop systematically the logical machinery needed to make such a theory workable, and to explore in some detail its inner ramifications, its consequences, and its uses. Understanding the coherence theory to aim at providing a criterion of truth, coherence considerations may be construed to furnish a *testing procedure* for separating truths from falsehoods in the context of a family of competing truth-candidates in the factual domain. Thus viewed, the theory calls in outline for subjecting an inconsistent mass of conflicting propositions to a screening process in terms of their 'coherence' with one another, a screening process designed to separate the unqualified truth-candidates from the duly qualified truths.

As just remarked, this organization of discordant data into a coherent system of truths is akin to finding the 'right' solution to a jigsaw puzzle with excess pieces. We start with a great mass of *inconsistent* claims to truth. By suitably heeding logical relations among these, we build up as large a cohesive structure as possible. Those data that form part of this optimal structure are classed as truths and those which—being incompatible therewith—cannot be reconciled with them are rejected as falsehoods.

The truthfulness of a truth-candidate is thus an issue for *contextual* determination and becomes a matter of fitting it in amongst others in its environment. As H. H. Joachim puts it, the coherence theory would have us judge as true that which 'is demanded by, fits in with, indispensably supplements, "the whole" [of the data at our disposal]'.[1] On this procedure, truth-determination is not direct, but oblique—carried out not by

---

[1] H. H. Joachim, *Logical Studies* (Oxford, 1948), p. 272.

scrutinizing an isolated proposition in separation from others but by assessing its claims indirectly in terms of its relationships of mutual adjustment to others. The procedure is such that truth comes to be sought not in item-determinative but in system-determinative factors. A *systematic* aspect thus comes to the fore in the coherence theory. In a manner analogous with finding 'the right place' for the pieces of the puzzle in terms of the systematic nature of the resulting structures, the determination of the truthfulness of propositions is made to hinge upon the systematic structures into which they can be placed. Accordingly, the standard of truth is conceived in terms of a proposition's 'fit' within the context of other supporting—or competing—propositions.

2. *The Non-classical Character of a Coherence Theory of Truth*

Once the truth of a proposition is viewed as residing in its 'coherence-fit' with certain others, there arises the possibility that *neither* the proposition itself *nor* its contradictory denial will have the proper fit to qualify as true. The classical Law of the Excluded Middle, that of a proposition and its denial one must be true, has to be abandoned or qualified in a coherence theory of truth, when truth is viewed 'internally', so to speak, from the inner perspective of a criterial theory that may fail to class either a proposition P or its denial $\sim P$ as truths. This at once brings in its wake the demise or modification of those other logical principles that hinge upon this law. Specifically, the Law of Bivalence—that every proposition is either true or false—also comes into question. There is no reason, however, to expect a coherence theory to violate any of those principles of the classical theory of truth that (like the Law of Contradiction, which holds no proposition can be both true and false) are independent of bivalence/excluded middle.[2]

To summarize, a viable coherence theory must satisfy certain generic conditions for any workable theory of truth. Its criterion of truth must work in such a way as to guarantee the satisfaction of the following conditions:

1. A proposition can never be both true and false [Law of Contradiction].
2. A proposition is either true or false—not in general, but in all 'standard cases'[3] [Law of Bivalence in a weakened form].

[2] The important considerations which this paragraph has treated all too sketchily are examined in considerable detail in Chapter V.

[3] The precise specification of how the 'standard cases' in question are constituted will depend on—and vary with—the specific features of the coherence theory at issue. We shall have to return to this matter in Chapter VI.

3. Of a proposition and its negation (denial) at most one can be true and at most one false [Law of Negation].
4. Of a proposition and its negation (denial) at least one will be true, and at least one false—not in general, but in all 'standard cases' [Law of Excluded Middle in a weakened form].

The difference between a classical and a non-classical theory of truth lies precisely in the failure to maintain principles 2 and 4 of this list in unqualified form. One could not but regard it as a most unfortunate defect if a coherence theory of truth departed from the 'classical' logical doctrines further than in these matters of bivalence/excluded middle, in regard to which already Aristotle himself may well have been a non-classicist.[4]

Moreover, with a coherence theory, the idea of a proposition's fitting more or less adequately into an over-all system at issue will be applicable, at least in principle. We here face not a simple dichotomy of 'the true' and 'the false', but rather shades and gradations over a range from adequate to inadequate. The theory thus points towards a concept of *degrees* of truth that must be explored, and whose entry would also endow this theory with a significantly non-classical aspect.

3. *Characteristic Features of a Coherence Theory of Truth*

Against the background provided by these general considerations, it is possible to set out the specific features that must be looked for in the coherence theory to be developed. There will clearly be certain conditions that will apply specifically and characteristically to a coherence theory of truth. The totality of these features provides *criteria of adequacy* for any proposed reconstruction of the theory—a check-list to which any acceptable version of the theory must conform. Specifically, the following conditions must be met by any workable *coherence* theory of truth:

1. The truth of a proposition is to be assessed in terms of its 'coherence' with others: whether or not it is to be classed as true depends largely or exclusively on its relationships of compatibility or conflict with others. Correspondingly,
2. The issue of the truth of a proposition is a *contextual* matter in the sense that one cannot in general determine whether or not a proposition is true by inspecting it in isolation, but

---

[4] See N. Rescher, 'Truth and Necessity in Temporal Perspective' in idem, *Essays in Philosophical Analysis* (Pittsburgh, Pa., 1969), pp. 271-302.

only by analysing it in the setting of other propositions. Accordingly,

3. The truth of propositions is crucially dependent on matters of *systematization*, that is, of their logical linkages with other propositions together with which they form a connected network.[5] Thus

4. Truths must constitute a *system* that is *consistent* and whose members are appropriately *connected*: they must be inter-related so as to form a single cohesive unit, whose very cohesiveness acts to exclude other possibilities.

5. Moreover, this systematic unit must be sufficiently large to embrace the domain of real fact; it must exhibit a certain completeness—nothing can be omitted without due warrant. Accordingly, the domain of truth is determined through contextual considerations of compatibility and conflict and must be 'systematic' in being consistent, comprehensive, and cohesively unitary. These several systematic facets must be predominant in the coherence determination of truth.

6. However, a coherence theory will be such that certain laws of the classical theory of truth cannot be accepted in their traditional form. In general—outside the boundaries of special circumstances—the Laws of Bivalence and of Excluded Middle can in particular be maintained only in a restricted, weakened form, and not their classically strong versions.

These six theses present positions integral to the traditions of the subject. They must be secured by the coherence theory that is to be developed here.

4. *Objections to be Circumvented*

It is useful to take one more measure of the task that lies ahead. One can readily glean from the literature of the subject certain *standard objections* to the coherence theory of truth, and it must be asked of our theory that these objections be either met or circumvented in some appropriate way.

(1) It is usually objected that coherence cannot be the standard of truth because in determining coherence we make use of the truths of logic and hence must *already* have a standard of truth.

[5] As one coherence theorist emphatically insists, truth forms an *organic whole* which is 'such that all its constituent elements reciprocally involve one another, or reciprocally determine one another's being as contributory features in a single concrete meaning' (H. H. Joachim, *The Nature of Truth* (Oxford, 1906), p. 66).

This objection can be met in two ways, the first of which is as follows. One grants that coherence makes use of the *principles* of logic—its *rules* of inference—but denies that it requires logical *theses* or truths as such. All logical principles are reconstrued as regulative, that is, as rules for reasoning or inference-licences—even when seemingly formulated as outright assertions. Correspondingly one denies the need for a prior resolution of the issue of logical truths. One then goes on to argue that the correctness of logical principles can be assessed by standards that involve no explicit reference to truth—for example, by *pragmatic* considerations. In this way the machinery of logic can be put at the disposal of the theory of truth without reliance on a previously fixed standard of logical truth.

However, a second way of meeting the objection is certainly more forthright and perhaps more plausible. This is to concede that the coherence theory makes use of logical truths, but then to maintain that it is intended as a *partial criterion* rather than as a *comprehensive standard* of truth, so that no vicious circularity is involved. It is thus conceded that for *logical* truths some further appropriate criterion distinct from coherence is indeed needed. C. D. Broad has put the thesis as follows:

A coherent system seems to be one whose members are related in accordance with logical principles. These principles are themselves, no doubt, members of the system; but, unless they satisfy the intellect *apart* from considerations of their coherence with the other members of the system, the fact that the system as a whole is coherent in accord with these principles will not make it satisfy the intellect. My conclusion is that the coherence theory cannot do without [logical] facts . . . and that these really do satisfy the intellect apart from their coherence with other propositions. My argument is that there must at any rate be independent knowledge of the fact and of the principles of coherence. . . .[6]

From this perspective one is led to the view that the coherence theory addresses itself to the problem of a criterion for *extra-logical* truths, the traditional truths of fact.

The impact of the first objection can be deflected by either of these tactics. However, the second approach is not only less devious but serves as a blunt reminder of fundamentals. Unless 'coherence' is to be construed in somehow figurative, aesthetic

[6] 'Mr. Bradley on Truth and Reality', *Mind*, 23 (1914), 349–70 (see p. 366). Again, A. C. Ewing registers as a standard objection to the coherence theory the contention that 'even if the criterion of coherence can be applied to subsidiary conclusions, it cannot be applied to the fundamental principles of logic and, in particular to the coherence principle itself' (*Idealism: A Critical Survey* (London, 1934), p. 237; cf. also p. 241).

terms, a coherence theory unavoidably needs to make use of the machinery of logic. Thus if there are to be truths of logic at all—from any viewpoint whatever—coherence becomes disqualified as a global standard by which the truths of all subjects and disciplines must be assessed. To avoid circularity, the truths of logic—if such there be—must be judged by a standard other than that of coherence, since they are themselves essential to the implementation of that standard. At best, a coherence analysis of truth can apply within the extra-logical domain of empirical truth.[7] The machinery of logic—broadly construed to embrace definitional and conceptual truths in addition to narrowly 'logical' ones, and so to include the theory of meaning (semantics) as well as the purely formal theory of inference (*logic* in the narrower sense)—must form part of the basis of coherence considerations rather than be a product of them. Reasons such as these give grounds for abandoning the thesis of A. R. White that 'What the coherence theory really does is to give the criteria for the truth and falsity of *a priori*, or analytic, statements.'[8]

A reader may well ask at this stage: 'But if it is to deal with specifically empirical truths, why is the book described as concerned with the theory of truth rather than the methodology of science?' The answer is this: the special theory of scientific truth is to the general theory of empirical truth as the special theory of scientific explanation or exposition is to the theory of explanation or exposition in general. In each case, the precepts of the special domain must be not only compatible with but actually conformable to those of the general, but would manifest the more graphic detail and specialized features attainable in a narrower domain. Epistemology is broader than the theory of scientific method, however large and important its role may be. In science, after all, one is primarily concerned with laws, that is, with *general* truths regarding the processes of nature; whereas our present concern is in equal measure with the *particular* facts regarding the concrete details of specific occurrences.

(2) An objection closely related to the preceding one is that coherence cannot afford a standard of truth because coherence considerations cannot be used to validate the criterion itself without vicious circularity. C. D. Broad has formulated this point as follows:

---

[7] And even here, its claims will, as we shall see, have to be subject to further limitation—the truths of mathematics being a case in point.

[8] A. R. White, 'Coherence Theory of Truth' in P. Edwards (ed.), *The Encyclopedia of Philosophy*, vol. 2 (New York, 1967), pp. 130–3 (see p. 132). I view this contention as somewhat idiosyncratic because it does not reflect the position of any writer of the coherentist tradition.

In the discussions on coherence it seems to me that the propositions involved in the very notion of a coherent system have been somewhat neglected. To take a very simple example: Is the judgment that coherence is the ultimate test of truth accepted simply because it is coherent with all other judgments? If so, have we not a vicious circle? Unless this judgment can be known to be true independent of its coherence with other judgments how will the fact of its coherence with them prove its truth? For, *until* we know that it is true, why should we think the members of a coherent system more likely to be true than those of an incoherent one?[9]

But once the coherence criterion is no longer regarded as altogether *universal* in scope, this objection collapses. The withdrawal of logical truths from its scope opens up the prospect of placing the coherence criterion itself into this very class, and looking for its justification elsewhere in considerations apart from coherence (e.g. in pragmatic considerations). These brief indications must eventually be followed up in greater detail. But they suffice to exhibit the general lines along which the impact of the charge of circularity can be avoided.

(3) Yet another objection to a coherence standard of truth is that coherence, as a highly general and abstract truth-determining factor, can potentially come into conflict with more specific and concrete considerations. Thus suppose that we have a very partial and limited but yet basic and reliable means for truth-determination that yields $P_1, P_2, \ldots, P_n, Q$ as true. However, when we examine the matter from a coherence standpoint we find that what best coheres with $P_1, P_2, \ldots, P_n$ is actually some R that is incompatible with Q. In such a case coherence would point the wrong way, as it were. How is this prospect to be excluded? In sum, what guarantee can there be that, when there is some independent, albeit limited, standard of truth-evaluation, an application of the coherence machinery will produce an accordant result? Clearly if coherence is to be viable as a higher-level criterion it *must agree* with the results arrived at at the lower level in special cases.

This formulates what is not so much an objection to the programme of developing a coherence theory of truth as a problem that must be resolved in the course of such a development. But one observation is immediately in order. As long as the coherence theory at issue is strictly criterial and is prepared to admit the possibility of an error of type II, the way remains open for the criterion on occasion to qualify as a truth a proposition which further or better consideration reveals to be

9 'Mr. Bradley on Truth and Reality', *Mind*, 23 (1914), 349–70 (see p. 365).

a falsehood. In this event, the present objection is seen to ask for a guarantee that will not—and in principle cannot—be forthcoming.

(4) It is sometimes objected that coherence cannot be the standard of truth because here we may well arrive at a multiplicity of diverse but equally coherent structures, whereas truth is of its very nature conceived of as unique and monolithic. Bertrand Russell, for example, argues in this way:

. . . there is no reason to suppose that only *one* coherent body of beliefs is possible. It may be that, with sufficient imagination, a novelist might invent a past for the world that would perfectly fit on to what we know, and yet be quite different from the real past. In more scientific matters, it is certain that there are often two or more hypotheses which account for all the known facts on some subject, and although, in such cases, men of science endeavour to find facts which will rule out all the hypotheses except one, there is no reason why they should always succeed.[10]

One must certainly grant Russell's central point: however the idea of coherence is articulated in the abstract, there is something fundamentally undiscriminating about coherence. A group of truths can be found to cohere with one another, but so can a group of falsehoods. Fiction can be made as coherent as fact. Coherence may well be—nay certainly is—a descriptive feature of the domain of truths: they cohere. But there is nothing in this to prevent propositions other than truths from cohering with one another. Truths surely have no monopoly of coherence. Indeed '. . . it is logically possible to have two different but equally comprehensive sets of coherent statements between which there would be, in the coherence theory, no way to decide which was the set of true statements'.[11] In consequence, coherence

[10] B. Russell, *The Problems of Philosophy* (London, 1912), p. 191. Or compare M. Schlick's formulation of this point: 'Since no one dreams of holding the statements of a story book true and those of a text of physics false, the coherence view fails utterly. Something more, that is, must be added to coherence, namely, a principle in terms of which the compatibility is to be established [sc. as factual], and this would alone then be the actual criterion' (M. Schlick, 'The Foundation of Knowledge', in A. J. Ayer (ed.), *Logical Positivism* (Glencoe, Ill., 1959), pp. 209–27 (see p. 216)).

[11] A. R. White, 'Coherence Theory of Truth' in P. Edwards (ed.), *The Encyclopedia of Philosophy*, vol. 2 (1967), pp. 130–3 (see p. 131). One critic of the coherence theory elaborates this important point with demonstrative clarity as follows: 'That in the end only one sufficiently comprehensive system of statements would be found consistent, is a suggestion which runs counter to obvious facts about the nature of consistency and of systems; probably it strikes us as plausible because we are such poor liars, and are fairly certain to become entangled in inconsistencies sooner or later, once we depart from the truth. A sufficiently magnificent liar, however, or one who was given time and patiently followed a few simple rules of logic, could eventually present us with any number of systems, as comprehensive as you please, and all of them including falsehoods. Insofar as it is possible to deal with any such

cannot of and by itself discriminate between truths and false-hoods. Coherence is thus seemingly disqualified as a means for *identifying* truths. Any viable coherence theory of truth must make good the claim that despite these patent facts considera-tions of coherence can—somehow—be deployed to serve as an indicator of truth.

The objection in view is thus an essentially technical one that hinges on the specific character of the particular coherence theory at issue. Does it or does it not admit of cohesive diversity in such a way as to engender a fragmentation of truth? Surely there is no reason why a coherence theory *must* inevitably do so. Accordingly, the weight of this objection will have to be assessed after a specific version of the theory has been presented.

(5) A further criticism is developed by pressing hard upon the question 'coherence with what?' Is this to mean coherence with *everything*—with *all* other propositions that can be enunciated? That is patently impossible: as a body, the totality of meaningful propositions is certainly inconsistent—and so incoherent. Is it merely coherence with *something*—i.e. with some *other* proposi-tions—that is asked for? That clearly will not do. A novel or science fiction tale or indeed any other sort of made-up story can be perfectly coherent. To say simply that a proposition coheres with *certain* others is to say too little. *All* propositions will satisfy this condition, and so it is quite unable to tell us anything that bears upon the question of truth. It would be quite senseless to suggest that a proposition's truth resides in 'its coherence' alone. Its coherence is of conceptual necessity a relative rather than an absolute characteristic. Coherence must always be coherence *with something*. The verb 'to cohere with' requires an object just as much as 'to be larger than' does. We do not really have a co-herence theory in hand at all, until the *target domain* of coherence is specified. Once this has been done, we *may* very well find that the inherent truth-indeterminacy of abstract coherence—its

---

notion as "the whole of the truth", it is the Leibnizian conception of an infinite plurality of possible worlds which is justified, and not the conception of the historical coherence theory that there is just one all-comprehensive system, uniquely deter-mined to be true by its complete consistency. . . . Thus if we start with any empirical [i.e., contingent] belief or statement "P", we shall find that one or other of every pair of further empirical statements, "Q" and "not-Q", "R" and "not-R", etc., can be conjoined with "P" to form a self-consistent set. And exactly the same will likewise be true of its contradictory "not-P". *Every empirical supposition, being a contin-gent statement, is contained in some self-consistent system which is as comprehensive as you please.* And as between the truth of any empirical belief or statement "P" and the falsity of it (the truth of "not-P") consistency with other possible beliefs or state-ments, or inclusion in comprehensive and self-consistent systems, provides no clue or basis of decision' (C. I. Lewis, *An Analysis of Knowledge and Valuation* (La Salle, Ill., 1962), pp. 340–1).

potential failure to yield a unique result—has been removed. Now it must be said in their defence that the traditional coherence theorists have not located truth in merely generic coherence *per se*, but have insisted that it is specifically 'coherence with our experience' that is to be the standard of truth.[12] The coherence theory of the British idealists has never abandoned altogether the empiricist tendency of the native tradition of philosophy.

(6) Moreover, it will clearly not do to say that it is coherence *with other truths* that is at issue in the coherence theory. For then we say too much! Some different, prior criterion will now clearly be needed to determine the truthfulness of these other truths. Then coherence could never serve as a primary truth-originative standard, but only as one that is secondary and truth-expansive.

Some philosophers take just this view. They argue that coherence, at any rate, is at best a means of amplifying our claims to truth: it cannot be a means for initiating truth-claims on a basis that affords no conceded truths as data:

> To reject a particular empirical statement like 'He saw a ghost' because it conflicts with the body of our beliefs is . . . [a step] made only because we think the body of our everyday beliefs has already been shown to be true of the world. Coherence of judgment with another is accepted as a practical test of truth only because the second judgment is independently accepted as true.[13]

It must be among the principal aims of a workable coherence theory of truth to provide a means of circumventing the thesis that *coherence of one proposition with others only constitutes a test of truth when these others are independently accepted as true.*[14]

[12] See A. C. Ewing, *Idealism: A Critical Survey* (London, 1934), p. 238, as well as his later essay on 'The Correspondence Theory of Truth' where he writes: 'that coherence is the test of truth can only be made plausible if coherence is interpreted not as mere internal coherence but as coherence with our experience' (*Non-Linguistic Philosophy* (London, 1968), pp. 203–4). For an author of the earlier period see H. H. Joachim who writes: 'Truth, we said, was the systematic coherence which characterized a significant whole. And we proceeded to identify a significant whole with "an organized individual experience, self-filling and self-fulfilled"' (*The Nature of Truth* [Oxford, 1906], p. 78).

[13] A. R. White, op. cit., p. 131.

[14] The operative issue is trenchantly formulated by one recent writer as follows: '. . . if a proposition is tested wholly or solely by its coherence or lack of coherence with a system *S*, the question arises as to how *S* itself is to be verified . . .: on what grounds do we regard or have regarded it as knowledge in the first place' (H. Khatchadourian, *The Coherence Theory of Truth: A Critical Evaluation* (Beirut, 1961), pp. 111–12). The result of this line of thought is put by C. I. Lewis as follows: 'Unless there are *some* empirical truths known otherwise than by their relations of consistency or inconsistency with others, no empirical truths can ever be determined by the criterion of consistency' (*An Analysis of Knowledge and Valuation* (La Salle, Ill., 1946), p. 341). H. H. Price has given an incisive statement of the key point: 'And clearly these new testimonies do strengthen . . . [a] story, *if* there is any independent reason for believing them to be true. In the case of the novel, on the other hand, there is *no* independent reason for thinking that any of the

In one interesting passage in his Carus Lectures for 1946 C. I. Lewis sketches a probabilistic variant of the coherence theory in the following terms:

... a possibility to be examined [is] that a body of empirical beliefs, each of which is less than certain and no one of which can be substantiated on empirically certain grounds, may nevertheless be justified as credible by their relation to one another ... [The case here is] fundamentally different ... from those theses, put forward by British post-Kantian idealism, which have the best right, historically, to the label 'coherence theory of truth'. In order to mark our departure from that historical conception, we shall speak of the *congruence* of statements, instead of coherence; and shall assign to this term 'congruence' a definite and limited meaning. *A set of statements, or a set of supposed facts asserted, will be said to be congruent if and only if they are so related that the antecedent probability of any one of them will be increased if the remainder of the set can be assumed as given premises.* This relation of congruence requires something more than merely the mutual consistency of a set of statements, but something less than that relation of a set or system such that each statement in it is logically deducible from the others, taken together as premises. If, however, we are not to repeat some of the fallacies of the historical coherence theory, it becomes vitally important to observe that neither mutual consistency throughout, nor what we call congruence of a set of statements, nor even that relation of a system in which every included statement is deducible from others which are included, can by itself assure even the lowest degree of probability for a body of empirical beliefs or suppositions in question. For that, it is absolutely requisite that some at least of the set of statements possess a degree of credibility antecedent to and independently of the remainder of those in question, and derivable from the relation of them to direct experience.[15]

One key aspect of Lewis's congruence theory is that congruence itself cannot provide a basis for accepting something as true: for truth-determination to be possible, the congruence

statements are true. The very naive reader may indeed have an inclination to take them for true, but that is not a reason. It is necessary to lay stress on this very obvious point because it does seem to be neglected by some advocates of the "coherence" theory of truth. A "coherent" system of propositions is presumably a system such that if any one proposition in it is true, it strengthens the probability of all the rest. But some people seem to conclude from this that any one proposition in the system strengthens the probability of the rest *whether it is itself true or not*' (*Perception* [New York, 1933], p. 183). It is, no doubt, this criticism more than any other that has led to the abandonment of the coherence theory of truth—even by writers deeply sympathetic to it. Thus A. C. Ewing writes in correspondence: 'I no longer give coherence nearly such an important place in thought as I used to, nor do I think any longer that it is an ultimate criterion. Where it is valid as a criterion I think it is always ultimately for some reason other than itself; e.g. if *p* and *q* are logically related so that the truth of *p* entails or makes probable the truth of *q*, then *p* is of course an argument for *q* on any theory, but their coherence can only serve as an argument in its favor because *p* is independently known.'

[15] *An Analysis of Knowledge and Valuation* (La Salle, Ill., 1962), pp. 338–9.

family must consist in statements independently established as true. Thus consider a congruence family of three propositions: p, q, r. Let us assume that these propositions are such that:

$$\Pr(p \ \& \ q \ \& \ r) = 0.6 \times 10^{-10}$$
$$\Pr(p \ \& \ q) = \Pr(p \ \& \ r) = \Pr(q \ \& \ r) = 0.7 \times 10^{-10}$$
$$\Pr(p) = \Pr(q) = \Pr(r) = 0.8 \times 10^{-10}.$$

Then it follows that:

$$\Pr(p/q \ \& \ r) = \Pr(q/p \ \& \ r) = \Pr(r/p \ \& \ q) = \tfrac{6}{7}$$
$$\Pr(p/q) = \Pr(q/p) = \Pr(p/r) = \Pr(r/p)$$
$$= \Pr(q/r) = \Pr(r/q) = \tfrac{7}{8}.$$

Throughout, the probabilities of the propositions in question are such that the propositions support each other—individually and collectively—to a very substantial extent indeed. All the same, all of these propositions are—individually and collectively— extremely improbable. The plain fact is that mutual concurrence just does not constitute any basis, however weak, for probable truth, let alone truth *per se*.

Moreover, we must already assume mutual consistency throughout the congruence family. Otherwise some of its member propositions would not be rendered relatively probable by the rest. Lewis's theory thus cannot meet that desideratum of a coherence theory that it bring order into logical chaos (i.e. inconsistency). Mutual consistency is its initial postulate.

This basic concept of coherence which underlies Lewis's *congruence*—i.e. the mutual support and reinforcement that a family of propositions lend to one another when all have a conjointly non-trivial probability (and so are *a fortiori* mutually consistent), and when each is rendered probable by the rest (i.e. *a posteriori* more likely with respect to them)—is an idea that recurs repeatedly in recent writings on epistemology. It is tantamount to what Arthur Pap calls 'coherence' or 'reciprocal confirmation';[16] and it amounts to what Roderick Chisholm calls 'concurrence', which he defines as follows: 'Any set of propositions that are mutually consistent and logically independent of each other (no one logically implies another) is *concurrent* provided that each member of the set is confirmed by the conjunction of all the other members of the set.'[17] All these concepts alike specify a coherence-analogous concept that:

[16] A. Pap, *Elements of Analytical Philosophy* (New York, 1949), p. 361.
[17] R. Chisholm, *Theory of Knowledge* (Englewood Cliffs, N.J., 1966), p. 53. Chisholm refers to C. I. Lewis's prior discussion of this concept in *The Theory of Knowledge and Valuation* (La Salle, Ill., 1946), as well as to the treatment of coherence in H. H. Price, *Perception* (New York, 1933).

1. is in principle only applicable to a consistent group of statements
2. requires all the statements at issue to be individually *and collectively* established by evidence, and so
3. requires prior development of an independent criterion of factual truth.

We are thus carried back to Lewis's basic theses that the establishment of truths requires a true foundation. The door is shut on the prospect of using this concept of *congruence* (Lewis) or *reciprocal confirmation* (Pap) or *concurrence* (Chisholm) as an *initiating* rather than as merely an *amplifying* criterion of truth.

This line of thought leads to the objection that the coherence standard is altogether disqualified as a fundamental criterion of truth by the fact that coherence can only then indicate the truthfulness of a proposition when it is *coherence with prior truths* that is at issue. One critic puts this point as follows: '. . . perfect coherence and comprehensiveness cannot be the ultimate *test* of truth. Only if the perfectly coherent and comprehensive system *is true* will the coherence of actual systems and propositions with it entail their truth, and their lack of coherence with it entail their falsity.'[18] Such an interpretation of 'coherence' as 'coherence with established truths' clearly admits no way of meeting the traditional demand upon a coherence theory of truth for the provision of an *initiating* standard of truth.

What is clearly wanted is a half-way house between coherence with *some* (i.e. *any*) propositions and coherence with *true* propositions. Essentially, what is needed is coherence with somehow 'the right' propositions. The coherence at issue in a coherence theory of truth must be construed as involving all in some way *appropriately qualified* propositions. This line of thought poses a task central to the construction of a workable coherence theory: that of specifying just what propositions are at stake when one speaks of determining the truth of a given proposition in terms of its 'coherence *with others*'. Which others are at issue? In answering this question we must introduce the key concept of a *datum*, thereby taking a large initial step towards the actual construction of the coherence theory to be presented.

5. *The Key Concept of a Datum*

Any adequate coherence theory of truth must resolve the objection: Why should coherence indicate truth? Regardless of

[18] H. Khatchadourian, *The Coherence Theory of Truth: A Critical Evaluation* (Beirut, 1961), p. 135.

how we resolve the issue of *defining* truth, truth is determined by the relation of a proposition *to the actual facts*. Coherence on the other hand, is a matter of the relation of propositions to each other. How, then, can we possibly pass from the one to the other? This objection too points to the (already mooted) consideration that it cannot be just abstract coherence that is at issue in a coherence theory of truth, but coherence with 'the right' propositions. Accordingly, the problem of the data that provide grist to the mill of coherence must be faced and resolved.

The concept of a datum, which is to play a pivotal role in the ensuing considerations, is something of a technical innovation. To be sure, the idea is one not *entirely* unrelated to the ordinary use of that term, nor to its (somewhat different) use among philosophers; yet it is significantly different from both.

A datum is a *truth-candidate*, a proposition to be taken not as true, but as potentially or *presumptively* true. It is a prima facie truth in exactly the sense in which one speaks of prima facie duties in ethics, a prima facie duty being one that is to represent an actual duty only provided that no countervailing conditions are operative. Similarly, a datum is a prima facie truth in that we should under the circumstances be prepared to class it as true provided that no countervailing considerations are operative. A datum is thus a proposition that one is to class as true *if one can*, that is, if doing so does not generate any difficulties or inconsistencies. A datum is not *established* as true, it is backed only by a *presumption* that it may turn out true 'if all goes well'. It lays a claim to truth, but it may not be able to make good this claim in the final analysis. (A datum is thus something altogether different from the basic, protocol truths that serve as foundation for an *Aufbau* of truth in the manner of the logical positivists.)

Such a datum is—in the traditional sense—a 'given'. But a proposition may be given in two ways:

(1) as a *truth* or as *actually* true; to be classed as true *sans phrase*.
(2) as a *truth-candidate*; as *potentially* or *presumptively* true; to be classed as true provided that doing so creates no anomalies.

A datum is a proposition that is 'given' not in the first, but only in this second mode: it is a *pretender* to truth whose credentials may well prove insufficient, a runner in a race it may not win. (And what is true of *givens* holds also for *assumptions*: a proposition can be assumed to be a truth [i.e. assumed as true] or assumed to be a truth-candidate [i.e. assumed as a datum]. A very different condition of things is posited in the two cases.)

For a proposition to count as a datum is altogether different from its counting as a truth, just as a man's being a presidential candidate is something far different from his being a president. Presidential candidates are not presidents; data are not truths. Truth-candidacy does not require or presuppose truth: quite different issues are involved. A potential truth is a truth no more than an egg-enclosed embryo is a hen. The 'acceptance' of a proposition as a truth-candidate is not *acceptance* at all but a highly provisional and conditional epistemic *inclination* towards it, an inclination that falls far short of outright commitment.

In taking a proposition to be a datum we propose to class it as true *whenever possible*, recognizing that this may not be possible because some data may contradict one another, so that we must consider some of them as non-truths. A datum is to be carried across the line from datahood to truth automatically whenever such a transfer is *unproblematic* (i.e. in no way involves a contradiction). A member of a group of data that meets with no rivalry from its fellows can immediately be accepted as true. Thus:

Given the data[19]	*We shall immediately obtain as a truth (relative to these data)*
(1) p, q	p, q
(2) $p, \sim p$	—
(3) $p, q, \sim q$	p
(4) $p, q, r, \sim p \lor \sim q, p \lor \sim p$	$r, p \lor \sim p$

Our stance towards data is unashamedly that of fair-weather friends: we adhere to them when this involves no problems whatsoever, but abandon them at the first sign of difficulties. But it is quite clear that such *loose* attachment to a datum is by no means tantamount to no attachment at all.[20]

The following objection might be made: How can you speak of asserting a proposition merely as a datum but not as a truth? If one is to assert (accept, maintain) the proposition in any way at all, does one not thereby assert (accept, maintain) it *to be true*? The answer to be made here is simply a head-on denial. To maintain P as a datum, as *potentially* or *presumptively* factual, is

---

[19] In this table propositional variables, p, q, r, etc., are to be thought to represent independent propositions.

[20] As I. Scheffler puts a similar point in the temporal context of a change of mind in the light of new information: 'That a sentence may be given up at a later time does not mean that its present claim upon us may be blithely disregarded. The idea that once a statement is acknowledged as theoretically revisable, it can carry no cognitive weight at all, is no more plausible than the suggestion that a man loses his vote as soon as it is seen that the rules make it possible for him to be outvoted' (*Science and Subjectivity* (New York, 1967), p. 118).

akin to maintaining P as *possible* or as *probable*: in no case are these tantamount to maintaining the proposition as true. Putting a proposition forward as 'possible' or 'probable' commits one to claiming no more than that it is *'possibly* true' or *'probably* true'. Similarly, to assert P *as a datum* is to say no more than that P is *potentially* or *presumptively* true—that it is a truth-candidate—but does not say that P is *actually* true, that it is a truth. As with assertions of possibility or probability, a claim of datahood definitely stops short—far short—of a claim to truth.

We do not intend the conception of a datum to 'open the floodgates' in an indiscriminate way. Not *everything* is a datum: the concept is to have *some* logico-epistemic bite. To be a datum is not just to be a proposition that *could conceivably* be claimed to be true but to be a proposition that (under the circumstances) can be claimed to be true with at least *some* plausibility: its claim must be well-founded. A proposition will not qualify as a datum without *some* appropriate grounding. Data are propositions that have a proper claim upon truth, and we must distinguish between truth-claims that can reasonably be made from those that are merely theoretically possible. (Not every human being is a possible winner in a race but only those who are genuinely 'in the running'.) A datum is a proposition which, given the circumstances of the case, is a *real prospect for truth* in terms of the availability of reasons to warrant its truth-candidacy. A datum is not merely something that is 'possibly true' or that is 'true for all I know about the matter'. To class a proposition as a datum is to take a definite and committal position with respect to it, so as to say 'I propose to accept it as true in so far as this is permitted by analogous and possibly conflicting commitments elsewhere'.

The final cautionary clause means that in point of truth datahood is not an isolated feature of a single proposition but a contextual feature of a group of propositions, that is, a *family* of data. The reference to a 'conflict with others' gives to an imputation of datahood a relative and context-involving aspect. A more ambitious claim to truthfulness characterizes such a family of data than any one member of it. No imputation of truth (as opposed to presumptive or candidate truth) attaches to any individual datum, but there is a definite implicit claim that the 'logical space' spanned by the data as a whole somewhere embraces the truth of the matter. To be sure, several mutually incompatible propositions can be 'introduced in evidence'—i.e. as potentially to be included among what is ultimately to be accepted—but it must remain our view that 'the real truth' is somehow present within this fabric of possibility, as the winner of a race must be sought among those 'in the running'.

Taken individually, the data are merely truth-*presumptive*, but taken collectively as a family they are to be viewed as truth-containing: admitting that they do not *pinpoint* where the truth lies, we are committed to the view that they *surround* the area where it is to be found.

We in general *know* that data cannot be identified with truths —that some of them must indeed be falsehoods—because they are generally incompatible with one another. Truth-candidates —like rival candidates for public office—can work to exclude one another: they are mutually exclusive and victory for one spells defeat for the others. Candidate-truths are not truths pure and simple because it is of the very nature of the case that matters must so eventuate that some of them are falsehoods.

Virtually all writers on the subject take the position that, as one recent authority puts it, 'acceptance as true is a necessary condition for acceptance as evidence'.[21] On this view, if something can only count as genuine and actual evidence when it is established as true, the weaker conception of *potential* evidence —as contradistinguished from evidence as such (the *actual* evidence)—comes closer to our conception of the data. But although *some* basis is required for counting as a datum, this basis need not be very strong by the usual epistemic standards. To be a datum is to be a truth-*candidate*. And to count as such, a proposition need be neither an *actual* truth, nor a *probable* truth: it need only be 'in the running' as a genuine candidate or a live possibility for truth. Such propositions are not truths, but make good a claim to truth that is at best tentative and provisional; by themselves they do not formulate truth but at most *indicate* it. Historically the tentativity of the experientially and mnemonically 'given' has always been recognized, and the deliverances of our senses and our memory are the traditional examples of this circumstance of merely *purported* truth.

One may well ask: 'How can coherence with the data yield truth if the data themselves are not individually true? How can something so tentative prove sufficiently determinative?' The answer can only be found in the detailed development of the machinery; at this preliminary stage we can do no better than give a rough analogy. Consider again the earlier example of a jigsaw puzzle with superfluous pieces. It is clear here that the

---

[21] I. Levi, *Gambling with Truth* (New York, 1967), p. 28. 'To accept H as evidence is not merely to accept H as true but to regard as pointless further evidence collection in order to check on H' (ibid., p. 149).

factor of 'suitably fitting in' will be determinative of a piece's place (or lack of place) in the correct solution. Not the (admittedly tentative) status of the individual pieces but their mutual relationships of systematic accord is the determinative consideration. Thus the issue is not that of how mere truth-candidacy itself can serve to confer truth but of how it can help to determine truth on the basis of certain systematic considerations. Of course the exact nature of these considerations remains to be considered, but the key fact at this stage is that there is an important epistemic category of claims to presumptive or provisional verisimilitude that carry truth-indicative weight, while yet stopping well short of claims to truth as such.

This underlines the sharp difference between *data* in the present sense and *evidence* as traditionally understood. Only what is conceded as true can count as evidence: a claim of truth must be conceded for whatever is to serve as evidence on the orthodox conception. But the relation of evidence to data in our sense is close to being an inverse one. Evidence consists in adducing truths by means of which the claims of a truth-candidate are to be supported. The data, by contrast, are the truth-candidates themselves from which truths are to be extracted. When a proposition is validated by evidence, other propositions are adduced as grounds for it; but when a proposition is validated by data, it itself (or propositions strong enough to entail it deductively)—as well as its prime alternatives—will in general be present among the data.[22] On the standard conception, the evidence cannot be inconsistent without cancelling itself out. The evidence—whatever it be—must be mutually compatible. Just this, we have insisted, is not to be so in the case of data. In this respect, an attempt 'to extract the truth from the evidence' is very different from one that sets out from data, where nothing need be claimed or conceded as true. And we must go beyond the orthodox conception that a reasonable claim to truth of the discursive type must be based upon evidence, and so require a prior concession of truth. The very core idea of our coherence analysis of truth is that truth-determinations can be based upon data that have *not* already been established, rather than upon evidence that has been. Unlike the introduction of evidence, that of data requires no prior concession of truth.

Articulated in these terms, the presently operative standard of truth will be essentially relative: the data used must play the

[22] The inclusion among the given data of the proposition *sub judice* is natural and may in general be expected. However, its presence among the given *evidence* is unnatural because it would vitiate the whole procedure as circular.

decisive role, and the truth extracted from them is truth 'relative to' or 'with respect to' the data. If the data are changed, this will affect the propositions they determine as true on a coherence analysis—in much the same way as in deductive logic when the premisses are altered, this may change the propositions they determine as true. Of course, as long as the premisses are maintained *as given premisses* the consequences they determine will remain fixed as (relative) truths. And as long as the data are maintained *as given data* the consequences they engender through a coherence analysis are determined as (relative) truths. But the analysis is—and must be—impotent to yield truths save on a foundation of data. We are dealing at the criteriological level with truth relative to a given basis—not with truth in some absolute sense. The resulting structure of truth will and must be such as to reflect (at least in part) the specific foundations on which it rests.

6. *Examples of Data*

Understanding that data are *potential* truths or truth-candidates, the question remains: what procedure is to be used in qualifying a proposition for datahood? This question does not admit of a single answer—different sorts of data-establishing considerations will be at issue in different contexts. The best course of procedure is by way of examples:

Example 1: Reports

A paradigm example of data is afforded by reports stemming from different sources, such as historical reports about some transaction of the past. In so far as they agree in mutual substantiation, we would not hesitate to accept them all as true; but often such reports do not agree—some contradict others. In this event they cannot be regarded as truths, but at best regarded as truth-candidates. It should be remarked that we are at this point dealing with the status of a certain author of contentions as *a source pure and simple*, and not necessarily as *a good source*—one that is accurate and reliable. This second item is one that affects his *merit* as a source (not his serving as a source as such). This cannot be resolved only in the course of applying a criterion of truth, but can become an operative issue only after such a criterion has been deployed.

Analogous cases arise in connection with information supplied by different data-sources regarding what goes on in some sector of the world—the different sensors of a servomechanism, for example, or a man's different senses. Thus sight may report that the stick under water is bent, touch that it is straight. Against the claims of the senses automatically to afford us the truth pure and simple one can deploy all of the traditional arguments of the sceptics, and take for our precept the dictum of Descartes: 'All that up to the present time I have accepted as most true and certain I have learned either from the senses or through the senses; but it is sometimes proved to me that these senses are deceptive, and it is wiser not to trust entirely to any thing by which we have once been deceived.'[23] But, of course, such arguments in support of the potential untruthfulness of sensory data serve only to re-emphasize their role as *data*—i.e. truth-*candidates* —in our sense, rather than outright *truths* as such. In our technical sense of these terms we must thus speak not of 'the *evidence* of our senses' but rather of 'the *data* of our senses'. (That potential fallibility proves actual falsehood and that these truth-candidates are in principle to be excluded from the realm of truth—in short that what is not known to be true is thereby known to be false—is something no sceptic has claimed to establish in even his most extravagant moments. And this being so, the door to truth-candidacy will remain open.) While in the face of potential inconsistencies among sensory (or other) reports one must yield up any insistence on truth, the factor of truth-*candidacy* yet passes by unscathed, and is not damaged by the fact that some candidates occasionally fail.

Example 2: Probable Consequences of Given Information

A second possibility is to approach the idea of truth-candidacy from a probabilistic direction. Accordingly, we might be prepared to count as a datum any proposition that is sufficiently probable relative to a given informational base. This policy is perfectly workable and is not impeded by the well-known difficulty of taking probability as a guide to truth as such.

Thus suppose that we are to toss a normal die, and that we are prepared to accept as a *presumptive* truth any proposition with probability greater than 0·8. The following would all qualify as data

The toss will not yield 1

The toss will not yield 2

.

.

.

The toss will not yield 6.

---

[23] *Meditations on First Philosophy*, No. I, tr. R. M. Eaton.

Note that these all qualify as a datum since each has a high probability ($\frac{5}{8}$ or 0·83). But it is perfectly clear that not *all* of these presumptively true propositions can possibly be actual truths. (For then their conjunction would be true—which is *ex hypothesi* impossible.)

Relating the conception of datahood to probable evidence, we might be prepared to count as a datum (truth-candidate) those propositions that a given item of evidence renders more likely *a posteriori* than they were *a priori*. But this seemingly natural approach also leaves open the possibility of the data once more being incompatible. Thus consider the following set:

$$\{\alpha, \beta, \gamma, \delta, 1, 2, 3, 4\}.$$

Let it be supposed that one element has been singled out at random. Consider now the evidence: 'The chosen element is a number.' With the approach indicated, this provides substantiating evidence *both* for

(1) The chosen element is an *odd* number

and

(2) The chosen element is an *even* number.

Both of these propositions initially had an *a priori* probability of $\frac{2}{8}$ or $\frac{1}{4}$ but now in the face of the evidence obtain an *a posteriori* probability of $\frac{2}{4}$ or $\frac{1}{2}$. The evidence thus serves to support each of these propositions by *doubling* its probability. But in the face of this example it is again quite clear that not *all* the data—truth-candidates on the present mode of datahood-determination—can possibly qualify as truths, since there will be inconsistencies.

Note that this second probabilistic construction of datahood does not require us to maintain that the data be probable *per se*. Thus consider an urn with three balls, each of them black or white. Three balls are drawn at random with replacement, and the 'evidence' is that all three so drawn were white. The family of propositions that interests us is:

$[i]$ = there are exactly i white balls in the urn ($i = 0, 1, 2, 3$). Accordingly we have four possibilities with the following probabilities:

$$\Pr([0]) = 0$$
$$\Pr([1]) = 0·07$$
$$\Pr([2]) = 0·29$$
$$\Pr([3]) = 0·64.$$

Now we might well choose to take probability-greater-than-0·01 as our criterion for datahood, and accordingly eliminate only

[0]. To qualify as a datum is to be a truth-*candidate*, and to possess '*some* prospect for truth', and this does not at all require a proposition to be probable *per se*. Thus in the above case, none of the propositions at issue qualifies as probable, but all of them, save for the eliminated [0], qualify as data.

Example 3: Counterfactuals

Consider a belief-contravening conditional such as: 'If this pat of butter had been heated, it would have melted.' Note that this conditional is put forward against the following context of background knowledge:

(1) This pat of butter has not been heated
(2) This pat of butter has not melted
(3) All pats of butter melt when heated.

The antecedent of the counterfactual explicitly instructs us to replace (1) by its negation

(1') This pat of butter has been heated.

From this premiss we can indeed get via (3) to 'This pat of butter has melted' as the counterfactual conditional insists. But this result explicitly contradicts (2). Thus the 'residuum' of our remaining knowledge after replacement of (1) by (1') constitutes an inconsistent set of propositions. In the setting of the new epistemic situation that results from the hypothesis we cannot now look upon these propositions as *truths* but at best as truth-candidates.

And this circumstance is general: whenever a counterfactual hypothesis is introduced into a context the result is a family of 'givens' that, being mutually inconsistent, can at best be regarded as truth-candidates but not as truths. Counterfactual hypotheses thus provide another road by which we may arrive at truth-candidates.

Example 4: Inductive Grounding

Let us begin with some given informational base, **B**, and consider the set **S** of the relevant alternatives that are inductively grounded by **B**, the various hypotheses that are *inductively possible* with respect to **B**. Thus letting ⊢ be the relationship of evidential grounding we form the set **S** such that whenever **B** ⊢ *P*, then *P* ∈ **S**. Clearly this procedure yields an inconsistent set. (The case is akin to that of probabilities.) For example, in a detective story all of the sleuth's conjectures on the basis of 'the given facts of the case' as to how the various suspects may have committed the crime will form such a set.

7. *The Determination of Datahood*

As the examples considered in the preceding section show, there are various distinct roads that lead to families of 'data' in the sense of our discussion: reports, belief-contravening assumptions and their epistemic neighbourhood, and inductively grounded alternatives, among others. A multiplicity of sources of data are indigenous to common sense and epistemological tradition: first-hand sense perceptions and memory, vicarious observation-reports, synthetic cognitive processes like assumption, supposition, conjecture, etc. And these, of course, are of variable plausibility. There is no one single uniform and monolithic *criterion of datahood*, no one sole basis for presumptive factuality. Many and various routes can lead to the same destination, presenting us with propositions which have an epistemic foundation sufficiently insecure to fail to establish their truth, but yet sufficient to warrant some claim to truth—a claim that must prevail in the total absence of counterindications. All in all, data vary drastically in nature—they are a jumble of facts, hypotheses, conjectures, and possibly even assumptions.

What fixes the potential truthfulness of the data in cases of sensation, of memory, of hypothetical reasoning, of reports, of scientific hypotheses, etc., is determined not by one single uniform general principle, but by case-specific, *ad hoc* considerations.[24] Data in our sense will be forthcoming in various contexts of inquiry through epistemic considerations diversified in type and different in nature. This lack of a single standard does not mean that the determination of truth-candidates need be complicated or even mysterious. Rather, the fact that we can so readily manage in these diverse cases without a unique standard points to the essential simplicity of the matter.

But if a coherence analysis calls for the use of data, and if a quite different procedure for the identification of 'the data' can be operative in different cases, how is it that the use of one particular method in a certain case or group of cases is justified? What validates the use of one specific 'criterion of datahood'? Clearly this cannot without baneful circularity be the thesis that this standard leads to the truth. Rather, it is an essentially *pragmatic* justification: that this standard 'works out best' in a problem situation of the sort at issue. The key factor is that of

---

[24] Consider but one example. Suppose that someone we know (on grounds extraneous to the present case) to be so colour-blind as to be unable to distinguish between green and blue (but otherwise visually normal) reports an object to be green. Then we cannot just enter his explicit report 'The item is green' alone among the data, clearly both this and 'The item is blue' will be truth-candidates.

experience which must prove decisive here. Historically speaking, the process is fundamentally one of Darwinian selection. There is no *theoretical* reason for excluding dreams, premonitions, and omens as potential data for our knowledge of the processes of nature. It is only because they fail us in the pragmatic context of our purposes—explanation, prediction, and control—that these 'data' are dismissed as not veridical, i.e. irrelevant in our search for truth.[25]

The development of this line of justification must await the more detailed presentation of the machinery of coherence analysis and the procedures for its application. (See Chapters IX–X below.) Yet one preliminary observation is in order. A datum is unlike the protocol truths of the positivists not only (as already emphasized) in its potential failure to be true, but also in that it is not essentially 'protocol'—data, that is, need not be cognitively primitive. That is, a 'datum' in our sense is not an epistemically fundamental and nondiscursive 'baseless basis'. There will, in general, be a rational warrant for counting something as a datum. If it be the case that 'we have reason to believe he was there, "on the spot"', then this, for example, provides a good basis for treating some person's declarations about a purported historical transaction as a datum regarding this transaction (though of course this 'foundation for datahood' is far removed from being an automatic justification of the truth of what he says). And in analogous ways the acceptance *as a datum* of a certain declaration can in general be supported by reasons. That a certain proposition should 'be counted among the data' of a particular problem of truth-determination is not a primitive fact but a rationally supportable contention (albeit one whose support need not go so far as to establish its truth). Datahood is certainly no matter of arbitrary convention but is subject to rational criteria whose credentials of legitimation form a crucial part of coherentist epistemology. But it is crucially important that the issue here is one of generic grounds for presumptive credibility rather than of specific grounds establishing the truth of particular claims.

8. *The Foundational Role of Data*

Data—construed along some such lines as that of the preceding discussion—must inevitably play a pivotal role in the articulation of a coherence-based criterion of truth. The entire drama

[25] This line of thought with its insistence on the co-ordination in the search for truth of the theoretical with the practical aspect of relevant purpose is developed in detail in Section 6 of Pt. III, 'Explanation, Scientific Understanding, and the Aim of Science' of the author's book on *Scientific Explanation* (New York, 1970).

of a coherence analysis will be played out within the sphere of propositions, in terms of the sorts of relationships they have to one another. Now there is—in any event—enough merit in a correspondence account of truth for a somehow appropriate relationship to obtain between 'the actual facts of the matter' and a proposition regarding them that can qualify as true. However, as long as we confine our attention entirely to the relationships among maintained propositions, then any such 'external' relationship will and must escape us. The propositions make claims, but the question of their factuality remains untouched. A basis of limitation to propositions that are to some extent 'appropriate in view of the facts' cannot be altogether dispensed with in a search for true propositions. And since this basis cannot be the *product* of a coherence analysis deployed purely in the abstract, it must be an *input* thereof. The task of the 'data' is to provide this required input for the coherence machinery. But having paid the devil—or rather, the correspondence theory—this due, we must also insist that the required external relationship need not and will not be one of correspondence to facts, and indeed that the data need not —and generally will not—be truths. Just this renders it not altogether incredible that a coherence criterion should have not only *truth-widening* applications to yield new truths from old ones, but even *truth-generating* applications that yield truths as output from a basis that includes no truths.

To the criticism why should mere coherence imply truth, we thus propose to reply: what is at issue here is not *mere* coherence, but coherence *with the data*. It is not with bare coherence as such (whatever that would be) but with data-directed coherence that a truth-making capacity enters upon the scene. But, of course, this basis of datahood is only a foundation for truth, not the structure itself. Coherence plays the essential role because it is to be through the mediation of coherence considerations that we move from truth-candidacy and presumptions of factuality to truth as such. And the procedure is fundamentally non-circular: we need make no imputations of truth at the level of data to arrive at truths through application of the criterial machinery in view.

In his exposition of the coherence theory, Brand Blanshard has written:

> Granting that propositions, to be true, must be coherent with each other, may they not be coherent without being true? . . . Again, a novel, or a succession of novels such as Galsworthy's *Forsyte Saga*, may create a special world of characters and events which is at once

extremely complex and internally consistent; does that make it the less fictitious? . . . This objection, like so many other annihilating criticisms, would have more point if anyone had ever held the theory it demolishes. But if intended to represent the coherence theory as responsibly advocated, it is a gross misunderstanding. That theory does not hold that any and every system is true, no matter how abstract and limited; it holds that one system only is true, namely the system in which everything real and possible is coherently included. How one can find in this the notion that a system would still give truth if, like some arbitrary geometry, it disregarded experience completely, it is not easy to see.[26]

This key passage, intended to answer a basic objection, leaves matters in a badly muddled state. Just where is coherence to be operative? In 'the system in which everything real and possible is coherently included'? But here—in this *all-inclusive* system— there is no difference drawn or to be drawn between the actually real and the merely possible with respect to coherence: this exactly is the force of the initial objection. Yet Blanshard's position is at bottom correct. The coherence theory would indeed be deficient if it held 'that a system would still give truth if . . . it disregarded experience completely'. Our recourse to data is intended to supply just this requisite of a recourse to 'experience'.

One acute critic has made the following charge against traditional formulations of the coherence theory:

It is on this point particularly that the historical coherence theory appears to be ambiguous; it seems never possible to be sure, in presentations of that conception, whether 'coherence' implies some essential relation to *experience*, or whether it requires only some purely logical relationship of the statements in question. Indeed, the so-called 'modern logic', associated with this theory, is such as totally to obscure the essential distinction between analytic truths of logic and those empirical truths we can only be assured by some reference beyond logic to given data of sense.[27]

Our own version of the coherence theory is immune to this criticism. The 'essential relation to *experience*' is provided by the essential reliance upon *data*—i.e. by restrictive use of only certain propositions as data. The 'purely logical relationship of the statements in question' in terms of which the conception of coherence is implemented comes into play only after these data are in hand, in providing the mechanism for determining some among them to be truths.

[26] B. Blanshard, *The Nature of Thought* (London, 1939), pp. 275–6.
[27] C. I. Lewis, *An Analysis of Knowledge and Valuation* (La Salle, Ill., 1962), p. 339.

The concept of a datum along the general lines explicated in the preceding discussion is certainly no newcomer to epistemology. Coherence theorists and others have articulated conceptions of much this same sort, F. H. Bradley himself being a prime case in point. In his essay 'On Truth and Coherence',[28] Bradley introduces the concept of a *fact* so as to have it play a role closely akin to that of a truth-candidate in our sense. First of all, Bradleyan 'facts'—let us call them B-facts—differ from everyone else's facts in not necessarily being factual, i.e. true. Typical, for Bradley, are the 'facts of perception and memory', which need not, of course, be true at all, but are at best purportedly or presumptively veridical:

These facts of perception [and memory], I further agree, are at least in part irrational [and so false]. . . . [Yet] I do not believe that we can make ourselves independent of these non-relational data. But, if I do not believe all this, does it follow that I have to accept independent facts [i.e., facts true independently of all other considerations]? Does it follow that perception and memory give one truths which I must take up and keep as they are given me, truths which in principle cannot be erroneous? This surely would be to pass from one false extreme to another. . . . I therefore conclude that no given fact is sacrosanct. With every fact of perception or memory a modified interpretation is in principle possible, and no such fact therefore is free from all possibility of error.[29]

Bradley espouses—with respect to the limited range of perception, memory, and the testimony of others—a notion of 'fact' according to which the facts do not automatically qualify as truths at all but at best as possible or potential truths.[30] Despite its limitations in scope, Bradley's conception of a 'fact' is clearly a precursor of—indeed almost a paradigm for—our own conception of a datum.[31]

---

[28] *Essays on Truth and Reality* (Oxford, 1914), ch. VII, pp. 202–18.

[29] Ibid., pp. 203–4. See also discussion of Bradley's position in A. C. Ewing, *Idealism: A Critical Survey* (London, 1934), especially pp. 239–40.

[30] Compare C. I. Lewis's thesis that 'whatever is remembered, whether as explicit recollection or merely in the form of our sense of the past, is *prima facie* credible because so remembered' (*An Analysis of Knowledge and Valuation* (La Salle, Ill., 1946), p. 334). This line of thought was developed earlier in substantial detail in A. Meinong's important essay 'Zur erkenntnistheoretischen Würdigung des Gedächtnisses' in his *Gesammelte Abhandlungen* (Leipzig, 1933). Meinong there argues that memory-derived judgments must be accorded 'immediate presumptive evidence' (p. 207). This conception of the *presumptively evident* is clearly yet another precursor of the conception of prima facie truth.

[31] Bradley's concept of the 'facts of sense' finds a faithful restoration in the following passage from E. W. Hall, who insists that: 'When I have the perceptual experience of a yellow pencil on the table before me I am [fully entitled] to assume that there probably is a yellow pencil on the table before me. Perhaps an analogy will help. In the American legal system, following the English in principle, there

Bradley's conception of the 'facts' of perception and memory itself has impressive historical credentials. The early Stoics manifested a tendency to take sense-perception as a standard of truth. This view was sharply criticized by Carneades of Cyrene (*c.* 213–129 B.C.), one of the leaders of the Platonic Academy and the most important of the 'Academic Sceptics'. The position of Carneades is sketched in considerable detail by Sextus Empiricus in his *Outlines of Pyrrhonism* and his tract *Against the Logicians*. One key passage reads as follows:

For all these factors together form the criterion namely, the probable presentation, and that which is at once both probable and irreversible and besides these that which is at once probable and irreversible and tested. And it is because of this that, just as in

are various rules of evidence of a man's guilt. If someone is on trial for having committed a crime, his lawyers will attempt to confute the evidence which the state brings against him or to have it disallowed by the court. But suppose a curious spectator from the continent should ask, "I notice that there is evidence against him and attempts to meet it, but where is the evidence in favor of him? Everyone seems to suppose him innocent, since he has not pleaded guilty, until proved otherwise." The appropriate answer would be "Exactly. This is basic in our whole system, that a man is assumed to be innocent until proved to be guilty." So in our empirical intentionalism a perception is to be assumed reliable until shown to be otherwise. Now, what sort of evidence can be brought to bear against the assertion constituting any given perception? Clearly only that presented by other, conflicting perceptions or generalizations based upon them. And we are justified in pronouncing a perception to be (most probably) incorrect in some respect only if some other perception, conflicting with it in this respect, is more coherent with the whole body of relevant perceptions' (E. W. Hall, *Our Knowledge of Fact and Value* (Chapel Hill, N.C., 1961), pp. 93–4).

Again, Bradleyan 'facts' and Stoic 'recognizable presentations' find an echo in the conception of *initial credibility* expounded by N. Goodman in one brief passage of a critique of C. I. Lewis's *An Analysis of Knowledge and Valuation*: 'Internal coherence is obviously a necessary but not a sufficient condition for the truth of a system; for we need also some means of choosing between equally tight systems that are incompatible with each other. There must be a tie to fact through, it is contended, some immediately certain statements. Otherwise compatibility with a system is not even a probable indication of the truth of any statement.

'Now clearly we cannot suppose that statements derive their credibility from other statements without ever bringing this string of statements to earth. Credibility may be transmitted from one statement to another through deductive or probability connections; but credibility does not spring from these connections by spontaneous generation. Somewhere along the line some statements, whether atomic sense reports or the entire system or something in between, must have initial credibility. So far the argument is sound. . . . Yet all that is indicated is credibility to some degree, not certainty. To say that some statements must be initially credible if any statement is ever to be credible at all is not to say that any statement is immune to withdrawal. For indeed, . . . no matter how strong its initial claim to preservation may be, a statement will be dropped if its retention—along with consequent adjustments in the interest of coherence—results in a system that does not satisfy as well as possible the totality of claims presented by all relevant statements. In the "search for truth" we deal with the clamoring demands of conflicting statements by trying, so to speak, to realize the greatest happiness of the greatest number of them. These demands [for credibility] constitute a different factor from coherence [itself] . . .' ('Sense and Certainty', *Philosophical Review*, 61 (1952), 160–7 (see 162–3)).

ordinary life when we are investigating a small matter we question a single witness, but in a greater matter several, and when the matter investigated is still more important we cross-question each of the witnesses on the testimony of the others—so likewise, says Carneades, in trivial matters we employ as criterion only the probable presentation, but in greater matters the irreversible, and in matters which contribute to happiness the tested presentation. Moreover, just as they adopt, they say, a different presentation to suit different cases, so also in different circumstances they do not cling to the same presentation. For they declare that they attend to the immediately probable in cases where the circumstances do not afford time for an accurate consideration of the matter. A man, for example, is being pursued by enemies, and coming to a ditch he receives a presentation which suggests that there, too, enemies are lying in wait for him; then being carried away by this presentation, as a probability, he turns aside and avoids the ditch, being led by the probability of the presentation, before he has exactly ascertained whether or not there really is an ambush of the enemy at the spot. But they follow the probable and tested presentation in cases where time is afforded for using their judgment on the object presented with deliberation and thorough examination.[32]

The 'irreversible' sense presentations are those which are 'uncontradicting' and 'concurring': each attests the same facts and none casts doubt upon any of the others. To illustrate Carneades' concept of mutually supportive data, Sextus cites a group of perceptions all concurring in the fact that a certain man is Socrates. 'We believe that this man is Socrates from the fact that he possesses all his customary qualities—colour, size, shape, converse, coat, and his position in a place where there is no one like him.' Concurrence is also illustrated in medical diagnoses: 'Some doctors do not deduce that it is a true case of fever from one symptom only—such as too quick a pulse or a very high temperature—but from a concurrence, such as that of a high temperature with a rapid pulse and ulcerous joints and flushing and thirst and analogous symptoms.'[33]

In the light of such criticism of the epistemic value of an uncritical acceptance of the 'facts of perception', the later Stoics revised the theory of their predecessors. Whereas the older Stoics held the doctrine that 'recognizable presentation' (*hē katalēptikē phantasia*) is the criterion of truth, the later Stoics added the crucial qualification 'provided that the recognizable

---

[32] *Against the Logicians*, tr. by R. G. Bury in vol. 2 of the Loeb Classical Library edition of Sextus Empiricus (Cambridge, Mass., 1933), 1. 184–7. A critical examination of the position of Carneades is given in R. Chisholm, *Theory of Knowledge* (Englewood Cliffs, N.J., 1956), pp. 41–52.

[33] Sextus Empiricus, *Against the Logicians*, 1. 178–9.

presentation has no obstacle'.[34] This proviso with respect to the needed absence of 'obstacles' puts the 'recognizable presentations' of the Stoics into the same category with Bradley's 'facts of sense'. Both concepts implement with respect to the data of sense-perception the basic idea of propositions that are not truths, but at best truth-*candidates* that will win out in the absence of countervailing considerations. Many recent writers have adopted these Bradleyan ideas in some form or fashion—generally without any explicit acknowledgement of their source.

The concept of a datum thus does a critically important job for the coherence theory of truth. It serves to provide an answer to the question 'Coherent with what?' without postulating a prior category of fundamental truth. It provides the coherence theory with grist to its mill that need not itself be the product of some preliminary determinations of truth. A reliance upon data makes it possible to contemplate a coherence theory that produces truth not *ex nihilo* (which would be impossible) but yet from a basis that does not itself demand any prior determinations of truthfulness as such. A coherence criterion can, on this basis, furnish a mechanism that is *originative* of truth—that is, it yields truths as outputs without requiring that truths must also be present among the supplied inputs.

9. *Summary*

This chapter has set out the tasks that a viable coherence theory of truth must be prepared to achieve and the obstacles it must be able to overcome. Specifically in the wake of the objections examined above we can make further additions to the earlier check-list of demands upon a reconstructed coherence theory given in Sect. 3:

1. The theory should provide a precise explication of the nature of 'coherence' to indicate just what relationships—and specifically relationships of logical consistency and interdependence—are involved.
2. The theory should articulate a conception of truth that is orderly and unitary despite any pluralism one might on first thought expect to inhere in the idea of coherence.
3. The theory should provide a mechanism for 'restoring consistency' into the inconsistent set of propositions represented by competing truth-candidates.

[34] For a discussion of the Stoic theory see J. M. Rist, *Stoic Philosophy* (Cambridge, 1970), ch. 8 ('The Criterion of Truth').

4. The theory should give a satisfactory answer to the question 'Coherent with what?' and should do so without a stultifying reliance upon *prior* truths already established as such.

Going beyond this, a coherence theory of truth must make clear the nature and extent of the extra-logical epistemic considerations that it deploys. For we must face—sooner or later—the question whether the coherence analysis of the truth-status of propositions is a matter of logic or of epistemology. As has been stressed repeatedly, the central issue is one of extra-logical truth, and this, of course, cannot be a strictly logical matter. Not only must logic as such fail to tell us what the data are, logic alone cannot distill coherent truths from inconsistent data. Given a group of inconsistent propositions logic can—and does—tell us *that* consistency must be restored, but does not go so far as to say *how* consistency is to be realized. Thus it is clear that something more than pure logic must be involved in the implementation of coherence considerations. Though we shall not concern ourselves—save in the sketching of examples—with 'material' (rather than 'formal') epistemic considerations of a specifically substantive kind, still the role of these considerations must be clarified, if only in a highly abstract and formal way. Basically, the enterprise is a matter of epistemico-logical methodology: of sketching at a high level of abstractness and generality (hence logic) how epistemic considerations (hence epistemology) will bear upon the rationally warranted determination of the truth-status of propositions. The whole topic belongs to the domain of *applied logic*—that is, of using the tools of theoretical logic, but with due extralogical supplementation to render them capable of resolving factual issues.

IV

THE LOGIC OF COHERENCE

1. *Approach to the Problem*

THE starting-point for the coherence theory of truth as we propose to develop it here is posed by the question: Coherence with what? This question—as already seen—is to be answered neither in terms of coherence with *all* propositions (nothing can be *that* flexible) nor in terms of coherence with *some* propositions (a feature of every proposition whatsoever that is not self-contradictory) nor in terms of coherence with *true* propositions (for that would make the criterion circular).[1] Rather, an appropriate answer can only be given in terms of a suitably articulated conception of coherence with *certain* propositions. But *which* propositions are to provide this basic point of reference, this fulcrum on which the lever of coherence is to rest? This question was answered in terms of the essentially technical conception of a datum as introduced in the preceding chapter. Thus a coherence approach to truth in terms of 'coherence with other propositions' will make two initial stipulations:

(1) that the propositions at issue must be truth-candidates or 'data' in the somewhat technical sense explained above,

and

(2) that the set of data providing this starting-point for a coherence-screening of truth must be sufficiently comprehensive in its canvassing of the relevant possibilities for there to be adequate rational warrant for holding that the 'true alternative' lies *somewhere* within the range covered by the data.

This aspect of the comprehensiveness of the data is crucial. Let some disputed question be such that there are five mutually exclusive and exhaustive alternatives: $A_1, \ldots, A_5$. If we introduce

---

[1] Though not viciously so. It would simply render the criterion a second-line device whose workings will have to hinge upon some other first-line criterion that provides 'prior' truths as grist to its mill.

only one of these upon the stage of analysis, as the sole truth-candidate available for contemplation, then it will obviously gain an uncontested victory. (By itself it is [*ex hypothesi*] consistent, and so will in itself satisfy the requirements of coherence in the minimal sense of consistency.) But if the other alternatives are to be 'genuine possibilities', then our coherence analysis must also take cognizance of them. The coherence standard of truth is a valid method only when *coherence is taken in a broader sense that includes comprehensiveness*, and calls for an accounting of all the appropriate relevant data. Partial coherence with some fragment of the data may well prove insufficient.

F. H. Bradley has put this matter in clear and trenchant terms:

> The test [of truth] which I advocate is the idea of a whole of knowledge as wide and as consistent as may be. In speaking of system [as the standard of truth] I mean always the union of these two aspects, and this is the sense and the only sense in which I am defending coherence. If we separate coherence from what Professor Stout calls comprehensiveness, then I agree that neither of these aspects of system will work by itself. . . . All that I can do here is to point out that both of the above aspects are for me inseparably included in the idea of system, and that coherence apart from comprehensiveness is not for me the test of truth or reality.[2]

Coherence in the narrow sense of consistency will only be a guide to truth when applied in the context of an approach which, by insisting on the amplitude of the data, seeks to maximize the sphere of truth.

It should be noted that two distinct sorts of comprehensiveness will be operative in a coherence standard of truth. One requires that the data themselves be sufficiently inclusive, which might be characterized as the *external comprehensiveness* of the data, i.e. their comprehensiveness *vis-à-vis* what falls outside. But then, once the data are given, the coherence theory seeks to identify as true the largest possible sector of what is contained *within* the data. This might be characterized as an *internal comprehensiveness* of the truths within the data. This dual striving of maximality is an essential aspect of a coherence criterion of truth.

Given that 'the data' are construed in this sense, the core of our coherence theory is accordingly formulated in the principle:

[2] 'On Truth and Coherence', *Essays on Truth and Reality* (Oxford, 1914), pp. 202–18. See pp. 202–3. Compare Leibniz's insistence that the actual (i.e. the best world) optimizes the combination of *lawfulness* (coherence, cohesiveness, orderliness, simplicity of hypothesis) with *variety* (comprehensiveness, content, richness of phenomena). (Cf. the author's discussion in *Essays in Philosophical Analysis* [Pittsburgh, Pa., 1969], pp. 166–9.] Leibniz's ontological insistence on these factors is a pre-Kantian analogue of Bradley's epistemicized version thereof.

'those propositions among the totality of relevant data that exhibit the best fit with the rest—that "maximally cohere with the data"—are (in the context of those data) to be classed as true'. But this is a mere foundation. To erect a structure upon it we must explicate the figurative idea of a 'fit' among propositions and specify just what is involved in 'coherence with the data' in general, and *maximal coherence* in particular.[3]

In deploying coherence as a test of truth, we must accord the conception of consistency a central role. It goes almost without saying that truths must be consistent with each other. But now we wish to use coherence and consistency not as an *ex post facto* feature of already established truths, but as a means for initially identifying the truths within a family of incompatible competitors. Those propositions warranted by the data are to qualify for classification as truths that as a system have the best fit with one another and with the data as a whole.

On this approach, the truths are to be identified as just those items among the truth-candidates that have the best systematic attunement with the rest. F. H. Bradley puts the matter as follows:

> I must depend upon the judgments of perception. Now it is agreed that, [since these may conflict,] if I am to have an orderly world, I cannot possibly accept all the 'facts' [= data]. Some of these must be relegated, as they are, to the world of error. . . . Facts for it [i.e., 'the view which I advocate'] are true just in so far as they work, just so far as they contribute to the order of experience. If by taking certain judgments as true, I can get more system into my world, then these 'facts' are so far true. . . . 'Facts' are justified because and as far as, while taking them as real [= true], I am better able to deal with the incoming new 'facts' and in general make my world wider and more harmonious. The higher and wider my structure, and the more that any particular fact or set of facts is implied in that structure, the more certain are the structure and the facts.[4]

The mark of truth, on this account, is a proposition's capacity to contribute to the systematic order that is to be imposed upon —or, better, extracted from—the mass of discordant truth-candidates. The family of truths is identifiable as an optimal construct from the data.

---

[3] Some writers use the word 'data' to indicate basic or 'protocol' truths on which other truths can be grounded. On this view, a 'datum' is a quintessential truth. Our present usage is clearly radically different from this—although, as matters turn out, both conform to the general formula that 'data are propositions on the basis of which the truthfulness of other propositions can be determined'.

[4] F. H. Bradley, 'On Truth and Coherence', *Essays on Truth and Reality* (Oxford, 1914), pp. 202–18; see pp. 210–11.

Let it for the moment be supposed that we are in the fortunate circumstance of a set **S** of data that is consistent. Then, on the standard conception of the matter, a proposition P will be true, relative to these data, just in case P is a *deductive consequence* of **S**: **S** ⊢ P. Now P may be said to *cohere* with **S**—in a weakish sense of that term—when P is *compatible* with **S**. However, P coheres *maximally* with **S** when $\sim P$ is incompatible with **S**. Now this is precisely the case when P follows from **S**. In this light 'maximal coherence' comes to view as coincident with 'following as a logical consequence'. And this seems natural enough. After all, a proposition cannot be better fitted to and in accord with others than when its denial is actually incompatible with them. Here, then, in the consistent case, truth relative to **S** and maximal coherence with **S**—in the specific sense of following as a consequence of **S**—patently coincide.

What we should like to be able to do is to apply exactly this same idea with respect to an inconsistent set of data, and to generalize to this case the precept:

> P is true (relative to the set **S** of data) whenever P is a consequence of **S**.

This thesis, in fact, presents the foundation on which the envisaged reconstruction of the coherence theory of truth is to be erected. But to implement this idea in the critical case of an inconsistent set of data requires having at one's disposal a theory of the consequences of an inconsistent set of propositions. The construction of such a theory is thus a prime requisite of this inquiry. Once this requisite is resolved, we can proceed in a manner essentially parallel to the approach of deductive logic. In deductive logic a proposition can be viewed as 'true relative to premisses' when it follows from them and so is to be taken as true *when these premisses are accepted as true*. On the coherence analysis a proposition is also 'true relative to premisses' and is to be taken as true if it follows from them *when these premisses are accepted as data*. A truth, as the coherence analysis sees it, is simply a proposition which 'follows' from the data. But in the present case these will, alas, generally be inconsistent, and this poses special and peculiar difficulties which must be overcome.

2. *The Need for a Theory of Inference From Inconsistent Premisses*

Throughout the history of logic up to the present day, the standard texts and treatises in the field have little or nothing to say on the subject of inference from inconsistent premisses. It would seem that a sort of *horror contradictionis* is endemic among logicians, and that it is the view of the guild that once a contradiction has been encountered nothing more remains to be done but to leave the scene with proper expressions of disapproval. Yet even a cursory survey of the range of applications suffices to bring out the extraordinary importance of this sphere of reasoning.

The process of argumentation by *reductio ad absurdum* represents the best-known instance of inference from mutually inconsistent premisses. Counterfactual inference, the process of inference in the presence of knowledge-contravening (or belief-contravening) suppositions is another case in point. A further example is the situation that arises in the case of conflicting reports from diverse sources, a situation particularly prominent—indeed commonplace—in the sphere of the historian. Taken as a whole, the data in such cases present an incompatible body of propositions from which one must draw one's inferences as best one can.

Again, we might be dealing with the case of inconsistent reports from a single source as in the case of an author who contradicts himself. At times he insists upon p, on occasion he argues that p entails q, somewhere he says that not-q. What are we to make of this? How should one reason in the face of these inconsistent premisses in order to extract from them a coherent interpretation of the presumptively consistent position that the charitable reader would assume to be hidden behind the surface layer of inconsistency?

A situation closely analogous to that of inconsistent reports is encountered in the case of centralized reporting of data derived from imperfect sensors—perhaps a sentient organism provided with conflicting information by different senses (say sight and touch),[5] or a servomechanism with sensors that provide redundant information but are not free from error. Here again a situation arises where reasoning must be carried on in the face of inconsistent data.

In other cases, it is not the body of initial information that is inconsistent, but the group of propositions that one is tempted to hold to be true on this basis. Thus consider the five pairs:

$$\{\alpha, 1\}$$
$$\{\alpha, 1\}$$
$$\{\alpha, 2\}$$
$$\{\beta, 2\}$$
$$\{\beta, 2\}.$$

[5] For example, sight reports that the half-submerged stick is bent, touch reports it to be straight.

Let it be supposed that a number has been chosen from one of these five pairs, selected at random. Then all of the following will *probably* be true (i.e. will obtain a probability greater than 0·5, and so will be more likely than not):

x is 2

x is chosen from an α-containing set

If x is chosen from an α-containing set, then x is 1.

Evidently if we here accept all of the propositions rendered probable by the information given, an inconsistent set results.[6] And this illustrates a general situation, viz. that in making inferences from the body of what is probably the case one generally reasons from an inconsistent set of premisses.

A situation closely comparable in its conceptual structure to that of the probabilistic case we have just considered arises in the context of the methodology of science when different methods are available for extending our information beyond the range of what is initially given. In projecting a curve, for example, one might well want to take incompatible results into equally serious account, say the results of linear extrapolation both of the curve itself and also of its derivative. But, of course, the concurrent application of a variety of methodologies will, in general, lead to an inconsistent diversity of results and so face us with a situation where reasoning must proceed from incompatible premisses.

In all such cases, and many others like them, we confront as a basis for reasoning a collection of premisses that are mutually inconsistent. The theory of inference from incompatible premisses is patently a matter of substantial and diversified philosophico-logical interest.

Note that neither deductive nor inductive logic (of the standard, probabilistic type) gives guidance in reasoning from an inconsistent set **S** of premisses. For as far as deductive logic is concerned *anything* follows from such a premiss set. Nor can we reason probabilistically from an inconsistent data-base. For consider the determination of the probability of some proposition P relative to the inconsistent set **S**:

$$\mathrm{pr}(P/\mathbf{S}) = \frac{\mathrm{pr}(P \ \& \ \mathrm{conj}[\mathbf{S}])}{\mathrm{pr}(\mathrm{conj}[\mathbf{S}])}$$

---

[6] This problem for a probabilistic acceptance rule has become known as the Lottery Paradox. See H. E. Kyburg, Jr., *Probability in the Logic of Rational Belief* (Middletown, Conn., 1961). Cf. also R. Hilpinen, *Rules of Acceptances and Inductive Logic* (Amsterdam, 1968; *Acta Philosophica Fennica*, fasc. 22), pp. 39–49. We shall return to this problem at some length below. See sect. 7 of Chapter IX.

where conj[**S**] is the conjunction over the set **S**. But due to the assumed inconsistency of **S** this fraction takes the value 0/0 and is consequently undefined.

Since the existing methods of inference do not resolve our problem of reasoning from inconsistent givens, we must endeavour to forge our own.

3. *Maximal Consistent Subsets, Innocent Bystanders, 'Culprits'*

The preceding sections have perhaps said enough—or more than enough—about the need for a logical mechanism of inference from inconsistent premisses. Let us now embark upon an inquiry into how such a mechanism can be constructed.

Let **S** be any set of propositions, $\mathbf{S} = \{p_1, p_2, \ldots\}$, be it consistent or not. Any subset $\mathbf{S}_i$ of **S** will be said to be a maximal consistent subset (m.c.s.) of **S** if it satisfies the following three conditions:

1. $\mathbf{S}_i$ is a non-empty subset of **S**
2. $\mathbf{S}_i$ is consistent
3. no **S**-element that is a non-member of $\mathbf{S}_i$ can be added to it without generating an inconsistency (so that for every proposition P in **S** which is not in $\mathbf{S}_i$, the set $\mathbf{S}_i \cup \{P\}$ is inconsistent).

The following consequences follow at once from this definition. Consider any propositional set **S**. Then:

(i) If **S** is consistent, then **S** has only one m.c.s., namely **S** itself.
(ii) No self-contradictory **S**-element occurs in any m.c.s. $\mathbf{S}_i$.
(iii) If there are no self-contradictory **S**-elements, then **S** is the union of its m.c.s.
(iv) If **S** is the union of the sets **S**′ and **S**″, where **S**″ is a set of propositions each of which is self-contradictory, then the m.c.s. of **S** and **S**′ are the same sets.
(v) If an **S**-element P is a tautology, then P is in every m.c.s. of **S** (since the addition of a tautology to a consistent set cannot affect its consistency). (The term 'tautology' is meant here to stand for logical truths in general.)

Note that an infinite propositional set (of self-consistent elements) can have infinite-sized m.c.s.:

$$\mathbf{S} = \{p, \sim p, p \ \& \ (q \supset q), \sim p \ \& \ (q \supset q), p \ \& \ (q \lor \sim q),$$
$$\sim p \ \& \ (q \lor \sim q), \ldots\}.$$

The infinite set consisting of all the odd members of the enumeration will be an m.c.s. of **S**, as also will be that consisting of all the even members. Nor need an infinite set have only finitely many m.c.s. Consider:

$$S = \{p, \sim p, q, \sim q, r, \sim r, s, \sim s, \ldots\}.$$

We construct an m.c.s. by selecting one element of each successive pair, which can be done in infinitely many ways.

(It should at this point be noted parenthetically that a preoccupation with maximality will prove of significance in the context of a coherence theory of truth. For stress is here placed on extracting from the data—an inconsistent set of premisses— the greatest possible amount of truth. This reflects an idea we had already touched on in connection with the factor of internal comprehensiveness whose workings characterize a coherence approach.)

We shall call an **S**-element P an *innocent bystander* (i.b.) of **S** if $P \in S_i$ for every m.c.s. of S_i of **S**. Hence, every tautology in **S** is an i.b. of **S**. The converse, however, does not hold in general. Thus let $S = \{p, q, s, s \supset t, \sim t\}$. The m.c.s. of **S** are in this case $S_1 = \{p, q, s, s \supset t\}$, $S_2 = \{p, q, s \supset t, \sim t\}$, $S_3 = \{p, q, s, \sim t\}$. All include both p and q which are therefore i.b.'s, although they are not tautologies.

We shall call a proposition P belonging to an inconsistent set **S** a *culprit* of **S** whenever this P is not an i.b. of **S**. (If P is a culprit of **S**, P may possibly, however, include an i.b. of **S** as a conjunct.)

With each m.c.s. S_i of **S** we shall associate the set $C(S_i)$ of all of its ⊢-consequences. This L-*consequence set* of S_i is such that a proposition P is in $C(S_i)$ iff it is the logical consequence of (the conjunction of all) the propositions of S_i, in short, if $S_i \vdash P$:

$$C(S_i) = \{P : S_i \vdash P\}.$$

Correspondingly we at once obtain:

(i) $S_i \subseteq C(S_i)$
(ii) $C(S_i)$ is consistent, and so if $P \in C(S_i)$ then $\sim P \notin C(S_i)$
(iii) $C(S_i)$ is deductively closed. That is: If
$P_1 \in C(S_i), P_2 \in C(S_i), \ldots, P_k \in C(S_i)$ and $P_1, P_2, \ldots, P_k \vdash Q$, then $Q \in C(S_i)$. In consequence:
(iv) $C(S_i) \vdash P$ iff $P \in C(S_i)$
(v) All the consequence-sets $C(S_i)$ of the m.c.s. of a given set **S** will have in common all tautologies, all the i.b. of **S**, and very possibly also other propositions.

Since obviously no self-contradictory proposition ever follows from a consistent set, the union of all the consequence-sets of the m.c.s. of a set **S** need not in general include **S** itself as a subset because **S** may contain self-contradictory elements. However, every element of **S** that is not self-contradictory must be contained in this union.

It is important to remark that the m.c.s. of a set **S** will depend upon the mode of formulation of the content of **S**. Thus consider the following four propositional sets all of which seemingly 'convey the same information':

$$\mathbf{S^1} = \{p, \sim p, q\}$$
$$\mathbf{S^2} = \{p \ \& \ \sim p, q\}$$
$$\mathbf{S^3} = \{p \ \& \ q, \sim p\}$$
$$\mathbf{S^4} = \{p \ \& \ \sim p \ \& \ q\}.$$

S⁴ has no m.c.s. whatsoever, since it contains no self-consistent elements. The m.c.s. of the other sets are:

$$\mathbf{S^1_1} = \{p, q\} \qquad \mathbf{S^2_1} = \{q\} \qquad \mathbf{S^3_1} = \{p \ \& \ q\}$$
$$\mathbf{S^1_2} = \{\sim p, q\} \qquad\qquad\qquad\quad \mathbf{S^3_2} = \{\sim p\}.$$

The 'mode of formulation' of an inconsistent propositional set is thus a matter of some importance on which significant consequences hinge. The problem of defining a normal form for propositional sets, including inconsistent sets—as well as the cognate issue of determining when two such propositional sets are equivalent—is dealt with in Appendices C and D.

4. Inevitable Consequence: Weak Consequence

As regards the *consequences* of an inconsistent propositional set it seems plausible to take the following position. In one (relatively strong) sense of 'consequence', the consequences of a (possibly inconsistent) set **S** of propositions will be the deductive consequences of *all* of its m.c.s.—each and every one of them. (For surely, if some inconsistent data are given, then something that follows on *each and every* attempt to reduce these to the point of consistency cannot but be accepted as a 'consequence' thereof.) In a much weaker sense of the term, a 'consequence' of the set **S** is a deductive consequence of *at least one* among the m.c.s. of **S**. Correspondingly, we may define two distinct notions of consequence.

First, *P* may be characterized as an *inevitable consequence* (I-consequence) of the set **S** if, for *every* m.c.s. $\mathbf{S}_i$ of **S**, *P* is a deductive consequence (L-consequence) of $\mathbf{S}_i$. In this event we shall write $S \vdash_I P$. Since, in the case where S is consistent, P is an I-consequence of S iff P is a deductive consequence of S, inevitable consequencehood is very closely related to the standard concept of L-consequence (logically deducible, deductive consequence).

Secondly, we shall say that P is a *weak consequence* (W-consequence) of the—possibly inconsistent—set S, and denote it by $S \vdash_W P$, if there is *some* m.c.s. S_i of S such that P is a logical consequence of S_i. Again, if S is consistent, a proposition is a W-consequence of S iff it is a logical (deductive) consequence of S. The set of all I-consequences of any propositional set S is a subset of the set of W-consequences of S. But the former is always a consistent set, while the latter need not be. Thus the set $S = \{p, \sim p, q\}$ has both p and $\sim p$ among its W-consequences, and so the set of all W-consequences of S is obviously inconsistent. However, this does not mean that the set of W-consequences of an inconsistent set S will include any and all propositions. In the example cited, the set S has two m.c.s. $S_1 = \{p, q\}$ and $S_2 = \{\sim p, q\}$. Hence, the set of W-consequences of S includes both p and $\sim p$, but it does not include p & $\sim p$, for this is a deductive consequence of neither S_1 nor S_2. And in general, no self-contradictory proposition is ever a W-consequence of any set S, even though mutually incompatible propositions may be W-consequences of S. Every S-element that is not self-contradictory will be a W-consequence of S. Thus when S is inconsistent, then the set of its W-consequences will also by and large be inconsistent.

Since—as we have seen—the m.c.s. of a propositional set S are determined not by the 'content' alone but by its 'mode of formulation' as well, the same will be true of its W-consequences and its I-consequences. Thus consider again the three sets:

$$S^1 = \{p, \sim p, q\}$$
$$S^2 = \{p \ \& \sim p, q\}$$
$$S^3 = \{p \ \& \ q, \sim p\}.$$

The m.c.s. generated by these sets are as follows:

$$S^1_1 = \{p, q\} \qquad S^2_1 = \{q\} \qquad S^3_1 = \{p \ \& \ q\}$$
$$S^1_2 = \{\sim p, q\} \qquad\qquad\qquad\quad S^3_2 = \{\sim p\}.$$

Note that q is an I-consequence of S^1 and S^2, but not of S^3, and that p is a W-consequence of S^1 and S^3, but not of S^2. Again, with S^1 we seemingly stand some chance of drawing $\sim p$ & q as a 'consequence', but we stand no chance of this with S^2 or S^3.

Appendices C and D should be consulted on this issue of the

mode of formulation of propositional sets. Here a 'normal form' reduction is defined for such sets, be they consistent or not, that can be used, when desired, to remove the effects of such 'stylistic arbitrariness'.

5. *Preferred m.c.s. and $\mathcal{P}$-Consequence*

The conceptions of the I-consequences and the W-consequences of propositional sets do not of themselves suffice to resolve our fundamental problem of the 'consequences' of an inconsistent set of data.

Given an inconsistent propositional set **S**, one would like to be able to answer the question: What actually follows from **S**? Consider the following example: let **S** be the set of the propositions presenting, say, the reports of a certain observer. Although a system of reports (and hence the set **S**) may involve some contradiction among its members, one does not ordinarily reject completely upon this sole ground the prospect of drawing conclusions from whatever information may otherwise be contained in the set. Correspondingly, the standard resolution of the question of the 'logical consequences' of inconsistent premises —which is too liberal, since it holds that *anything and everything* follows therefrom—is not to be adopted. Nor is it sufficiently restrictive to fall back upon the W-consequences. For the W-consequences of **S**—though to be sure a narrower group— are also too much for comfort, since they can again form an inconsistent set. The preceding considerations may seem to incline in tendency to resolve the question of which proposition can unproblematically qualify as the 'consequences' of an inconsistent propositional set in a certain minimal sense: namely those which are the (inevitable) deductive consequences of *all* of its maximal consistent subsets. But we should certainly not, in general, want to restrict ourselves to the I-consequences of **S** alone. For whereas the standard resolution of the question of the 'consequences' of inconsistent premises is too liberal (since it holds that everything follows therefrom), this mooted conception of 'consequences' is too restrictive (since it confines these only to the consequences that are inevitable in the sense of following from each and every m.c.s., and this is too much to ask). Thus given the premiss-set $S = \{p \ \& \ q, \ \sim p\}$ we should be strongly— and I think rightly—inclined towards drawing the conclusion q, even though the m.c.s. of **S**, viz. $S_1 = \{p \ \& \ q\}$ and $S_2 = \{\sim p\}$ are not such that this result is inevitably forthcoming from them. On the anything-follows approach we have an embarrassment of riches; on the I-consequence approach a too drastic scarcity. A third alternative must be developed.

But we are now at once put into a position to delimit more realistically the concept of 'consequence' we have in mind in the context of an inconsistent set **S** of (mutually incompatible) propositions: one should not be prepared to accept P as a 'consequence' of **S** if P does not follow from *at least one* m.c.s. of **S**. And one cannot but accept P as a 'consequence' of **S** if it follows from *every one* of its m.c.s., so that no matter how we tried to reduce **S** to consistency we would find ourselves confronted with P.

This policy at least enables us to avoid the trivializing result that 'everything' follows from inconsistent premisses. Thus consider the inconsistent propositional set:

$$\mathbf{S} = \{p, p \supset q, \sim q\}.$$

It has three m.c.s.

$\mathbf{S}_1 - \{p, p \supset q\}$ whose consequences are axiomatized by p & q

$\mathbf{S}_2 = \{p, \sim q\}$ whose consequences are axiomatized by p & $\sim q$

$\mathbf{S}_3 = \{p \supset q, \sim q\}$ whose consequences are axiomatized by $\sim p$ & $\sim q$.

We are now at least entitled to say definitively that, e.g. $(p$ & $q) \vee (p$ & $\sim q) \vee (\sim p$ & $\sim q)$ *must* count as a 'consequence' of **S**—since this proposition follows from each of its m.c.s. And— more helpfully—we are entitled to say that $\sim p$ & q is surely *not* a 'consequence' of **S**—since this proposition is incompatible with each of its m.c.s. The indicated approach to the 'consequences' of an inconsistent set thus has some logical 'bite' to it.

One would accordingly be reluctant to regard as 'the content' of **S** either all of its W-consequences or merely its I-consequences: the former group is too liberal, the latter too restrictive. The prospect of some sort of intermediate resolution—some 'half-way house' position—must be explored. Let us designate this as yet unspecified intermediate concept of consequence a $\mathscr{P}$-consequence, for preferential or plausible consequence (and correspondingly adopt the notation $\mathbf{S} \vdash_{\mathscr{P}} P$).

In seeking to articulate the conception of the $\mathscr{P}$-consequence of an inconsistent set of propositions, any acceptable solution must be confined within the limits of certain 'conditions of the problem'. Specifically, to accommodate the policy stated above, the resultant $\mathscr{P}$-consequence has to meet two conditions:

(1) Whenever a statement is an I-consequence of a propositional set **S**, then it must also be a $\mathscr{P}$-consequence; that is, any proposition that follows from *all* of the m.c.s. must

certainly be a $\mathscr{P}$-consequence: Every I-consequence is a $\mathscr{P}$-consequence (though the converse is not necessarily the case).

(2) Whenever a statement is a $\mathscr{P}$-consequence of a propositional set **S**, then it must also be a W-consequence; that is, no proposition can be a $\mathscr{P}$-consequence that does not follow from *some* m.c.s.: Every $\mathscr{P}$-consequence is a W-consequence (though the converse is not necessarily the case).

Correspondingly, the $\mathscr{P}$-consequences of a set **S** must lie in the region intermediate between its I-consequences and the W-consequences. Now since the I-consequences are the propositions that follow deductively from *every* m.c.s. and the W-consequences those that follow deductively from *some* m.c.s., the obvious way to get an intermediate concept is to have it be that the $\mathscr{P}$-consequences are those that follow deductively from *certain* m.c.s.—those which we may characterize by some such special designation as 'preferred' or 'eligible'.

Thus if we suppose the availability of a criterion of preference enabling us somehow to restrict the range of the m.c.s. of a propositional set **S** that need to be taken into account, we shall obtain exactly what is needed. For suppose **S** has the m.c.s., $\mathbf{S}_1, \ldots, \mathbf{S}_n$, and that, according to some given preferability criterion, $\mathbf{S}^1, \ldots, \mathbf{S}^m$ $(m < n)$ are those m.c.s. of **S** which are *eligible*. Now we can specify as a preferential consequence ($\mathscr{P}$-consequence) of **S** any proposition P such that for every *eligible* m.c.s. $\mathbf{S}^i$ of **S** we have it that $\mathbf{S}^i \vdash P$. This definition will clearly meet all of the desiderata specified above. And thus the problem as to what is to count as 'the consequential content' of any propositional set **S** can be reduced to finding a suitable criterion for preference among the m.c.s. of **S**.[7]

We must be quite clear as to the nature of the eligibility or 'preference' that is at issue. It categorically does *not* mean that we should like it better if a certain alternative among the m.c.s. is true. Rather it means that the m.c.s. at issue is (objectively) to be preferred as a candidate for truth, that its truth-claims are stronger. Any affective sort of preference of the liking-better type is wholly beside the point; only preferability in point of truth-potential is at issue, *alethic* preferability to give it a name (from the Greek *aletheia* = truth). And accordingly, if the preference standard singles out one alternative m.c.s. as

---

[7] This line of approach to finding the 'consequences' of an inconsistent set of premisses through the isolation of certain preferred m.c.s. subsets was originally developed in N. Rescher, *Hypothetical Reasoning* (Amsterdam, 1964).

uniquely preferred, then the coherence process commits us to classing its membership as true. This feature of the coherence analysis means that the preference mechanism must revolve solely about preferability in point of truth. In so far as the eligibility-criterion $\mathscr{P}$ narrows the range of alternatives, the workings of this standard must be such that we are entitled to take the view that this narrowing represents a narrowing around the truth.

All this, of course, leaves open the critical residual issue of how such a criterion is to be devised. This problem will provide the focus of the next chapter. For the present let us merely explore the consequences that follow once a solution is in hand.

In line with the indicated approach, we are to resolve the problem of the consequences of an inconsistent set **S** of (self-consistent) propositions by the following procedure:

1. We determine the family $\mathbf{S_1}, \mathbf{S_2}, \ldots, \mathbf{S_k}$ of the m.c.s. of **S**.
2. Within this family $\mathbf{S_1}, \mathbf{S_2}, \ldots, \mathbf{S_k}$ we determine the subfamily $\mathbf{S}^1, \mathbf{S}^2, \ldots, \mathbf{S}^m$ $(m \leqslant k)$ of certain m.c.s. that qualify—by a criterion yet to be specified—as (alethically) *preferred* m.c.s. relative to a criterion $\mathscr{P}$.
3. A $\mathscr{P}$-consequence of **S** is then to be any proposition that follows from every $\mathscr{P}$-preferred m.c.s. of **S**:

   $$\mathbf{S} \vdash_{\mathscr{P}} P \text{ iff } \mathbf{S}^i \vdash P \text{ for every } \mathscr{P}\text{-preferred S-m.c.s. } \mathbf{S}^i.$$

An example is in order. Let:

$$\mathbf{S} = \{r \,\&\, p, p \supset q, \sim q\}.$$

Then the m.c.s. of **S** will be as follows:

$\mathbf{S_1} = \{p \,\&\, r, p \supset q\}$ which is axiomatized by $p \,\&\, q \,\&\, r$

$\mathbf{S_2} = \{p \supset q, \sim q\}$ which is axiomatized by $\sim p \,\&\, \sim q$

$\mathbf{S_3} = \{p \,\&\, r, \sim q\}$ which is axiomatized by $p \,\&\, \sim q \,\&\, r$.

The I-consequences of **S** will certainly not include r, since we do not have $\mathbf{S_2} \vdash r$. In fact, the I-consequences are axiomatized by $(p \,\&\, r) \vee (\sim p \,\&\, \sim q)$, and this is as far as we can go in specifying S-consequences without recourse to preferential considerations. But let it now be supposed that $\mathbf{S_1}$ and $\mathbf{S_3}$ are to be the *eligible* m.c.s. Then r will clearly be a $\mathscr{P}$-consequence of **S**, as indeed $p \,\&\, r$ will. This illustrates the potential of preferential considerations for providing a more definite answer to the question of the consequences of an inconsistent datum-set of premisses, and so for determining the truths relative to that set.

The preceding example has been drawn from propositional logic, and this will be the case with virtually all the examples given. This course is followed solely for reasons of simplicity and ease of exposition. Quite obviously, there is no reason why the initial set **S** could not be chosen, for example, from the sphere of syllogistic, categorical propositions, say

S = {all X is Y, all Y is Z, all Z is W, some X is not W}.

In any such situation, the determination of maximal consistent subsets and the application of preferential machinery could be carried through in a way strictly parallel with the procedure in the propositional case.

A brief digression is warranted on the kinship between the logical modalities and the preceding modes of consequence. On the standard conception, a proposition P is:

(1) necessary if it obtains in *every* possible world
(2) possible if it obtains in *some* possible world
(3) actual if it obtains in *the uniquely 'preferred'* (i.e. the actual) world.

At present, given a set **S** of data we have it that a proposition P is:

(1) an I-consequence if it follows from *every* m.c.s. of **S**
(2) a W-consequence if it follows from *some* m.c.s. of **S**
(3) a $\mathscr{P}$-consequence if it follows from *all the preferred* m.c.s. of **S**.

The determination of m.c.s. can be viewed as a process along the lines of the Leibnizian idea of sorting an incoherent mass of possibilities into consistent possible worlds. On this analogy, the mechanisms at issue in our discussion can be viewed as founding a basis not merely for the actual truth of certain propositions (relative to a set **S** of data and a preferential criterion $\mathscr{P}$), but of their possible and necessary truth as well. Accordingly, the approach can also provide a basis for the introduction of modal ideas—that is, of relative modalities with respect to a given set **S**. In this regard it differs from the position of many coherence theorists in the idealistic tradition who deny the validity of modal distinctions, and for whom the actual is as such alone possible and is thus necessary. With our approach, it is only when all the data are compatible—so that all the presumptive truths can be classed as actual truths without anomaly—that a collapse of modal distinctions takes place.

6. *The Effect of Different Modes of Consequence/Incompatibility*

Before proceeding, it is essential to emphasize one point. In the previous pages our discussion and examples have always proceeded in terms of *logical* inconsistencies and consequences (a practice to which we shall continue to adhere in what follows). But to develop the machinery of m.c.s., and of W, I, and $\mathscr{P}$-consequences, we need merely *some* concept of inconsistency and consequence:[8] specifically, empirical inconsistency and consequence would do the trick. By way of example consider a belief-contravening supposition. Consider the situation:

Beliefs: (1) Napoleon lost the battle of Waterloo.
   (2) Napoleon attempted to flee France on an American ship a fortnight after the battle of Waterloo.
   (3) Napoleon was captured by the British and sent into imprisonment on St. Helena about a month after the battle of Waterloo.
   (4) Napoleon died in exile on St. Helena some six years after the battle of Waterloo.
Supposition: Assume Napoleon won the battle of Waterloo.

Clearly item (1) must be negated in the face of the counterfactual supposition at issue (being logically at odds with it). However, the (very real) incompatibility of (2) and (3) with the assumption at issue is certainly not logical, but rather 'empirical' in character. Such a basis of extra-logical inconsistency would provide a perfectly adequate foundation for the m.c.s.-based analyses of the preceding discussion.[9]

It is of interest to note the divergencies arising with different modes of consequence. Assume we have different but related modes of consequence $\vdash_1$ and $\vdash_2$ connected by the relationship:

$$P_1, P_2, \ldots, P_n \vdash_1 Q \text{ whenever } P_1, P_2, \ldots, P_n \vdash_2 Q \text{ (though not}$$

$$\text{necessarily vice versa).}$$

Logical and physical consequence can provide one example, and classical versus strict entailments another.

---

[8] Actually either one of this pair will do, since the other member can be defined in terms of it.

[9] There is, however, every reason to suppose that such 'extra-logical' inconsistency can always be reduced to outright logical inconsistency of a relative rather than absolute sort—i.e. inconsistency in the presence of certain empirical givens. In this way the case of empirical coherence can simply be dealt with as a matter of 'logical' coherence in the general manner of the analysis, provided that this is taken as coherence with certain empirical theses that are postulated (i.e. taken as so plausible as to be exempt from question in the context of discussion).

With respect to each type of consequence we obtain a corresponding concept of m.c.s. ($\vdash_1$-m.c.s. and $\vdash_2$-m.c.s.) and corresponding types of W, I, and $\mathscr{P}$-consequences. It is not difficult to show that—surprising though this may seem on first thought —none of the relationships we might expect will obtain in general. Specifically we shall not have any one of the following: for any propositional set **S**, and any fixed preferential criterion $\mathscr{P}$:

1. Whenever P is a W_1-consequence of **S**, it is a W_2-consequence of **S**.
2. Whenever P is a W_2-consequence of **S**, it is a W_1-consequence of **S**.
3. Whenever P is an I_1-consequence of **S**, it is an I_2-consequence of **S**.
4. Whenever P is an I_2-consequence of **S**, it is an I_1-consequence of **S**.
5. Whenever P is a $\mathscr{P}_1$-consequence of **S**, it is a $\mathscr{P}_2$-consequence of **S**.
6. Whenever P is a $\mathscr{P}_2$-consequence of **S**, it is a $\mathscr{P}_1$-consequence of **S**.

In short, if the concept of consequence/incompatibility is changed—even if only slightly, in a way that leaves it seemingly still closely related to the initial version—one will have 'to go back to Square 1' and recommence from the very start the matter of m.c.s. specification and the determination of W, I, and $\mathscr{P}$-consequences.[10]

7. *A Coherence Theory of Truth Based on $\mathscr{P}$-Consequences*

It is useful to review in a systematic way the coherence theory of truth that results from putting together the lines of thought developed above:

1. We begin with a mass of incoherent data, data incoherent in the strong sense of being logically inconsistent. These data are certainly not given as true; they are not truths at all, but at the very best truth-candidates.
2. By determining the various m.c.s. inherent in these data, we obtain a view of the spectrum of the alternative consistent and coherent subordinate data-groupings.
3. A proposition is certainly to be viewed as a 'consequence' of the initial set of data—in *any* plausible sense of that term

[10] The materials of sections 2–6 of the present chapter are drawn in part from N. Rescher and R. Manor, 'On Inference from Inconsistent Premisses', *Foundations of Language*, 1 (1970), 179–217.

—if it inevitably follows from each and every one of these m.c.s., i.e. if it is an I-consequence. Moreover, we may still regard it as a 'consequence' ($\mathscr{P}$-consequence) of these data if it invariably follows from all those m.c.s. in whose favour a suitable prior criterion of eligibility has ruled. (This obviously relativizes the consequences obtained to the preferential criterion at issue. This matter is, for the moment, left open. The next chapter will be devoted to it.)

4. We now apply the idea that one proposition coheres with a group of others if it is consistent with them, and that it coheres maximally with them if its contradictory is inconsistent with them—i.e. that it follows from them.

5. Finally, in accordance with these ideas, we implement the principle of standard logic that a proposition must count as true relative to a set of premisses when it is a consequence thereof. But the premisses now at issue need not form a consistent set and the notion of 'consequence' is accordingly readjusted.

This outline presents in essentials the proposed reformulation of the coherence theory of truth.

This approach to truth has the following rationale. If

$$S = \{P_1, P_2, \ldots\}$$

is an inconsistent set of truth-candidates, then its m.c.s. $S_1, S_2, \ldots$ represent the very best that we can do to identify the various 'alternative possibilities for truth'. Given the P_i as truth-candidates, one or another of the S_i cannot fail to capture 'the truth of the matter'. By treating all the S_i disjunctively (through a disjunction of their axioms) we 'go for safety' in disjunctively canvassing all of these alternatives for truth. (When considerations of alethic preference enable us to eliminate some of these alternatives as 'unrealistic', then in 'going for safety' we canvass disjunctively merely all of the *realistic* alternatives.)

The relationship that obtained on this approach between the 'consequences' of the (inconsistent) data and the truth needs re-emphasis, since the use of this method as a coherence criterion of truth can be justified only through this relationship. For our starting-point we began (*ex hypothesi*) with a set S of data as truth-candidates in the previously specified sense. We then canvassed all of the possible alternatives for 'the truth' as determined by these data, namely the m.c.s. of S. Next, considerations of alethic preference were deployed to eliminate some of these theoretically *possible* alternatives for truth (i.e. the m.c.s. or—more conveniently—their propositional axioms) as not being substantively *real* alternatives (i.e. the $\mathscr{P}$-preferred m.c.s.). Given the status of the initial propositions of $\mathbf{S}$ as data, we are committed to the position that the truth lies somewhere within the range spanned by these alternatives. As the final step of truth-determination we then 'go for safety' by the simple device of forming the disjunction of these alternatives. Given that we were initially serious about viewing $\mathbf{S}$ as a set of data (in the specified sense), and about viewing $\mathscr{P}$ as a standard of alethic eligibility, we cannot avoid the consequence that 'the truth of the matter' is to be located in this way.

The workings of this coherence analysis of truth are best clarified by some illustrative examples. Consider the following set of data (say more or less reliable reports):

$$\mathbf{S} = \{p \vee q, \sim p, \sim q\}.$$

The m.c.s. of $\mathbf{S}$ are as follows

$\mathbf{S_1} = \{p \vee q, \sim p\}$ which is axiomatized by $\sim p \mathbin{\&} q$

$\mathbf{S_2} = \{p \vee q, \sim q\}$ which is axiomatized by $p \mathbin{\&} \sim q$

$\mathbf{S_3} = \{\sim p, \sim q\}$ which is axiomatized by $\sim p \mathbin{\&} \sim q$.

With respect to the initial set of data one or another of these m.c.s. must obtain: our view is simply that one of the reports must be in error. We can thus 'play safe' in the identification of the truth by disjoining the axioms of the m.c.s. to obtain $(\sim p \mathbin{\&} q) \vee (p \mathbin{\&} \sim q) \vee (\sim p \mathbin{\&} \sim q)$ or equivalently $\sim p \vee \sim q$. Now let it be supposed that some preferential machinery is operative but eliminates only a single case among the m.c.s.

(1) Suppose this is $\mathbf{S_1}$. Then the truths are determined as the consequences of $\mathbf{S_2}$ and $\mathbf{S_3}$. These are axiomatized by $(p \mathbin{\&} \sim q) \vee (\sim p \mathbin{\&} \sim q)$, that is, $\sim q$. Looking back to $\mathbf{S}$ we realize that this leaves the truth-status of $\sim p$ and $p \vee q$ unsettled. As regards these two $\mathbf{S}$-elements, we are faced by a choice. We can have one but not both, for we know that it is now a truth that $[\sim q \mathbin{\&} (p \vee q)] \vee [\sim q \mathbin{\&} \sim p]$. We find ourselves in a fundamentally disjunctive situation.

(2) Suppose that it is $\mathbf{S_3}$ that is preferentially eliminated. Then the truths are axiomatized by $(\sim p \mathbin{\&} q) \vee (p \mathbin{\&} \sim q)$ or equivalently $(p \vee q) \mathbin{\&} (\sim p \vee \sim q)$. Again we know that one $\mathbf{S}$-element is true (viz. $p \vee q$) and the other two $(\sim p \sim q)$, and remain in a disjunctively related but undetermined truth-status.

Of course when application of the preference machinery leads to a single, unique m.c.s., then every $\mathbf{S}$-element will either be true or false (since incompatible with truths). But when the preference mechanisms are less definitive and lead to several m.c.s., then by the disjunctive nature of the approach some of the **S**-elements will—as the example shows—fail to obtain a determinate truth-status (i.e. not be true or false). In general, the theory will thus violate the classical Laws of Bivalence and Excluded Middle even as regards only the elements of the basic set **S** of data.

Again, consider the following set of data:

$$\mathbf{S} = \{p, p \supset q, q \supset r, \sim r, \sim p \vee \sim q\}.$$

The m.c.s. of **S** are as follows:

$\mathbf{S_1} = \{p, p \supset q, q \supset r\}$ which is axiomatized by $p \,\&\, q \,\&$

$\mathbf{S_2} = \{p, p \supset q, \sim r\}$ which is axiomatized by $p \,\&\, q \,\&\, \sim r$

$\mathbf{S_3} = \{p, q \supset r, \sim r, \sim p \vee \sim q\}$ which is axiomatized by $p \,\&\, \sim q \,\&\, \sim r$

$\mathbf{S_4} = \{p \supset q, q \supset r, \sim r, \sim p \vee \sim q\}$ which is axiomatized by $\sim p \,\&\, \sim q \,\&\, \sim r$.

Let it be assumed that whatever preferential machinery we have eliminates the last two of these sets. Then the 'consequences' of **S** (its $\mathscr{P}$-consequences) will be exactly the members of $C(\mathbf{S_1}) \cup C(\mathbf{S_2})$ which will be axiomatized by

$$(p \,\&\, q \,\&\, r) \vee (p \,\&\, q \,\&\, \sim r),$$

or equivalently by $p \,\&\, q$. Accordingly, the truths determined by **S** (relative to the preferential criterion at issue) will be exactly those propositions that follow from $p \,\&\, q$—the set $C(\{p, q\})$.

Note that this procedure divides the membership of the initial set **S** of data into three groups, as may be illustrated by the preceding example:

(1) truths (namely $p, p \supset q$)
(2) falsehoods—those propositions whose contradictories follows from the truths (namely $\sim p \vee \sim q$)
(3) undetermined propositions—those neither true nor false (namely $q \supset r, \sim r$).

As this case shows, the theory of truth at issue is fundamentally three-valued.

The example is misleading in one respect. It suggests that our theory is identical with what might be called the naïve coherence theory based on the following alternative procedure:

1. As before, we begin with an inconsistent set **S** of initial data.
2. By some appropriate procedure we single out a certain consistent subset (not necessarily maximal) **S'** of **S** as representing the eligible sector of **S**.
3. We class a proposition as true (relative to **S**) when it belongs to or follows from **S'**.

That this naïve version of the theory is *not* identical with ours is most clearly shown by a further example. Thus let

$$\mathbf{S} = \{p, q, \sim p \vee \sim q\}.$$

Then the m.c.s. are as follows:

$\mathbf{S_1} = \{p, q\}$ which is axiomatized by $p \mathbin{\&} q$

$\mathbf{S_2} = \{p, \sim p \vee \sim q\}$ which is axiomatized by $p \mathbin{\&} \sim q$

$\mathbf{S_3} = \{q, \sim p \vee \sim q\}$ which is axiomatized by $\sim p \mathbin{\&} q$.

Let us suppose that whatever preferential mechanisms may be at work are ineffective at eliminating any one of these m.c.s. Then the 'consequences' of **S** will be exactly those of

$$(p \mathbin{\&} q) \vee (p \mathbin{\&} \sim q) \vee (\sim p \mathbin{\&} q).$$

Thus there will be various truths—for instance $p \vee (\sim p \mathbin{\&} q)$—and various falsehoods (e.g. $\sim p \mathbin{\&} \sim q$). But not a single member of the initial set **S** itself is now determined either to be true or false. We find ourselves in the seemingly anomalous but perfectly intelligible position—one that cannot but be considered as appropriate in view of the indicated rationale—where a set of data that contains no truths can yield truths. It is just this critical fact that illuminates decisively the fundamental distinction between taking something as a datum and accepting it as true. By the application of the coherence machinery here presented we do not necessarily become committed to the truth of any of the data that can nevertheless provide a basis for truth. Starting from truth-candidates alone we may thus arrive at truths. Its present version is able to overcome one of the standard objections to the traditional coherence theory that 'consistency cannot serve as a test of truth unless we already know that some proposition or theory, with which the proposition to be tested is consistent, is itself true'.[11]

[11] H. Khatchadourian, *The Coherence Theory of Truth : A Critical Appraisal* (Beirut, 1961), p. 128.

One amendment must be added. Whenever preferential machinery enters upon the scene so as to *eliminate* certain of its m.c.s. and moreover is *sufficiently* eliminative, then some of the **S**-elements will come to assume the status of truths. Clearly, if some single m.c.s. is uniquely preferred, then all its members will be truths belonging to **S**. Nor is it necessary that the elimination of m.c.s. be that extensive. It is readily shown, for example, that if **S** is itself a minimal inconsistent set, then the elimination of any one of its m.c.s. $\mathbf{S}_j$ will verify (i.e. render true) that unique **S**-element which does not belong to $\mathbf{S}_j$ (but will belong to all the other $\mathbf{S}_i$). On the other hand, it is not true in general that the preferential elimination of one of the m.c.s. of a set **S** must verify some **S**-element. Thus consider

$$\mathbf{S} = \{p, q, \sim p, \sim q\}.$$

Its m.c.s. are:

$$\mathbf{S}_1 = \{p, q\}$$
$$\mathbf{S}_2 = \{p, \sim q\}$$
$$\mathbf{S}_3 = \{\sim p, q\}$$
$$\mathbf{S}_4 = \{\sim p, \sim q\}.$$

Note that even the elimination of both $\mathbf{S}_1$ and $\mathbf{S}_4$ will not render true any single element of **S**—i.e. leave it as a consequence of all remaining $\mathbf{S}_i$.

These considerations do, however, show that, when the preferential machinery operates so as to provide for m.c.s. elimination in a sufficiently extensive way, then our own coherence theory coincides in effect with the workings of what we have termed the naïve version of the theory. From this angle, our theory may indeed be looked upon as providing a plausible mechanism for implementing the basic idea of the naïve version, or rather—and perhaps better—it may be seen as a broader framework within which that theory can be subsumed.

It is of interest in connection with the preceding observations regarding the 'naïve version' of the coherence theory to observe that the decision-theory of truth-acceptance differs radically from the decision-theory of alternative courses of action. Given the inconsistent set $\mathbf{S} = \{P_1, P_2, \ldots, P_n\}$

of prima facie desirable objects of choice or courses for action, the obviously appropriate method of procedure is to determine that unique m.c.s. which optimizes the resultant good (i.e. 'maximizes utility'). Here we *must* opt for a unique m.c.s., because their disjunctive combination is infeasible. There can be no disjunctive combination of mutually incompatible objects of choice or courses of action (outside the probabilistic area). Theoretical and practical reasoning are significantly different from one another in this regard. With truth-acceptance we can 'play it safe' and 'have it both ways' by *disjunctively* accepting *all* of several incompatible alternatives.

One result that is already implicit in the preceding examples deserves to be made explicit. The approach at issue is exactly suited to illustrate the important fact that the idea of 'coherence with prior truths' provides an *ampliative* criterion of truth—one capable of extending the boundaries of what has already been accepted as true. Thus suppose that in circumstances where $p \vee (q \not\equiv r)$ has already been established we are confronted with the following set of further data:

$$S = \{p, q, \sim r, q \; \& \; r, (p \vee q) \supset (\sim p \; \& \; r)\}.$$

The m.c.s. of **S** are as follows:

$S_1 = \{p, q, \sim r\}$ which is axiomatized by $p \; \& \; q \; \& \; \sim r$

$S_2 = \{p, q, q \; \& \; r\}$ which is axiomatized by $p \; \& \; q \; \& \; r$

$S_3 = \{q, q \; \& \; r, (p \vee q) \supset (\sim p \; \& \; r)\}$ which is axiomatized

by $\sim p \; \& \; q \; \& \; r$

$S_4 = \{\sim r, (p \vee q) \supset (\sim p \; \& \; r)\}$ which is axiomatized

by $\sim p \; \& \; \sim q \; \& \; \sim r$.

According to prior hypothesis, compatibility with $p \vee (q \not\equiv r)$ may be taken to serve as our criterion of preference $\mathscr{P}$ among the S_i. Thus, since S_3 and S_4 are incompatible with $p \vee (q \not\equiv r)$, we may eliminate them and identify S_1 and S_2 as preferred m.c.s. This leads to the result that the $\mathscr{P}$-consequences are axiomatized by $(p \; \& \; q \; \& \; \sim r) \vee (p \; \& \; q \; \& \; r)$ or equivalently $p \; \& \; q$. Given that $p \vee (q \not\equiv r)$ has (by hypothesis) already been established as a truth, the family of truths determined by coherence considerations from the set **S** of initial data is to be axiomatized by $p \; \& \; q$. This finding goes far beyond our starting-point, the postulated truth of $p \vee (q \not\equiv r)$.

Our coherentist truth-determination procedure is thus 'ampliative' in the precise sense that, starting from the combination of the postulated truth of certain propositions and a given set of data that are *not* truths (but are at best truth-candidates) we are able to deploy coherence considerations to extend the boundaries of the true, or rather, and more accurately, of what —relative to these 'conditions of the problem'—is reasonably to be classed as such. But, of course, we do not here generate truths *ex nihilo*. We extract the new truths not from the old truths (as in deductive logic) but from *the data*. The status of datahood does not, of course, presuppose truthfulness as such, but it does nevertheless involve a certain commitment as to truth-relevant considerations.

8. *The Pivotal Role of Data*

The basis for the application of a coherence analysis of truths is thus to be a *set of data*, subject to the conception of a 'datum' set forth in the preceding chapter. Accordingly, the standard of truth to be deployed will be articulated in terms of 'coherence with the data'. But, of course, not just *any* set of data will serve: it must be a sufficiently comprehensive set, that includes all of those propositions relevant to the matter at issue that we are prepared to recognize as genuine prospects for truth. Specifically, a set of data is inadequate if we are not willing to concede 'on general principles' that the actual truth is somehow comprehended within it. For example, let the following set be put forward as representing the data for a coherence analysis:

$$S = \{p \,\&\, q, p \,\&\, {\sim}q, {\sim}p \,\&\, q\}.$$

Note that (in the absence of any specifically more delimitative preferential criterion) the 'consequence'

$$(p \,\&\, q) \vee (p \,\&\, {\sim}q) \vee ({\sim}p \,\&\, q),$$

or more simply ${\sim}({\sim}p \,\&\, {\sim}q)$, will emerge from these data. The omission of the (clearly highly relevant) alternative '${\sim}p \,\&\, {\sim}q$' from the data must be taken to indicate that this is explicitly excluded from the truth-candidates, so that ${\sim}({\sim}p \,\&\, {\sim}q)$ can on this basis be taken as a definite truth. Had we wanted to block this view of the matter, and wished 'to keep the door open' as regards the possible truth of '${\sim}p \,\&\, {\sim}q$', we should have had to add this proposition to S as yet another truth-candidate ($=$ datum).

The failure of some relevant possibilities to figure in the data can be tantamount to their elimination. The set S of data need not be 'complete' in any absolute sense but must be complete enough to enable us to view this set *as a set of data*, and take the stance that as much as can consistently be accepted from S must be true. If this stance is inappropriate—e.g. if S gives an admittedly incomplete list of alternatives—then the requisite conditions for a coherence analysis of truth do not apply. Thus to characterize a group of propositions as a set of data in our technical sense is to make a certain special sort of 'completeness' claim on their behalf.

Membership of the set of data must be *truth-presumptive*, and reflect our determination to take all **S** members as true in so far as is possible. And this leads immediately to the element of completeness emphasized in the first section of the present chapter. Thus consider the case when **S** contains a group of mutually exclusive (albeit individually self-consistent) alternatives:
$$\mathbf{S} = \{A_1, A_2, \ldots, A_n\}.$$

No matter how the process of $\mathscr{P}$-consequence determination proceeds, we are going to validate the I-consequence:

$$A_1 \vee A_2 \vee \ldots \vee A_n.$$

On the coherence analysis of truth, mutual exhaustiveness follows from the collective exclusiveness of the data. By setting the A_i up as the data for a truth-analysis, we are, in effect, saying that they are the only alternatives there are, that they exhaust the range of the *real* alternatives. The 'argument from silence' is definitely valid with respect to a family of truth-candidates. A possibility not envisaged by the data is for all practical purposes eliminated by our postulated determination 'to accept as much from among the data as we consistently can'. The status of datahood, as repeatedly stressed, carries a significant burden of epistemic weight.

It follows that the *systematic* aspect of a 'family' of data plays an important role. In setting up a certain collection of 'given' theses as 'the data of the problem' we adopt the stance of an implicit extremal principle to the effect that these are *all* the data—that our survey of the relevant truth-candidates is in suitable measure *complete*. The data map out the domain of what we are prepared to recognize—in the given cognitive circumstances—as genuine possibilities for an outcome with respect to the question at issue; they serve to delimit our epistemic horizons, so to speak. This has important implications for all applications of the procedure of coherence analysis, because it endows all results obtained on this basis with a certain tentativity.

If the coherence analysis is to yield a worthwhile upshot, this range of alternatives must not be too broad. Suppose we are to toss a (normal) die. Let a proposition regarding the outcome count as a datum if its probability exceeds 0·5. The data will then be as follows:

1-or-2-or-3-or-4-or-5-or-6
1-or-2-or-3-or-4-or-5 and all the other five quintuples
1-or-2-or-3-or-4 and all the other quadruples.

These combine into m.c.s. whose axioms are all the pairs:

1-or-2, 1-or-3, etc.

The I-consequences will be axiomatized by the disjunction of *all* these: 1-or-2-or-3-or-4-or-5-or-6. Since our initial data left us in a position of substantial ignorance, we had no choice but, in effect, to 'canvass all the possibilities'. In such cases of totally non-discriminatory data our coherence analysis of the truths resulting from them will not (in the absence of all eliminative machinery of preference) carry us to any significantly interesting upshot. If the coherence analysis is to have any profitable result, the 'data' must have some epistemic bite: they certainly need not tell us just where the truth lies, but they should not be *altogether* non-committal with respect to the alternatives.

The coherence analysis thus presents the mechanisms through which the given family of 'data' (of the sort explained above) is determinative of the resulting truth. It is important to stress that as regards the coherence process datahood is an *a priori* input into the analysis and in this respect differs radically from truth, which is its *a posteriori* output. From the standpoint of the coherence machinery, datahood remains an external and *prior* issue that must be resolved *ab initio* by other means. But of course datahood is *a priori* only relative to truths, and not in any absolute sense. As the discussion has shown, datahood can—as in the case of the 'data of the senses'—definitely be a matter of empirically *a posteriori* considerations. Indeed just this is the basis for the epistemic bite which the data can possess—and, as we have seen, *must* possess if the coherence analysis is to produce a worthwhile product.

V

CRITERIA OF ALETHIC ELIGIBILITY
AND EPISTEMIC DECISION THEORY

1. *The Problem of Alethic Preference*

IN the preceding chapter it was shown how the problem of the $\mathscr{P}$-consequences (preferential consequences) of an inconsistent set **S** of premisses can be resolved once certain among the m.c.s. $S_1, S_2, \ldots, S_n$ of **S** are classified as alethically preferred to the rest.[1] This leads to the question: upon what sort of rational foundation can one base such a preference for some m.c.s. over others? This is the problem to be examined in the present chapter.

One point must be reiterated at the very outset. The mode of 'preference' that is at issue throughout this discussion is *alethic* or truth-oriented preference. Preference of the *affective* sort is not in question. The issue is what is preferable in point of *being* true, and not what someone would prefer to *have* true. We wish to avoid any taint of a confusion to which some careless exponents of pragmatism may on occasion have succumbed. As we shall see, preferability judgments are not somehow extracted *ex nihilo* by wishful thinking, but are themselves conditioned by prior knowledge or postulation.

A word as to the nature of the task. The basic issue that confronts us can be seen in the light of a problem in *epistemic decision theory*. Given an inconsistent set of premisses, say

$$\mathbf{S} = \{p, p \supset q, \sim q\},$$

we know that we cannot rationally accept all of its consequences (e.g. both p and $\sim p$). And yet logic itself does not resolve the dilemma of selection that confronts us. Theoretical logic alone is not in a position to tell us more than that one must make choices: it will not—indeed cannot—tell us what particular choices are to be made. The venture being embarked upon here

---

[1] It should by now have become clear that alethic preference is in general a matter of preferring one group of alternatives to another, and need not be one of preferring a single alternative to all the rest. It is in general apposite to speak of *a* preferred m.c.s. rather than *the* preferred m.c.s.

is thus inevitably one not of theoretical but of applied logic, or perhaps rather of epistemic methodology. The choice among the members of an inconsistent set of premisses must in the very nature of things be motivated by extra-logical considerations, considerations to be drawn from the specific and characteristic epistemic features of the setting in which particular problems arise.

No attempt will be made here to provide one solitary monolithic solution. We view the situation as fundamentally pluralistic: there is no one single criterion of m.c.s. preference that by itself provides the sole rationally viable and invariably appropriate procedure. A variety of methods for establishing alethic eligibility is available, each with its own distinctive points of advantage and disadvantage and each peculiarly fitted for application to a certain range of uses. We shall now describe some of the most important of these diverse criteria. Throughout, it must be borne in mind that the adoption of one of these procedures rather than another cannot be argued on general principles but must be settled in the light of the specific features of particular problem-situations. In view of this diversity, it is more accurate to speak in the plural of the instrumentalities of the coherence analysis of truth, to indicate a family of related procedures rather than one single uniform process. All one can do here is make a general survey of methods; the circumstances of the case do not permit one to survey a general method.

2. *Method I: Propositional Pivot-Points*

Assume, by way of illustration, that the data providing the starting-point are statements put forward by a certain source, and that these form an inconsistent propositional set S. Let it be the case that some (consistent) subset of these propositions yields a particular consequence P. And let us now suppose further that we have external grounds for postulating that P is something that this source could not possibly have intended or could not possibly have accepted. Then we would be in a position to 'disqualify' all of those m.c.s. of S that yield P as a consequence—or, equivalently, all those that are incompatible with $\sim P$. Accordingly, we should 'prefer' the rest of the m.c.s. over these $\sim P$-incompatible ones. One does in actual practice proceed on some such lines when one says of a certain writer who, being dead, cannot explain what he would have done if he had noticed an inconsistency: 'At any rate he couldn't possibly have meant to say that p'—so that whatever he could reasonably be taken to have meant must be consistent with $\sim p$. This line of thought presents the general features of our first method for the selection of preferred m.c.s., which actually has two versions, one stronger and one weaker.

Method I
(Weaker Form)

Given an inconsistent propositional set **S**, to prefer those m.c.s. of **S** that do not conflict (i.e. are consistent) with certain 'designated' (or postulated) theses. Thus if P is 'designated', $\mathbf{S}_i$ is preferred whenever:

$$\text{Not: } \mathbf{S}_i \vdash \sim P.$$

(Stronger Form)

Given an inconsistent propositional set **S**, to prefer those m.c.s. of **S** that yield as consequence (i.e. entail) certain 'designated' (or postulated) theses. Thus if P is 'designated', $\mathbf{S}_i$ is preferred whenever:

$$\mathbf{S}_i \vdash P.$$

The 'designated' theses at issue constitute—as it were—fixed pivot-points around which the other considerations must be made to revolve.

An illustration of this method can be provided by the set:

$$\mathbf{S} = \{p \,\&\, q \,\&\, r, q \supset r, \sim q \,\&\, \sim r, \sim p \,\&\, (q \vee r)\}.$$

The m.c.s. of this set are:

$\mathbf{S}_1 = \{p \,\&\, q \,\&\, r, q \supset r\}$ which is axiomatized by $p \,\&\, q \,\&\, r$

$\mathbf{S}_2 = \{\sim q \,\&\, \sim r, q \supset r\}$ which is axiomatized by $\sim q \,\&\, \sim r$

$\mathbf{S}_3 = \{\sim p \,\&\, (q \vee r), q \supset r\}$ which is axiomatized by $\sim p \,\&\, r$.

Suppose it resolved that q has been so 'designated' that the possibility of maintaining it is to be kept open, so that anything inconsistent with q must go. Since $\mathbf{S}_2$ is inconsistent with q, this set is now to be dropped in favour of the 'preferred' sets $\mathbf{S}_1$ and $\mathbf{S}_3$. The $\mathscr{P}$-consequences of **S** with respect to this present criterion will thus be exactly those propositions that follow from both $\mathbf{S}_1$ and $\mathbf{S}_3$, a set axiomatized by $(p \,\&\, q \,\&\, r) \vee (\sim p \,\&\, r)$ or equivalently $r \,\&\, (p \supset q)$.

The preceding example shows that a 'designated' thesis will not itself invariably be a $\mathscr{P}$-consequence when Method I is applied in its weaker form. (Note that q, though designated, is not a $\mathscr{P}$-consequence.) A designated thesis need not be postulated in the sense of being 'stipulated to be true'. Indeed it need not even be a truth-candidate or datum. It may only play the part of 'an option to be kept open'. We may be led to it by considerations not of truth as such, but merely of plausibility.

By way of contrast with the preceding example, let us suppose it to be resolved that q must be maintained, and that only those m.c.s. of **S** that yield q can be admitted; in short, that q is postulated. Then we are reduced to S_1 alone, and the $\mathscr{P}$-consequences of **S** with respect to this criterion will be axiomatized by $p \mathbin{\&} q \mathbin{\&} r$. (That q is now a $\mathscr{P}$-consequence is a foregone conclusion.)

The second form of the coherence approach typifies the amplificatory and truth-extending applications of the method, in contrast with those applications that are actually truth-originative in generating truths without the provision of input-truths. Here the designated or postulated theses are, in effect, 'prior truths' to which we have already become committed by some independent procedure deployed at an earlier stage.

The preferential criterion at issue may, of course, fail altogether to be effective in some circumstances. Thus if, in the previous example, it had been our policy to prefer those m.c.s. that do not conflict with $\sim q \vee r$, then *all* the m.c.s. would qualify as 'preferred', and the criterion becomes unable to narrow the range of possibilities.

An important point must now be observed. Let us suppose that the datum-set

$$\mathbf{S} = \{p,\ \sim p,\ q \supset p,\ r \supset p,\ q \mathbin{\&} r\}$$

is being considered in a context where Method I is to be applied with respect to $\sim p$ as 'designated'. The m.c.s. of **S** are:

$S_1 = \{p,\ q \supset p,\ r \supset p,\ q \mathbin{\&} r\}$ axiomatized by $p \mathbin{\&} q \mathbin{\&} r$

$S_2 = \{\sim p,\ q \supset p,\ r \supset p\}$ axiomatized by $\sim p \mathbin{\&} \sim q \mathbin{\&} \sim r$

$S_3 = \{\sim p,\ q \mathbin{\&} r\}$ axiomatized by $\sim p \mathbin{\&} q \mathbin{\&} r$.

With either form of the method, S_1 is eliminated, and the $\mathscr{P}$-consequences of **S** will be axiomatized by

$$(\sim p \mathbin{\&} \sim q \mathbin{\&} \sim r) \vee (\sim p \mathbin{\&} q \mathbin{\&} r)$$

or equivalently $\sim p \mathbin{\&} (q \equiv r)$.

But consider now the cognate set **S′** obtained from **S** by breaking up the conjunction $q \mathbin{\&} r$:

$$\mathbf{S'} = \{p,\ \sim p,\ q,\ r,\ q \supset p,\ r \supset p\}.$$

The m.c.s. of **S′** are:

$S_1' = \{p,\ q,\ r,\ q \supset p,\ r \supset p\}$ axiomatized by $p \mathbin{\&} q \mathbin{\&} r$

$S_2' = \{\sim p,\ q,\ r \supset p\}$ axiomatized by $\sim p \mathbin{\&} q \mathbin{\&} \sim r$

$\mathbf{S}_3' = \{\sim p, r, q \supset p\}$ axiomatized by $\sim p \;\&\; \sim q \;\&\; r$

$\mathbf{S}_4' = \{\sim p, q, r\}$ axiomatized by $\sim p \;\&\; q \;\&\; r$

$\mathbf{S}_5' = \{\sim p, q \supset p, r \supset p\}$ axiomatized by $\sim p \;\&\; \sim q \;\&\; \sim r.$

The m.c.s. that survive elimination with respect to $\sim p$ as designated (on either version) are $\mathbf{S}_2'$, $\mathbf{S}_3'$, $\mathbf{S}_4'$, and $\mathbf{S}_5'$. Accordingly the $\mathscr{P}$-consequences of $\mathbf{S}'$ with respect to this present criterion are axiomatized by

$$(\sim p \;\&\; q \;\&\; \sim r) \;\vee\; (\sim p \;\&\; \sim q \;\&\; r) \;\vee$$
$$\vee \;(\sim p \;\&\; q \;\&\; r) \;\vee\; (\sim p \;\&\; \sim q \;\&\; \sim r)$$

or equivalently $\sim p$. In this revised case, the given preferential criterion provides, in effect, no output whatsoever when applied to $\mathbf{S}'$, apart from the favoured $\sim p$ itself.

The preceding example makes explicit a phenomenon we had certainly expected to encounter. The way the 'content' of an inconsistent set of premisses is formulated in general affects the m.c.s. that result, and will correspondingly affect decisively the 'consequences' of the set in any of the senses at issue—and not only the W-consequences and I-consequences, as we have seen above, but also the $\mathscr{P}$-consequences, as the present example shows.

The preferential method under consideration is excellently fitted to illustrate the difference between assuming a proposition as a truth and assuming it as a datum. Thus let an initially given set of data be as follows:

$$\mathbf{S} = \{p \vee q, \sim q\}.$$

Now let $\sim p$ also be given, but given as a truth (and so of course 'designated' in the sense of the method). First we must transform $\mathbf{S}$ into:

$$\mathbf{S}' = \{p \vee q, \sim q, \sim p\}.$$

The m.c.s. are:

$\mathbf{S}_1' = \{\sim q, \sim p\}$ which is axiomatized by $\sim p \;\&\; \sim q.$

$\mathbf{S}_2' = \{p \vee q, \sim p\}$ which is axiomatized by $\sim p \;\&\; q$

$\mathbf{S}_3' = \{p \vee q, \sim q\}$ which is axiomatized by $p \;\&\; \sim q.$

But since $\mathbf{S}_3'$ is $\sim p$-incompatible, we can eliminate this m.c.s. by the present method, and, accordingly axiomatize the $\mathscr{P}$-consequences of $\mathbf{S}$ as $(\sim p \;\&\; \sim q) \vee (\sim p \;\&\; q)$ and so simply as $\sim p$. On the other hand, if we had assumed $\sim p$ merely as an additional datum—and not as a fixed truth to which all else must be adjusted—we should have been left with all three of the m.c.s., and accordingly axiomatized the $\mathscr{P}$-consequences of S' by $\sim p \vee \sim q$. This example shows that assumption as merely another added datum, as a presumptive truth, places a proposition upon a very different, less demanding—and also less conclusive—footing than its assumption as a definite truth.

3. Method II: Majority Rule

Under some circumstances it may be reasonable to prefer those m.c.s. that yield more elements as I-consequences of S than do the others. We thus arrive at

Method II

Given an inconsistent propositional set S, to prefer those m.c.s. of S that contain more S-elements than the others.

Consider, for example, the set:

$$S = \{p \ \& \ q, \ \sim p \ \& \ r, \ q \ \& \ \sim r\}.$$

The m.c.s. of this set are:

$S_1 = \{p \ \& \ q, q \ \& \ \sim r\}$ which is axiomatized by $p \ \& \ q \ \& \ \sim r$

$S_2 = \{\sim p \ \& \ r\}$ \qquad which is axiomatized by $\sim p \ \& \ r$.

According to the criterion of the method now at issue we should prefer S_1, since it contains two S-elements, whereas S_2 contains only one. Accordingly, the $\mathscr{P}$-consequences of S would, on this criterion, be axiomatized by $p \ \& \ q \ \& \ \sim r$.

It is worth observing that this criterion operates so as to magnify the effect of certain redundancies. Let the inconsistent set at issue contain certain elements that follow from one given element, as in the indicated set the last element follows from the first:

$$S = \{p, q, \sim p \vee \sim q, p \vee \sim q\}.$$

Note that p will also carry $p \vee \sim q$ along into any m.c.s. that contains it, and thus the present method will endow these sets with a substantial (and in some circumstances perhaps unmerited) advantage. The m.c.s. of this set S are:

$S_1 = \{p, q, p \vee \sim q\}$ \qquad which is axiomatized by $p \ \& \ q$

$S_2 = \{p, \sim p \vee \sim q, p \vee \sim q\}$ which is axiomatized by $p \ \& \ \sim q$

$S_3 = \{q, \sim p \vee \sim q\}$ \qquad which is axiomatized by $\sim p \ \& \ q$.

Here S_3 is eliminated by the present method and the $\mathscr{P}$-consequences are axiomatized by $(p \ \& \ q) \vee (p \ \& \ \sim q)$ which is equivalent to p. Thus p emerges victorious in S—but does so merely through the presence of its redundant consequence $p \vee \sim q$. For—by way of contrast—note that in

$$S' = S - \{p \vee \sim q\} = \{p, q, \sim p \vee \sim q\},$$

we have
$$S_1' = \{p, q\}$$
$$S_2' = \{p, \sim p \vee \sim q\}$$
$$S_3' = \{q, \sim p \vee \sim q\}.$$

Here none of the m.c.s. is preferable by the present criterion, so that p is not now a $\mathscr{P}$-consequence. In cases where one wishes to deny consequential efficacy to the presence of such redundancies, the present method is not to be applied. However, if one is minded to make redundancies count favourably towards establishing 'consequences', then the present method has its appeal. For example, one would presumably want to use it when the data represent independent reports by equally reliable observers, so that redundant reports are mutually reinforcing through reciprocal substantiation.

One seemingly analogous approach to the matter of preferential consequences is, however, to be blocked off: we cannot consistently adopt the policy that a proposition is to count as a preferred consequence of a propositional set S if it follows from *most* of its m.c.s. (i.e. from more than not). This is shown by the example:
$$S = \{p, q, \sim q, p \supset q\}.$$

The m.c.s. of S are as follows:

$S_1 = \{p, q, p \supset q\}$ which is axiomatized by $p \& q$

$S_2 = \{p, \sim q\}$ which is axiomatized by $p \& \sim q$

$S_3 = \{\sim q, p \supset q\}$ which is axiomatized by $\sim p \& \sim q$.

Note that p belongs to—and so follows from—most of the m.c.s. (viz. all but one), as do $\sim q$ and $p \supset q$ also. Thus the group of 'consequences' in *this* sense can once again form an inconsistent set.

4. *Method III: Probabilistic Preference*

Every m.c.s. of a given propositional set S is axiomatized by a (self-consistent) proposition, which is characteristic of it in not being equivalent to—indeed in being inconsistent with—the axiomatization of any other m.c.s. Thus *if* we had information about the probabilities of the relevant propositions we could assign probability-values also to the m.c.s. via their axioms, and then use these m.c.s. probabilities as a basis for preferential selections.

Now the critical fact is that we can in suitable circumstances use a propositional set **S** itself as a basis for establishing an assignment of probability-values to propositions. The best way to describe the procedure at issue here is to illustrate it in a simple case. Consider the set:

$$\mathbf{S} = \{p, p \supset q, \sim q\}.$$

Through the well-known procedure for reducing propositional complexes to disjunctive normal form, each of the propositions of **S** can—in all such cases—be represented as a disjunction of the possible-world descriptions (state descriptions) in terms of the basic propositional variables at issue. Thus with two propositional atoms (p and q) we shall obtain four possible worlds:

$$W_1: p \ \& \ q$$
$$W_2: p \ \& \sim q$$
$$W_3: \sim p \ \& \ q$$
$$W_4: \sim p \ \& \sim q.$$

Accordingly, we have the equivalences:

p is equivalent to $W_1 \vee W_2$

$p \supset q$ is equivalent to $W_1 \vee W_3 \vee W_4$

$\sim q$ is equivalent to $W_2 \vee W_4$.

Every **S**-element is thus uniquely correlated with that group of W_i which figure in its normal-form representation. Let us now suppose some distribution of *a priori* probability-values over the W_i to be in hand. (In the absence of counter-indications, one could assume a 'principle of indifference' and give the same probability to the W_i.) For any **S**-element P we may distribute a total probability of 1 over those W_i that figure in P's disjunctive normal form, the distribution being made in proportion with the W_i probability values, as in the following two examples:

Case 1

Possible World	A Priori Probability	Propositional Weighings		
		p	$p \supset q$	$\sim q$
$W_1 = p \ \& \ q$	$\frac{1}{4}$	$\frac{1}{2}$	$\frac{1}{3}$	
$W_2 = p \ \& \sim q$	$\frac{1}{4}$	$\frac{1}{2}$		$\frac{1}{2}$
$W_3 = \sim p \ \& \ q$	$\frac{1}{4}$		$\frac{1}{3}$	
$W_4 = \sim p \ \& \sim q$	$\frac{1}{4}$		$\frac{1}{3}$	$\frac{1}{2}$

Case 2

Possible World	A Priori Probability	Propositional Weighings		
		p	$p \supset q$	$\sim q$
$W_1 = p \mathbin{\&} q$	$\frac{1}{6}$	$\frac{1}{2}$	$\frac{1}{5}$	
$W_2 = p \mathbin{\&} \sim q$	$\frac{1}{6}$	$\frac{1}{2}$		$\frac{1}{4}$
$W_3 = \sim p \mathbin{\&} q$	$\frac{1}{6}$		$\frac{1}{5}$	
$W_4 = \sim p \mathbin{\&} \sim q$	$\frac{3}{6}$		$\frac{3}{5}$	$\frac{3}{4}$.

We can now obtain a new series of W_i-values—determined with reference to the propositions of **S**—by finding the sum corresponding to each W_i-row, and then normalizing these values to 1:

Case 1

Possible World	Sum (Σ) over S-Propositions	Σ Normalized (Σ*)
$W_1 = p \mathbin{\&} q$	$\frac{1}{2}+\frac{1}{3} = \frac{5}{6}$	$\frac{5}{18}$
$W_2 = p \mathbin{\&} \sim q$	$\frac{1}{2}+\frac{1}{2} = \frac{6}{6}$	$\frac{6}{18}$
$W_3 = \sim p \mathbin{\&} q$	$\frac{1}{3} = \frac{2}{6}$	$\frac{2}{18}$
$W_4 = \sim p \mathbin{\&} \sim q$	$\frac{1}{3}+\frac{1}{2} = \frac{5}{6}$	$\frac{5}{18}$

Case 2

Possible World	Sum (Σ) over S-Propositions	Σ Normalized (Σ*)
$W_1 = p \mathbin{\&} q$	$\frac{1}{2}+\frac{1}{5} = \frac{14}{20}$	$\frac{14}{60}$
$W_2 = p \mathbin{\&} \sim q$	$\frac{1}{2}+\frac{1}{4} = \frac{15}{20}$	$\frac{15}{60}$
$W_3 = \sim p \mathbin{\&} q$	$\frac{1}{5} = \frac{4}{20}$	$\frac{4}{60}$
$W_4 = \sim p \mathbin{\&} \sim q$	$\frac{3}{5}+\frac{3}{4} = \frac{27}{20}$	$\frac{27}{60}$.

In every such case the result is a new set of W_i-weighings (the Σ*-values) that can serve as *a posteriori* probabilities of the W_i relative to the data of **S**. The idea is that each proposition of **S** gives to each world W_i a certain individual weight (essentially the probability relative to that proposition of this world being the case, as assessed in the light of the *a priori* probabilities). And these individual weights can in turn be combined to give an over-all group weight relative to all the propositions of **S**. (Treating all the propositions of **S** as equals we can once more —in the absence of counter-indications—simply give each of them equal emphasis in the process of combination.)

On this basis we can now introduce a third, probabilistic method for the determination of preferred m.c.s.:

Method III

We begin with an inconsistent propositional set **S** and a (given or postulated) *a priori* probability distribution over the relevant possible worlds W_i (state descriptions). (These *a priori* probabilities come *ab extra* as externally supplied to the problem. They can, however, be based upon a 'principle of indifference' in the absence of any counter-indications.) In the manner described, we calculate a revised set of internally determined **S**-relativized *a posteriori* probabilities for the W_i, drawing our guidance specifically from the elements of **S**. We then use these **S**-derived *a posteriori* probability-values to compute a probability value for each m.c.s. S_i, namely that of its axiom. The resulting S_i-probabilities are finally our guide for preferring some S_i to others in accordance with the magnitude of their probabilities.

A detailed example will help to make these abstract considerations clearer. Let us return to the previous example:

$$S = \{p, p \supset q, \sim q\}.$$

The m.c.s. of this set are as follows:

$S_1 = \{p, p \supset q\}$ which is axiomatized by $p \,\&\, q \equiv W_1$

$S_2 = \{p, \sim q\}$ which is axiomatized by $p \,\&\, \sim q \equiv W_2$

$S_3 = \{p \supset q, \sim q\}$ which is axiomatized by $\sim p \,\&\, \sim q \equiv W_4$.

The resulting S_i-probabilities—already computed above—are as follows:

Case 1	Case 2
S_1: $\frac{5}{18}$	S_1: $\frac{14}{60}$
S_2: $\frac{6}{18}$	S_2: $\frac{15}{60}$
S_3: $\frac{5}{18}$	S_3: $\frac{27}{60}$.

In Case 1 we merely arrive at a slight preference of S_2 over the rest; but in Case 2 our initial (*a priori*) penchant towards

$$\sim p \,\&\, \sim q = W_4$$

results in a distinct preference for S_3 (whose axiom is just this proposition).

One prospect is to use this procedure *iteratively*, beginning with indifference among the W_i, and calculating *a posteriori* W_i probabilities on this basis with reference to **S**. Then we should use these probabilities as *a priori* inputs into a second round of the same procedure, and so on.

Thus consider the results of Case 1 above, where we did begin with an initial supposition of indifference, and let us recalculate on the basis of the resulting W_i-probabilities

World	'New' A Priori Probability	Propositional Weighings			Σ	Σ*
		p	$p \supset q$	$\sim q$		
$W_1 = p \,\&\, q$	$\frac{5}{18}$	$\frac{5}{11}$	$\frac{5}{12}$		$\frac{5}{11}+\frac{5}{12} = \frac{115}{132}$	$\frac{115}{396}$
$W_2 = p \,\&\, \sim q$	$\frac{6}{18}$	$\frac{6}{11}$		$\frac{6}{11}$	$\frac{6}{11}+\frac{6}{11} = \frac{144}{132}$	$\frac{144}{396}$
$W_3 = \sim p \,\&\, q$	$\frac{2}{18}$		$\frac{2}{12}$		$\frac{2}{12} = \frac{22}{132}$	$\frac{22}{396}$
$W_4 = \sim p \,\&\, \sim q$	$\frac{5}{18}$		$\frac{5}{12}$		$\frac{5}{12}+\frac{5}{11} = \frac{115}{132}$	$\frac{115}{396}$.

Note that in the first round (Case 1) the four W_i came out with probabilities 0·27, 0·33, 0·11, and 0·27 respectively, whereas corresponding second-iteration values are 0·29, 0·36, 0·05, and 0·29. S_2 has managed to strengthen its lead over S_1 and S_3 somewhat. By this device of using the data themselves as a basis for obtaining a 'new' schedule of (second order) *a priori* probabilities we can to some extent overcome the seemingly unfortunate apriorism inherent in a dogmatic stance of indifference as to the W_i. When this is done repeatedly, it can be shown by analytic methods that with reasonable generality this iterative procedure will produce a limited number of distinct possible outcomes (or even a unique outcome), regardless of the initial distribution of (non-zero) *a priori* probabilities. We are thus not as much at the mercy of the seemingly arbitrary initial *a priori* probabilities as it might seem on first view.

Let us have one final look at a set $\mathbf{S} = \{p, p \supset q, \sim q\}$ from another perspective. Suppose we were to view $\sim p$ to be *a priori* more likely than p, and q than $\sim q$, so that the relative *a priori* probability-weights of the four possible worlds were something like: 0·2, 0·1, 0·5, 0·2. Then the situation would be

W_i	A Priori Probability	Propositional Weighings			Σ	Σ*
		p	$p \supset q$	$\sim q$		
$p \,\&\, q$	$\frac{2}{10}$	$\frac{5}{11}$	$\frac{5}{12}$		$\frac{115}{132} \times \frac{2}{10}$	$\frac{230}{714}$
$p \,\&\, \sim q$	$\frac{1}{10}$	$\frac{6}{11}$		$\frac{6}{11}$	$\frac{144}{132} \times \frac{1}{10}$	$\frac{144}{714}$
$\sim p \,\&\, q$	$\frac{5}{10}$		$\frac{2}{12}$		$\frac{22}{132} \times \frac{5}{10}$	$\frac{110}{714}$
$\sim p \,\&\, \sim q$	$\frac{2}{10}$		$\frac{5}{12}$	$\frac{5}{11}$	$\frac{115}{132} \times \frac{2}{10}$	$\frac{230}{714}$.

The 'preferred' m.c.s. would now be S_1 and S_3, so that the $\mathscr{P}$-consequences of S would be axiomatized by:

$$(p \,\&\, q) \vee (\sim p \,\&\, \sim q)$$

or equivalently $p \equiv q$. The entry of different *a priori* judgments has had some effect. They have forced us to change our mind: at first we inclined to S_2 over the rest of the m.c.s.; now we must prefer the others to S_2. Thus the altered *a priori* probabilities have blocked our initial inclination to axiomatize the consequences of S by $p \,\&\, \sim q$.

As this analysis has shown, the machinery of a 'statistical' or probabilistic analysis of state-description distributions affords yet another possible—and in suitable circumstances readily workable—approach to the problem of selecting the preferred m.c.s. of an inconsistent set of premises.

In using probabilities as a basis for m.c.s. selection, Method III in a way effects a forced marriage between alien procedures that does violence to the natural inclinations of the two. Consider once again a propositional set:

$$S = \{p, p \supset q, \sim q\}.$$

One proposition that by no means counts as a 'consequence' of S—indeed whose negation is an I-consequence thereof—is $\sim p \,\&\, q$. The entire m.c.s. analysis of consequences cries out that, relative to S, $\sim p \,\&\, q$ must count as impossible; that $\sim p \,\&\, q$ is not compatible with S, since $\sim(\sim p \,\&\, q)$ is its I-consequence. Yet, on the other hand, all of the probabilistic analyses considered yield $\sim p \,\&\, q$ not as impossible, but rather as possible though improbable. The probabilistic approach insists that $\sim p \,\&\, q$ is a possible result of the data, though one of low probability, to be sure. To combine probabilities with the coherence process so as to eliminate by the latter what the former merely classes as improbable goes against the grain of the natural tendency of each conception. (For a probability-like concept whose workings mesh smoothly with the inherently non-probabilistic nature of the m.c.s. analysis with its surgically neat case-eliminations we must await the conception of plausibility indexing to be introduced in the context of Method IV in the next section.)

One important further point needs to be made about the probabilistic version of the coherence method. The reader has presumably by now grown accustomed to the circumstance that in reasoning from an inconsistent set of premises the specific 'mode of formulation' given to 'the content' of this set must play a decisive role in determining the 'consequences' that follow from the set. This general phenomenon is once again operative with regard to the derivation of probabilities. Thus consider the set $S = \{p, p \supset (q \& r), \sim r\}$. The m.c.s. of this set are:

$S_1 = \{p, p \supset (q \& r)\}$ which is axiomatized by $p \& q \& r$

$S_2 = \{p, \sim r\}$ which is axiomatized by $p \& \sim r$

$S_3 = \{p \supset (q \& r), \sim r\}$ which is axiomatized by $\sim p \& \sim r$.

The calculation of probabilities proceeds as follows (assuming the *a priori* equi-probability of the possible worlds):

	p	$p \supset (q \& r)$	$\sim r$	Σ	Σ^*
$p \& q \& r$	$\frac{1}{4}$	$\frac{1}{5}$		$\frac{9}{20}$	$\frac{9}{60}$
$p \& q \& \sim r$	$\frac{1}{4}$		$\frac{1}{4}$	$\frac{10}{20}$	$\frac{10}{60}$
$p \& \sim q \& r$	$\frac{1}{4}$			$\frac{5}{20}$	$\frac{5}{60}$
$p \& \sim q \& \sim r$	$\frac{1}{4}$		$\frac{1}{4}$	$\frac{10}{20}$	$\frac{10}{60}$
$\sim p \& q \& r$		$\frac{1}{5}$		$\frac{4}{20}$	$\frac{4}{60}$
$\sim p \& q \& \sim r$		$\frac{1}{5}$	$\frac{1}{4}$	$\frac{9}{20}$	$\frac{9}{60}$
$\sim p \& \sim q \& r$		$\frac{1}{5}$		$\frac{4}{20}$	$\frac{4}{60}$
$\sim p \& \sim q \& \sim r$		$\frac{1}{5}$	$\frac{1}{4}$	$\frac{9}{20}$	$\frac{9}{60}$.

Correspondingly, the three m.c.s. obtain the following probabilities: $\quad S_1: \frac{9}{60} \quad S_2: \frac{20}{60} \quad S_3: \frac{18}{60}.$

Adopting the clearly indicated step of eliminating S_1, the (probabilistic) $\mathscr{P}$-consequences of S are accordingly axiomatized by $(p \& \sim r) \lor (\sim p \& \sim r)$ or equivalently simply $\sim r$.

Consider now by way of contrast the 'variant' formulation of S as: $\qquad S' = \{p, p \supset q, p \supset r, \sim r\}.$

The m.c.s. of S' are:

$S'_1 = \{p, p \supset r, p \supset q\}$ which is axiomatized by $p \& q \& r$

$S'_2 = \{p, \sim r, p \supset q\}$ which is axiomatized by $p \& q \& \sim r$

$S'_3 = \{p \supset q, p \supset r, \sim r\}$ which is axiomatized by $\sim p \& \sim r$.

The calculation of probabilities now proceeds as follows (assuming again the *a priori* equi-probability of the possible worlds):

	p	$p \supset q$	$p \supset r$	$\sim r$	Σ	Σ^*
$p \& q \& r$	$\frac{1}{4}$	$\frac{1}{6}$	$\frac{1}{6}$		$\frac{14}{24}$	$\frac{14}{96}$
$p \& q \& \sim r$	$\frac{1}{4}$	$\frac{1}{6}$		$\frac{1}{4}$	$\frac{16}{24}$	$\frac{16}{96}$
$p \& \sim q \& r$	$\frac{1}{4}$		$\frac{1}{6}$		$\frac{10}{24}$	$\frac{10}{96}$

	p	$p \supset q$	$p \supset r$	$\sim r$	Σ	$\Sigma*$
$p \ \& \sim q \ \& \sim r$	$\frac{1}{4}$			$\frac{1}{4}$	$\frac{12}{24}$	$\frac{12}{96}$
$\sim p \ \& \ q \ \& \ r$		$\frac{1}{6}$	$\frac{1}{6}$		$\frac{8}{24}$	$\frac{8}{96}$
$\sim p \ \& \ q \ \& \sim r$		$\frac{1}{6}$	$\frac{1}{6}$	$\frac{1}{4}$	$\frac{14}{24}$	$\frac{14}{96}$
$\sim p \ \& \sim q \ \& \ r$		$\frac{1}{6}$	$\frac{1}{6}$		$\frac{8}{24}$	$\frac{8}{96}$
$\sim p \ \& \sim q \ \& \sim r$		$\frac{1}{6}$	$\frac{1}{6}$	$\frac{1}{4}$	$\frac{14}{24}$	$\frac{14}{96}$.

Correspondingly, the three m.c.s. obtain the following probabilities:

$$\mathbf{S}'_1 : \tfrac{14}{96} \qquad \mathbf{S}'_2 : \tfrac{16}{96} \qquad \mathbf{S}'_3 : \tfrac{28}{96}.$$

We now seem to have warrant in opting for $\mathbf{S}'_3$ alone, and should accordingly axiomatize the $\mathscr{P}$-consequences of $\mathbf{S}'$ by $\sim p \ \& \sim r$. The 'reformulation' of $\mathbf{S}$ as $\mathbf{S}'$ has enabled us to achieve a different—and in this case emphatically more definite—result regarding the 'consequences' that ensue. In dealings with inconsistent sets, such 'reformulation' is never a matter of 'merely grammatical' differences, but generally has far-reaching logical repercussions.

5. *Method IV: From Propositional Plausibility to Set Preference*

Suppose that one were somehow to obtain an indexing of the relative acceptability of the data constituting a propositional set $\mathbf{S}$, an indication of the respective weight of their cognitive claims to adoption as truths. Specifically, suppose this relative plausibility of the $\mathbf{S}$-elements to be graded in terms of some such scheme as:

1 = highly plausible

2 = moderately plausible

3 = minimally plausible

4 = highly implausible.

A plausibility-grading of this sort is often warranted by relevant information regarding the circumstances, by background knowledge, by analogy with previously considered cases, or the like. One can without irrationality accord varying degrees of epistemic favour to even an inconsistent family of propositions for each of which there is some warrant to support a positive inclination short of outright acceptance (for that would be irrational). The point is that data are merely candidates for truth, 'real possibilities' that are in the running, and it is clearly necessary to supplement such considerations of *possibility* by considerations of *plausibility*. The establishment of a plausibility-grading scheme in terms of the characteristics of these candidates—for example, in the case of reports, a reference to the question of how reliable the sources from which they come have been in other instances —can clearly prove both useful and warranted. Even in the epistemically paradigmatic case where the data are the products of sense perception and memory it is clear that differential plausibilities are also warranted by changing conditions of reliability (the man has just emerged from sleep and is scarcely awake, he is under the influence of alcohol or drugs, his observations are made under the pressure of haste or fear, etc.).

Granted a plausibility-grading scheme, one could make use of it by the following procedure:

Method IV

Given an inconsistent propositional set **S** and indexing of the relative acceptability or plausibility of its members, to prefer those m.c.s. of **S** which

(A) are compatible with the 1-obtaining (highly plausible) elements of **S**. (Note that these must be assumed to form a consistent set.)

and

(B) have as their most implausible elements more plausible propositions than the most implausible elements of the others. (This criterion is best applied to m.c.s. after they have been denuded of innocent bystanders. It amounts to the a-chain-is-no-stronger-than-its-weakest-link principle.)

and/or

(C) have elements that are *on the average* more plausible than those of the others.

The 'standard form' of this fourth method would be first to apply (A) and (B) to select *some* m.c.s. as preferred to others, and then apply (C) to effect a yet more refined preferential choice among these.

For an example of this procedure, consider the inconsistent set:
$$\mathbf{S} = \{p \vee q, q \supset r, r \supset p, \sim p\}.$$

Let it be supposed that the index values of a grading in plausibility are as follows:

$$|p \vee q| = 3$$
$$|q \supset r| = 2$$
$$|r \supset p| = 4$$
$$|\sim p| = 1.$$

The situation with regard to the m.c.s. of **S** may be tabulated thus:

m.c.s.		index values	maximum	average
$S_1 =$	$\{p \vee q, q \supset r, r \supset p\}$	(3, 2, 4)	4	3
$S_2 =$	$\{p \vee q, q \supset r, \sim p\}$	(3, 2, 1)	3	2
$S_3 =$	$\{p \vee q, r \supset p, \sim p\}$	(3, 4, 1)	4	$2\frac{2}{3}$
$S_4 =$	$\{q \supset r, r \supset p, \sim p\}$	(2, 4, 1)	4	$2\frac{1}{3}$.

Here S_1 is at once eliminated, since it is incompatible with a 1-obtaining **S**-element (viz. $\sim p$). S_2 alone among the other S_i succeeds in avoiding the maximally disfavoured **S**-element $r \supset p$. Moreover, S_2 fares best in a comparison of average plausibilities. Thus S_2 qualifies as the 'preferred' m.c.s. on the present criterion, and we should accordingly axiomatize the $\mathscr{P}$-consequences of **S** by $\sim p$ & q & r. (Note that the only **S**-element falsified by this procedure is the 4-indexed proposition $r \supset p$; all the rest would be classed as true.)

Such a mechanism for the assessment of propositional plausibilities must differ in various fundamental respects from a measure of probabilities. This is clear from the basic nature of the method at issue. One cannot use just the probabilities of their respective members to judge between groups of propositions because to do so would be to ignore crucial interdependencies.

Thus consider the following case:

Possible World	Probability (By hypothesis)
p & q	0·25
p & $\sim q$	0·35
$\sim p$ & q	0·15
$\sim p$ & $\sim q$	0·25.

Consider now the propositional sets:

Set	Probability of Members
$S_1 = \{p, \sim p \vee q\}$	(0·60, 0·65)
$S_2 = \{\sim p \vee q, \sim q\}$	(0·65, 0·60)
$S_3 = \{p, \sim q\}$	(0·60, 0·60).

In any direct comparison of the probabilities of the elements, S_3 must lose to S_1 and S_2. But this is misleading and mistaken. To take account of interdependencies we must consider the *axioms* of the sets:

Set	Axiom	Probability of Axiom
$S_1 = \{p, \sim p \vee q\}$	$p \,\&\, q$	0·25
$S_2 = \{\sim p \vee q, \sim q\}$	$\sim p \,\&\, \sim q$	0·25
$S_3 = \{p, \sim q\}$	$p \,\&\, \sim q$	0·35.

Now in *this* solely correct and appropriate method of probabilistic comparison, S_3 is the clear winner over S_1 and S_2.

Thus, probabilities do not yield a basis for a set-comparison on the basis of the status of the several separate elements. And therefore whatever can so serve—namely a plausibility measure —must be of a character substantially different from a measure of probability. To implement this conception, a probability-like mechanism quite different from the actual machinery of probability theory will be needed.

Everything said so far, however, leaves open the questions of whether and whence and how such an index of propositional acceptability can be obtained. These questions, whose resolution is critical for the effective implementation of this fourth method for establishing m.c.s. preferabilities, must now be dealt with.

6. *Plausibility Indexing*

It is necessary to explore in considerable detail the prospects of providing a plausibility indexing of propositions capable of guiding a preferential selection among the maximal consistent subsets of an inconsistent set of propositions. Let us begin at the beginning, with a more precise explanation of just how a plausibility index is to work.

(i) *Plausibility Indexing*

Given a set **S** of propositions, a plausibility indexing of **S** is to consist in assigning to the elements of **S** integers from the list $0, 1, 2, \ldots, n$. This assignment is to be such as to implement the intuitive idea that the values play the following roles:

1. 0 represents maximal plausibility (or logical certainty)
2. 1 represents high plausibility (or effective or virtual certainty)
3. $0, 1, \ldots, m$ represent decreasing degrees of positive plausibility (where $m < n$)
4. $m, m+1, \ldots, n$ represent increasing degrees of implausibility
5. n represents high or maximal implausibility.

In general, when $i < j$, then i indicates a higher degree of plausibility than j (and j a higher degree of implausibility than i).

The terminal value n is to be large enough to permit drawing all the plausibility distinctions necessary to the case in hand.

Formally, this numerical assignment is to conform to the following rules: There is to be an indexing (called a *plausibility indexing* for the set **S**) assigning for every proposition $P \in$ **S** an index value $|P|$ where $0 \leqslant |P| \leqslant n$. This indexing is to be such that the following conditions hold:

(P1) Every proposition in **S** obtains a plausibility value. For every $P \in$ **S**, there is some value k, with $0 \leqslant k \leqslant n$, such that $|P| = k$

(P2) Logical truths are maximally plausible; indeed they constitute the category of the maximally plausible:
$$\vdash P \text{ iff } |P| = 0$$

(P3) All the propositions classed as highly plausible must be mutually compatible. The set: $\{P \mid |P| = 1\}$ is to be consistent

(P4) When a certain (consistent) group of propositions entails some proposition, then this proposition cannot be less plausible than the least plausible among them. If $P_1, \ldots, P_r \vdash Q$ (with $r \geqslant 1$), and $P_1, \ldots, P_r$ are mutually consistent, then $|Q| \leqslant \max_{1 \leqslant i \leqslant r} |P_i|$.

From (P4) it follows at once that: If $P \vdash Q$, then $|Q| \leqslant |P|$.

This entails that interdeducible propositions must have the same plausibility ranking.

Moreover, one can readily establish the following result for mutually compatible propositions P and Q:

$$|P \& Q| = \max [|P|, |Q|].$$

The proof goes as follows:

(1) Since $P \& Q \vdash P$, we have by the preceding result that $|P| \leqslant |P \& Q|$. And analogously, $|Q| \leqslant |P \& Q|$. Consequently $\max [|P|, |Q|] \leqslant |P \& Q|$.

(2) Since $P, Q \vdash P \& Q$ we have it by (P4) that
$$|P \& Q| \leqslant \max [|P|, |Q|].$$

(3) The desired equality relation now follows at once from (1) and (2).

One of the best ways of conceptualizing a plausibility indexing is to think of inferences made from a group of premises belonging to very different epistemic categories, ordered in point of solidity and security. On the principle that 'a chain is no stronger than its weakest link', the status of a conclusion will clearly be determined by that of its 'weakest' premiss. The old principle of modal logic, that the conclusion follows the weakest premiss becomes applicable (*sequitur conclusio peiorem partem*).[2]

It will be shown in Appendix E that such a mechanism of plausibility indexing is in essentials equivalent to the machinery of modal categories as developed in the author's *Hypothetical Reasoning* (Amsterdam, 1964). Also, Appendix F will examine the relationship of this conception to cognate ideas proposed by G. L. S. Shackle and C. L. Hamblin in the 1950s.

A plausibility-indexing is roughly analogous to an assignment of probabilistic likelihoods. But there are certain crucial and decisive exceptions, among which the following two are pre-eminent: (1) when statements of equal probability are conjoined the *probability* of the resultant conjunction is (in general) diminished. But—by the above reasoning—the plausibility of the conjunction is in such cases to remain unaltered. (2) When the probability of P is given, that of $\sim P$ is determined, and so determines that if P is rather probable (i.e. has relatively high probability) then $\sim P$ is rather improbable (i.e. has relatively low probability). By contrast, the plausibility of $\sim P$ bears no necessary relationship to that of P: in principle both can together obtain relatively high or relatively low plausibility values. The fact is that plausibility is a distinct concept in its own right and is something altogether different from probability as explicated by the mathematical calculus of probabilities.

The aim of a plausibility indexing is to codify the comparative extent of our epistemic commitment to propositions. The informal ideas at issue here are not difficult to explain. To say

² The technical conception of plausibility at work in this discussion differs from the use of the same term in various other writers. In G. Polya's *Patterns of Plausible Inference* (Princeton, N.J., 1954) plausibility plays the role of a probability that is merely comparative rather than fully quantitative. In a recent paper by W. C. Salmon on 'Bayes' Theorem and the History of Science' in vol. 5 (*Historical and Philosophical Perspectives of Science*) of the *Minnesota Studies in Philosophy of Science* (Minneapolis, Minn., 1970), the concept of plausibility is also prominent. However, Salmon's plausibility is also a probability of a certain kind, viz. *a priori* probability for use in a Bayesian analysis of posterior probabilities. All the same, the specific ways in which Salmon proposes to use historical analogies to obtain these prior probabilities (= *his* plausibility) in the consideration of scientific hypotheses are highly suggestive for and relevant to the considerations from which plausibilities in *our* sense can be obtained. Again, various writers on scientific reasoning speak comparably about credibility. For example, in B. Russell's *Human Knowledge* (New York, 1948), the concept of 'intrinsic credibility' (see Pt. II, ch. 12, and Pt. V, chs. 6–7). N. Goodman speaks similarly of 'initial credibility' ('Sense and Certainty', *The Philosophical Review*, 61 (1952), 160–7). But it seems that here too the thinking proceeds on essentially probabilistic lines, and that such credibility is, as with Salmon's analogous notion, an essentially probabilistic concept, rather than being fundamentally non-probabilistic, like the present plausibility.

that a proposition is relatively plausible is *not* to say that it is true, but only that its epistemic claims are to be viewed as relatively strong: that if it were to be true this would not surprise us, but would be something that we should welcome (from the epistemic point of view—not necessarily from others). Plausibility is a sort of potential commitment: if we regard a statement as highly plausible we are saying that *if* we were to accept it as true, then we should be prepared to give it a very comfortable and secure place among the truths. And the more plausible the statement, the more deeply we should commit ourselves to accepting it as true if we did in fact so accept it. The allocation of plausibility-index values to a group of statements is thus a reflection of our relative degree of attachment to these statements—be it actual attachment or hypothetical attachment in the context of a certain analysis. In giving one statement a better plausibility classification than another we are saying that if in the last resort we *had* to make a choice between them, we should prefer the more plausible statement.

These remarks help to motivate the characteristic features of plausibilities as compared with probabilities. Even if $P_1, P_2, \ldots,$ P_k are all highly probable, their conjunction can be very improbable indeed, but if they are all very plausible—if we are 'very definitely inclined' to accept each of them—we cannot in logical honesty be any the less minded to accept their conjunction.

The usefulness of plausibility considerations is readily illustrated. Against the charge that coherence is an inadequate standard of truth because fiction and fancy can be made as coherent as any reality, Bradley replied as follows: when fictions are introduced, he insists, then

. . . you cannot confine yourself within the limits of this or that fancied world, as suits your pleasure or private convenience. You are bound to recognize and to include the opposite fancy . . . The fancied world not only has opposed to it the world of perception. It also has against it any opposite arrangement or any contrary part which I can fancy . . . Nothing, therefore, will be left to outweigh the world as perceived, and the imaginary hypothesis will be condemned by our criterion.[3]

But, of course, in this mutually annihilating balance of fiction against fiction from which 'fact' emerges victorious, its victory is not gained by default through the absence of fact-contradictory possibilities. Fact can prevail only by outweighing its fictional alternatives. We can *imagine* what we like, hypothetical possibilities 'come cheap', but—for example—any *perception*

[3] F. H. Bradley, *Essays on Truth and Reality* (Oxford, 1914), pp. 214–15.

(however fallible) must carry special weight in the quest for truth; any 'presumptive observation'—however potentially erroneous and corrigible—must bear a greater weight of plausibility than any 'mere hypothesis'.

There are, of course, many possible epistemological bases for a plausibility indexing of propositions: evaluations of *a priori* likelihood, assessments of simplicity, structural considerations of relative generality, degree of analogy with accepted statements, and the like. Various specific approaches will be considered in detail below.

(ii) *Establishment of a Full-Scale Plausibility Index from a Minimal Plausibility Index*

One natural and simple way of obtaining a plausibility index for a set of propositions **S** is to begin with what might be called a *minimal plausibility indexing* of **S**. An indexing that assigns to each element P of a given propositional set **S** an integral value $\|P\|$ such that $0 \leqslant \|P\| \leqslant n$ is to be so characterized if it satisfies the following three conditions:

(M1) For all $P \in \mathbf{S}$ we have $\|P\| = k$ for some $0 \leqslant k \leqslant n$

(M2) $\vdash P$ iff $\|P\| = 0$

(M3) $\{P: \|P\| = 1\}$ is a consistent set.

These three (conjointly very weak) conditions are in effect identical with (P1)–(P3) above. They provide a framework of rather minimal demands for indicating the plausibilities of a group of propositions under consideration.

Now, given any such minimal indexing for any finite set **S**, one can in fact construct from it a full-scale plausibility indexing by means of the following *index-revision rule*:

Whenever $P_1, \ldots, P_k \vdash Q$ (where $P_1, \ldots, P_k, Q \in \mathbf{S}$) and $P_1, \ldots, P_k$ are mutually consistent, then reduce the index of Q to that of the largest index value of the P_i (where $1 \leqslant i \leqslant k$), whenever such reduction is possible.

The proof that this procedure must terminate is as follows: since **S** is a finite set of propositions, and each of the propositions has as its index an integer not greater than n, it follows that any process in which each step results in reducing an index of at least one proposition will have to come to an end after a finite number of steps. Hence, in order to show that the result of applying the index revision rule whenever possible will yield a plausibility indexing of **S**, it suffices to note the (obvious) fact that at each step of the application of this rule the resulting indexing will still be a minimal index. When this process is ended, namely, when the index-revision rule can be applied no more, the resulting index must obviously be a plausibility index. It is shown in Appendix G that in any given case all of the various possible applications of this procedure must in fact terminate in one single, uniquely defined, full-scale plausibility index.

A minimal index is a plausibility index in embryo: it provides only crude and unrefined discriminations of plausibility. But a careful logical screening can transform these imperfect indications into a full-scale plausibility indexing of the propositions at issue, through implementation of the index-revision rule.[4]

(iii) *Illustration of the Procedure*

Consider the propositional set

$$\mathbf{S} = \{p \mathbin{\&} r, p \mathbin{\&} s, r \mathbin{\&} s, p \supset q, \sim q, \sim p\}$$

and suppose a (minimal) plausibility indexing of $\mathbf{S}$ to be given:

$$\|p \mathbin{\&} r\| = 3 \qquad \|p \supset q\| = 2$$
$$\|p \mathbin{\&} s\| = 2 \qquad \|\sim q\| = 3$$
$$\|r \mathbin{\&} s\| = 1 \qquad \|\sim p\| = 1.$$

We then have the following entailments:

(1) $p \mathbin{\&} r, p \mathbin{\&} s \vdash r \mathbin{\&} s$ so in this case $3, 2 \vdash 1$

(2) $p \mathbin{\&} r, r \mathbin{\&} s \vdash p \mathbin{\&} s$ so in this case $3, 1 \vdash 2$

(3) $p \mathbin{\&} s, r \mathbin{\&} s \vdash p \mathbin{\&} r$ so in this case $2, 1 \vdash 3$

(4) $\sim p \vdash p \supset q$ so in this case $1 \vdash 2$

(5) $\sim q, p \supset q \vdash \sim p$ so in this case $3, 2 \vdash 1.$

Hence, we must apply the index-revision rule to (3), which will result in lowering $\|p \mathbin{\&} r\|$ to 2, yielding (3') $2, 1 \vdash 2$. This revision leads to the further revision of (1) and (2) to

(1') $2, 2 \vdash 1$

(2') $2, 1 \vdash 2$

which of themselves require no further adjustments. Moreover, we must apply the index-revision rule to (4), lowering $\|p \supset q\|$ to 1, so as to yield (4') $1 \vdash 1$. This changes (5) to

(5') $3, 1 \vdash 1$

---

[4] It should be noted that any plausibility-indexing of a finite set $\mathbf{S}$ can readily be utilized to provide one for the set of all W-consequences of $\mathbf{S}$ by the rule that whenever Q is a W-consequence of $\mathbf{S}$ then $/Q/$ is to be the minimum of the $\max_{1 \leqslant i \leqslant k} \{/P_1/, /P_2/, \ldots, /P_k/\}$ for all sequences $P_1, P_2, \ldots, P_k$ such that (1) all the $P \in \mathbf{S}$, (2) all the P_i are mutually compatible, and (3) $P_1, P_2, \ldots, P_k \vdash Q$.

which requires no further adjustments. Observing that all of (1′), (2′), (3′), (4′), (5′) will now conform to (P4), we conclude that we are done, and obtain from the initial minimal indexing the following full-scale plausibility indexing:

$$|p \; \& \; r| = 2$$
$$|p \; \& \; s| = 2$$
$$|r \; \& \; s| = 1$$
$$|p \supset q| = 1$$
$$|\sim q| = 3$$
$$|\sim p| = 1.$$

Note that this of itself assures us of $\sim p \; \& \; r \; \& \; s$, (in virtue of index assignments of 1) and leaves for the coherence machinery only the task of determining the status of q. Now the one and only m.c.s. of **S** that is compatible with the 1-obtaining elements is
$$\mathbf{S_1} = \{r \; \& \; s, p \supset q, \sim q, \sim p\}.$$

Accordingly, the $\mathscr{P}$-consequences of **S** are axiomatized by $\sim p \; \& \; \sim q \; \& \; r \; \& \; s$. Hence on the present procedure $\sim q$ is indeed a $\mathscr{P}$-consequence, notwithstanding its low plausibility assessment in the initial indexing.

An important point can be brought to light in terms of this example, namely that there is no direct relationship between plausibility and truth. A proposition that is unproblematically true relative to certain data **S**—an I-consequence of **S**, for example—can have a very low plausibility. This is shown by the case of an innocent bystander that is very implausible (i.e. has a large plausibility index). On the other hand, a proposition rated as highly plausible can fail to be true. Consider the propositional set:

$$\mathbf{S} = \{p \; \& \; q, q \; \& \; r, p \supset r, p \supset q, \sim r, \sim q \; \& \; r\}$$

where the following plausibility indexing of **S** is given:

$$|p \; \& \; q| = 3$$
$$|q \; \& \; r| = 2$$
$$|p \supset r| = 2$$
$$|p \supset q| = 2$$
$$|\sim r| = 2$$
$$|\sim q \; \& \; r| = 3.$$

S has the following four m.c.s.:

$S_1 = \{p \ \& \ q, q \ \& \ r, p \supset r, p \supset q\}$ with axiom $p \ \& \ q \ \& \ r$

$S_2 = \{p \ \& \ q, p \supset q, \sim r\}$ with axiom $p \ \& \ q \ \& \sim r$

$S_3 = \{p \supset q, p \supset r, \sim r\}$ with axiom $\sim p \ \& \sim r$

$S_4 = \{p \supset q, p \supset r, \sim q \ \& \ r\}$ with axiom $\sim p \ \& \sim q \ \& \ r$.

Now consider $\sim p \ \& \ q \ \& \ r$. No matter how we resolve the issue of preference among the S_i, this proposition is going to be falsified: every S_i is incompatible with it, and so $\sim(\sim p \ \& \ q \ \& \ r)$ is an I-consequence of **S**. But $\sim p \ \& \ q \ \& \ r$ ranks high in plausibility. Its plausibility index value is calculable as 2, and no nontautologous W-consequences of **S** whatsoever could possibly do better than that. Just as a proposition can be improbable but true (or probable but false) so it can be implausible but true (or plausible but false).

(iv) *Further Examples*

Some further examples of the use of a plausibility index for m.c.s. selection may prove helpful.

Let us return to the propositional set already considered above: $S = \{p \ \& \ r, p \ \& \ s, r \ \& \ s, p \supset q, \sim q, \sim p\}$.

But let us now suppose the plausibility indexing:

$$|p \ \& \ r| = 2$$
$$|p \ \& \ s| = 2$$
$$|r \ \& \ s| = 1$$
$$|p \supset q| = 1$$
$$|\sim q| = 3$$
$$|\sim p| = 2.$$

Here the m.c.s. of **S** are

$S_1 = \{p \ \& \ r, p \ \& \ s, r \ \& \ s, p \supset q\}$ which is axiomatized by
    $p \ \& \ q \ \& \ r \ \& \ s$

$S_2 = \{p \ \& \ r, p \ \& \ s, r \ \& \ s, \sim q\}$ which is axiomatized by
    $p \ \& \sim q \ \& \ r \ \& \ s$

$S_3 = \{r \ \& \ s, p \supset q, \sim q, \sim p\}$ which is axiomatized by
    $\sim p \ \& \sim q \ \& \ r \ \& \ s$.

Note first of all that S_2 can be eliminated at once as incompatible with the 1-indexed elements (specifically $p \supset q$).

For the remaining two sets, we obtain the following pattern of index values:

m.c.s.	Plausibilities	Maximum	Average
S_1	(2, 2, 1, 1)	2	$1\frac{1}{2}$
S_3	(1, 1, 3, 2)	3	$1\frac{3}{4}$.

Thus by Method IV, S_1 is the preferred m.c.s., and the $\mathscr{P}$-consequences of S are accordingly axiomatized by p & q & r & s. Note that the sole difference from the first example of the preceding section was the change in the index value of $\sim p$ from 1 to 2, a change that not only resulted in making p a $\mathscr{P}$-consequence in place of $\sim p$, but also—because of coherence interconnections—in making q a $\mathscr{P}$-consequence, instead of $\sim q$.

For another example, consider the set

$$S = \{p, \sim p, q, \sim q, q \supset r, p \supset \sim r\}.$$

Let us assume these propositions to be subject to the indicated assignment of (minimalistic) plausibility values:

Proposition		Index
(1)	p	4
(2)	$\sim p$	3
(3)	q	3
(4)	$\sim q$	2
(5)	$q \supset r$	4 (goes to 2—see below)
(6)	$p \supset \sim r$	4 (goes to 3—see below).

The following implications obtain so as to necessitate the indicated index revisions:

(2) ⊢ (6)	3 ⊢ 4	∴ (6) goes to 3
(4) ⊢ (5)	2 ⊢ 4	∴ (5) goes to 2
(3), (5), (6) ⊢ (2)	3, 4[2], 4[3] ⊢ 3	
(1), (5), (6) ⊢ (4)	4, 4[2], 4[3] ⊢ 2.	

The revised index values yield a full-scale plausibility indexing. The m.c.s. of S are as follows—and now obtain the indicated plausibility values:

m.c.s.	Index Values	Maximum	Average
$S_1 = \{p, q, q \supset r\}$	(4, 3, 2)	4	3
$S_2 = \{p, q, p \supset \sim r\}$	(4, 3, 3)	4	$3\frac{1}{3}$
$S_3 = \{p, \sim q, q \supset r, p \supset \sim r\}$	(4, 2, 2, 3)	4	$2\frac{3}{4}$
$S_4 = \{\sim p, q, p \supset \sim r, q \supset r\}$	(3, 3, 3, 2)	3	$2\frac{3}{4}$
$S_5 = \{\sim p, \sim q, q \supset r, p \supset \sim r\}$	(3, 2, 2, 3)	3	$2\frac{1}{2}$.

Here the m.c.s. S_1–S_3 may be eliminated, and the $\mathscr{P}$-consequences of S are accordingly axiomatized by $\sim p$ & $(q \supset r)$. The truth-status of all the S-elements apart from q and $\sim q$ is thus decided (and this despite the high plausibility of $\sim q$).

As with coherence considerations in general, the plausibility indexing of a propositional set is sensitive to its 'mode of formulation'. Thus consider the set $S = \{p$ & $q, \sim p$ & q, p & $\sim q\}$. The indexing

$$|p \text{ \& } q| = 8$$
$$|\sim p \text{ \& } q| = 6$$
$$|p \text{ \& } \sim q| = 7$$

clearly constitutes a full-scale plausibility index. But now consider a set formed by adding to S nothing but the logical consequences of some of its own members:

$$S^+ = \{p \text{ \& } q, \sim p \text{ \& } q, p \text{ \& } \sim q, p, q\}.$$

Note that the following consequences ensue:

$$p \text{ \& } \sim q \vdash p \qquad \therefore |p| \leqslant 7$$
$$\sim p \text{ \& } q \vdash q \qquad \therefore |q| \leqslant 6$$
$$p, q \vdash p \text{ \& } q \qquad \therefore |p \text{ \& } q| \leqslant 7.$$

Thus, once p and q are imported into the set, the index-revision rule calls for changes in the assignment which, in the initial set S, provided a full-scale plausibility index. The subtle role in the coherence analysis of 'mere differences in the mode of formulation of data' is once again made manifest.

7. *Probabilities and Plausibilities*

As already remarked, plausibilities behave very differently from probabilities. If the probability of p is the same as that of q, the probability of p & q will in general be different and indeed less. Uniform plausibility status, on the other hand, is preserved in conjunction. In consequence of this basic difference, the results of probability and plausibility analyses will in general not be the same.

Consider the set: $S = \{p, p \supset q, \sim q\}$. Let it be that p is viewed as more plausible than $p \supset q$ or $\sim q$. Say that we have:

$$|p| = 2$$
$$|\sim q| = 3$$
$$|p \supset q| = 3.$$

Then in the plausibilistic analysis we have

$S_1 = \{p, p \supset q\}$ corresponding to (2, 3) with maximum 3 and average 2·5

$S_2 = \{p \supset q, \sim q\}$ corresponding to (3, 3) with maximum 3 and average 3

$S_3 = \{p, \sim q\}$ corresponding to (2, 3) with maximum 3 and average 2·5.

Here S_1 and S_3 are to be preferred to S_2 but are essentially indifferent between themselves.

Let us contrast this result with a probabilistic approach. Now we shall suppose that p is viewed as more probable than $p \supset q$ or $\sim q$. To assure this consider

State Description	Probability
p & q	x
p & $\sim q$	y
$\sim p$ & q	z
$\sim p$ & $\sim q$	w.

Now

(1) $\Pr(p) > \Pr(p \supset q)$, i.e. $x+y > x+z+w$ or $y > z+w$

(2) $\Pr(p) > \Pr(\sim q)$, i.e. $x+y > y+w$ or $x > w$.

To meet these conditions let us assume that $x = \frac{3}{12}$, $y = \frac{5}{12}$, $z = \frac{3}{12}$, and $w = \frac{1}{12}$ as *a priori* probabilities for the state descriptions. We may now calculate the *a posteriori* probabilities relative to **S** as follows:

State Description	A Priori Probability	S-elements p	$p \supset q$	$\sim q$	Σ	Σ^*
p & q	$\frac{3}{12}$	$\frac{3}{8}$	$\frac{3}{7}$		$\dfrac{3\times42+3\times48}{8\times7\times6}$	$\frac{270}{1008}$
p & $\sim q$	$\frac{5}{12}$	$\frac{5}{8}$		$\frac{5}{6}$	$\dfrac{5\times42+5\times56}{8\times7\times6}$	$\frac{490}{1008}$
$\sim p$ & q	$\frac{3}{12}$		$\frac{3}{7}$		$\dfrac{3}{7}$	$\frac{144}{1008}$
$\sim p$ & $\sim q$	$\frac{1}{12}$		$\frac{1}{7}$	$\frac{1}{6}$	$\dfrac{6+7}{7\times6}$	$\frac{104}{1008}$

But now consider:

S_1 is axiomatized by p & q which obtains probability $\frac{270}{1008}$

S_2 is axiomatized by $\sim p$ & $\sim q$ which obtains probability $\frac{104}{1008}$

S_3 is axiomatized by p & $\sim q$ which obtains probability $\frac{490}{1008}$.

Again S_1 and S_3 are to be preferred to S_2, but now S_3 obtains a distinct preferential advantage over S_1. The results of this probabilistic analysis thus differ substantially from those of the previous plausibilistic analysis.

The reasons for such discrepancies are not far to seek. In taking the initial comparative evaluations (p over $p \supset q$, p over $\sim q$) to relate to probabilities rather than plausibilities we have implicitly loaded in a good deal of extra information. Probabilities and plausibilities given a very different account of propositional relationships. Such variant informational inputs will, of course, introduce diversities whose presence on the scene can be expected to make a difference.

We might contemplate translating plausibilities into probabilities. This cannot in general be accomplished. Thus consider our preceding example of $S = \{p, p \supset q, \sim q\}$ with the following assignment of plausibility values:

$$|p| = 2$$
$$|\sim q| = 3$$
$$|p \supset q| = 3.$$

In line with this specification of plausibilities, we should—on the approach presently envisaged—try to set up something like the following assignment of probabilities:

Pr(p) is relatively high (say > 0.6)
Pr($\sim q$) is relatively low (say < 0.4)
Pr($p \supset q$) is relatively low (say < 0.4).

But consider the possibilities for meeting these conditions:

State Description	Probability
p & q	x
p & $\sim q$	y
$\sim p$ & q	z
$\sim p$ & $\sim q$	$1-(x+y+z)$

Pr(p) $= x+y > 0.6$
Pr($\sim q$) $= y+1-(x+y+z) = 1-(x+z) < 0.4 \therefore 0.6 < x+z$
Pr($p \supset q$) $= x+z+1-(x+y+z) = 1-y < 0.4 \therefore 0.6 < y.$

This is manifestly impossible, for since $x+y+z \leqslant 1$ we cannot have $1 \cdot 2 < x+y+z$.

Plausibility assignments thus cannot be construed in directly probabilistic terms. Something quite different is at issue in the two cases; owing to the fundamentally different nature of the concepts they do not commingle smoothly; each must be treated in its distinct, characteristic manner.

There remains, however, an oblique way of using a probabilistic approach as a means to obtaining plausibility values. Here we assume, as a starting-point, that certain probability values are given for the data, and then proceed to use these as a basis for the assignment of plausibility values. In illustrating this process let us suppose the set of data:

$$\mathbf{S} = \{p \vee q, \sim p, \sim q\}.$$

The probability-status of the state descriptions will be assumed to be as follows:

State Description	Given Probability
$p \ \& \ q$	$\frac{3}{12}$
$p \ \& \sim q$	$\frac{5}{12}$
$\sim p \ \& \ q$	$\frac{3}{12}$
$\sim p \ \& \sim q$	$\frac{1}{12}$.

(Such probability-values could even have been derived from the initial set of data $\mathbf{S}$ itself by the procedures considered above.) The probabilities of the $\mathbf{S}$-elements are consequently

$$\Pr(p \vee q) = \tfrac{11}{12}$$
$$\Pr(\sim p) \ = \tfrac{4}{12}$$
$$\Pr(\sim q) \ = \tfrac{6}{12}.$$

We now give a (minimal) indexing of plausibility values by evaluating the plausibility of a proposition P as follows:

$$2 \text{ for } \tfrac{2}{3} < \Pr(P) \leqslant 1$$
$$3 \text{ for } \tfrac{1}{3} < \Pr(P) \leqslant \tfrac{2}{3}$$
$$4 \text{ for } 0 \leqslant \Pr(P) \leqslant \tfrac{1}{3}.$$

Thus the $\mathbf{S}$-elements will obtain the following plausibility values:

$$|p \vee q| = 2$$
$$|\sim p| = 4$$
$$|\sim q| = 3.$$

Given such plausibility values, the procedures of Method IV can now be applied in the usual way. Here both this plausibilistic and the directly probabilistic analysis would lead to the same result: the preferential elimination of the m.c.s. $\{\sim p, \sim q\}$.

The key fact to be noted, however, is that (contrary to the upshot of *this* example) there is no guarantee of any agreement between

     (1) the use of probabilities to effect a direct preferential selection among the m.c.s.

and (2) the use of probabilities as basis for a plausibility indexing of the propositions at issue, which in turn can then serve as a basis for a preferential choice among the m.c.s. in accordance with Method IV.

The fact is that plausibilities are so different from probabilities that even if plausibilities are assigned on probabilistic grounds, the resulting plausibilistic analysis may well differ radically from the results of a direct probabilistic analysis.

Thus let us give an (indifferentist) probabilistic analysis of the by now familiar example: $\mathbf{S} = \{p, p \supset q, \sim q\}$. The m.c.s. are

$$\mathbf{S_1} = \{p, p \supset q\} \quad \text{which is axiomatized by } p \,\&\, q$$
$$\mathbf{S_2} = \{p \supset q, \sim q\} \quad \text{which is axiomatized by } \sim p \,\&\, \sim q$$
$$\mathbf{S_3} = \{p, \sim q\} \quad \text{which is axiomatized by } p \,\&\, \sim q.$$

The probabilistic analysis proceeds as follows:

Possible World	A Priori Probability	p	$p \supset q$	$\sim q$	Σ	Σ^*
$p \,\&\, q$	$\frac{1}{4}$	$\frac{1}{2}$	$\frac{1}{3}$		$\frac{5}{6}$	$\frac{5}{18}$
$p \,\&\, \sim q$	$\frac{1}{4}$	$\frac{1}{2}$		$\frac{1}{2}$	$\frac{6}{6}$	$\frac{6}{18}$
$\sim p \,\&\, q$	$\frac{1}{4}$		$\frac{1}{3}$		$\frac{2}{6}$	$\frac{2}{18}$
$\sim p \,\&\, \sim q$	$\frac{1}{4}$		$\frac{1}{3}$	$\frac{1}{2}$	$\frac{5}{6}$	$\frac{5}{18}$.

Here $\mathbf{S_3}$ emerges as the distinctly preferable m.c.s.

But the probabilities of the **S**-elements relative to the use of Σ^*-values as probabilities are:

$$\Pr(p) = \tfrac{11}{18}$$
$$\Pr(p \supset q) = \tfrac{12}{18}$$
$$\Pr(\sim q) = \tfrac{11}{18}.$$

Accordingly we might rate the plausibilities involved as something like

$$|p| = 4$$
$$|p \supset q| = 3$$
$$|\sim q| = 4.$$

The plausibility results from the m.c.s. would then be

S_1: (4, 3) with maximum 4 and average 3·5
S_2: (3, 4) with maximum 4 and average 3·5
S_3: (4, 4) with maximum 4 and average 4.

Accordingly we should drop S_3 as the least favoured m.c.s. This result is the exact reverse of that of the probabilistic analysis—even though the plausibilities were assigned on the basis of the probability values obtained from that analysis. The lesson is clear: probabilities and plausibilities work in entirely different ways. Even probabilistically motivated plausibilities stay 'true to type', and behave as plausibilities must, yielding results that may be altogether different from those obtained by a probabilistic analysis.

It was maintained earlier in the present section that the relative plausibilities of propositions cannot be translated in any direct way into probabilities. This point is correct: yet it is one we wish not to qualify but to supplement. Consider the inconsistent propositional set:

$$\mathbf{S} = \{p \supset q, q \supset \sim p, p\}.$$

Recall our procedure for deriving *a posteriori* probabilities of the **S**-elements relative to **S**:

Possible World	*A Priori Probability*	*S-elements* $p \supset q$	$q \supset \sim p$	p	Σ		Σ^*
p & q	$\frac{1}{4}$	$\frac{1}{3}$		$\frac{1}{2}$	$\frac{5}{6}$	$\frac{5}{18}$	$= 0.28$
p & $\sim q$	$\frac{1}{4}$		$\frac{1}{3}$	$\frac{1}{2}$	$\frac{5}{6}$	$\frac{5}{18}$	$= 0.28$
$\sim p$ & q	$\frac{1}{4}$	$\frac{1}{3}$	$\frac{1}{3}$	$\frac{4}{6}$	$\frac{4}{18}$	$= 0.22$
$\sim p$ & $\sim q$	$\frac{1}{4}$	$\frac{1}{3}$	$\frac{1}{3}$	$\frac{4}{6}$	$\frac{4}{18}$	$= 0.22$

The Σ^*-values now furnish a basis for allocating *a posteriori* probabilities to the elements of **S**. But note that in the tabulation the weight given to each of the **S**-elements is precisely the same. To take account of the relative plausibilities of the **S**-elements we could proceed by giving to each **S**-element a differential weight depending upon its plausibility, ranging, say, from near 0 for extreme implausibility to 1 for maximal plausibility. In this way the calculations of probabilities could be so conducted as to take account of the plausibilities of the propositions in view.

Thus let us suppose that in the example the plausibilities at issue are

$$|p \supset q| = 5$$
$$|q \supset \sim p| = 4$$
$$|p| = 3.$$

Then the weights might be fixed as follows:

$$p \supset q: \tfrac{1}{10}$$
$$q \supset \sim p: \tfrac{2}{10}$$
$$p: \tfrac{5}{10}.$$

The calculation would now proceed as indicated in the tabulation:

Possible World	A Priori Probability	S-elements/weight $\frac{1}{10}$ $p \supset q$	$\frac{2}{10}$ $q \supset \sim p$	$\frac{5}{10}$ p	Σ	Σ*
p & q	$\frac{1}{4}$	$\frac{1}{3}$		$\frac{1}{2}$	$\frac{1}{3} \times \frac{1}{10} + \frac{1}{2} \times \frac{5}{10}$	$\frac{17}{48} = 0.36$
p & $\sim q$	$\frac{1}{4}$		$\frac{1}{3}$	$\frac{1}{2}$	$\frac{1}{3} \times \frac{2}{10} + \frac{1}{2} \times \frac{5}{10}$	$\frac{19}{48} = 0.40$
$\sim p$ & q	$\frac{1}{4}$	$\frac{1}{3}$	$\frac{1}{3}$		$\frac{1}{3} \times \frac{1}{10} + \frac{1}{3} \times \frac{2}{10}$	$\frac{6}{48} = 0.12$
$\sim p$ & $\sim q$	$\frac{1}{4}$	$\frac{1}{3}$	$\frac{1}{3}$		$\frac{1}{3} \times \frac{1}{10} + \frac{1}{3} \times \frac{2}{10}$	$\frac{6}{48} = 0.12$

These four Σ*-values must be compared with 0·28, 0·28, 0·22, 0·22, which would result in the absence of the plausibilistic weighting of S-elements. The situation regarding the m.c.s. of **S** is as follows:

m.c.s.	Axiomatization	Probability Aplausibilistic	Probability Plausibilistic
$S_1 = \{p \supset q, q \supset \sim p\}$	$\sim p$	0·44	0·24
$S_2 = \{p \supset q, p\}$	p & q	0·28	0·36
$S_3 = \{q \supset \sim p, p\}$	p & $\sim q$	0·28	0·40

As we should expect from a cursory examination of the assigned plausibilities, the plausibilistic analysis rules in favour of $S_3 = \{p, q \supset \sim p\}$. The explicit introduction of differential plausibilities into the probabilistic calculation has changed the status of S_1 from being the most to the least promising candidate among the m.c.s.

To summarize: probabilities and plausibilities are different in conception and different in effect. Even when probabilities are determined by the use of plausibility-considerations, or when plausibilities are assigned on the basis of probabilistic information, the two modes of analysis will subsequently proceed on their own separate ways. The key points of difference are:

(1) Plausibility status is preserved in conjunction (with uniform —and compatible—conjuncts), but probability status not.
(2) The assignment of probability values to propositions determines those of their negations, with plausibility values this need not inevitably be so.
(3) Plausibility assignments take implicational relationships into account more extensively than probabilities do.

The sharp difference between these two modes of propositional valuation in the context of the present analysis may be highlighted thus: consider two propositions P and Q and suppose that we have information about their acceptability *separately*, but seek to have information about their acceptability *jointly*. If this information is given in probabilistic terms we may find ourselves left at the starting gate. Thus if we know simply that both P and Q are relatively probable (say each has probability > 0.4), then we know nothing about the probability of their conjunction (it may be 0 if $\Pr(P) = 0.45$ and $Q = \sim P$; again it may be 1 if $\Pr(P) = 1$ and $Q = P$). Separate probabilities do a very incomplete job of taking account of the logical relationships that emerge from conjunctions. With a probabilistic approach to selecting the propositions of a set **S** we cannot look at these propositions separately and seriatim, we must always look at them also conjunctively so as to take interactions into account. With plausibilities, on the other hand, it is a defensible procedure to proceed with reference to separate propositions because in the assignment of plausibility numbers the logical interrelationships among the propositions that arise in conjunction have already been taken into account. Thus given that some set **S** has an m.c.s. consisting of three elements, P, Q, R, that are all 'very probable'—say with probabilities $\frac{3}{4}$, $\frac{2}{3}$, $\frac{2}{3}$, respectively—we know little about the probability of the set as a whole. Its 'axiom' P & Q & R could have a probability as great as $\frac{8}{12}$ or as little as $\frac{1}{12}$ and could range from 'rather probable' to 'very improbable'. But in terms of plausibilities, if we know that all three elements are 'very plausible' then we know that the set as a whole—or rather its 'axiom' P & Q & R—must also be very plausible.

The pivotal fact is that the usual rule of probabilistic degradation in conjunctions—according to which $\Pr(P \ \& \ Q)$ is in general substantially less than $\Pr(P)$ or $\Pr(Q)$—envisages the case of conjoining claims that function in an essentially separate and discrete way. By contrast, the plausibilistic principle of conjunction envisages the case of *systematic interdependence*, where the acceptability of one component is part and parcel with that of the whole to which it belongs. Plausibilistic combination is not modelled on the aggregation of discrete units but in that of the accession of an entire systematic whole, with a view to the acceptance not of this or that separate item, but of a whole network of interlocked and interdependent parts. Here the whole rests on the same footing as its parts—they stand or fall together, and have a common and *shared* status of credibility. The status of a large-scale scientific theory or discipline provides a guiding analogy—a system of physical geometry, for example, must be accepted *en bloc* as a whole, its acceptability cannot be motivated as a compilation of discrete and separately confirmed bits and pieces. (Recall once more the teachings of Duhem on this head.) Thus quite different paradigms are at issue in the plausibilistic and probabilistic spheres. The probabilistic mode of combination addresses itself to the essentially *aggregative* case whose model is the distributive acceptance of discrete items, whereas the plausibilistic mode of combination addresses itself to the essentially *systematic* case whose model is the collective acceptance of a unified whole, each of whose components is effectively interlocked with the rest. (This factor of systematic interdependence renders the plausibilistic approach profoundly congenial to the spirit of the coherence theory.)

8. *Method V: A Pragmatic Approach to m.c.s. Preference*

The pragmatic theory of truth—as we have characterized it in Chapter I—would have us class as true those propositions whose acceptance has (practical) consequences that outweigh the (practical) consequences of their rejection. The weight of these consequences—positive or negative—is to be assessed in terms of a suitable measure of utility. We have already advanced various objections against this doctrine's serving as a theory of truth, and shall have occasion to bring up more in the chapter to follow. At present, however, our aim is to note that—and how—a pragmatic approach can be articulated so as to provide a means for resolving the fundamental problem of the present chapter: a preferential selection among the m.c.s. of an inconsistent set **S** of data.

The starting-point of this inquiry must be a body of machinery providing for a theory of propositional utility. Specifically we shall assume that for every proposition P six quantities are given, as follows:

	We class P as true	We refrain from classing P as either true or false	We class P as false
P is the case	$T^+(P)$	$I^+(P)$	$F^+(P)$
P is not the case	$T^-(P)$	$I^-(P)$	$F^-(P)$

The six numbers occurring within such a 'utility matrix' are to be real numbers, positive or negative. They are to be subject to the following four utility-allocation conditions, reflecting a basic assumption about the workings of the utility-concept at issue:

(U1) $T^+(P)$ and $F^-(P)$ are both positive (i.e. we cannot but do well by being right)

(U2) $T^-(P)$ and $F^+(P)$ are both negative (i.e. we cannot but do ill by being wrong)

(U3) $T^+(P) > I^+(P) > F^+(P)$ ⎞ (i.e. the righter the better, the

(U4) $T^-(P) < I^-(P) < F^-(P)$ ⎠ wronger the worse.)

Apart from conforming to these conditions, the numbers are in principle to be independent of one another.

Some of the logical rules governing such utility matrices are as follows:

I. *Negation*

If the u.m. of P is $\dfrac{x_1}{y_1}\bigg|\dfrac{x_2}{y_2}\bigg|\dfrac{x_3}{y_3}$, then that of $\sim P$ is $\dfrac{y_3}{x_3}\bigg|\dfrac{y_2}{x_2}\bigg|\dfrac{y_1}{x_1}$

II. *Conjunction*

If P, Q are independent, and the u.m. of P is $\dfrac{x_1}{y_1}\bigg|\dfrac{x_2}{y_2}\bigg|\dfrac{x_3}{y_3}$

and that of Q is $\dfrac{v_1}{w_1}\bigg|\dfrac{v_2}{w_2}\bigg|\dfrac{v_3}{w_3}$, then the u.m. of P & Q is

of the usual form with entries not in general determinable if no further specific information is given.

Given such information regarding propositions, the usual choice-strategy familiar from modern decision-theory is applicable. Specifically we could adopt any of the following policies, adapting some standard decision-theoretic strategies to our purposes.[5]

(1) *Minimax Loss Rule*: To implement that column for which the maximum loss is minimal. In virtue of (U1)–(U4) this rule amounts to:

$$\text{To class } P \text{ as } \begin{cases} \text{true} \\ \text{false} \\ \text{either (indifferently)} \end{cases} \text{ according as}$$

$$\begin{cases} F^+(P) < T^-(P) \\ T^-(P) < F^+(P) \\ \text{neither, i.e. } F^+(P) = T^-(P) \end{cases}$$

The shortcoming of this rule is that in settling for minimax loss we may sacrifice a tremendous potential gain to a very small advantage in point of possible losses.

(2) *Maximin Gain Rule*: To implement that column for which the minimum gain is maximal. In virtue of (U1)–(U4) this rule amounts to:

$$\text{To class } P \text{ as } \begin{cases} \text{true} \\ \text{false} \\ \text{either (indifferently)} \end{cases} \text{ according as}$$

$$\begin{cases} T^+(P) > F^-(P) \\ F^-(P) > T^+(P) \\ \text{neither, i.e. } T^+(P) = F^-(P) \end{cases}$$

The shortcoming of this rule is that in going for the maximin gain we may risk a tremendous potential loss to secure very small advantage in point of possible gains.

(3) *Minimax Regret Rule*: Here we first compute the 'regret matrix' resulting from a given utility matrix as follows:

	We class P as true	We refrain from classing P as either true or false	We class P as false
P is the case	$T^+(P) - T^+(P) = 0$	$T^+(P) - I^+(P)$	$T^+(P) - F^+(P)$
P is not the case	$F^-(P) - T^-(P)$	$F^-(P) - I^-(P)$	$F^-(P) - F^-(P) = 0$

[5] For further details on the basic issues of decision-theory the reader is referred to R. D. Luce and H. Raiffa, *Games and Decisions* (New York, 1964) (see chs. 1, 2, 13, and 14), and R. M. Thrall, C. H. Coombs, and R. L. Davis, *Decision Processes* (New York, 1960).

We now implement that column for which the maximum entry is a minimum.

In virtue of (U1)–(U4) this policy of playing safe means that we shall inevitably refuse to class any proposition as either true or false. This is so since we shall always have

$$T^+(P) - I^+(P) \leqslant T^+(P) - F^+(P)$$
$$\text{(since } F^+(P) \leqslant I^+(P)\text{).}$$
$$F^-(P) - I^-(P) \leqslant F^-(P) - T^-(P)$$
$$\text{(since } T^-(P) \leqslant I^-(P)\text{)}$$

Thus for each entry of the second column, one of the others has one just as large (or larger), so that the minimax entry must lie in this central column. Unhappily the play-safe policy of minimax regret invariably results in a suspension of judgment.

All three of these rules have serious shortcomings, as we have seen. Their principal weakness, however, is that they ignore the relative probabilities of the various outcomes. The aim of the fourth rule is to repair this defect.

(4) *Expected Value Rule*: We suppose a measure of propositional probabilities to be in hand. Using this we can define the 'expected value' of each of the three options as follows:

  i. $V_T(P)$, the 'expected value of classing P as true' is given by

$$V_T(P) = \Pr(P) \times T^+(P) + \Pr(\sim P) \times T^-(P)$$

or equivalently, since $T^-(P) = F^+(\sim P)$,

$$= \Pr(P) \times T^+(P) + \Pr(\sim P) \times F^+(\sim P)$$

  ii. $V_I(P)$, the 'expected value of refraining from classing P as either true or false' is given by:

$$V_I(P) = \Pr(P) \times I^+(P) + \Pr(\sim P) \times I^-(P)$$

  iii. $V_F(P)$, the 'expected value of classing P as false', is given by

$$V_F(P) = \Pr(P) \times F^+(P) + \Pr(\sim P) \times F^-(P)$$

or equivalently, since $F^-(P) = T^+(\sim P)$,

$$= \Pr(P) \times F^+(P) + \Pr(\sim P) \times T^+(\sim P).$$

The decision-rule at issue instructs us to implement that column whose corresponding expected value is the greatest.

For example, let P be such that $\Pr(P) = \frac{1}{3}$ and the utility matrix for P is

$$\frac{2 \quad | \quad 1 \quad | \quad -1}{-2 \quad | \quad -1 \quad | \quad 3}.$$

Then
$$V_T(P) = \frac{1}{3} \times (+2) + \frac{2}{3} \times (-2) = -\frac{2}{3}$$
$$V_I(P) = \frac{1}{3} \times (+1) + \frac{2}{3} \times (-1) = -\frac{1}{3}$$
$$V_F(P) = \frac{1}{3} \times (-1) + \frac{2}{3} \times (+3) = +\frac{5}{3}.$$

According to this rule we should classify P as false, since the corresponding V-value is clearly the largest.

This Expected Value Rule is the gateway to a pragmatic approach to m.c.s. preference. We begin, as usual, with a (standardly inconsistent) set S of data.

$$S = \{P_1, P_2, \ldots, P_n\}.$$

We assume that we have in hand (1) a probability value $\Pr(P_i)$ for every $P_i \in S$, which, if necessary, we can calculate on the basis of S itself in the way now familiar, and (2) a utility matrix for each $P_i \in S$. Note now that any m.c.s. S_j of S serves to divide S into (1) those S-elements that are true relative to itself (viz. all the $P_i \in S$ that belong to S_j) and (2) those S-elements that are false relative to itself (viz. all the $P_i \in S$ that do not belong to S_j). Accordingly we can define for every m.c.s. S_i of S its aggregated expected utility. One way of doing so is by means of a simple summation formula:

$$V(S_i) = \sum_{p \in S_i} V_T(P) + \sum_{p \in (S - S_i)} V_F(P).$$

The summation formula just stated has it that the utility value of an m.c.s. is the sum-total of the V_T values of all the S-elements that it *verifies* or determines as (relatively) true (i.e. includes), together with the sum-total of the V_F values of all the S-elements that it *falsifies* or determines as (relatively) false (i.e. excludes). Because no m.c.s. is neutral with respect to any S-elements, but divides them exhaustively into the (relatively) true and the (relatively) false, the V_I-values do not enter into the calculation here. Accordingly, we can for subsequent purposes suppress the central column of the utility matrices of the propositions in question.

It should be noted that this formula represents just one *modus operandi*. Other possibilities for utility aggregation are also possible, and will be considered below.

Along the general line of our approach here, we can now formulate the generically pragmatic procedure of Method V.

Method V

Given an inconsistent propositional set **S**, to prefer those m.c.s. of **S** that obtain a high score in a comparative evaluation of expected utilities.

An example of this procedure is in order. Consider the propositional set $\mathbf{S} = \{p, q, \sim p \vee \sim q\}$. Using the familiar procedure we can derive from **S** itself the following propositional probabilities:

$$\Pr(p) = \tfrac{11}{18}$$
$$\Pr(q) = \tfrac{11}{18}$$
$$\Pr(\sim p \vee \sim q) = \tfrac{12}{18}.$$

Let the utility-matrices be as follows:

p		q		$\sim p \vee \sim q$	
$+1$	-2	$+2$	-3	$+1$	-5
-1	$+2$	-1	$+3$	-1	$+5$

The propositions to enter into calculation will accordingly obtain the following expected values:

$$V_T(p) = \frac{11}{18} \times (+1) + \frac{7}{18} \times (-1) = \frac{+4}{18}$$

$$V_F(p) = \frac{7}{18} \times (-2) + \frac{11}{18} \times (+2) = \frac{+8}{18}$$

$$V_T(q) = \frac{11}{18} \times (+2) + \frac{7}{18} \times (-1) = \frac{+15}{18}$$

$$V_F(q) = \frac{7}{18} \times (-3) + \frac{11}{18} \times (+3) = \frac{+12}{18}$$

$$V_T(\sim p \vee \sim q) = \frac{12}{18} \times (+1) + \frac{6}{18} \times (-1) = \frac{+6}{18}$$

$$V_F(\sim p \vee \sim q) = \frac{6}{18} \times (-5) + \frac{12}{18} \times (+5) = \frac{+30}{18}.$$

The m.c.s. of **S** are as follows:

$$\mathbf{S_1} = \{p, q\}$$
$$\mathbf{S_2} = \{p, \sim p \vee \sim q\}$$
$$\mathbf{S_3} = \{q, \sim p \vee \sim q\}.$$

The expected values for these sets are as follows:

$$V(S_1) = \frac{+4}{18} + \frac{+15}{18} + \frac{+30}{18} = \frac{+49}{18}$$

$$V(S_2) = \frac{+4}{18} + \frac{+6}{18} + \frac{+12}{18} = \frac{+22}{18}$$

$$V(S_3) = \frac{+15}{18} + \frac{+6}{18} + \frac{+8}{18} = \frac{+29}{18}$$

Thus S_1 is far-and-away the preferred choice among the S_i according to the present criterion.

The preceding mode of utility-aggregation however has a certain deficiency in its simply additive combination of element utilities into set utilities. Thus suppose one of the m.c.s. of a set S to be as follows:

$$S_1 = \{p \ \& \ q, p, q \supset r\}.$$

Presumably it can happen in such cases (although it perhaps does not have to happen) that the contribution of p to the over-all utility result is included in that of p & q. Say that this is so because p and q are essentially independent so that p and q make their contributions to the joint utility separately:

$$u(p \ \& \ q) = u(p) + u(q).$$

Now in computing $V(S_1)$ according to the preceding procedure we form the sum

$$V(S_1) = u(p \ \& \ q) + u(p) + u(q \supset r)$$
$$= u(p) + u(q) + u(p) + u(q \supset r).$$

Thus we in effect count $u(p)$ twice, ignoring the fact that p has already made its utility-contribution as part of p & q. As this example shows, the procedure is unbalanced in favour of redundancies. If such imbalance is to be avoided—as would in general be preferable—the determination of aggregated set utilities must be made in some other way.

The most promising approach here would be to apply an expected-value calculation to the m.c.s. S_i directly—that is to say to their axioms—rather than indirectly through the several propositions that constitute their elements.

To see an example of the use of Method V in this form, consider once again the set:

$$S = \{p, q, \sim p \ v \sim q\}.$$

The possible-world probabilities to which **S** gives rise are determined as follows:

Possible Worlds	A Priori Probability	S-elements p	$q \sim p \vee \sim q$		Σ	Σ^*
p & q	$\frac{1}{4}$	$\frac{1}{2}$	$\frac{1}{2}$		$\frac{6}{6}$	$\frac{6}{18}$
p & $\sim q$	$\frac{1}{4}$	$\frac{1}{2}$		$\frac{1}{3}$	$\frac{5}{6}$	$\frac{5}{18}$
$\sim p$ & q	$\frac{1}{4}$		$\frac{1}{2}$	$\frac{1}{3}$	$\frac{5}{6}$	$\frac{5}{18}$
$\sim p$ & $\sim q$	$\frac{1}{4}$			$\frac{1}{3}$	$\frac{2}{6}$	$\frac{2}{18}$

The m.c.s. of **S** are

$\quad$ **S**$_1$ = $\{p, q\}$ $\qquad$ which is axiomatized by p & q

$\quad$ **S**$_2$ = $\{p, \sim p \vee \sim q\}$ which is axiomatized by p & $\sim q$

$\quad$ **S**$_3$ = $\{q, \sim p \vee \sim q\}$ which is axiomatized by $\sim p$ & q.

Then the expected-value utilities of these **S**$_i$ are

$\quad$ **S**$_1$: $V_T(p \,\&\, q) = \frac{6}{18} \times T^+(p \,\&\, q) + \frac{12}{18} \times T^-(p \,\&\, q)$

$\quad$ **S**$_2$: $V_T(p \,\&\, \sim q) = \frac{5}{18} \times T^+(p \,\&\, \sim q) + \frac{13}{18} \times T^-(p \,\&\, \sim q)$

$\quad$ **S**$_3$: $V_T(\sim p \,\&\, q) = \frac{5}{18} \times T^+(\sim p \,\&\, q) + \frac{13}{18} \times T^-(\sim p \,\&\, q)$.

If the appropriate utility-values are known, then these expected values are readily calculated. Thus let it be supposed that the utilities at issue are as given in the following three u.m.:

$$
\begin{array}{cc}
p \,\&\, q \\
\begin{array}{c|c} +3 & -1 \\ \hline -1 & +2 \end{array}
\end{array}
\qquad
\begin{array}{cc}
p \,\&\, \sim q \\
\begin{array}{c|c} +4 & -1 \\ \hline -2 & +2 \end{array}
\end{array}
\qquad
\begin{array}{cc}
\sim p \,\&\, q \\
\begin{array}{c|c} +1 & -1 \\ \hline -1 & +1 \end{array}
\end{array}
$$

We now have:

$$\textbf{S}_1: \quad V_T(p \,\&\, q) = \frac{6}{18} \times (+3) + \frac{12}{18} \times (-1) = \frac{+6}{18}$$

$$\textbf{S}_2: \quad V_T(p \,\&\, \sim q) = \frac{5}{18} \times (+4) + \frac{13}{18} \times (-2) = \frac{-6}{18}$$

$$\textbf{S}_3: \quad V_T(\sim p \,\&\, q) = \frac{5}{18} \times (+1) + \frac{13}{18} \times (-1) = \frac{-8}{18}.$$

Given these results, the criterion now at issue rules emphatically in favour of **S**$_1$.

This illustration exhibits workings of Method V in its present version of an expected utility comparison among the axioms of the m.c.s.

An interesting fact emerges in the light of these considerations: it is possible to articulate a workable version of the pragmatist theory of truth *within* the framework of the coherence theory developed here. An essentially pragmatic formulation of the coherence theory of truth can be devised. Our coherence analysis deploys considerations of alethic preferability to narrow the range of the eligible m.c.s. arising from a body of inconsistent data. There is no reason of principle why the indeterminacy so left open cannot be resolved on pragmatic grounds and the choice among the m.c.s. be made through an evaluation of their comparative utilities. A pragmatist could certainly use our coherence analysis as a vehicle for the application of his favoured doctrine that the true is to be located with reference to the utile.[6]

Another possible pragmatist approach, a variant of Method IV above (based on plausibility considerations), must also be recognized; namely, to take a pragmatic, propositional-utility approach to plausibility indexing. Consider William James's thesis that 'we cannot reject any hypothesis if consequences useful to life flow from it'.[7] If 'reject' here is construed (as seems only natural) in the sense of 'reject as *plausible*', rather than 'reject as *true*', a pragmatist version of our coherence theory results directly.

It must be recognized, however, that the standard objection to a pragmatic theory of truth still remains pertinent with undiminished force: the normative considerations of practical utility do not provide a theoretically satisfying basis for determining what the true facts of the matter actually or plausibly are. Why should what is preferred in point of value be preferred in point of truth? Surely the rationale at work here is no better than a theoretical systematization of wishful thinking: is there not an illicit step here from better *if* true to better *as* true? Why is the preferred-for-value to be preferred-for-truth? The pragmatic approach employs a perfectly good criterion outside the range of its proper application: the standard of 'working out better' and 'superiority in its effects' is a perfectly good criterion for choosing among instrumentalities, procedures, tools, and methods, but *not* for choosing among truth-candidates (propositions, claims, and purported facts).

---

[6] Such a version of pragmatism, however, envisages a pragmatic theory of truth framed on essentially criterial rather than definitional lines, a position which only a few among the lesser pragmatists have been willing to take, but (to all appearances) not the major figures like W. James and F. S. C. Schiller. Cf. B. Russell, *Philosophical Essays* (London, 1910), pp. 132, 137–8.

[7] *Pragmatism* (New York, 1909), p. 273.

Thus recognition that a pragmatic method of m.c.s. selection *can* be employed must be tempered by recognition that there are no theoretical grounds for regarding this mode of resolution as especially satisfactory, let alone as superior to others.

It remains, however, to take account of the special case of an intellectualized pragmatism of purely cognitive utilities. Here we are to abstract ourselves wholly from the pragmatic issue of actual *practical* effects of accepting certain propositions as true, and admit only the strictly *intellectual* effect of being right or being wrong. Accordingly, every proposition is to have one and the same uniform utility matrix:

$$\frac{+1 \mid 0 \mid -1}{-1 \mid 0 \mid +1}.$$

The expected utility of a proposition is now as follows:

$$V_T(P) = \Pr(P) \times (+1) + \Pr(\sim P) \times (-1)$$
$$= \Pr(P) \times (+1) + [1 - \Pr(P)] \times (-1)$$
$$= 2\Pr(P) - 1.$$

Utilities are now merely a renormalization of probabilities to the interval from -1 to $+1$ through the linear transformation: $x \to 2x - 1$. In effect, we simply return to reliance upon probabilities.

In consequence, the method just described of preferential selection among the m.c.s. in question on grounds of their comparative utilities is, in this special case of purely cognitive utilities, tantamount to and identical in effect with the workings of Method III, according to which a preferential choice was to be made on the basis of an assessment of their comparative probabilities. With a purely epistemic pragmatism of 'being right' as the only benefit and 'being wrong' as the only penalty, we are carried back to the actually pre-pragmatic issues of relative probabilities. Our truth-decision procedure no longer warrants the designation of 'pragmatic'—it has become transformed into one that is straightforwardly probabilistic.[8]

---

[8] See also pp. 164-5 below.

VI

A REAPPRAISAL OF TRADITIONAL THEORIES OF TRUTH

1. *The Task of Reappraisal*

THE task in this chapter will be to assess the capacity of various traditional criteria of truth to provide an adequate foundation for a theory of truth. To make the filiation of ideas more perspicuous, it is helpful to outline in advance the methodology of the inquiry:

(1) First an inventory will be made of the general formal conditions that must invariably be satisfied by any adequate theory of truth. This inventory will include both a version of what may be called 'the full classical theory of truth' and the more limited set of conditions for an 'orthodox non-classical theory of truth'.

(2) Whenever a specific criterion of truth is under consideration, the formal requirements that are admitted under (1) can then be transposed into corresponding, more specifically defined, conditions upon this particular criterion of truth.

(3) Each of the various major criteria of truth that have figured in our discussion must consequently be reappraised in the light of the transposed conditions: once these transposed conditions are in hand, the ability of various criteria of truth to meet them can be subjected to critical scrutiny.

This general outline represents the procedure now to be followed. It puts at the forefront the specification of general conditions for a theory of truth, a task to which we shall turn shortly. But one preliminary remark must first be made. It will transpire that all of the traditional theories of truth that have been considered—correspondence, intuitionist, pragmatic, and coherence—can be articulated in ways that satisfy all the various adequacy conditions to be developed. Thus no eliminations can be made: all the theories—coherence specifically included—are qualified to be 'in the running' so far as the generic requirements of a theory of truth are concerned. It is therefore necessary to examine minutely the relative advantages and disadvantages of each, and to identify the specific work to which these various theories of truth are particularly suited. In the course of this investigation it will be our special task to assess the strengths and weaknesses not only of the coherence theory but of its rivals as well.

2. *Conditions of Adequacy for a Theory of Truth*

We now turn to the task of making an inventory of the conditions governing a theory of truth, conditions of adequacy that must be met if any particular theory is to qualify as a theory *of truth*. We shall construe the theory in the criterial sense, as affording rules for determining truth-values for propositions. The conditions will stipulate that this determination must as 'a matter of principle' observe certain proprieties—that it cannot, for example, class a given proposition as *both* true *and* false. Actually, not one but two lists of conditions will be given: (1) those for a full classical theory of truth—including certain controversial principles that turn specifically on two-valuedness (bivalence), such as the law of excluded middle—and (2) those for a non-classical but yet orthodox theory that is to be identical with the former in all respects except in those matters that hinge upon two-valuedness. Both inventories will be given in a single list, but the conditions to be dropped in the move from the classical to the non-classical theory will be indicated by starring.

We presuppose as basis for the discussion a set $\mathbf{D}$ of propositions and a set $\mathbf{V}$ of truth-values. As notation for the truth-value of a proposition P, we adopt the convention that this be represented through the use of slashes: thus $|P|$ is to be the truth-value of P.[1] The conditions we require may now be formulated in the following rules:

I. *Conditions Governing the Content of* $\mathbf{V}$

(I*a*) $\mathbf{V}$ contains at least the two distinct truth-values T and F:

$$T \in \mathbf{V} \text{ and } F \in \mathbf{V} \text{ and } T \neq F.$$

This may be called the *condition of pluri-valuedness.*

---

[1] Thus throughout the present chapter $|P|$ is used to represent the *truth*-value of a proposition P and not, as in Chapter V, its *plausibility*-value.

(I*b*)*   **V** contains just the two distinct truth-values T and F, and no others:

If $v \in \mathbf{V}$, then either $v = T$ or $v = F$.

This may be called the *condition of two-valuedness*.

II. *Conditions Governing Truth-Value Assignments*

(II*a*)   Every $P \in \mathbf{D}$ has at least one truth-value $|P| \in \mathbf{V}$:

There is a $v \in \mathbf{V}$ such that $|P| = v$.

This may be designated as the *existence condition*.

(II*b*)   Every $P \in \mathbf{D}$ has at most one truth-value $|P| \in \mathbf{V}$:

If both $|P| = v$ and $|P| = v'$, then $v = v'$.

This may be designated as the *uniqueness condition*.

III. *Normalcy Conditions for Propositional Connectives*

(III*a*)   Contradictories satisfy the normalcy conditions:

(i) $|P| = T$ iff $|\sim P| = F$

(ii) $|\sim P| = T$ iff $|P| = F$.

Taken together, this pair may be said to represent the *condition of negation*.

(III*b*)   A conjunction is true iff both conjuncts are:

$|P \& Q| = T$ iff both $|P| = T$ and $|Q| = T$.

This may be called the *condition of conjunction*.

(III*c*i)   If either disjunct is true, then their disjunction is also true:

If $|P| = T$ or $|Q| = T$, then $|P \vee Q| = T$.

(III*c*ii)* If a disjunction is true, one of its disjuncts must be true:

If $|P \vee Q| = T$, then $|P| = T$ or $|Q| = T$.

(III*d*i)   If either conjunct is false, their conjunction is false:

If $|P| = F$ or $|Q| = F$, then $|P \& Q| = F$.

(III*d*ii)* If a conjunction is false, then one of the conjuncts must be false:

If $|P \& Q| = F$, then either $|P| = F$ or $|Q| = F$.

* An asterisk marks those conditions that are to be dropped in the formation of the 'orthodox non-classical' theory of truth to be discussed below.

(IIIe)   A disjunction is false iff both disjuncts are false:

$|P \vee Q| = F$ iff both $|P| = F$ and $|Q| = F$.

IV. *Conditions Governing Logical Deduction*

(IVa)   All logical theses are invariably true:

If $\vdash P$, then $|P| = T$ identically, for every assignment of truth-values to the propositional variables of P (or its other variables, if any).

This may be called the *condition of tautology*.

(IVb)   Logical processes are truth-preserving, i.e. from true premises they can only lead to true conclusions. (This may—from another angle—be looked upon simply as a part of the *definition* of a 'valid logical process'):

If $P_1, P_2, \ldots, P_n \vdash Q$ and $|P_1| = |P_2| = \ldots = |P_n| = T$, then $|Q| = T$.

This requirement that a deductive conclusion drawn from true premises must be true may be called the *condition of deductive closure*. It warrants remark that in the light of IIIa this condition has the consequence that truths must always be consistent with one another:

If $|P_1| = |P_2| = \ldots = |P_n| = T$, then not:

$P_1, P_2, \ldots, P_{n-1} \vdash \sim P_n$.

This principle may be called the *condition of consistency*.

This completes the inventory of basic conditions for the assignment of truth-values in a workable theory of truth. It remains only to repair one seeming omission: nothing has been said about normalcy conditions for quantifiers. We shall suppose here that the substitution interpretation for quantifiers is adopted so that:

(∀) $(\forall x)(\ldots x \ldots)$ is to amount to the claim that $(\ldots a \ldots)$ obtains for any and every a in the domain of ∀. The ∀-quantifier is thus essentially conjunctive, and is to be interpreted in line with the normalcy conditions for conjunctions.

According to this condition we shall have $|(\forall x)(\ldots x \ldots)| = T$ iff $|\ldots a \ldots| = T$ for *all the individuals* a in the domain of ∀.

(∃) $(\exists x)(\ldots x \ldots)$ is to amount to the claim that $(\ldots a \ldots)$ obtains for some a in the domain of ∃. The ∃-quantifier is thus essentially disjunctive, and is to be interpreted in line with the normalcy conditions for disjunctions.

According to this condition we shall have $|(\exists x)(\ldots x \ldots)| = T$ iff $|\ldots a \ldots| = T$ for some individual a in the domain of $\forall$.

3. The Traditional Laws of Truth and Their Congeners

It is now readily verified that the several 'laws of truth' familiar from the traditional discussions of the subject are all forthcoming as immediate consequences of the conditions listed for the classical theory of truth in the preceding section. Some, however, must fail in an orthodox non-classical theory (and will accordingly be starred). The details are as follows:

(1) *The Law of Contradiction* (LC)

A proposition is never both true and false: never both $|P| = T$ and $|P| = F$, or equivalently:

$$|P| \neq T \text{ or } |P| \neq F.$$

Proof: By (Ia), (IIb).

(2) *The Law of Identity* (LI)

Provably equivalent propositions are identical in point of truth. If P and Q are interdeducible, then one is true iff the other is:

If $P \vdash Q$ and $Q \vdash P$, then $|P| = T$ iff $|Q| = T$.

Proof: By (IVb).

(3)* *The Law of Excluded Middle for Truth* (LEM-T)

Of a proposition and its contradictory, one must always be true: $\quad |P| = T \text{ or } |\sim P| = T.$

Proof: If $|P| = T$, we are home. So assume $|P| \neq T$. Then by (Ib) $|P| = F$. And so by (III$a$ii) we have $|\sim P| = T$. Q.E.D. (Note: through its use of (Ib) this proof relies critically upon a starred principle.)

(4)* *The Law of Excluded Middle for Falsity* (LEM-F)

Of a proposition and its contradictory, one must always be false: $\quad |P| = F \text{ or } |\sim P| = F.$

Proof: If $|P| = F$, we are home. So assume $|P| \neq F$. Then by (Ib) we have $|P| = T$. And so by (IIIai) we have $|\sim P| = F$. Q.E.D.

(5)* *The Law of Excluded Middle* (LEM)

Of a proposition and its contradictory, one is true and the other false:

$$(|P| = T \text{ and } |\sim P| = F) \text{ or } (|P| = F \text{ and } |\sim P| = T).$$

Proof: This version of LEM is simply a compilation of the preceding two.

(6) *The Law of Negation* (LN)

A proposition and its contradictory cannot both be true, nor can they both be false.[2]

$$\text{Not both: } |P| = T \text{ and } |\sim P| = T$$
$$\text{Not both: } |P| = F \text{ and } |\sim P| = F.$$

Or equivalently:

$$|P| \neq T \text{ or } |\sim P| \neq T$$
$$|P| \neq F \text{ or } |\sim P| \neq F.$$

Proof: By (Ia), (IIIa). (Note that the proof of this law—unlike its predecessor—involves no starred principles.)

(7)* *The Law of Bivalence* (LB)

A proposition must always be either true or false:

$$|P| = T \text{ or } |P| = F.$$

Proof: By (Ib), (IIa).

It should be remarked that only three of these seven traditional 'laws of truth' will obtain in an orthodox non-classical theory of truth: the laws of contradiction, identity, and negation. The bivalence principle and everything that depends upon it fall to the ground.

It is worth remarking, however, that although the 'external' excluded middle principle for truth (LEM-T),

$$\text{either } |P| = T \text{ or } |\sim P| = T,$$

fails in an orthodox non-classical theory, we must, by IVa, here have an 'internal' excluded middle principle of the form:

$$|p \lor \sim p| = T.$$

---

[2] Some writers call one (or both) of these principles the Law of Contradiction, in place of (1) above. (See, for example, A. Tarski, *Logic, Semantics, Metamathematics* (Oxford, 1956), p. 197.) For a survey of alternative formulations of the laws of contradiction and excluded middle see N. Rescher, *Many-Valued Logic* (New York, 1969), pp. 148–54.

A word regarding terminology seems in order. The nomenclature 'orthodox non-classical' has been used to mark two facts: (i) that the theory is non-classical in that it omits the Principle of Bivalence and everything that turns upon it (LEM in particular), and (ii) that in all other respects the theory conforms to the traditional principles of the theory of truth that have figured in discussions of these issues since Aristotle's day.

It is of interest to consider whether or not it is a condition upon truth that the set of all truths must be *saturated* in the sense that the addition to it of any non-member (i.e. non-truth) creates a logical inconsistency. In view of the condition of conjunction (IIIb), this comes down to requiring that whenever P is a non-truth (i.e. $|P| \neq T$), then there is at least one true proposition Q (viz. the conjunction of all the P-relevant truths) which is inconsistent with P (and so deductively entails the contradictory of P):

Whenever P is such that $|P| \neq T$, then

there is a Q such that $|Q| = T$ and $Q \vdash {\sim}P$.

Now given this principle, the condition of deductive closure (IVb) at once yields the result:

Whenever $|P| \neq T$, then $|{\sim}P| = T$.

And by the condition of negation (IIIa) this yields

Whenever $|P| \neq T$, then $|P| = F$.

But this is simply a statement of the condition of two-valuedness. Thus to insist upon the saturation of the set of all truths is tantamount to taking a two-valued view of truth and correspondingly holding to the classical theory of truth.

4. *The Orthodox Non-Classical Theory of Truth and Many-Valued Logic*

According to the classical theory the truth-value of a proposition must be T or F. With the orthodox non-classical theory, however, propositions with an intermediate truth-status must be contemplated. Failure of bivalence assures that we encounter the case of a proposition P such that $|P| \neq T$ and $|P| \neq F$.

Examples of this non-classical position are familiar from the history of logic. The most famous is the discussion of future contingents in Chapter 9 of Aristotle's *De Interpretatione* (*On Interpretation*). According to many interpreters—ancient and modern alike—Aristotle here holds that propositions about future contingent matters, such as the sea battle that may (or may not) take place tomorrow, are presently indeterminate in truth-status, and neither true nor false.[3] Again, certain logicians have maintained that predications of non-existents (e.g. 'The present King of France is bald') are neither true nor false, but 'undefined' in truth status.[4] Moreover, some writers have motivated a departure from two-valuedness by mathematical applications. They have in mind a mathematical predicate ϕ (i.e. a propositional function) of a variable x ranging over a domain D where '$\phi(x)$' is defined for only a part of this domain. For example, we might have it that $\phi(x)$ iff $1 < 1/x < 2$. Here $\phi(x_1)$ will be:

(1) *true* whenever x_1 lies within the range from $\frac{1}{2}$ to 1

(2) *undefined* (or undetermined) when $x_1 = 0$

(3) *false* in all other cases (i.e. when either $1 < x_1$ or $[(x_1 \neq 0)\ \&\ (x_1 < \frac{1}{2})]$.

Here too we arrive at a basically non-bivalent situation.[5] Yet another important mode of non-bivalence is represented by the conception of relatively determined truth, that is, truth with respect to a given (consistent) basis of information. Thus with respect to the basis **B** we shall have

$$|P| = T \text{ iff } \mathbf{B} \vdash P$$

$$|P| = F \text{ iff } |{\sim}P| = T \text{: that is } \mathbf{B} \vdash {\sim}P.$$

Since the case will arise (whenever **B** is *incomplete*) that neither **B** $\vdash P$ nor **B** $\vdash {\sim}P$, a non-bivalent situation will arise. It is readily shown that all of the conditions for an orthodox non-classical theory of truth will obtain in this case and the preceding ones.

It is useful to undertake a detailed scrutiny of the logical structure of a non-classical theory of truth in the specifically three-valued case:
$$\mathbf{V} = \{T, F, I\}.$$

[3] For a discussion of the problem with references to the literature see 'Truth and Necessity in Temporal Perspective' in N. Rescher, *Essays in Philosophical Analysis* (Pittsburgh, Pa., 1969), pp. 271–302. See also D. Frede, *Aristoteles und die 'Seeschlacht'* (Göttingen, 1970; Hypomnemata (classical monograph series), vol. 27).

[4] See 'The Concept of Nonexistent Possibles' in N. Rescher, *Essays on Philosophical Analysis* (Pittsburgh, Pa., 1969), pp. 73–110.

[5] See the discussion of the three-valued system of S. C. Kleene in N. Rescher, *Many-Valued Logic* (New York, 1969), pp. 34–6.

(A) Consider the truth-table for negation:

P	$\sim P$
T	(1)
I	(2)
F	(3)

Note that:

(1) must be F by (IIIai)
(2) must be I by elimination (IIIa precludes T or F)
(3) must be T by (III$a$ii).

(B) Consider next the truth-table for conjunction

P/ \\ /Q/	T	I	F
T	T*	(3)	F†
I	(1)	(2)	F†
F	F†	F†	F†

/Q/   /P & Q/

    * Fixed by (IIIb)   † Fixed by (IIIdi)

Note that by (IIIb), (1)–(3) cannot be T, and so must be I or F. But in the absence of (III$d$ii) we cannot make any more specific determination, and so arrive at the quasi-truth-functional[6] truth-table:

P/ \\ /Q/	T	I	F
T	T	(I, F)	F
I	(I, F)	(I, F)	F
F	F	F	F

/Q/   /P & Q/

By a wholly analogous process the truth-table for disjunction now becomes:

P/ \\ /Q/	T	I	F
T	T	T	T
I	T	(T, I)	(T, I)
F	T	(T, I)	F

/Q/   /P v Q/

[6] So called because certain entries are left indeterminate. See N. Rescher, *Many-Valued Logic* (New York, 1969), pp. 166–84.

Thus in the three-valued case, the conditions for an orthodox non-classical theory of truth will dictate the system of truth-tables that can arise almost but not quite completely, since a (restricted) indeterminacy remains in the binary connectives.[7] (Note that these truth tables throughout meet a basic condition of normalcy: they agree completely with the two-valued, classical tables when only the classical values T and F are involved.)

It should be observed that the multi-valued situation envisaged in the preceding discussion occurs at the meta-level, and arises when the truth-values of propositions are at issue, rather than simply these propositions themselves. There is thus no reason why our logic at the object-language level should not be two-valued, and this is the posture we shall standardly assume for reasons of simplicity (though not of principle). There is nothing whatsoever inconsistent about this superposition of a multi-valued semantical metasystem upon a system whose internal logic is essentially two-valued and classical.

This is perhaps the best place to take at least passing notice of the aberrant, albeit not insignificant, *doctrine of twofold truth*, the double-truth theory that passes under the name of *Averroism*.[8] According to this theory there are distinct standpoints from which the matter of truth can be viewed, and what is true from one may be false from the other. (In its traditional version, two particular standpoints, the religious and the scientific, are primarily at issue.) Such a theory of truth is the very antithesis of the classical, countenancing that a proposition can be *both* true and false. But although the doctrine of twofold truth seems

---

[7] Suppose that into an orthodox non-classical theory we introduce the concept of what might be called semi-truth, subject to the idea that a proposition is semi-true if its contradictory is not true:

$$|p| = T^* \text{ iff } |\sim p| \neq T.$$

For the corresponding falsehood we have

$$|p| = F^* \text{ iff } |p| \neq T^* \text{ iff } |\sim p| = T.$$

Then, clearly, any proposition will have to be either (semi) true or (semi) false. But the resulting two-valued theory of truth will not in general be classical. Classically we have the normalcy condition:

$$|P| = T \text{ iff } |\sim P| = F.$$

But examine

$$|P| = T^* \text{ iff } |\sim P| = F^*$$

or equivalently

$$|\sim P| \neq T \text{ iff } |\sim \sim P| = T$$
$$\text{iff } |P| = T.$$

This will not obtain in general, but hold only when the basic truth values T and F are themselves classical.

[8] The classic study of Averroism is E. Renan, *Averroès et l'averroïsme* (Paris, 1859; rev. edn. by H. Psichari, Paris, 1949). See also M. Maywald, *Die Lehre von der zweifachen Wahrheit* (Berlin and Munich, 1871); W. Betzendörfer, *Die Lehre von der doppelten Wahrheit im Abendlande* (Tübingen, 1924).

at first sight to go wholly and entirely against all our conceptions of the nature of truth, matters are not quite so bad as this. The double-aspect perspective itself saves the day. Although the two aspects can indeed prove mutually discordant, once we assume the 'internal' perspective of a particular one of them, the truth-theoretical situation is, presumably, restored to a classical order.[9]

5. The Machinery for Criteriological Analysis

The criteriological analysis of truth we propose now to cultivate is based on the supposition that some criterion of truth is to be made available and takes the generic form:

$$\text{(T)} \quad |P| = T \text{ iff } C(P).$$

Because condition (Ib) of the preceding section is crucial, we take the view that a classical formulation of the criteriological analysis is to be obtained only when (T) is conjoined with the following rule for F:

$$\text{(F/C)} \quad |P| = F \text{ iff } |P| \neq T \text{ (or equivalently: not-}C(P)).$$

By contrast, the non-classical analysis will be presumed to result when the rule for F is based on condition (III$a$ii) above:

$$\text{(F/NC)} \quad |P| = F \text{ iff } |\sim P| = T \text{ (or equivalently: } C(\sim P)).$$

On the classical analysis, T and F are the only possible truth-values; on the non-classical analysis, T and F are but two truth-values among (presumably) others.

We propose now to check the requirements that must be imposed upon the condition C if the various truth-rules (I)–(IV) of Section 2 are to be satisfied.

Rule	Restriction on C for the Classical Analysis Based on (T) and (F/C)	Restriction on C for the Presumptively Non-Classical Analysis Based on (T) and (F/NC)[10]
(Ia)	None (the condition is automatically satisfied)	None (the condition is automatically satisfied)

[9] Along essentially analogous lines A. Rose has constructed an eight-valued ($8 = 2^3$) system of geometric propositions, the truth-values indicating their respective truth-status in the three systems of Euclidean, Riemannian, and Lobatchevskian geometry. See his 'Eight-Valued Geometry', *Proceedings of the London Mathematical Society*, series 3, vol. 2 (1952), pp. 30–44. See also the discussion in N. Rescher, *Many-Valued Logic* (New York, 1969), pp. 111–16.

[10] The word 'presumptively' is inserted here because, even on the basis of (T)/(F/NC), the full classical theory can result when C is such as to satisfy all the special conditions indicated for the starred rules.

Rule	Restriction on C for the Classical Analysis (T) and (F/C) (cont.)	Restriction on C for the Presumptively Non-Classical Analysis (T) and (F/NC) (cont.)[10]
(Ib)*	None (the condition is automatically satisfied)	This condition is presumably not satisfied *ex hypothesi*. (It will, however, be satisfied in the special case that either $C(P)$ or $C(\sim P)$ always holds, so that we are, in effect, thrown back to the classical case.)
(IIa)	None (the condition is automatically satisfied)	Special provisions must be made for assigning truth-values when neither $C(P)$ nor $C(\sim P)$
(IIb)	None (the condition is automatically satisfied)	P cannot assume two distinct truth-values; specifically $C(P)$ is incompatible with $C(\sim P)$, so that a conjunctive realization of both $|P| = T$ and $|P| = F$ is ruled out.
(IIIai)	$C(P)$ iff not-$C(\sim P)$	$C(P)$ iff $C(\sim\sim P)$
(III$a$ii)	$C(\sim P)$ iff not-$C(P)$	None (the condition is automatically satisfied)
(IIIb)	$C(P \,\&\, Q)$ iff $C(P)$ and $C(Q)$	$C(P \,\&\, Q)$ iff $C(P)$ and $C(Q)$
(IIIci)	If $C(P)$ or $C(Q)$, then $C(P \lor Q)$	If $C(P)$ or $C(Q)$, then $C(P \lor Q)$
(III$c$ii)*	If $C(P \lor Q)$, then $C(P)$ or $C(Q)$	If $C(P \lor Q)$, then $C(P)$ or $C(Q)$
(IIIdi)	If not-$C(P)$ or not-$C(Q)$, then not-$C(P \,\&\, Q)$ If $C(P \,\&\, Q)$ then $C(P)$ and $C(Q)$	If $C(\sim P)$ or $C(\sim Q)$, then $C(\sim[P \,\&\, Q])$
(III$d$ii)*	If not-$C(P \,\&\, Q)$, then not-$C(P)$ or not-$C(Q)$ If $C(P)$ and $C(Q)$, then $C(P \,\&\, Q)$	If $C(\sim[P \,\&\, Q])$, then $C(\sim P)$ or $C(\sim Q)$

10 See p. 151.

Rule	Restriction on C for the Classical Analysis (T) and (F/C) (cont.)	Restriction on C for the Presumptively Non-Classical Analysis (T) and (F/NC) (cont.)[10]
(IIIe)	$\begin{cases}\text{Not-}C(P \vee Q) \text{ iff both} \\ \text{not-}C(P) \text{ and not-}C(Q) \\ C(P \vee Q) \text{ iff } C(P) \text{ or } C(Q)\end{cases}$	$C(\sim[P \vee Q])$ iff both $C(\sim P)$ and $C(\sim Q)$
(IVa)	If $\vdash P$, then $C(P)$	If $\vdash P$, then $C(P)$
(IVb)	If $P_1, P_2, \ldots, P_n \vdash Q$, and $C(P_1), C(P_2), \ldots, C(P_n)$, then $C(Q)$.	If $P_1, P_2, \ldots, P_n \vdash Q$, and $C(P_1), C(P_2), \ldots, C(P_n)$, then $C(Q)$.

First we reiterate two basic ground-rules: (1) For a classical theory of truth, *all* the conditions must be satisfied, while for an orthodox non-classical theory we are to except the starred ones. (2) A classical theory of truth is to be based on ('T') and (F/C), and a non-classical theory on (T) and (F/NC).

The situation that results from a scrutiny of this tabulation may now be summarized as follows. For *both* theories the basic criterion C must be such that:

(1) If $\vdash P$, then $C(P)$ IVa

(2) If $P_1, P_2, \ldots, P_n \vdash Q$

     and $C(P_1), C(P_2), \ldots, C(P_n)$,

     then $C(Q)$ IVb

Considering that

$$P, Q \vdash P \;\&\; Q$$
$$P \;\&\; Q \vdash P$$
$$P \;\&\; Q \vdash Q$$

condition (2) at once yields

(3) $C(P \;\&\; Q)$ iff $C(P)$ and $C(Q)$

with the result that (IIIb) is inevitably satisfied when (1)–(2) obtain.

Let two propositions P, Q be termed *provable equivalents* when they are interdeducible, that is, when $P \vdash Q$ and $Q \vdash P$ both obtain. Note that (2) will have the consequence that

(4) When P and Q are provable equivalents,
     then $C(P)$ iff $C(Q)$.

This result will prove useful.

[10] See p. 151.

What further conditions, additional to (1)–(2), must the criterion C satisfy to assure a non-classical theory based on (T) and (F/NC)? There are just two, namely:

(NC1) If $C(\sim P)$, then not-$C(P)$

(NC2) If $C(P)$ or $C(Q)$, then $C(P \vee Q)$.

Let us check down the list, remembering that the starred conditions all drop out. There is no difficulty about (Ia) and (IIa). Stipulation (NC1) suffices to assure (IIb). Condition (IIIai) follows from (4). Condition (IIIaii) creates no difficulties. Condition (IIIb) has already been assured. Stipulation (NC2) assures condition (IIIdi) in the presence of (4). (3) assures condition (IIIe) in the presence of (4). And this completes the verification.

By an analogous process, it is easy to verify that the following two conditions over and above (1)–(2) suffice to assure that the criterion C will yield a fully classical theory based on (T) and (F/C), namely the principles:

(C1) $C(\sim P)$ iff not-$C(P)$

(C2) $C(P \vee Q)$ iff $C(P)$ or $C(Q)$

A comparison of (C1)–(C2) with (NC1)–(NC2) once again shows that the non-classical orthodox theory amounts—as it should—simply to an impoverished counterpart to the classical theory.

The critical fact now is:

> Given any proposed criterion of truth C, we can apply the classical (T)/(F/C) or the non-classical (T)/(F/NC) rules for truth-values and then determine—in terms of (1)–(2) plus either (C1)–(C2) or (NC1)–(NC2), respectively—whether the resultant theory of truth is of the classical or of the orthodox non-classical type.

This principle is the key to what we shall characterize as the *criteriological analysis* of theories of truth.

6. *Criteriological Analysis of the Correspondence Theory*

For present purposes, we shall construe 'the correspondence theory of truth' in a criteriological manner, basing it upon the 'Tarski condition of truth':

$$C(P) \text{ iff } P.$$

According to this postulation, we have it that:

$$|P| = T \text{ iff } P.$$

It is now readily determined that the entire classical theory of truth results when we adopt the rule (F/C) as the governing condition for falsity. Conditions (1)–(2) become

[1] If $\vdash P$, then P

[2] If $P_1, P_2, \ldots, P_n \vdash Q$ and

$P_1, P_2, \ldots, P_n$, then Q.

It is obvious from the very nature of the consequence-operator $\vdash$ that both these conditions must be satisfied. Let us go on to check (C1)–(C2), that is:

[C1] $\sim P$ iff not-P

[C2] $P \vee Q$ iff P or Q.

These requirements too are obviously met, given the intended interpretation of the connectives at issue.

This completes the demonstration that the postulated version of the correspondence theory—based on the specified Tarski-type criterion—meets all of the stipulated conditions and therefore yields the full classical theory of truth.

7. Criteriological Analysis of the Intuitionist Theory

As formulated above, the intuitionist theory of truth is based on a criterion of truth that amounts to derivability from a (logically self-consistent) set of basic truths. That is, a proposition P is to be classed as true ($|P| = T$) or otherwise in accordance with the following conditions:

(i) $P \in \mathbf{T}_0$

(ii) P follows from truths; that is, there are propositions $P_1, P_2, \ldots, P_n$ such that $|P_1| = |P_2| = \ldots = |P_n| = T$ and $P_1, P_2, \ldots, P_n \vdash P$

(iii) $|P| \neq T$ whenever $|P| = T$ does not obtain on the above basis.

These three conditions can be consolidated in terms of the deductivist truth-criterion:

$$C(P) = {}_{\text{DF}} \mathbf{T}_0 \vdash P.$$

The intuitionist theory takes a foundationalist approach to truth in taking the criterial stance that truth is built up by inference

from a starter set T_0 of primitive truths. Let us explore the consequences of this criterion.

We shall first show that once we adopt the rule (F/NC) as the governing condition for falsity, all of the conditions for an orthodox non-classical theory of truth will be met.[11] Conditions (1)–(2) become:

[1] If ⊢ P, then T_0 ⊢ P

[2] If $P_1, P_2, \ldots, P_n$ ⊢ Q and
$$T_0 ⊢ P_1, T_0 ⊢ P_2, \ldots, T_0 ⊢ P_n$$
then T_0 ⊢ Q.

It is obvious that these requirements are satisfied. All that remains is to check (NC1)–(NC2), that is

[NC1] If T_0 ⊢ $\sim P$, then not: T_0 ⊢ P

[NC2] If T_0 ⊢ P or T_0 ⊢ Q, then T_0 ⊢ $P \vee Q$.

It is obvious that both of these conditions are also satisfied.

This completes the demonstration that the specified version of an intuitionist theory of truth meets all of the conditions needed to obtain a theory of truth of the orthodox non-classical type.

This theory cannot, however, be strengthened to the full classical theory. Consider the conditions (C1) and (C2) which would now become

[C1] T_0 ⊢ $\sim P$ iff not: T_0 ⊢ P

[C2] T_0 ⊢ $P \vee Q$ iff T_0 ⊢ P or T_0 ⊢ Q.

Let T_0 be deductively incomplete so that it in some case entails neither P nor $\sim P$. Then [C1] is clearly violated, as is [C2], which can be seen by letting Q be $\sim P$. (Of course, *in the special case* that T_0 is deductively complete and [C1]–[C2] are satisfied, it will indeed happen that the intuitionist truth-criterion will yield the full classical theory of truth.)

The preceding version of the intuitionist criterion is essentially deductivist. A variant version in terms of a weakened form of inductive grounding (⊧ in place of ⊢) is also viable. Here we should adopt the truth-criterion:

$$C(P) =_{\text{DF}} T_0 \vDash P.$$

It is also possible, provided we introduce consistency screening, to assure that the set of all propositions that are ⊧-consequences

[11] We shall show below that there is no point of adopting (F/C) for falsity and trying for the full classical theory, since condition (IIIaii) is violated.

of a self-consistent proposition will be mutually consistent. Certain principles must be stipulated for ⊨; specifically

(1) $P \vDash Q$ whenever $P \vdash Q$ and P is consistent (and so $\vDash P$ whenever $\vdash P$).

(2) If P is itself consistent and $P \vDash \sim Q$, then not $P \vDash Q$. (It is here that we need the consistency screening.)

(3) If $P \vDash Q$ and $P \vDash R$, then $P \vDash Q \,\&\, R$.

(4) If $P \vDash Q$ and $Q \vdash R$, then $P \vDash R$.

Given these principles, it is readily shown that the inductivist version of the intuitionist criterion is also orthodox non-classical.[12]

These considerations show that in general the theory of truth appropriate to an intuitionist approach is of the orthodox non-classical type.

8. *Criteriological Analysis of the Pragmatic Theory*

In considering the pragmatic theory of truth we shall reverse our usual procedure. Heretofore we have begun with a definite version of the theory, and then tested its specific capacity to satisfy the conditions for truth. Instead we shall now begin almost *in vacuo* and consider how a theory of truth of the generically pragmatic type must be articulated to meet the conditions of a non-classical orthodox theory of truth.

The guiding idea of the pragmatic theory of truth may be taken to reside in the criterial precept that a proposition is to count as true if its utility is sufficiently great, that is, if 'the utility of classing it as true' exceeds some designated magnitude. Accordingly, we shall suppose that for some measure of propositional utility we may stipulate a truth-criterion of the following type:

$$C(P) \text{ iff } u(P) \geqslant c$$

where $u(P)$ stands for the utility measure of the proposition P, and c is a constant that represents some specified threshold value. The question that now confronts us is: what must be the character of the utility measure u if the specified criterion is to generate a non-classical orthodox theory of truth?

By applying the list of conditions developed in Section 5, we

---

[12] We leave open the question of the plausibility of these principles—especially (4)—under the intended interpretation of ⊨.

note that u must be such that the following requirements are met:

[1] If $\vdash P$, then $u(P) \geqslant c$

[2] If $P_1, P_2, \ldots, P_n \vdash Q$ and $u(P_1) \geqslant c, u(P_2) \geqslant c, \ldots,$
    $u(P_n) \geqslant c$, then $u(Q) \geqslant c$

[NC1] If $u(\sim P) \geqslant c$, then $u(P) < c$

[NC2] If $u(P) \geqslant c$ or $u(Q) \geqslant c$, then $u(P \vee Q) \geqslant c$.

The key point to be made is that any propositional utility measure that satisfies these four conditions will result in an orthodox non-classical theory of truth.

An example of such a utility measure is in order, and is indeed needed to settle the question of possible existence. Let us stipulate an assignment of utility-values to propositions conforming to the following rule:

(U1) Every proposition P of the domain D obtains a utility-value from the range -1 to $+1$: $-1 \leqslant u(P) \leqslant +1$.

(U2) Whenever $\vdash P$, then $u(P) = 1$.

(U3) The utilities of contradictories are so arranged that $u(\sim P) \leqslant -u(P)$.

(U4) Whenever $P_1, P_2, \ldots, P_n \vdash Q$, then $u(Q) \geqslant \min_i u(P_i)$.

It is readily shown that any utility-measure conforming to these rules must satisfy the four requirements listed above:

[1] is identical with (U2).

[2] is assured by (U4).

[NC1] is assured by (U3) *provided that $c > 0$.*

Proof: Suppose $u(\sim P) \geqslant c$. Then $-u(P) \geqslant c$. Hence

$$u(P) \leqslant -c.$$

But if $c > 0$, then $c > -c$. Hence $u(P) < c$. Q.E.D.

[NC2] Since $P \vdash P \vee Q$, we have it by (U4) that

$$u(P \vee Q) \geqslant u(P).$$

And analogously $u(P \vee Q) \geqslant u(Q)$. Hence if either $u(P) \geqslant c$ or $u(Q) \geqslant c$, then $u(P \vee Q) \geqslant c$. Q.E.D.

It follows that any propositional utility measure so designed that (U1)–(U4) are satisfied must assure a theory of truth of at least the orthodox non-classical type.

The question remains: what conditions need to be added to make the resulting theory of truth fully classical? The answer is: it will be fully classical only when the converses of [NC1] and [NC2] are also added, yielding

[C1] $u(\sim P) \geqslant c$ iff $u(P) < c$

[C2] $u(P \vee Q) \geqslant c$ iff either $u(P) \geqslant c$ or $u(Q) \geqslant c$.

It follows by [C2] and [1] that every contradictory pair P, $\sim P$ must be such that either $u(P) \geqslant c$ or $u(\sim P) \geqslant c$, and then from [C1] that exactly one of these must always obtain. A utility measure meeting these further conditions is possible, but extremely restrictive. Thus the orthodox non-classical theory of truth again appears as the 'natural' resolution for this case.

Variant versions of a pragmatic criterion of truth are also possible. Basically, a pragmatic truth-criterion can take three forms, in specifying different conditions for accepting a proposition P as true:

(A) it works out very well to accept P:

$u(\text{accepting } P) \geqslant c$

(B) it works out better to accept P than to accept $\sim P$:

$u(\text{accepting } P) > u(\text{accepting not-}P)$

(C) it works out better to accept P than not to accept P:

$u(\text{accepting } P) > u(\text{not accepting } P)$.

The preceding discussion has focused on version (A). But suppose we had adopted the variant version (B):

$C(P)$ iff $u(P) > u(\sim P)$.

Let us once more adopt the preceding utility rules (U1)–(U4). We note, to begin with, that by (U3):

$u(P) > u(\sim P)$ iff $u(P) > 0$.

Hence the present criterion is virtually reduced to a special case of that initially considered.

Finally, suppose we had adopted the variant version (C):

$C(P)$ iff $u(\alpha P) > u(\sim \alpha P)$

where α is a special acceptance operator. To assume an orthodox non-classical theory of truth it would now suffice to assume a (u/α)-calculus in which the following principles held:

[1] If $\vdash P$, then $u(\alpha P) > u(\sim \alpha P)$.

[2] If $P_1, P_2, \ldots, P_n \vdash Q$ and always $u(\alpha P_i) > u(\sim \alpha P_i)$, then $u(\alpha Q) > u(\sim \alpha Q)$.

[NC1] If $u(\alpha P) > u(\sim \alpha P)$, then $u(\alpha \sim P) \leqslant u(\sim \alpha \sim P)$.

[NC2] If $u(\alpha P) > u(\sim \alpha P)$ or $u(\alpha Q) > u(\sim \alpha Q)$, then

$$u(\alpha[P \vee Q]) > u(\sim \alpha \sim [P \vee Q]).$$

That all these conditions *can* (in principle) be assured is shown by the fact that this case reduces to the preceding under the assumptions that:
$$u(\alpha P) = u(P)$$
$$u(\sim \alpha P) = u(\sim P).$$

It follows that the variant versions (B) and (C) of the pragmatic criterion are also such that a non-classical orthodox theory of truth can be made to result more or less naturally.

9. *Criteriological Analysis of the Coherence Theory*

The coherence theory of truth as developed above is somewhat more complex in its articulation than those that have concerned us to this point. With the coherence theory one proceeds—as with the intuitionist theory—from a certain prior basis; a foundation, however, now not of basic *truths* but of basic *data*. We begin with a propositional set **S** (in general inconsistent) of truth-candidates or data. Moreover, we stipulate on the basis of prior extralogical considerations a certain standard of propositional preference $\mathscr{P}$. We then specify the idea of propositions 'to-be-classed-as-true relative-to-**S**-and-$\mathscr{P}$' as follows:

$T_{\mathbf{S},\mathscr{P}}(P)$ iff $\mathbf{S}_i^* \vdash P$ for every m.c.s. $\mathbf{S}_i^*$ of **S** that is preferred (over certain other m.c.s.) according to $\mathscr{P}$.

Correspondingly we obtain a basic criterion of truth that may be articulated as follows:

$C(P) =_{\mathrm{DF}} P$ is a logical consequence of *all* of the $\mathscr{P}$-preferred m.c.s. of the basic set **S** of data.

Since we shall now clearly *not* have 'If not-$C(\mathbf{S})$, then $C(\sim \mathbf{S})$' the corresponding theory of truth is at best of the orthodox non-classical type based on the rule (F/NC) for falsity. Let us verify that this is indeed the case:

Conditions (1)–(2) now become:

[1] If $\vdash P$, then $\mathbf{S} \vdash_{\mathscr{P}} P$.

[2] If $P_1, P_2, \ldots, P_n \vdash Q$ and
$\mathbf{S} \vdash_{\mathscr{P}} P_1, \mathbf{S} \vdash_{\mathscr{P}} P_2, \ldots, \mathbf{S} \vdash_{\mathscr{P}} P_n$, then $\mathbf{S} \vdash_{\mathscr{P}} Q$.

Both of these will obviously have to be satisfied owing to the construction of the consequence-relationship $\vdash_{\mathscr{P}}$.

It remains only to check (NC1)–(NC2):

[NC1] If $S \vdash_{\mathscr{P}} \sim p$, then not: $S \vdash_{\mathscr{P}} P$.

[NC2] If $S \vdash_{\mathscr{P}} P$ or $S \vdash_{\mathscr{P}} Q$, then $S \vdash_{\mathscr{P}} (P \vee Q)$.

Both of these are also obviously satisfied owing to the nature of $\vdash_{\mathscr{P}}$.

Could we strengthen the theory of truth to be fully classical? Could we have also the converses of [NC1] and [NC2] and so obtain

[C1] $S \vdash_{\mathscr{P}} \sim P$ iff not $S \vdash_{\mathscr{P}} P$

[C2] $S \vdash_{\mathscr{P}} (P \vee Q)$ iff $S \vdash_{\mathscr{P}} P$ or $S \vdash_{\mathscr{P}} Q$?

Again, this could happen only in the (very special) case of a set S of data that is $\mathscr{P}$-*complete* in the technical sense that for any pair of contradictories P, $\sim P$ it yields exactly one as a $\mathscr{P}$-consequence.[13] Though not inconceivable, this situation represents an extreme and implausible special circumstance.

Thus the version of the coherence theory of truth presented in the preceding chapters will—as expected—naturally yield a theory of truth of the orthodox, non-classical variety.

10. *The Strengths and Weaknesses of the Several Criterial Theories*

Four distinct truth-criteria have been examined in the preceding discussion:

Name	Criterion, C(P)	Resulting Theory of Truth
1. Correspondence	P	classical
2. Intuitionist		
(a) Deductivist Version	$T_0 \vdash P$	orthodox non-classical
(b) Inductivist Version	$T_0 \vDash P$ + a consistency screening	orthodox non-classical
3. Pragmatic	$u(P) \geqslant c$	orthodox non-classical
4. Coherence	$S' \vdash P$ whenever S' is a preferred m.c.s. of S	orthodox non-classical

[13] Specifically, this could happen when $S = \{$all propositions$\}$ and $\mathscr{P}$ is such that it yields exactly one m.c.s. as preferred. (For now if $\mathscr{P}$ countenanced two distinct m.c.s., S_1 and S_2, then there would be a proposition P such that $P \in S_1$ and $P \notin S_2$, so that $\sim P \in S_2$. And then neither P nor $\sim P$ will be $\mathscr{P}$-consequences of S.) A full classical theory of truth would result in a coherentist approach in this special case.

Furthermore, we have determined that the following situation obtains with respect to the possibility of errors of Type I and Type II:

Criterial Theory	Type I Error $(P$ but not $C(P))$	Type II Error $(C(P)$ but not $P)$
Correspondence	cannot occur	cannot occur
Intuitionist (Deductive)	possible	cannot occur[14]
Intuitionist (Inductive)	possible	possible
Pragmatic	possible	possible
Coherence	possible	possible

A criterial theory of truth may be characterized as *ampliative* if its output of (purported) truth can be greater than the input of given truths, that is, if the criterion can so operate as to class as true propositions that are not merely the logical consequences of what has already been determined as such. Moreover, a criterial theory of truth may be characterized as *originative* if it can initiate findings of truth: a criterion lacks this feature if its employment requires a prior resolution of questions of truth. (A *non-originative* criterion accordingly always moves from certain admitted truths to other propositions it purports to be true.)

The situation of the five theories with regard to these characteristics are:

	Criterial Theory	Ampliative ?	Originative ?
1.	Correspondence	no	?[15]
2a.	Intuitionist (Deductive)	no	no
2b.	Intuitionist (Inductive)	yes	no
3.	Pragmatic	yes	yes
4.	Coherence	yes	yes

A comparison of these tabulations rightly suggests that the ampliative character of a criterial theory is intimately connected with the possibility of a Type II error. If the theory is ampliative it must so operate as to be able 'to tell us that something is true about the truth of which we previously were genuinely ignorant or undecided'. Any theory that admits of a Type II error and can lead us into falsehood at least has the capacity to carry us beyond the domain of established truth, and is thus inherently ampliative. (The reverse is, of course, not so: there is no reason of fundamental logical principle why an ampliative criterion

---

[14] We may suppose that all members of the basic set T_0 are in fact truths.

[15] It is problematic whether or not one should be prepared to count the correspondence criterion as 'originative'.

could not be invariably truth-producing and so avoid Type II errors.)

The advantage of the correspondence theory *vis-à-vis* all the others is that it alone avoids the prospect of errors of both Type I and II. This point of undoubted strength from a *definitional* standpoint, however, is matched by a corresponding weakness from the *criterial* standpoint. In applying the relevant standard as a criterion to determine that a proposition P is true we must establish that P is the case, and so must in effect settle pre-criterially the truth of P. This places the originative character of the theory in a problematic light. Furthermore, the correspondence criterion is clearly not ampliative. The correspondence theory thus has serious shortcomings from the criteriological point of view.

Moreover, how are we to implement the correspondence standard as an operative criterion? The correspondence criterion would have us maintain '"P" is true' when, but only when, we have determined P to be the case. It stipulates a comparison of the truth-claim with the facts. But how are we to 'confront the facts' in order to effect such a comparison in the traditional range of problematic cases? (The difficulties that arise here have already been canvassed in Chapter I.)

The points of strength and weakness of the correspondence theory are in large measure matched by the deductive version of the intuitionist theory. It too avoids Type II errors, but this advantage is offset by the non-ampliative and non-originative nature of the criterion. To use it to establish the truth of a proposition P we must just have settled this very issue with respect to a proposition that logically comprehends (deductively entails) P itself.

The intuitionist theory gains ampliative force in its inductive version, but does so at a price to its integrity as a viable theory: in going from deductive to inductive implication (from $\vdash$ to $\not\vdash$), we lose our hold on the pivotal factor of consistency. As we shall see with the Lottery Paradox (in Chap. X), a proposition can provide strong inductive (probabilistic) evidence for each of a group of others that are logically incompatible. The inductivist version of the intuitionist theory thus cannot provide a theory of truth unless supplemented by a consistency screening. But the systematic imposition of such a screening must carry us over into the threshold of coherence theory: we arrive at an inductivist or probabilistic version of the coherence theory. To get a workable version of the theory we must, in effect, abandon it.

The pragmatic standard shares with that of coherence (alone) the criteriological advantage of being both originative and ampliative. From the criterial standpoint it accordingly manifests substantial points of merit.

The essential criticisms of the pragmatic theory of truth are well known and relatively straightforward. Their main impetus bears upon an equivocation in the conception of 'working out' or 'positive effects' or 'utilities' that is altogether basic to the pragmatic theory. This conception can be construed in two ways, according to whether the issue is taken to be one of

(i) *practical utilities* having to do with the concrete effects for the conduct of the affairs of life, be they beneficial or malign, or

(ii) *cognitive utilities* that are purely theoretical and have to do not with success in practical matters, but only with cognitive success in 'being right' in one's judgments and in being effective in the construction of explanatory mechanisms and in yielding verifiable (i.e. correct) predictions.

In terms of this distinction, a critique of the pragmatic theory can be formulated as a dilemma:

(1) If it is *practical* utilities that are to be at issue, then the bridge from utility to truth is broken. There is no reason in principle why acceptance of a falsehood should not be enormously benefit-conducive, or why something that is benefit-conducive should be true.[16] There may well be *some* positive correlation between the truth of propositions and the practical utility of their espousal, but this is by no means enough to warrant taking the one as a criterion for the other.[17]

(2) If it is *cognitive* utilities that are to be at issue, then the link between utility and truth is indeed maintained, but pragmatism is effectively abandoned as an ultimate standard of truth, since the conception of 'working out' in the specifically cognitive sense of 'being correct' can only

---

[16] The literature of the subject is replete with examples of the following sort: a man mistakenly believes he has a certain disease and mistakenly believes a certain medicinal preparation is called for by way of treatment. Unbeknown to himself he actually has another malady against which this medicine is highly effective. If he 'knew the truth' he would suffer badly being altogether ignorant of any remedy for his actual condition. For variations on this theme see 'Pragmatic Justification' in N. Rescher, *Essays in Philosophical Analysis* (Pittsburgh, Pa., 1969), pp. 303–7.

[17] In the first decade of this century, this line of objection was heavily pressed against W. James by A. O. Lovejoy in 'The Thirteen Pragmatisms', *The Journal of Philosophy*, 5 (1908), 1–12 and 29–39, and by B. Russell in *Philosophical Essays* (London, 1910). Even J. Dewey, his own pragmatist ally, criticized James to the effect that he had confounded the intellectual issues of what can satisfy the inquiring mind with the issue of human values.

be implemented through an *independent* criterion of truth of an essentially non-pragmatic character. In going over to the view that 'having positive effects' and 'working out' are to come down to 'being right' and 'being correct', we for all practical purposes short-cut the pragmatic formulation and go over to a different, apparently correspondence-style criterion of truth. In so far as the practical utilities are abandoned in favour of the cognitive, the characteristic genius of the pragmatic theory is simply ignored.

These considerations point to the dilemma that we either (1) maintain the link between utility and truth through the cognitive construction of utilities, but then abandon an essentially pragmatic approach; or else (2) maintain an authentically pragmatist perspective through the genuinely practical construction of utilities, but then sacrifice the prospect of a warrant for the move from utility-maximization to truth. This critical —and ultimately fatal—tension between the role of purely cognitive satisfactions (utilities, etc.) and those that are strictly practical has never been fully resolved by the pragmatists.[18]

This brief assessment of weaknesses of the rivals to the coherence theory must be supplemented by an evaluation of this theory itself. The following chapter will be devoted to this task. First, however, it is desirable—and in fairness necessary—to recognize explicitly the useful work that these various theories can accomplish in their different ways.

11. *The Characteristic Work of the Several Theories of Truth*

The preceding discussion has maintained the superior qualifications of the coherence theory as a criterion of contingent

[18] William James, for example, sometimes wrote as though the purely cognitive, theoretical satisfactions were the principal issue: 'But particular consequences can perfectly well be of a theoretic nature. Every remote fact which we infer from an idea is a particular theoretic consequence which our mind practically works towards. The loss of every old opinion of ours which we see that we shall have to give up if a new opinion be true, is a particular theoretic as well as a particular practical consequence. After man's interest in breathing freely, the greatest of all his interests (because it never fluctuates or remits, as most of his physical interests do), is his interest in *consistency*, in feeling that what he now thinks goes with what he thinks on other occasions. We tirelessly compare truth with truth for this sole purpose. Is the present candidate for belief perhaps contradicted by principle number one? Is it compatible with fact number two? and so forth. The particular operations here are the purely logical ones of analysis, deduction, comparison, etc.; and altho general terms may be used *ad libitum*, the satisfactory *practical working* of the candidate-idea consists in the consciousness yielded by each successive theoretic consequence in particular. It is therefore simply idiotic to repeat that pragmatism takes no account of purely theoretic interests' (*The Meaning of Truth: A Sequel to Pragmatism* (New York, 1909); quoted from A. Rorty (ed.), *Pragmatic Philosophy* (New York, 1966), p. 188).

a posteriori truth, truth in the context of factual data. The merits of the coherence theory in this regard have been stressed at the expense of its rivals. But this must not be taken to imply that these rivals are in themselves defective and useless. Quite the reverse. The fact is that each of the traditional theories of truth has its own distinct and characteristic work—each one has a specific job that it alone is pre-eminently fitted to accomplish.

As has been clear from the outset, any application of the coherence theory requires a body of *logical* machinery of consequence and consistency. Thus when it comes to the formulation of a criterion for *logical* truth, the coherence theory is not in the running. Here the pragmatic theory comes into its own. For the essential role of logic is as an instrument of reasoning and inquiry. And in this area, in relation to instruments, tools, methods, and procedures, the pragmatic theory is in its native element. Here the theme of results and effects—pivoting around the question 'How well does it work towards accomplishing the tasks in hand?'—is at the forefront. In this respect, then, as a means for choosing among alternative logics, and so, in effect, determining what is to count as true in logic, the pragmatic theory is on home ground in its natural habitat, and performs an essential and indispensable service.[19]

The peculiar merit of the correspondence theory in comparison to its rivals lies in its capacity to implement the traditional definition of the true as 'what answers to the facts'. Its very defects from the criteriological angle—the circumstance that it is neither ampliative nor originative—are strengths that bolster its claims to adequacy in the matter of definitional explication. The special merits of the correspondence theory relate to its capacity to provide the scaffolding for a realization of a certain definitional blueprint of truth.

The intuitionist theory of truth—at any rate in its deductive form—has its natural application in the domain of pure mathematics. In so far as an axiomatic basis is required here to go beyond purely logical considerations (and the extent to which this is so is, of course, a matter of dispute) mathematics is evolved on basic input-truths that are not themselves the product of any mechanism for the warrant of truths, but whose justification is conceived to be somehow immediate.

There are, of course, those who would argue that there are no

---

[19] This point of view has been argued for at considerable length in the chapter on 'The Question of Relativism in Logic' in N. Rescher, *Many-Valued Logic* (New York, 1969), pp. 213–35.

extralogical truths whatever in axiomatic mathematics, by reasoning as follows:

Mathematics only asserts *hypothetical* truths: the mathematician does not make any *categorical* assertions. Mathematical axioms are not put forward as truths, but as *stipulations* assumed to elicit their consequences. All that he ever asserts is that *if* the axioms are accepted, *then* the theorems follow from them. The only truths he asserts are those of a strictly logical nature.

This formalist standpoint, while certainly apposite with respect to the different types of geometry or various algebraic systems, is difficult and problematic with respect to arithmetic. Here at least, mathematics does seem committed to a categorically assertive position, so an intuitionist approach appears natural in this quintessential branch of mathematics. (Of course, a pragmatic mode of justification could also be considered as a possibility here.) Thus in so far as the domain of mathematical truth is taken to be a matter of logical proliferation from basic axiomatic truths, the intuitionist approach (in the deductive mode) exactly provides the theory of truth corresponding to it.

In its inductive form, the intuitionist theory of truth implements the—or at any rate a—standard programme of inductive logic. This is conceived of along the following lines. Somehow —by some hook or crook—we gain a starter-set of truths. These truths are 'immediate'—or, as we may say, intuited—precisely because as members of the starter-set they are not themselves discursively warranted in terms of some other truths. Then, given these elemental or protocol truths, we may proceed to apply inductive considerations in order to establish further truths. The conception of an ultimate starting-point is, of course, highly problematic. This line of thought leads into matters we shall pursue in detail in a later chapter (Chapter IX). At present, having noted the strengths and weaknesses of its rivals, it is time to resume consideration of the coherence theory itself.

VII

CHARACTERISTIC FEATURES OF THE COHERENCE THEORY

1. *Truth as a System*

THE preceding chapter sought to show that the coherence theory conforms to the basic conditions universally demanded of a theory of truth, and to assess the comparative capacity of the coherence theory—*vis-à-vis* its rivals—to meet the general desiderata of an explication of truth. There remains the more specific question of seeing if our coherence theory of truth can overcome the difficulties and be defended from the objections traditionally charged against the coherence approach to truth.

The conception that all truths form one comprehensive and cohesive system in which everything has its logically appropriate place, and in which the interrelationships among truths are made duly manifest, is one of the many fundamental ideas contributed to the intellectual heritage of the West by the ancient Greeks. The general structure of the concept can already be discerned in the Presocratics, especially in the seminal thought of Parmenides.[1] The conception that all knowledge—that is all of truth as humans can come to have epistemic control of it—forms a single comprehensive unit that is capable of a deductive systematization on essentially Euclidean lines is the guiding concept of Aristotle's theory of science as expounded in *Posterior Analytics*.

This tradition found new life through its restatement in Kant's Copernican Revolution, and the idea that in espousing the

[1] 'The thing that can be thought and that for the sake of which the thought exists is the same; for you cannot find thought without something that is, as to which it is uttered. And there is not, and never shall be, anything besides what is, since fate has chained it so as to be whole and immovable. . . . Since, then, it has a furthest limit, it is complete on every side, like the mass of a rounded sphere, equally poised from the centre in every direction; for it cannot be greater or smaller in one place than in another. For there is nothing that could keep it from reaching out equally, nor can aught that is be more here and less there than what is, since it is all inviolable. For the point from which it is equal in every direction tends equally to the limits. Here shall I close my trustworthy speech and thought about the truth' (Frag. 8, Diels; tr. J. Burnet).

dictum that 'truth is a system' what we are actually claiming to be systematic is not the world as such, but rather our *knowledge* of it. Accordingly, it is what is known to be true regarding 'the facts' of nature that is systematized, and systematicity is thus in the first instance a feature rather of knowledge than of its subject-matter. The idea of system can, indeed must, be applied by us to nature, but not to nature in itself but rather to 'nature insofar as nature conforms to our power of judgment'.[2] Correspondingly, system is at bottom not a constitutive conception descriptive of reality *per se*, but a regulative conception descriptive of how our thought regarding reality must proceed.

Kant's successors tended to turn their backs upon his regulative and epistemological approach. They wanted to 'overcome' Kant's residual allegiance to the Cartesian divide between our knowledge and its object. Waving the motto that 'The real is rational' aloft on their banners, they sought to restore system to its Greek position as a fundamentally ontological—rather than 'merely epistemological'—concept. In this setting, however, the concept of the systematization of truth played the part of a controlling idea more emphatically than ever.

Even so bare a sketch may suffice to show the longevity and vitality of the idea that truth as we can know it is a *system* (regardless of whether systematicity is a feature of its own nature or of our knowledge of it). This systematic feature of truth is central in the thinking of coherence theorists. As Bradley bluntly puts it, the aim of the coherence theory of truth is to establish 'the claim of system as an arbiter of fact'.[3]

It is thus desirable to view the coherence theory of truth in the light of an explication of the way in which the idea that 'truth is a system' is to be understood. Three things are at issue: the set Γ of truths—of propositions which one must recognize as truths in the setting of a coherence criterion—must have the features of *comprehensiveness*, *consistency*, and *cohesiveness* (unity).

Here comprehensiveness is a complex conception that has several aspects. The first of these indicates what might be characterized as an inferential mode of self-sufficiency:

(1) *Inferential closure.* The set Γ of true propositions is inferentially closed in being self-contained with respect to entailment or derivation. That is, we have the principle:

If $p_1, p_2, \ldots, p_n \in \Gamma$ and $p_1, p_2, \ldots, p_n \vdash q$, then $q \in \Gamma$.

[2] Introduction to Kant's *Critique of Judgment*, *Werke*, Vol. V; Academy edition (Berlin, 1920), p. 202.
[3] 'Coherence and Contradiction' in *Essays on Truth and Reality* (Oxford, 1914), pp. 219–44, see p. 219.

Inferential closure clearly counts as a mode of systematic comprehensiveness in the sense of self-sufficiency: the propositional set Γ is sufficiently rich in content to embrace all its own logical consequences.

Clearly, the specific coherence theory articulated above is such that this condition is guaranteed: a closure requirement is a basic constituent of the proposed formulation of the coherence criterion.

A second aspect of comprehensiveness is represented by the requirement of including all of the theses of logic:

(2) *Logical inclusiveness.* The set Γ of true propositions is logically inclusive in that this set must contain every thesis of logic (a requirement which is, in effect, a consequence of the preceding one):

$$\text{Whenever } \vdash P, \text{ then } P \in \Gamma.$$

The need to have the set Γ of truths observe this particular mode of 'comprehensiveness' is too obvious to require comment. That our coherence theory satisfies this condition is likewise obvious.

The requirement of completeness imposes a very strong condition of richness upon a propositional set **S**. A propositional set **S** qualifies as *complete* (i.e. unrestrictedly complete or *saturated*) if if always includes either a proposition itself or its contradictory:

$$\text{Whenever } P \notin \mathbf{S}, \text{ then } \sim P \in \mathbf{S}.$$

A coherence theory of truth certainly need not—and ours does not—satisfy this comprehensiveness condition in this, its very strong and unrestricted form. But it does meet the condition in a weakened form:

(3) *Restricted completeness.* The set Γ of true propositions is *restrictedly complete* in that whenever certain 'standard' conditions are met by a proposition P, then $\sim P$ must be a Γ-element whenever P fails to be:

$$\text{In 'standard cases', if } P \notin \Gamma \text{ then } \sim P \in \Gamma.[4]$$

It is clear that restricted completeness guarantees the applicability of an at least limited form of the Laws of Bivalence and of Excluded Middle. We are, of course, left hanging in the air until told what this 'standardness' involves. It will be recalled

---

[4] The converse of this thesis, viz. that

$$\text{If } \sim p \in \Gamma, \text{ then } p \notin \Gamma$$

is, of course, assured by the consistency of Γ.

(from Chapter III) that a combination of two conditions will serve here: (i) that the proposition in question is an element of the set **S** of initial data, and (ii) that the criterion of preference is such as to lead to a unique m.c.s. as preferred. If a case is classed as *standard* when these two conditions are met, then the completeness requirement is at once guaranteed for all cases conforming to this circumstance.

The general idea of *comprehensiveness* that underlies and unites all of these various considerations is absolutely fundamental to the traditional conception of a coherence theory of truth. F. H. Bradley, for example, writes:

> The test which I advocate is the idea of a whole of knowledge as wide and as consistent as may be. In speaking of system I mean always the union of these two aspects, and this is the sense and the only sense in which I am defending coherence. If we separate coherence from what Prof. Stout calls comprehensiveness, then I agree that neither of these aspects of system will work by itself. . . . All that I can do here is to point out that both of the above aspects are for me inseparably included in the idea of system, and that coherence apart from comprehensiveness is not for me the test of truth or reality.[5]

Thus the contentual richness of the family of 'coherent' propositions at issue represents an essential feature of the coherence theory.

It deserves note that, on the present construction of a coherence analysis, this insistence that a coherent set 'should include as much as possible' finds its systematic counterpart in the insistence that the subsets of the data whose claims on truthfulness are to be considered must be not only consistent but *maximal*. With such a stipulation of completeness, the coherence theory pays tribute to the classical theory of truth with its provision for the principles of bivalence and excluded middle.

Suppose we are determined to accept as true as much as is logically possible and accordingly enter into a situation marked by two features: (1) the set **S** of data is full enough to be unrestrictedly complete (*saturated*) in that we unqualifiedly have

$$\text{If } P \notin \textbf{S}, \text{ then } {\sim}P \in \textbf{S}$$

so that we stipulate the maximum feasible external comprehensiveness for **S**, and (2) the preferential criterion $\mathscr{P}$ in hand is strong enough to single out one particular m.c.s., so that we provide for the maximum feasible internal comprehensiveness

---

[5] 'On Truth and Coherence', in *Essays on Truth and Reality* (Oxford, 1914), pp. 202–18; see pp. 202–3. 'Truth', as Bradley says in another place, 'must exhibit the mark of expansion and all-inclusiveness.'

for **S**.[6] Under these conditions, and in this special, certainly extreme, and perhaps 'ideal' case—the coherence analysis must (as we shall shortly see) yield the 'all-inclusiveness' of which Bradley speaks, and will give rise to a theory of truth that is altogether classical.

So much, then, for aspects of the comprehensiveness of Γ. The consistency of Γ, that is, its self-consistency is the subject of the next requirement:

> (4) *Consistency*. The set Γ of propositions is consistent (negation-consistent) if (or rather *since*) it never contains a proposition together with its contradictory:

Whenever $P \in \Gamma$, then $\sim P \notin \Gamma$; and whenever $\sim P \in \Gamma$ then $P \notin \Gamma$.

The modes of comprehensiveness serve to assure that the contents of Γ are rich enough in having a sufficiently large membership. In contrast, the consistency condition assures that this content does not get to be too large for logical comfort.

The condition of consistency assures that Γ never contains incompatible elements, so that we do not have in Γ propositions P and Q such that $P \vdash \sim Q$. To show this, let it be assumed for *reductio ad absurdum* that $P \in \Gamma$, $Q \in \Gamma$, and $P \vdash \sim Q$. Then by deductive closure $\sim Q \in \Gamma$, which contradicts consistency. Thus consistency guarantees the Law of Contradiction. Moreover Γ can contain no logical falsehoods (i.e. contradictories of logical theses); since by the condition of logical inclusiveness it includes all the theses of logic.

Another important consequence of consistency has already been foreshadowed. Together with restricted completeness it yields the result that the Law of Bivalence holds in all the 'standard' cases:

$$\sim P \in \Gamma \text{ iff } P \notin \Gamma.$$

This principle guarantees that the full classical theory of truth will have to be operative in all of the 'standard' cases. The traditional laws of truth are thus closely connected with the concept that 'truth is a system' and specifically a system that combines the features of consistency and completeness.

We turn now to the third systematic aspect of the coherence theory, that of the cohesiveness of the set of truths according to the theory. This brings us to the central and most quintessential

---

[6] It warrants restatement (of a consideration in Chapter III) that the 'external comprehensiveness' of a set of data is a matter of its inclusion of *conceivably relevant* data, and the 'internal comprehensiveness' of the truths determined by data is a matter of the extent to which these data become acknowledged truths. This double aspect of comprehensiveness is a key facet of the coherence theory of truth.

feature of the coherence theory, one so important as to deserve a separate section for itself.

2. The Cohesiveness of Truth

The various systematic aspects of truth dealt with in the preceding section do not really capture the most characteristic aspect of the coherence theory: they are for the most part operative with respect to other theories of truth as well. The essential distinctiveness of the coherence theory lies in its utilization of the following precepts:

(I) The truth of a proposition is to be determined in terms of its relationships to other propositions in its logico-epistemic environment. And consequently,

(II) The true propositions form one tightly knit unit, a set each element of which stands in logical interlinkage with others so that the whole forms a comprehensively connected and unified network.

This way of describing the matter is obviously figurative: further analysis is needed to introduce clarity and precision.

It might seem on first thought that (II) is to be explicated as follows:

The propositional set Γ exhibits the feature of inferential interlinkage in that every Γ-element is inferentially dependent upon at least some others: Whenever $Q \in \Gamma$, then there are elements $P_1, P_2, \ldots, P_n \in \Gamma$ (all suitably distinct from Q) such that:

$$P_1, P_2, \ldots, P_n \vdash Q.$$

Accordingly, a set Γ would exhibit inferential interlinkage if it contained no inferentially independent propositions—that is, contained no propositions not derivable from other Γ-elements.

Coherence theorists have sometimes talked in a way that lends credence to the view that they have such inferential interlinkage in mind in the explication of thesis (II). But a detailed scrutiny of the matter brings out the inadequacy of this view. For example, consider the set $\{p \ \& \ q, \ q \ \& \ r, \ p \ \& \ r\}$. This certainly exhibits deductive interlinkage, every one of its elements being derivable from the other two. But—as this example clearly shows—this feature is at bottom merely a matter of sufficient redundancy. As such, it is not very interesting, and is clearly not what is wanted in the present context.

Thus according to H. H. Joachim, systematic coherence demands

> ... a 'significant whole' or a whole possessed of meaning for thought. A 'significant whole' is such that all its constituent elements involve one another, or reciprocally determine one another's being as contributory features on a single concrete meaning. The elements thus cohering constitute a whole which may be said to control the reciprocal adjustment of its elements, as an end controls its constituent means.[7]

Redundancy, clearly, is not a suitable means 'to control the reciprocal adjustment' of the elements of a coherent set. Inferential interlinkage simply fails to do justice to the network aspect of the coherence theory.

To say this is not, of course, to deny that inferential interlinkage does and must characterize truths. Assume that p and $\sim q$ are both true (and so q false). Then clearly both of the following will also be truths: $p \lor q$, $q \supset (r \ \& \sim r)$. And so if our initial two propositions were excised from the set that represents the truths, they would both still be derivable from the remainder. The set of all truths does indeed exhibit this sort of *systematic constrictiveness* that makes each element inferentially redundant. But the presence of this redundancy that is undeniably present within the realm of truth, precisely because it must obtain on essentially trivial logical grounds alone, will not exhaust the relevant aspects of cohesiveness.

To see how our present version of the coherence theory accommodates this aspect of cohesiveness, it is best to go back to its basis in the contextual determination of truth. According to the approach set out above, the starting-point for a coherence analysis is afforded by a (presumably inconsistent) set **S** of initial data. Let us review the method in the context of an example. Consider the set of data:

$$\mathbf{S} = \{p, q, \sim p \lor \sim q\}.$$

Once such an inconsistent set is at hand, we form its m.c.s.:

$$\mathbf{S}_1 = \{p, q\} \qquad \text{axiomatized by } p \ \& \ q$$
$$\mathbf{S}_2 = \{p, \sim p \lor \sim q\} \ \text{axiomatized by } p \ \& \sim q$$
$$\mathbf{S}_3 = \{q, \sim p \lor \sim q\} \ \text{axiomatized by } \sim p \ \& \ q.$$

Given some criterion of preference $\mathscr{P}$ we determine the 'truths given **S** (relative to $\mathscr{P}$)' by using $\mathscr{P}$ to eliminate some of the m.c.s., and then proceeding to class as truths all those propositions that

---

[7] H. H. Joachim, *The Nature of Truth* (London, 1906), p. 66.

follow from *all* the remaining m.c.s. In this process the reciprocal adjustment of the **S**-elements to one another clearly becomes the controlling factor in the determination of truths.

It is only in this broader, systematic context of procedure that the interlinkage among the propositions at issue comes to light. There is not—we are free to postulate—any relationship in content between the p and q of the above example: they are (we are free to suppose) logically and contentually quite independent of one another. But in the setting of the data-family **S** they immediately obtain a deeper-rooted mutual relevance. For example, given $\sim p$ as true we can immediately conclude that q (for given $\sim p$ we arrive uniquely at S_3). Furthermore, if the preferential standard $\mathscr{P}$ enters so as to rule out S_1, then given p we can immediately conclude that $\sim q$. Such factors establish a systematic relationship between the propositions of **S** even when there is no content-relationship and correspondingly no deductive relationship. The procedures of the analysis introduce quasi-logical contextual interrelationships among the truth-standing of propositions even where, from another angle, there are no mutual relations at all so far as the assertoric content of the propositions at issue is concerned.

In general, the acceptance as true or rejection as false of any one **S**-element has far-reaching repercussions for the truth or falsity of the rest within the framework. On our theory the idea of contentual interlinkage of a deductive sort becomes replaced by one of contextual interlinkage:

> The propositions classed as true in the context of the original set of inconsistent data **S** stand in a mutual dependency relative to **S**: every truth here stands in a characteristic relation of interdependence with its fellows in the hypothetical sense that if the truth-status of some of these were different (i.e., if they were to be classed as false instead of true) then its own truth-status might well be affected.[8]

It is in this sense—rather than that of deductive interlinkage —that the coherence theory we have presented accommodates the coherence-theorists' standard conception of the cohesiveness of truth. Coherence has traditionally been conceived in terms of a combination of (i) logical consistency and (ii) mutual implication. The present characterization of the theory is perfectly attuned to the spirit of this conception, even though the mechanism involved may in some respects depart from the traditional approaches, as a result of its somewhat more complex approach.

[8] That is, could certainly be affected if the proposition in view were not an I-consequence of the original set **S**.

3. *Coherence and the Unity of Truth*

One objection that has (as observed in Chapter II) been advanced against the appeal to coherence as a criterion of truth turns on the prospect of a variety of equally adequate but mutually discordant coherent structures. If coherence is thought of figuratively on the analogy of a puzzle, there seems no reason why the pieces should not fit together in several different ways. Or think of the closer epistemic analogue of the inductive problem of constructing a theory to account for certain findings: different—and conflicting—theories may well account for the same data. Why should the coherence approach to truth not lead to a similar indeterminacy?

To see how our coherence theory circumvents this objection it is best to consider an example. To begin with, it must be granted that the theory does indeed encounter a certain type of basic indeterminateness. Consider an (inconsistent) set of initial data such as: $$S = \{p \vee q, \sim p, \sim q\}.$$

There are indeed several different 'families of possible truths' here—namely those based on the various m.c.s.:

$$S_1 = \{p \vee q, \sim p\} \quad \text{axiomatized by } \sim p \;\&\; q$$
$$S_2 = \{p \vee q, \sim q\} \quad \text{axiomatized by } p \;\&\; \sim q$$
$$S_3 = \{\sim p, \sim q\} \quad \text{axiomatized by } \sim p \;\&\; \sim q.$$

But despite this indeterminacy, our theory provides a unique and unambiguous result. It does so by proceeding

(i) *eliminatively* when certain cases are ruled out through the employment of the preference machinery. (For the sake of example let us suppose this rules out S_3.)

(ii) *disjunctively* in that the only propositions admitted as truths in the face of the diverse possibilities remaining after stage (i) are those yielded by their disjunction. (On the preceding assumption the truths would—in the example—be based on S_1 and S_2 and would correspondingly be axiomatized by $(\sim p \;\&\; q) \vee (p \;\&\; \sim q)$ or equivalently $\sim p \equiv q$. This being equivalent to

$$(p \vee q) \;\&\; (\sim p \vee \sim q)$$

we are in effect told to retain one S-element, viz. $p \vee q$, and to choose between the other two $(\sim p, \sim q)$.)

As the analysis of this example shows, our coherence theory is such that there may indeed be 'indeterminacy' in the sense that there will be some propositions among our data that we are not able to class as true or false. But there is nothing in this *disjunctive* sort of indeterminacy to confront us with alternative discordant bodies of truth in such a way as to render the theory itself unworkable. In sum, the analysis does not drive us into any vicious indeterminacy. The whole procedure is designed to lead systematically to one single and consistent result—a result whose definiteness, however, will hinge on the selective power of the preferential criterion at issue.

Yet it might still be objected that one sort of indeterminateness remains as an intrinsic feature of our analysis: that of alternative preferential schemes; in so far as a plurality of preferential eliminations of the m.c.s. of an inconsistent set **S** is always possible, so correspondingly there will be different results to our coherence analysis. To this objection we reply: (1) that in general the context of a coherence problem will indicate the appropriateness of one specific preferential criterion $\mathscr{P}$, and so removes the sting from the existence of possible rivals, but (2) that, in so far as no preferential criterion can warrantedly be accorded primacy, we simply have no choice but to proceed without eliminations, and so, letting all the rival m.c.s. remain in the picture, still proceed to a unique (albeit alternative-embracing) solution to the problem. In either case there is no sort of indeterminacy to vitiate the viability of the method.

4. *Coherence and the Issue of Logical Truth*

It is clear and indeed obvious that the machinery of deductive logic is an input and not a product of the coherence theory of truth we have expounded. That all 'theses of logic' must perforce be counted as truths is an automatic feature of the theory. Since logical truth is thus not determined but presupposed by our coherence criterion, the truthfulness of the truths of logic is an issue that must be resolved by other means—the coherence theory articulated here does not furnish any instruments for this work. From its standpoint, the truths of logic remain *sui generis*. Accordingly, the question of the criterial source and status of the theses of logic is left open and untouched by our theory. Because logic is presupposed by it, our 'coherence criterion of truth' must be understood as a criterion for extralogical truth.[9]

---

[9] One might perhaps be tempted to the policy of classing as logical truths those theses that will *invariably and inevitably* cohere with others, and so attempt to characterize logical truth in terms of coherence. But how are we to construe 'coherence' here? It must mean that these truths cannot *possibly* conflict with others, that they obtain under all possible circumstances and 'in all *possible* worlds'. And any attempt to indicate the sort of 'possibility' at issue here already presupposes the availability of logical machinery.

Another point must be made—or rather, restated—in this connection: The matter of how we resolve the issue of exactly which logic is to be employed will have a decisive effect upon the results of the coherence analysis carried out by its means. With different logical tools one obtains different relationships of consistency and consequence. (Thus p and $\sim(q \to p)$ are incompatible in the system of material implication but compatible in that of strict implication.) Consequently the inventory of the m.c.s. of one and the same inconsistent set will vary with the logical ground-rules that are brought to bear. And therefore the final results of a coherence analysis can be altogether different when a different system of logic is used as basis. However, as explained in Chapter VI, our standard procedure (adopted only for reasons of simplicity) is that the logic operative at the basic, object-language level is simply the classical, two-valued system.

In consequence, we cannot avoid recognizing—and indeed stressing—the fact that our coherence theory of truth is designed to operate in the extralogical realm. The issue of the 'truths of logic' is something the machinery of this coherence analysis does not itself resolve, but rather requires to be settled in advance. From the standpoint of our theory, the criteriology of logical truth is a separate and prior issue.[10]

5. *The Need for Extralogical Mechanisms in a Coherence Analysis*

One possible line of objection to a coherence theory as here formulated runs as follows: 'The truth-explicating mechanisms of the theory are not logically self-sufficient. They specifically require two extralogical items:

(1) A *factual* element, namely the truth-candidates. There must be an input of—and hence separate criterion for—data.

(2) A *normative* element, namely a mechanism for implementing the conception of an alethic preference among m.c.s.

In the face of these factors, the theory foregoes any pretentions to being a purely logical resource.'

The appropriate stance towards this objection is one not of refutation but frank concession. The coherence mechanisms of the present discussion are intended not as a criterion of truth in general, but as a criterion of specifically factual truth. This factual orientation of the theory requires it to step beyond the domain of purely logical considerations.

10 For the author's (essentially pragmatistic) views on the subject see the chapter on 'The Question of Relativism in Logic' in his *Many-Valued Logic* (New York, 1969).

It is inevitable that a coherence criterion of the type at issue here should go outside the logical realm. Logic alone cannot provide a sufficient basis for the coherence analysis of truth and falsity along the lines presently envisaged. This is already quite clear even if coherence is construed in only the absolutely minimal sense of consistency. To see this, it suffices to consider a simple case in which three data are given: p, q, $\sim p \vee \sim q$. Of course, logic here immediately tells us that one must be given up. But there are clearly three possible ways of restoring consistency and restoring a coherent situation so as to satisfy the demands of logic. It is clear that no amount of purely logical analysis of this case can of itself tell us which of the three alternatives to adopt. The very most that theoretical logic alone can tell us is *that* a revision is necessary; it cannot possibly give us an answer to the question of *which* revision ought to be made. All logic can do is to enjoin us to assure the consistency of what we accept; necessarily maintaining an utter, strict silence on the question of what this ought specifically to be.

When inconsistent alternatives are at issue the role of logic within the framework of our reasoning must be of a limited and restricted character. This point has been clearly stated by L. J. Savage: 'Logic . . . is . . . incomplete. Thus if my beliefs are inconsistent with each other, logic insists that I amend them, without telling me how to do so. This is not a derogatory criticism of logic but simply a part of the truism that logic is not a complete guide to life.'[11] The point is well taken: logic alone affords no sufficient touchstone of truth.[12] Logic is hypothetical and formal; factual truth is categorical and material. Though it provides indispensable help and guidance towards answering the question we face in regard to truth, it does not provide the answers as such. There is no shirking the fact that as an instrumentality for the determination of factual truth the theory belongs not to logic but to epistemology, and its essential mechanisms of reasoning belong not to theoretical but to applied logic.

For the purposes of a workable coherence criterion of truth, the consistency machinery of pure logic must be supplemented by considerations along some such lines as those of plausibility. From a set of inconsistent data (such as: p, q, $\sim p \vee \sim q$) we can take no steps to determine where the truth lies on the basis of pure logic alone. So far as 'the logic of the situation' goes, we

---

[11] *Foundations of Statistics* (New York, 1954), p. 59.

[12] Neither, incidentally, does the standard machinery of probability theory—as may be seen from the Lottery Paradox already considered above.

are left with a radical indeterminacy (in the example: p & q *or* p & $\sim q$ *or* $\sim p$ & q). To remove (or reduce) this indeterminacy we turned to considerations of alethic plausibility. We appeal to plausibilities as an extralogical resource to fill an epistemic gap. But they are something we ourselves bring to the coherence problem: they are not part of what can be extracted (without further auxiliary assumptions) from the problem itself, but must be brought to it *ab extra* as a means towards its resolution. To say this, is definitely not to categorize these plausibility considerations as haphazard, arbitrary, or devoid of rational warrant. On the contrary, it is to stress their importance and to recognize rather than to deny that they must be accorded a proper systematic footing.

Any viable theory of factual truth must recognize the overriding role of extralogical factors drawn from the epistemological sphere. In this light, the fact that the theory 'loses its claims to be a purely logical resource' is not a defect but a merit. Its stress on the extralogical issues of data and the machinery of alethic preference thus represents an essential strength of our coherence theory, rather than a point of weakness.

6. *Another Objection to the Coherence Theory*

A further (by now familiar) objection to our coherence theory of truth runs thus: 'With the approach at issue, it will make a substantial difference for truth-determinations how the basic data are formulated. Surely questions of truth should not hinge upon a merely grammatical issue of this kind.'

Once more an incorrect interpretation is pressed upon a correct premiss. The man who states 'p & $\sim p$ & q' puts forward but one single proposition (albeit one of conjunctive form), a proposition that is bound to be nonsense (in the technical sense of self-inconsistency) so that there is no possibility that what is said could be true. On the other hand, the man who states 'p' and '$\sim p$' and 'q' puts forward three distinct propositions some of which may well turn out true. When the issue of the truth of what is declared or maintained is before us, the mode of formulation is not a grammatical irrelevancy but a definitive aspect of the problem. The very nature of 'coherence', as we have approached it, is conceived of in terms of a coherence among propositions—viz. those advanced as data. And here the issue of formulation is absolutely critical—even for something as rudimentary as that most basic factor for determining how many propositions are to be at issue. In dismissing matters ot formulation as merely grammatical refinements without properly substantive bearing, the objection begs the question in a very mistaken and misleading way.

7. *'The Real Truth' as an Idealization*

A further possible objection to the coherence theory as formulated here goes as follows: 'The criterion operative in the theory (for the factual claims at issue) does not explicate "is true" in an absolute way, but only "is true relative to a certain basis"—namely, a basis of data. This coherence theory therefore deals not with factual truth as such, but with relative factual truth, truth with respect to certain data.'

Now the present coherence theory does indeed deal with (factual) truth on a basis. However, the proposed interpretation of the implications of this fact goes amiss. The concept of 'is true (*simpliciter*)' can legitimately be viewed as an essentially relative conception throughout the area of empirical fact. In the factual cases at issue, categorical truth can legitimately be viewed as relative truth on a certain basis—it is 'relative truth once all the possibly relevant returns are in'. This, of course, is an idealization that in general we shall be unable to realize—all of the relevant data may never actually be in hand. A hypothetical interpretation in terms of a subjunctive conditional is in order: 'If all the returns were in and a determination of relative truth made on this all-comprising basis, then the actual or categorical truth could not but be identical with the relative truth so determined.' Such a construction of categorical truth as truth relative to a basis (only, however, the *complete* basis) shows that the theoretical structure of the two concepts is fundamentally identical. Moreover, it explains and legitimizes the view of the relative truth as we can determine it as an approximation to an underlying idealization, the categorical truth pure and simple.

Inevitably on a coherentist approach '*our* truth' is a provisional truth, a truth relative to the data in hand. Thus the coherentist construes

X's (warranted) claim that P is true

as amounting at best to

P is true on the basis of the (suitably constituted) body of data available to X.

Now, of course, 'X warrantedly claims that P is true' does not entail 'P is true'. People can be rationally warranted in maintaining the things they do and yet be mistaken. The distinction between what is warrantedly maintained and what is actually so is not to be wiped out. Accordingly, the coherentist sees '*our truth*' as at best an approximative approach to 'the *real* truth', an ideal as it were, to whose actual attainment we cannot lay claim but which nevertheless plays an important regulative role in the process of inquiry.

Philosophers have sometimes objected that concern with truth *per se* is misleading because truth is conceived of as something fixed and unchanging whereas our knowledge is ever changing, and the 'truths' of yesteryear become 'falsehoods' of today. William James above all insisted that truth is not fixed and crystalline but something that involves change and process: 'The truth of an idea is not a stagnant property inherent in it. Truth *happens* to an idea. It *becomes* true, is *made* true by events. Its verity *is* in fact an event, a process, the process namely of its verifying itself, its veri*fication*.'[13] In viewing the criteriology of truth as an essentially relational matter—with truth-determinations as the product of a *fixed* relationship to *potentially changing* data—our coherence theory is able to combine the classical insistence upon the constancy of *the truth* with the latter-day stress upon the dynamism of man's transitory *truths*. John Dewey wanted to abandon the concept of *truth* in favour of *warranted assertability*. A careful heed of the criteriological mode of approach induces us to acknowledge the utility of the latter without jettisoning the former conception. They do, after all, run very close together: there is little harm in assimilating truth to warranted assertability so long as one is prepared to distinguish between the *actually accessible* warrant that is at hand and the *ultimately available* warrant that is *in principle* obtainable. In giving up the view that an adequate conception of factual truth must be based upon a statically true, axiom-like foundation, our coherence theory can accommodate a pragmatist aversion to the classical fixity of truth without abandoning conceptual stability and usefulness of the idea of truth upon which the classical tradition quite properly placed stress.

This view of the actual (categorical) truth as an idealization that cannot be realized in fact does not make this conception of truth otiose and useless. To be sure, a coherentist cannot accompany his claims of (factual) truth with the iron-clad guarantee that they will never—come what may—need retraction or amendment. But the fact that he cannot be irrevocably dogmatic about what is true does not mean that he has no use whatever for this conception. Quite the reverse, the very concept of the truth as an (unattainable) idealization leads him to

13 W. James, *Pragmatism* (New York, 1909), p. 201.

endow this idea with a special importance. It leads him to regard the conception of truth as a regulative principle (in Kantian terminology): throughout his pursuit of factual inquiries he is guided by the notion that an ever more adequate basis of evaluation will lead him ever closer towards the idealization at issue—without, of course, ever actually and finally reaching it.[14] The coherentist's *regulative* conception of truth accords this concept a place in the epistemic scheme no less important than the *descriptive* role it plays in other theories.

It must be re-emphasized in this connection that our criterion is not one of relative truth with respect to an arbitrary basis of randomly specified propositions, but one of relative truth with respect to the data, that is, propositions having a certain definite epistemic warrant (as explained at length in the previous exposition of this technical conception). Now someone might object: 'It is truths *simpliciter* that are in question, not truths relative to such-and-such premises or data. If the analysis provides simply the latter, it fails to respond to the real issue.' Now, of course, the move of detachment going from 'true relative to premises' to 'true pure and simple' is crucial. And this move pivotally hinges upon the concept of datahood. Just as in deductive logic this step from relative to categorical truth is warranted by the truth of the premises, so on the coherence analysis this step is warranted by the very nature of truth-candidacy. The validation of the move from 'true relative to givens' to unqualifiedly 'true' must lie in the nature of the 'givens'. It is because this concept of a datum is such that datahood has a definitely truth-related character, that 'detachment' from the basis of the relevant data is possible. Reliance on the data in the specified sense makes it legitimate to speak simply of the truth of the derived result (rather than having to continue to speak of the truth as relative to such-and-such propositions).

The standard distinction between 'the real truth' of a factual matter and 'the truth as best we can determine it here and now' thus continues to be important and relevant to the coherence theory. For the coherence theorist, the real or actual truth is the ultimate truth: what is determined as true once this determination is made appropriately on the basis of all the data (i.e. all of the proper data, properly evaluated). This relativistic approach notwithstanding, the actual truth is a perfectly distinct and distinctive conception, albeit an idealization. Our

---

[14] For a most informative discussion of the idea of truth as a regulative principle —though one that sets out from a point of departure rather different from ours— see K. R. Popper, *Conjectures and Refutations* (London, 1963), pp. 225–31.

partial, interim truth-determinations are at best imperfect approximations to this ideal. Our approach thus preserves intact the crucial difference between 'the real truth' and 'our truth'. The former affords an idealization to indicate where one winds up when all is said and done (which it never is); the latter always remains provisional, in however slight a measure.

In this regard, the coherentist view of the matter differs sharply from the architectonic approach of the intuitionist, for whom the matter of development is simply one of successive addition. With the growth of knowledge through the acquisition of new data, we get through the coherence approach not only a fuller view of the truth, but also a better view of it: progress is not merely a matter of growth at the boundaries, but of revision in the interior.

This approach accounts also for the position that three-valuedness in the approximating view of truth is compatible with two-valuedness at the level of what is approximated. Once 'all the returns are in' the coherence analysis too will yield a two-valued picture of the truth. Even for the coherentist, the *ideal* theory of truth—operative to be sure only in the ultimate case of complete data definitively evaluated—is provided by the classical theory. At this level, the truth-status situation will be fully bivalent so as to yield the full classical theory. A classical, bivalent situation will obtain in 'the standard cases' where (1) the propositions at issue themselves (or their negations) are part of the data, and (2) one single m.c.s. is preferred. Thus if the data are sufficiently complete (i.e. include every proposition or its negation) and if our preferential criterion is sufficiently powerful to yield a unique m.c.s., then in this 'ideal' case the theory of truth for this 'real truth' must be altogether classical. While at the interim level of truth-determination neither P nor its contradictory $\sim P$ may qualify as true on a coherence criterion, this is without import for the ultimacy of the matter. Thus even a coherentist is in a position to grant primacy to the classical theory of truth as an ultimate ideal and to think of 'the domain of truth' as the label of a well-defined realm, albeit one to which entry is not feasible in the practical nature of things.

But a problem remains. If—as we have conceded—the essential core of 'the real truth' lies in the correspondence conception of an agreement with the facts, then what guarantee is there that the ideal implementation of a coherence methodology in the ultimate circumstance of 'complete data appropriately evaluated' will indeed yield the real truth in the sense of fact-conformity? The only guarantee lies in the pivotal word 'appropriately'. If absolute assurance is wanted, then as with all logical guarantees we must put into the premises what we extract from the conclusion and the sought-for guarantee becomes the guarantee of circularity. The potential discrepancy in view canbe realized only if one envisages a discord between coherentist and correspondentist truth. One must postulate a case in which (1) the real truth of the matter is somehow determined, (2) the apparent truth of the matter is determined by a sufficiently appropriate and ultimate application of coherence mechanisms, and (3) there is a disagreement between (1) and (2). But this situation is in principle impossible. If —and in so far as—we can apply the correspondence standard to truth-determinations we could only concede as appropriate those applications of the coherence standard (in its ultimate form) that yield an accordant outcome. If we take seriously the position that coherence provides our sole standard of factual truth the envisaged discrepancy just cannot arise.

8. *Conclusion*

The main task of this chapter has been to re-examine the traditional objections to a coherence theory of truth formulated in Chapter II. In appraising these objections in the context of the particular version of the theory expounded in the intervening chapters, we have seen how this formulation of the theory is able to overcome these obstacles. It appears that our specific version of the coherence theory is able to meet or circumvent all the traditional arguments against the viability of a coherence theory of truth.

In closing, it is fitting to review briefly those aspects of the coherence theory that qualify as its strong points in a comparison with its rivals.

(1) In contrast to the correspondence theory, the coherence theory yields a working criterion of truth. It is thus in a position to render some service in that vast group of cases where—due to the inherent impossibility of 'confronting the facts'—the correspondence theory is criteriologically of no avail in coming to a decision as to whether or not a given proposition is to be classed as true.

(2) In contrast to the pragmatic theory, implementation of the coherence theory demands only the prior judgment of plausibility (or perhaps of *a priori* probability—since plausibility judgments *could* be made on this basis). A pragmatic theory requires not only the assessment of *probabilities* but also—and wholly in addition—an assessment of *utilities* (or preferabilities).

It is, correspondingly, a more complex and a more dubious instrument to employ. The pragmatic theory of truth has a certain aura of unwarranted—and unwarrantable—optimism. For on just what grounds can one justify accepting the maximally useful alternative as true?

(3) In contrast to the intuitional theory, the coherence theory is able to dispense with a foundation of basic truths. It has no need for a hard core of elemental and unquestionable truths outside logic. It adopts the epistemic stance that every extralogical truth is defeasible. This far-reaching point needs fuller analysis and will receive in later chapters the further attention it deserves.

VIII

EPISTEMOLOGICAL RAMIFICATIONS OF THE COHERENCE THEORY

1. *Epistemic* v. *Ontic Views of Truth*

IN elucidating the workings of the coherence theory it is useful to take more explicit note of its direction of approach to truth. There are several distinct perspectives upon the true:

(1) the *ontic* perspective, which is a matter of what *is in fact true*—wholly regardless of its being thought or accepted or believed to be so by anyone.

(2) the *descriptively epistemic* perspective, which is a matter of what *is actually thought* or accepted or believed or opined (etc.) to be true. This is person-relative and biographical: it is always a matter of someone's so thinking (etc.).

Between these two lies the half-way house of

(3) the *normatively epistemic* perspective, which is a matter of what is *rationally to be thought* or *rationally to be accepted* or *rationally to be believed* (or the like), regardless of anyone's actually so thinking.

This is a half-way house because it has an epistemic component in its reference to what is thought and an ontic, factual component in its reference to what is rationally warranted. Finally there is

(4) the *criteriological* perspective, which is a matter of what—through the deployment of an appropriately supported criterion for the assessment of truthfulness—*is justifiedly to be classed* as true.

Approaches (3) and (4) have a definite and close relationship. If the criterion at issue in (4) is one that implements the idea of rational acceptance, and if (3) is construed in terms specifically of acceptance-as-true (rather than, say, opinion or belief) then (3) and (4) come together as one. In view of this relationship, there is—or, rather, can be—a close kinship between the criteriological and the normatively epistemic approaches to truth. This relationship warrants closer examination.

We shall, for the present, adopt the notation:

$T(P), F(P)$ for 'P is true (false) in the ontic mode', that is: it is in fact the case that P is true (false).

$T^*(P), F^*(P)$ for 'P is true (false) in the normatively epistemic mode', that is: there is a proper rational warrant (given everything we know—or for that matter could know—by way of available data) for holding P to be true (false).

Note first of all that T and T^* (and also F and F^*) are in fact logically independent of one another. Though P is in fact true, we may lack all evidence that could warrant our thinking so, and thus there is no valid inference from $T(P)$ to $T^*(P)$. Again while there may be a proper rational warrant for holding P to be true, this may be one of those sad cases where 'things go wrong', and hence there is no valid inference from $T^*(P)$ to $T(P)$—that is, there is no valid *deductive* inference, though there will, of course, be an appropriate '*presumptive* inference'.

While the ontic truth-values T and F can plausibly be viewed as a truth-status dichotomy that conforms to the whole spectrum of relationships of the full classical theory of truth,[1] this is certainly not possible with T^* and F^*. The Law of Excluded Middle (and its cognates and dependants) will assuredly fail for T^* and F^*. Thus we shall clearly not have

$$\text{If} \sim T^*(P), \text{ then } T^*(\sim P)$$

A (rationally warranted) state of ignorance or agnosticism is certainly possible, a state in which, for some proposition p, neither $T^*(p)$ nor $T^*(\sim p)$ is warranted. To stipulate the entailment under consideration would be to gainsay this perfectly genuine possibility. It is, accordingly, a characteristic feature of the normatively epistemic mode of truth that it is non-classically orthodox. In view of its kinship with the criteriological perspective, these considerations regarding the normatively epistemic approach help to illuminate the characteristic features of the coherentist view of truth. Any criteriological theory of truth whose criterion is incomplete (in the sense that neither $C(P)$ nor $C(\sim P)$ may obtain for some propositions) also leads to the result that the excluded-middle principle will fail.

---

[1] Though not necessarily so, however. For example, a theory of the truth-indeterminacy of future contingents might not rest satisfied with an epistemological view of the matter ('not *known* to be true or false') but insist upon a genuinely ontic indeterminacy of truth-status.

2. *Fallibilism and the Growth of Knowledge: Aspects of the Dynamics of Truth-Reclassification on the Coherence Theory*

On any contextualistic truth-criterion—and specifically the normatively epistemic approach—a classical theory of truth will only obtain when 'in the limit' we reach a situation of completeness, when 'all returns are in', when our data-base or information-base is so adequate that the truth-status of *every* proposition becomes determinate. Like the epistemological view of truth, any contextual criterion—be it pragmatic or coherence-based or what have you—takes a potentially dynamic view of the matter. On a static conception of truth, a thesis that is determined to be true in one inquiry cannot become untrue in another: truth is something once-and-for-all. By contrast, any contextual criterion in general—and the coherence theory specifically—shares the feature of viewing truth-determinations as essentially dynamic: what is found to be true in the context of one information-basis need not at all continue so when the data-base changes. Whenever we proceed on a criterial approach to truthfulness where criterion-satisfaction is a context-sensitive issue, then the issue of our entitlement to class something as a truth itself becomes context-dependent. As the contextual basis changes, the criterion will operate in such a way as to lead us to reappraise the truth-claims of propositions (exactly as in the case of acceptance on the basis of a changing information base).

Unlike the ontic once-and-for-all view of truth on which what is once found to be true will continue so for ever, the coherence approach is inherently fallibilistic. Its considered position is that a changing context can always force a reclassification of the truth-status of a proposition. Coherence theorists have always stressed the provisional character of man's knowledge of the truth—our systematization of knowledge falls short of the complete coherence of an ideal system '. . . if only for the reason that it is growing in time'.[2] Accordingly, the coherentist has it that *our* factual truth is ever corrigible in principle. This does not eliminate the difference in meaning between *true* and *probably true*, nor even imply that this difference is one of degree only (since probability introduces yet another—and quite different—set of considerations). But it does have the consequence that whatever factual thesis we maintain to be true *simpliciter* (relative to our warranting ground) is in actuality never established as more than probably or (very probably) true in virtue of this. Of course when I warrantedly say '*P* is true' I don't say (or

[2] H. H. Joachim, *The Nature of Truth* (London, 1906), p. 14.

mean) 'P is very probably true', but this is nevertheless all that anybody is actually entitled—under these circumstances—to infer regarding P. The situation is exactly parallel with that when I (candidly) say 'P is true'. Then I don't say (or mean) 'Rescher thinks that P is true', although this is in fact all that anybody is actually entitled to infer regarding P.

A key aspect of the traditional coherence theory relates to its conception of man's inherently imperfect epistemic control over the domain of truth. The traditional coherence theory has always stressed that our mastery of factual truth is not only incomplete but contingent. On the classical model of 'derivation from the data'—with the data conceived of as truths—the addition of new data inevitably spells merely a growth of knowledge: a newly added item of (current) information cannot entail the subtraction of an old one. But with a coherence theory whose data are truth-candidates rather than truths, the addition of new data can have profound repercussions for the truth-status of the old. This poses a group of issues to which closer consideration must eventually be given.

Now when one contemplates the process of reclassifying the truth-status of a proposition two sorts of changes can be conceived of. First, there is the type of truth-status revision that we might characterize as *evolutionary*. This occurs when one reclassifies some proposition as T or F whose truth-status was previously indeterminate. There is also the more drastic type of truth-status change that we might characterize as *revolutionary*. This occurs when we class something as T that was previously classified as F, or the reverse. Both types of change are envisaged as perfectly possible prospects within the framework of the coherence theory of truth.

Let us see how this is so. The coherence theory expounded above envisages three sorts of changes that could induce a reclassification of the truth-status of propositions:

(i) new 'internal' data (i.e. additions to the set of data)
(ii) new 'external' data or *evidence* (i.e. determinations of truth-status as derived from another context altogether)
(iii) new preferability-evaluations.

Any satisfactory theory of truth must be prepared to shed light upon the rational mechanisms by which the growth of knowledge makes its impact on the critical evaluation of the truth-status of propositions. With the coherence theory here in view, this problem can be treated under the three headings that have been indicated.

The nature and import of the third case—that of new preferability-evaluations—are matters by now too familiar to need further discussion. Suffice it to say (1) that here we have the prospect of completely revolutionary changes in our assessment of the truth-status of propositions, and (2) that this can come about without introducing any new findings (data), but simply through such new information as will—for example—justify a revision of plausibility-assessments. The coherence mechanism is in this way able to provide a model for a certain—neither far-fetched nor uncommon—type of scientific progress. In the context of an apparently discordant conceptual situation this can consist, not in the accumulation of new experimental findings about the phenomena at issue, but in revising the assessment of relative plausibilities, so as to arrive at a 'new integration' of the 'seeming facts' of the matter. The replacement of the occult-influence view of the workings of witchcraft or the 'evil eye' by the theory of autosuggestion is but one example among others. Many episodes in the history of science can be regarded illuminatingly from this perspective. The divergence between Newton and Leibniz regarding gravitation occurred despite agreement on all relevant scientific facts because they viewed these facts from wholly different plausibility-perspectives (due to Newton's willingness to accept—unlike Leibniz—the prospect of action at a distance). Again, the dispute between Lavoisier and Priestley as to the nature of combustion affords another example. Both recognized the same body of scientific observations regarding combustion and its cognate processes. But their different perspectives of theoretical commitments led them to place entirely different plausibility-valuations on the key theses relating to the explanatory rationalization of these facts.

The best way to clarify the effect of new data at issue in the first two points is by means of examples. Suppose we begin— once again—with the following simple set of (mutually inconsistent) data: $\mathbf{S} = \{p \vee q, \sim p, \sim q\}$.

The m.c.s. of $\mathbf{S}$ are:

$\mathbf{S}_1 = \{p \vee q, \sim p\}$ as axiomatized by $\sim p$ & q

$\mathbf{S}_2 = \{p \vee q, \sim q\}$ as axiomatized by p & $\sim q$

$\mathbf{S}_3 = \{\sim p, \sim q\}$ as axiomatized by $\sim p$ & $\sim q$.

This example is familiar from previous discussion and, we may recall, leads—on the probabilistic analysis—to the position that the truths are axiomatized by the conjunction $\sim p$ & $\sim q$. There is, of course, the prospect that we might arrive—on the basis of considerations outside the foregoing statement of the problem—at plausibility assessments that would rank S_1 ahead of S_2 and S_3, so as to yield a family of truths axiomatized by $\sim p$ & q. In this case we would have to 'change our mind' about q. Nothing more need be said about this now-familiar process.

Suppose, however, that we obtain p as a new datum. Treating this new datum as 'internal' to the data at issue we simply add it to the previous S as yet another member, and so obtain:

$$S' = \{p \vee q, \sim p, \sim q, p\}.$$

The m.c.s. of S' are exactly as before (in the sense of having the same axiomatizations):

$S_1' = \{p \vee q, \sim p\}$ as axiomatized by $\sim p$ & q

$S_2' = \{p \vee q, \sim q, p\}$ as axiomatized by p & $\sim q$

$S_3' = \{\sim p, \sim q\}$ as axiomatized by $\sim p$ & $\sim q$.

But now the probabilistic analysis yields:

	$p \vee q$	$\sim p$	$\sim q$	p	Σ	Σ^*
p & q	$\frac{1}{3}$			$\frac{1}{2}$	$\frac{5}{6}$	$\frac{5}{24}$
p & $\sim q$	$\frac{1}{3}$		$\frac{1}{2}$	$\frac{1}{2}$	$\frac{8}{6}$	$\frac{8}{24}$
$\sim p$ & q	$\frac{1}{3}$	$\frac{1}{2}$			$\frac{5}{6}$	$\frac{5}{24}$
$\sim p$ & $\sim q$		$\frac{1}{2}$	$\frac{1}{2}$		$\frac{6}{6}$	$\frac{6}{24}$

Correspondingly we arrive at the position where S_2 is preferred and where the truths are axiomatized by p & $\sim q$. On the basis of this revised analysis as engendered by an additional datum we should, in effect, 'change our mind' about the truth-status of p.

The preceding analysis proceeded on the basis of an 'internal' addition of p to the set of data. We might also, however, have added p in an 'external' way by *postulating* p (a step we could be motivated to take on grounds external to those envisaged in the preceding statement of the problem). Correspondingly, we should then limit ourselves to those m.c.s. of the initial set S that are not incompatible with p (on the lines of Method I of Chapter IV). Here again we should have arrived at S_2 and at a family of truths axiomatized by p & $\sim q$.

It is illuminating in the present connection to note some facets of the acquisition of internal data that involve no new variables. Again, the general points can be brought out by a specific example:

Original Situation Before Addition (of $\sim p \lor q$ as a new datum)
$$S = \{p \lor q, \sim p, \sim q\}.$$

$S_1 = \{p \lor q, \sim p\}$ which is axiomatized by $\sim p \,\&\, q$
$S_2 = \{p \lor q, \sim q\}$ which is axiomatized by $p \,\&\, \sim q$
$S_3 = \{\sim p, \sim q\}$ which is axiomatized by $\sim p \,\&\, \sim q$.

Possible World	A Priori Probability	$p \lor q$	$\sim p$	$\sim q$	Σ	Σ^*	(A Posteriori Probability)
$p \,\&\, q$	$\frac{1}{4}$	$\frac{1}{3}$			$\frac{2}{6}$	$\frac{2}{18}$	$= 0\cdot11$
$p \,\&\, \sim q$	$\frac{1}{4}$	$\frac{1}{3}$		$\frac{1}{2}$	$\frac{5}{6}$	$\frac{5}{18}$	$= 0\cdot28$
$\sim p \,\&\, q$	$\frac{1}{4}$	$\frac{1}{3}$	$\frac{1}{2}$		$\frac{5}{6}$	$\frac{5}{18}$	$= 0\cdot28$
$\sim p \,\&\, \sim q$	$\frac{1}{4}$		$\frac{1}{2}$	$\frac{1}{2}$	$\frac{6}{6}$	$\frac{6}{18}$	$= 0\cdot33$

Resultant Situation After Addition (of $\sim p \lor q$ as a new datum)
$$S' = \{p \lor q, \sim p, \sim q, \sim p \lor q\}.$$

$S'_1 = \{p \lor q, \sim p, \sim p \lor q\}$ axiomatized by $\sim p \,\&\, q$
$S'_2 = \{p \lor q, \sim q\}$ axiomatized by $p \,\&\, \sim q$
$S'_3 = \{\sim p, \sim q, \sim p \lor \sim q\}$ axiomatized by $\sim p \,\&\, \sim q$.

Possible World	A Priori Probability	$p \lor q$	$\sim p$	$\sim q$	$\sim p \lor q$	Σ	Σ^*	(A Posteriori Probability)
$p \,\&\, q$	$\frac{1}{4}$	$\frac{1}{3}$			$\frac{1}{3}$	$\frac{4}{6}$	$\frac{4}{24}$	$= 0\cdot17$
$p \,\&\, \sim q$	$\frac{1}{4}$	$\frac{1}{3}$		$\frac{1}{2}$		$\frac{5}{6}$	$\frac{5}{24}$	$= 0\cdot20$
$\sim p \,\&\, q$	$\frac{1}{4}$	$\frac{1}{3}$	$\frac{1}{2}$		$\frac{1}{3}$	$\frac{7}{6}$	$\frac{7}{24}$	$= 0\cdot29$
$\sim p \,\&\, \sim q$	$\frac{1}{4}$		$\frac{1}{2}$	$\frac{1}{2}$	$\frac{1}{3}$	$\frac{8}{6}$	$\frac{8}{24}$	$= 0\cdot33$

A comparison of these tabulations shows a marked shift in the *a posteriori* probabilities of the possible worlds. The following observations are now in order:

(1) A new internal datum (in the same propositional variables) added to an inconsistent set cannot possibly reduce the number of m.c.s. For in each case we shall get as new m.c.s. the old m.c.s. plus (if consistently addable) the new datum). However, we might obtain additional new m.c.s. —as would have been the case in the preceding example if we had added $p \,\&\, q$ to **S**. Therefore—in the absence of case-eliminating plausibility considerations, when we are

confined to looking for *inevitable* consequences—added data (in the same variables) can only 'confuse the issue' further by reducing the range of I-consequences (by adding disjuncts to the disjunctive proposition that axiomatizes them) so as to force us to retract (never deny!) old 'truths'. The alethic uncertainty inherent in the original inconsistent set can only be increased by a new datum (in the same variables). This situation is in complete contrast with that of the consistent case when a new consistent datum is added to a set of consistent data. (Thus let $S = \{p \vee \sim q, \sim p \vee q\}$ and let S' result from adding $p \vee q$: $S' = \{p \vee \sim q, \sim p \vee q, p \vee q\}$. Now S was axiomatized by $(p \& q) \vee (\sim p \& \sim q)$, while S' is axiomatized by $p \& q$. The uncertainty has been diminished by reducing the number of disjuncts in the disjunctive normal form of the axiom of the propositional set.) But in the absence of plausibility considerations, this helpful effect of further data fails to be matched in the inconsistent case.

(2) Added data can definitely prove helpful for truth-determination when they serve as a basis for changed plausibilities. Thus consider the probabilistic plausibility approach to the above-given example. In the case of the original set S above there was little to choose between the S_i, their Σ^* values all lying within 20 per cent of the maximum. Here we could well be reluctant to prefer any of the S_i. If, correspondingly, we retain all the S_i, then the consequences of S are axiomatized by:

$$(\sim p \& q) \vee (p \& \sim q) \vee (\sim p \& \sim q)$$

or equivalently $\sim p \vee \sim q$. But with S' this situation is altered. The Σ^*-value of S'_2 is now sufficiently low relative to that of the others that we may feel free to prefer them to it. Then the consequences of S' would be axiomatized by $(\sim p \& q) \vee (\sim p \& \sim q)$ or equivalently $\sim p$. A considerable reduction in alethic uncertainty has been effected by the added datum, though only through its effect upon the probabilistic plausibilities.

(3) The most important lesson of the preceding analysis can be spelled out by drawing a technical distinction between *evidence* or what is given as true on the one hand, and *data* or what is given as a truth-candidate upon the other. As long as we proceed wholly in terms of factual evidence, any additions to this can indeed *extend* the realm of truth, but never *revise* it: when what is 'given' is given as

true, then new 'givens' cannot undo old truths. But when what is 'given' is given as a truth-candidate, then new 'givens' can definitely lead us to a change of mind regarding the truth of propositions. To 'change our mind' regarding the truth-status of propositions in the context of *evidence*, we cannot merely add something but must also make retractions (i.e. must actually delete items from the body of evidence). However, in the context of *data*, such changes can be induced merely by the addition of new items. When the growth of knowledge is viewed as simply the accumulation of new evidence the matter is viewed in an inherently evolutionary way in terms of simple accretions. But by considering new information in the light of data (in our technical sense) the possibility of genuinely revolutionary changes arises.

It is worthwhile to note some general characteristics of the case of 'new data' (of the internal variety). Let **S** be an inconsistent set of propositions and let

$$\mathbf{S'} = \mathbf{S} \cup \{P\} \text{ where } P \notin \mathbf{S}.$$

Then we shall have:

(i) Every W-consequence of **S** is a W-consequence of **S'**.

But the converse of (i) clearly does not obtain (P itself is presumably no W-consequence of **S**). And neither of the two following theses will obtain nor will their converses:

(ii) Every I-consequence of **S** is an I-consequence of **S'**.
(iii) Every $\mathscr{P}$-consequence of **S** is a $\mathscr{P}$-consequence of **S'**.

A counter-example to the first thesis—from which one to the second is readily provided—is as follows:

$$\mathbf{S} = \{p \ \& \ q, \ {\sim}p \ \& \ q\}$$
$$\mathbf{S'} = \{p \ \& \ q, \ {\sim}p \ \& \ q, \ {\sim}q\}.$$

Here q is an I-consequence of **S** but not of **S'**. Again, that the converse of (ii) is no thesis is shown by the example:

$$\mathbf{S} = \{p, \ {\sim}p\}$$
$$\mathbf{S'} = \{p, \ {\sim}p, \ q\}.$$

Here q is an I-consequence of **S'** but not of **S**. (This example, incidentally, does yield new I-consequences for **S'**, in seeming conflict with point (1) above. But the 'new datum', viz. q, is not one formulated in the same propositional variables.)

These considerations serve to emphasize a point that is crucial—though not surprising but only to be expected: the pivotal role of data in our control over truth. The addition of fundamentally new data or a revision of the old data by deletion or replacement can make a decisive difference for the results of deploying the criterion of truth. We generally lack—if indeed we ever have—'the whole story' of all the relevant data. To say all this is only to reassert the old platitude of the inherently provisional nature of our knowledge of extralogical truth.

3. *Verification and Falsification*

How does the coherence methodology fit into the dispute between the Popperians and the Carnapians over the merits of falsificationism $v.$ verificationism as the basic control over factual knowledge? In its conceptual structure it is closer to the falsificationist line. Consider the familiar example of the datum set:

$$S = \{p \vee q, \sim p, \sim q\}.$$

When we turn to an inventory of the indicated possibilities we arrive at the m.c.s.:

$$S_1 = \{p \vee q, \sim p\} \text{ as axiomatized by } \sim p \ \& \ q$$
$$S_2 = \{p \vee q, \sim q\} \text{ as axiomatized by } p \ \& \ \sim q$$
$$S_3 = \{\sim p, \sim q\} \ \text{ as axiomatized by } \sim p \ \& \ \sim q.$$

Supposing that considerations of alethic preferability enable us to eliminate one of these—say S_2—we then arrive at

$$(\sim p \ \& \ q) \vee (\sim p \ \& \ \sim q),$$

or equivalently simply $\sim p$, as the axiomatic basis for the set of truths relative to these data. As this example suggests, this whole approach in the 'search for truth' has a heavily falsificationist aspect. Relying heavily upon an *eliminative* line of attack we 'look for a weak spot' in the range of possibilities delineated by the data. The coherence analysis so proceeds that it is at bottom only because certain possibilities are rejected ('falsified') that we are able to reach those ultimate results recognized as truths. The Popperian dictum that 'verification proceeds through falsification' is thus a thesis which can also be used to characterize our own procedure—albeit from a rather different point of view.

4. *Degrees of Truth*

In considering the idealist doctrine of 'degrees of truth' we must at the very outset try to avoid misunderstanding by pointing out what *is not* at issue. First of all, in speaking of 'degrees of truth', no reference whatever to *degrees of probability* is intended. No one wants to quarrel with the contention that statements can have various degrees of likelihood or probability, in the sense that 'There will be a sunny day in Miami in June of next year' is highly probable *per se*, and is vastly more probable than 'There will be a snow-storm in Miami in June of next year'. To be sure, there are various proposals regarding the *interpretation* or the logical analysis of such probability statements. Nevertheless, there is substantial agreement that probability assertions in no manner impute to statements a status other than truth or falsity: they do not contradict *per se* the thesis that truth and falsity are exclusive and exhaustive alternatives for classifying statements. Probability assertions have to do, not with the truth-status of statements, but with the extent to which, on the evidence, a rational person is entitled to assert the truth or the falsity of the statements, or to give odds for or against them. The whole matter of probability, then, has no real bearing on the question of 'degrees of truth'. If a case is to be made out on behalf of the concept of degrees of truth, it must be done, not by invoking the concept of probability, but in some fundamentally different way.

The concept of degrees of truth could be construed as referring to adequacy in the use or presentation of information. On this approach, the 'degree of truth' of a body of discourse would derive from its success in conveying information regarding its object of reference. This thesis can perhaps be best explained by analogy with the process of *description*. *Webster's Dictionary* defines the verb 'describe' as 'to represent by words'. Now representation is in its very nature something that can be done well or badly. The validity of a description, then, does not depend merely upon the truth of the various statements of which it is comprised; a description can be wholly 'true' and yet entirely inadequate. In describing a particular man we can list at pleasure attributes common to all men, thus not advancing one jot the business of description, while uttering nothing but truth relevant to the object of discussion. Accordingly, the 'degree of truth' of a body of discourse would be conceived not merely with reference to its avoidance of falsehood, but also through consideration of the extent to which it did justice to the object under discussion. Discourse which has a 'high degree of truth' in this sense must, in the familiar legal jargon, not simply 'tell the truth and nothing but the truth', but it must also succeed in good measure in telling 'the whole truth'. On this proposal, then, the *degree of truth* of a body of discourse is to be assessed by (1) the negative but absolute requirement of avoidance of explicit falsehood, and (2) the positive but graduated and comparative extent to which this discourse conveys information regarding its object of reference.

Important though it unquestionably is, this mode of 'degrees of truth' in the sense of representative adequacy in description is not in any way a specifically characteristic issue with respect to the coherence theory. In the present context of truth as coherence, the definitive features of 'degrees of truth' must be articulated in terms of *the extent of coherence*. The present, coherentist perspective appears to call for something distinct from probabilities and to point towards the idea of one or more truth-statuses genuinely distinct from and 'intermediate between' truth and falsity.[3] If our determination of truth is a matter of coherence with the data, the coherence of a contemplated proposition with these data can vary in extent. Coherence being a matter of fit and accord, it is clear on the very surface that this will be a matter of comparative extent, of more or less, of relative degrees. In the context of a coherence analysis of truth, the prospect of degrees of truth is an inevitable fact: coherence being a matter of degree, so—on a coherence theory of truth—must truthfulness be also. (And *this* approach to degrees of truth is wholly independent of a second degree-indicating consideration, viz. that only the data we possess at the time can come into play at any given juncture, and that they will vary with the passage of time.) The coherentist will have to be in a position to make some proper sense of the seemingly paradoxical idealist doctrine that 'all [or at any rate *most*] judgments are partly true and partly false'.[4]

The doctrine of degrees of truth in just this sense is among the most characteristic aspects of the traditional coherence theory of truth. And just this has caused alarm and objection. 'Surely', the objectors have argued, 'it is nonsense to speak of *degrees of*

---

[3] Various writers have articulated a conception of 'partial truth' along essentially probability-involving lines. See H. Reichenbach, *Experience and Prediction* (Chicago, Ill., 1962), and M. Bunge, *The Myth of Simplicity* (New Jersey, 1963). In these cases—as in others—the idea of 'degrees of truth' is based on a correspondence theory of truth. Regarding this idea of 'degrees of truth' as representing approximations to correspondentist truth see K. R. Popper, *Conjectures and Refutations* (London, 1963), p. 232.

[4] A. C. Ewing, *Idealism: A Critical Survey* (London, 1934), p. 208.

truth. If a proposition is true, it is true; and if not, if it somehow falls short of being true, then it is untrue. What could be plainer than that?' This argument, however, overlooks the crucial difference between a *precriterial* and a *postcriterial* perspective upon truth.

From the postcriterial point of view, once a proposition has been correctly determined to be true in terms of some appropriate criterion, then *ex hypothesi* it cannot also fail to be true on the approach at issue. This idea can be enshrined in such a principle as:

$$|p| = T \supset \sim(\exists v)[v \neq T \,\&\, |p| = v].$$

That 'being true' is on–off and degreeless in *this* way is something that has never for a moment been denied in the preceding discussion.

But there is also the precriterial point of view, when the very issue of the proposition's meeting the criterion is still *sub judice*. All depending on the nature of the criterion at issue, this can very conceivably turn out to be a matter of degree. Specifically this is bound to be so in the case of coherence, where the criterial question is one of 'how well' a proposition fits into a context of others. Such 'fitting' will obviously be such as to admit the question of the *adequacy* of the fit, of one proposition's fitting better than another. As such it would be a matter of degree, of various shades of grey, rather than being a dichotomous issue of black or white or yes or no. Thus put, the matter is, however, formulated in rather figurative terms. It is necessary to examine with greater precision just how these somewhat metaphorical considerations bear on the coherence theory formulated here. This task will be undertaken in Appendix H.

In the preceding discussion the conception of differing degrees of truth has been considered with respect to a given and fixed data-base **S**. The approach has, of course, manifested features peculiarly characteristic of the coherence analysis in that the data at issue were presumably inconsistent. But apart from this difference—a very important one, to be sure—the analysis has much the same structure that can arise in the consistent and orthodoxly inductive case, when we are considering the relative degree of the probable truth of alternative possibilities with respect to a given body of evidence. Any test-procedure for truths that proceeds in terms of a basis of evidence or data takes an inherently fragmentistic view of our determinations of truth: the possibility of new truths based on new data will always be open. This analogy points to a yet different conception of degrees of truth, namely that based upon the relative complete-ness of the data. For it is a seemingly natural supposition that our conclusions should grow truer as the body of evidence that is their basis grows larger and more complete.

5. The 'Preface Paradox' and a Thesis of F. H. Bradley's

One quite intriguing epistemological problem discussed re-cently in philosophical literature can effectively be explicated and resolved by use of the coherence analysis. This problem—the *Preface Paradox*—has been formulated by D. C. Makinson in the following terms:

> Consider the writer who, in the Preface to his book, concedes the occurrence of errors among his statements. Suppose that in the course of his book a writer makes a great many assertions, which we shall call $s_1, ..., s_n$. Given each one of these, he believes that it is true. . . . However, to say that not everything I assert in this book is true, is to say that at least one statement in this book is false. That is to say that at least one of $s_1, ..., s_n$ is false, where $s_1, ..., s_n$ are the state-ments in the book; that $(s_1 \& ... \& s_n)$ is false; that $\sim(s_1 \& ... \& s_n)$ is true. The author who writes and believes each of $s_1, ..., s_n$ and yet in a preface asserts and believes $\sim(s_1 \& ... \& s_n)$ is, it appears, behaving very rationally. Yet clearly he is holding logically incompatible beliefs: he believes each of $s_1, ..., s_n, \sim(s_1 \& ... \& s_n)$, which form an inconsistent set. The man is being rational though inconsistent.[5]

That a cogent account can be given of how a man can be 'rational though inconsistent' may on first sight seem very problematic if not altogether impossible. However, from the standpoint of the coherence approach this aura of paradox is readily dispelled.

Let us examine the Preface Paradox in the light of a co-herence analysis of truth. We may begin with the series of statements in the text or main body of the book: $s_1, s_2, . . ., s_n$. For the sake of convenience it may be supposed that there are just three of these: s_1, s_2, s_3.

Now the preface insists that some of these are false, and so maintains that they will not all be true:

$$\sim(s_1 \& s_2 \& s_3).$$

The book as a whole advances all these propositions together, and so apparently confronts us with the following set of data:

$$\mathbf{B} = \{s_1, s_2, s_3, \sim(s_1 \& s_2 \& s_3)\}.$$

[5] D. C. Makinson, 'The Paradox of the Preface', *Analysis*, 25 (1964), 205–7.

Towards this set **B** we can take the standard stance of our coherence analysis and treat it as a collection of assertions all of which are put forward as prima facie truths, recognizing that they may differ among themselves in plausibility. For concreteness, let us suppose that all the text statements are to be regarded (i) as equally plausible, but (ii) as less plausible than the preface statement. Specifically, let $s^* = \sim(s_1 \,\&\, s_2 \,\&\, s_3)$ be given the plausibility value of 2, while s_1, s_2, and s_3 themselves all obtain a plausibility value of 3.

Now the m.c.s. of **B** are as follows, and obtain the indicated plausibilities:

			maximum	*average*
$\mathbf{B_1} = s_1, s_2, s_3$	with plausibilities $(3, 3, 3)$		3	3
$\mathbf{B_2} = s_1, s_2, s^*$	with plausibilities $(3, 3, 2)$		3	$2\frac{2}{3}$
$\mathbf{B_3} = s_2, s_3, s^*$	with plausibilities $(3, 3, 2)$		3	$2\frac{2}{3}$
$\mathbf{B_4} = s_1, s_3, s^*$	with plausibilities $(3, 3, 2)$		3	$2\frac{2}{3}$.

By the appropriate criterion of preference $\mathscr{P}$ operative here, we have it that $\mathbf{B_1}$ is eliminated, and the preferred m.c.s. of **B** are $\mathbf{B_2}$, $\mathbf{B_3}$, $\mathbf{B_4}$. As a result the $\mathscr{P}$-consequences of **B** are axiomatized by:

$$(s_1 \,\&\, s_2 \,\&\, \sim s_3) \;\vee\; (s_1 \,\&\, \sim s_2 \,\&\, s_3) \;\vee\; (\sim s_1 \,\&\, s_2 \,\&\, s_3),$$

that is: '*exactly one* of the s_i is false and all the rest are true'. Now *this* analysis of the upshot of placing the preface-statement into the context of the rest of the book does not seem to be correct. The intention of the preface is surely to say that *some* text statements are false and not—as the preceding m.c.s. analysis has it—that *exactly one* is false. To arrive at this, the 'natural' result, we must modify the set of propositions at issue to broaden the spectrum of outcomes we are prepared to contemplate. Thus let:

[*i*] = exactly *i* of s_1, s_2, s_3 is false ($i = 0, 1, 2, 3$).

Then consider:

$$\mathbf{B'} = \{s_1, s_2, s_3, s^*, [0], [1], [2], [3]\}.$$

With respect to the constituents of **B'** we intend, in view of the conditions of the problem, that (a) s^* is highly plausible, (b) all the s_i are equally plausible but less so than s^*, (c) the [*i*] are differentially plausible, with both [0] and [3] as *very* implausible and the intervening [*i*] somewhat more plausible—say, for simplicity, almost equally so. We thus arrive at a result somewhat as follows with respect to the plausibility values of the various statements at issue:

$$s_i: \ 3$$
$$s^*: \ 2$$
$$[0]: \ 6$$
$$[1]: \ 4$$
$$[2]: \ 4$$
$$[3]: \ 6.$$

The situation regarding the m.c.s. of **B′** is now as follows:

$\mathbf{B}'_1 = \{[0], s_1, s_2, s_3\}$ with average plausibility $3\frac{3}{4}$

$\mathbf{B}'_2 = \{[1], s^*, s_1, s_2\}$ with average plausibility 3

$\mathbf{B}'_3 = \{[1], s^*, s_2, s_3\}$ with average plausibility 3

$\mathbf{B}'_4 = \{[1], s^*, s_1, s_3\}$ with average plausibility 3

$\mathbf{B}'_5 = \{[2], s^*, s_1\}$ with average plausibility 3

$\mathbf{B}'_6 = \{[2], s^*, s_2\}$ with average plausibility 3

$\mathbf{B}'_7 = \{[2], s^*, s_3\}$ with average plausibility 3

$\mathbf{B}'_8 = \{[3], s^*\}$ with average plausibility 4.

If we eliminate **B′₁** and **B′₈** on this basis, we arrive simply at 'Some but not all of the s_i are false.' And just this result would seem to be the natural upshot of the Preface Paradox. As this treatment of the problem suggests, the pivotal crux in the resolution of the paradox lies in deploying once more the distinction between actual truths and prima facie truths (data, truth-candidates).

It has been shown in some detail above that a proposition can be 'given' in either of two modes, either as *evidence* or as a *datum*—as an *actual* or as a *presumptive* (prima facie) truth—and a great deal will hinge on the distinction. Exactly the same holds for all forms of acceptance. A proposition can be accepted (or believed or advanced) in either of two modes:

(i) as an actual truth; as being definitely and unquestionably the case; as in fact true without proviso.

(ii) as a prima facie truth; as being presumably the case; as true with the proviso that its placement in the setting of other beliefs does not prove a source of difficulty.

Correspondingly, there will be two distinct modes in which someone can be said to believe a proposition to be true, viz.

A-belief or belief as *actually* and definitely true and *P-belief* or belief as *presumably* true, i.e. belief in the status of a prima facie truth.

In the terms of this distinction, no actual irrationality will arise from inconsistency so long as the conflict arises within the domain of *P*-beliefs, the *A*-beliefs by themselves remaining consistent. The 'paradoxical' author accordingly is guilty of no irrationality whatever if he would be prepared to categorize as a specifically *P*-belief his belief in some or all of the propositions he puts forward in the body of his work. And in fact this categorization is precisely what he is apparently concerned to effect by the phraseology of the preface.

A resolution of the Preface Paradox—the seemingly hopeless task of maintaining the rationality of beliefs in the face of inconsistency of what is believed—can accordingly be achieved by distinguishing definite from presumptive truths and then drawing a corresponding distinction between *A*-beliefs and *P*-beliefs. Specifically we should have to maintain that

(i) The preface-statement $\sim(s_1 \ \& \ s_2 \ \& \ \ldots \ \& \ s_n)$ represents an *A*-belief.

(ii) Among the text-statements $s_1, s_2, \ldots, s_n$ certain ones *but not all* may also represent *A*-beliefs.

(iii) The *remainder* of the text-statements all represent *P*-beliefs (doubtless with differential plausibilities).

By their very nature, *P*-beliefs—as beliefs in the prima facie truth of the propositions at issue (unlike the *A*-beliefs in their actual truth)—need not be mutually consistent, not even for the strictest rationality. Accordingly it becomes possible to reconcile the demands of rationality for consistency among the *A*-beliefs with the presence of inconsistency within the group of beliefs as a whole.[6]

Among the seemingly paradoxical views about truth espoused by F. H. Bradley is his insistence upon the self-contradictory character of what man knows or indeed can know in the ordinary course of things. Surveying the discussion of Book I of *Appearance and Reality*, Bradley writes:

And the whole result of this Book may be summed up in a few words. Everything so far, which we have seen [i.e. all man's purported

---

[6] The same objectives could also be accomplished by an analogous distinction between *A*-acceptance (acceptance as *actually* true) and a probabilistic *L*-acceptance as *very likely* true. But of course there remains the decisive difference between a relatively non-committal 'acceptance as *probably true*' (with some specified degree of likelihood), and 'acceptance as *true provisionally*' (with some specified degree of plausibility). And this difference gives the plausibilistic approach a better fit to the circumstances of the case than the probabilistic.

knowledge of things and their properties, of space, time, and causation, of agents and persons, etc.], has turned out to be appearance. It is that which, taken as it stands, proves inconsistent with itself, and for this reason cannot be true of the real.[7]

What Bradley has in mind is neither the dynamic aspect of our knowledge of purported truths (the prospect of reclassing old or past truths as new or future falsehoods in the light of fuller information) nor its fragmentaristic aspect (as falling short of and presumptively conflicting with the ideal of the real truth as determinable only 'when all the returns are in' since our partial 'truth' contains falsehoods). Rather, what Bradley appears to have in view, *inter alia*, is the far less truistic and commonplace conception that the totality of what we are minded to maintain as knowledge at this point *in medias res* does not (and indeed *cannot*) constitute a totally consistent whole. We are forced to admit the inconsistency of what we vaunt as 'our knowledge' when once the inevitable recognition of our liability to error and the general imperfection of our epistemic control of truth itself comes to constitute—as it must—a part of the body of acknowledged knowledge.

The epistemically crucial point is that the linkage between *rationality* and *consistency* is not as tight as theoretically minded logicians would have us believe. In actual fact people are often not rigidly consistent. To be sure, the psychological study of the phenomenology of this very real circumstance of persons entertaining mutually discordant beliefs with varying degrees of attachment remains in a surprisingly rudimentary state,[8] but this does not gainsay the realities of the situation. And from the normative point of view there is nothing intrinsically improper about a man's conjoint entertainment of inconsistent beliefs with varying degrees of credence: the 'objective facts' may very well be such as to warrant this. As long as our acceptance is taken to remain in the presumptive or plausibilistic mode as making claims to prima facie truth, there is nothing so horrendous about 'falling into an inconsistency'.[9]

The issues that arise here are saliently illustrated in the Preface Paradox and the merit of Bradley's position can be

[7] *Appearance and Reality* (2nd edn., Oxford, 1897; paperback edition with an introduction by Richard Wollheim, 1969), p. 114.

[8] One recent discussion of relevant issues is Leon Festinger, *A Theory of Cognitive Dissonance* (New York, 1957; reissued in Stanford and London, 1962).

[9] This circumstance of logical inconsistency among our beliefs (*P*-beliefs) contrasts importantly and interestingly with those discordances generated when belief-*contravening* suppositions are introduced into the framework of what we accept. For the problems posed by this latter, very different case, see Chap. XI below.

made manifest from the vantage-point of our analysis of this problem. If truth is regarded from an epistemic light as *human* truth—what epistemically imperfect men are prepared to claim (and indeed have rational justification for claiming) to be true —then the domain of such truth will be actually inconsistent, since it cannot but include a recognition of the imperfections of our information, i.e. the knowledge that 'our knowledge' contains falsehoods. Once the totality of 'what is taken to be true' includes the recognition that some of our known 'truths' are actual falsehoods we are precisely in the position of the Preface Paradox so that what the right hand of the text gives us (the specific items we 'take to be true') the left hand of the preface takes away (the 'general principle' recognizing the partial falsity of what 'we take to be true'). The domain of our 'knowledge', as best we can claim to have epistemic control over it, is outright inconsistent. Herein lies the vindication of a Bradleian insistence on the failure of our commonplace knowledge to achieve that mutual consistency which sets reality apart from appearance. Its capacity to function effectively in the midst of this paradoxical situation affords a vivid illustration of the power and usefulness of the line of approach characterizing the coherence analysis of truth.

IX

INDUCTIVE REASONING AND THE JUSTIFICATION OF THE COHERENCE THEORY OF TRUTH

1. *The Coherence Analysis as Ampliative*

THE definitive feature of valid deductive reasoning is that it is *truth-preserving*: the truth of the premisses *guarantees* that of the conclusion, and so the content of the conclusion cannot go beyond the informative range of the premisses. In valid deductive inference no substantially new content, over and above what is logically implicit in the premisses, can (*ex hypothesi*) be provided by the conclusion. By contrast, the essential feature of sound inductive reasoning is generally viewed as being *ampliative* in extending the information at our disposal: the content-output of inductively warranted (presumptively true) conclusions can be greater than the content-input of the given premisses. In an inductive argument the assertive content of the conclusion can go beyond the premisses to state more than that for which the premisses provide a strictly logical (i.e. deductive) warrant.

The coherence analysis of course exhibits exactly this inductive feature, as is readily brought out by an example. Consider the following basic situation:

Given as truths: $p \supset q$

Given as data: p, $p \supset q$, $\sim q$. (Note: the given truth $p \supset q$ must, of course, be included among the data.)

The m.c.s. of the set **S** of all these data are:

$$\mathbf{S}_1 = \{p, p \supset q\} \quad \text{axiomatized by } p \,\&\, q$$
$$\mathbf{S}_2 = \{p, \sim q\} \quad \text{axiomatized by } p \,\&\, \sim q$$
$$\mathbf{S}_3 = \{p \supset q, \sim q\} \text{ axiomatized by } \sim p \,\&\, \sim q.$$

If we eliminate $\mathbf{S}_2$ as incompatible with the given truths, we are left with $\mathbf{S}_1$ and $\mathbf{S}_3$, resulting in a family of truths axiomatized by $(p \,\&\, q) \vee (\sim p \,\&\, \sim q)$ or equivalently $p \equiv q$. In the face of the given data, the coherence analysis has enabled us to 'extend' the realm of the true by precisely $q \supset p$. And so the output of 'resultant truths' goes beyond what is logically contained in the truths among the given premises.

Regarded from this point of view, the coherence analysis is seen to share fundamentally in the characteristic feature of the modes of reasoning classed as *inductive*. The derivation of truths by the coherence route exhibits an essential affinity rather with inductive than with deductive logic. In consequence, it is particularly worth while to examine the workings of the coherence machinery from the vantage-point of the methodology of inductive reasoning.

2. *The Originative Character of the Coherence Analysis and the Critique of Foundationalism*

The essential difference between the coherence theory and any foundationalist approach to truth lies in the fact that on such an approach every discursive (i.e. reasoned) claim to truth requires *truths* as inputs. If a presumptively true result is to be obtained, the premises on which it rests must themselves be true (or assumed to be so). The only strictly originative provider of truths is the intuition which yields the 'immediate' truths of the starter-set. The decisive difference of the coherence theory is its capacity to extract truths discursively from a basis that includes no conceded truths whatsoever—i.e. from data that are merely truth-candidates and not truths. The foundationalist requirement for basic truths is something that the coherence theory developed here—proceeding as it does from a basis of data that need be neither compatible nor true—has been designed to overcome. The motto 'Truth without true foundations' may properly be inscribed on the banner of the coherence theory of truth.

The foundationalist approach in epistemology is deep-rooted throughout the western tradition from Aristotle through Descartes to C. I. Lewis and R. M. Chisholm. It implements an ancient and enduring idea—based ultimately on the Greek concept of science as a Euclidean system—that *truth is a structure that must have foundations*. There must be a starter set of *primitive* (ungrounded, immediate, 'intuitive') truths and, outside this special category, truths can only be established from or grounded upon other truths. We are given an essentially recursive picture of the epistemic process of truth establishment. There is a special set Ξ that is the axiomatic starter-set of truths, and a grounding process $\propto$ for validating certain truth-claims in terms of others. The domain **T** of truths is then to be built up by the following recursion:

1. If $P \in \varXi$, then $P \in \mathbf{T}$

2. If $P_1 \in \mathbf{T}$, $P_2 \in \mathbf{T}$, . . ., $P_n \in \mathbf{T}$, and

   $P_1, P_2, \ldots, P_n \propto Q$ then $Q \in \mathbf{T}$.

There are two obvious difficulties with this conception. The first relates to the axiomatic starter-set of basic protocol truths. This is a point that has been touched upon repeatedly; we need not pursue it further here. The second difficulty relates to the grounding relationship $\propto$. This clearly cannot simply be a matter of *deductive* consequence. For then we should never be able to go beyond the purely logical implications of the basic protocols. And considering the sorts of propositions that have been cast in this role (confined in the empirical area to first-hand reports of perception) confinement within deductive limits would make it impossible to take even the smallest steps towards the truths of science and of everyday life. Accordingly the grounding relationship $\propto$ must be *inductive* in character. This points to the conception of an *inductive* logic, able to provide the means for a rationally warranted extension of the starter-set of truth-claims so as to widen the area of what may be taken as true.

Such a conception of an inductive *Aufbau* of truth on protocol foundations seems to have been the motivating starting-point of Carnap's monumental work in the foundations of inductive logic. And it seems to me that Carnap's persistence in this project, after his having for a time (in the early 1930s) joined forces with Neurath against Schlick's espousal of his own (i.e. Carnap's) earlier defence of protocol truth, is to some extent paradoxical. (Was Carnap put off by the fallibilist turn given to Neurath's position by Popper?) Had Carnap not been repelled by what he doubtless viewed as unsavoury metaphysical associations of the coherence theory, and had he in his later work followed the lead of Neurath rather than Schlick to construct an 'inductive logic' in the coherentist rather than foundationalist mould, something much like the theory developed in this book might well have appeared a generation earlier. For the coherence theory presented here is, in effect, the non-foundationalist's functional equivalent of an 'inductive logic' along Carnapian lines.

The relationship between such an inductivist *Aufbau* of the domain of truth and that of the coherence analysis can be made graphic in diagrammatic form:

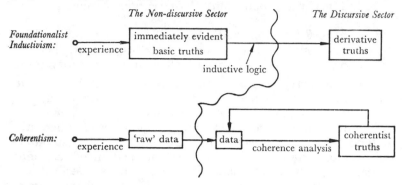

This diagram makes plain the basic similarities between the two approaches, but also brings out their significant differences, which are as follows:

1. On the F/I (foundationalist/inductivist) approach there are two distinct sorts of truths, the immediate and the derivative, while for the coherentist all truth is of a piece.
2. On the F/I approach experience is called upon to provide truths (i.e. immediately evident truths), while for the coherentist it only provides 'raw' data.
3. On the F/I approach all discursive—inductive or deductive—processes require an input of truth if truths are to be an output (which is exactly why an immediate, non-discursive route to truth must be postulated). The coherence analysis differs fundamentally in this regard.
4. On the F/I approach the initial 'givens' are wholly non-discursive and fixed invariants, while on the coherence approach the data represent a *mixture* of experiential and discursive elements. And thus, the non-discursive 'raw' data are, for the coherentist, only one part of the total data; they are by no means fixed and sacred but subject to reappraisal and revision. Accordingly:
5. On the F/I approach nothing whatever that happens at the epistemically later stages of the analysis can possibly affect the starting-point of basic truths, while on the coherentist approach there is a feed-back loop through which the data themselves can be conditioned by the outcome of a co-herence analysis (in other contexts) and their status is subject to re-evaluation in the light of new insights regarding their plausibility.

6. Unlike the F/I approach the coherence analysis does not require a sharp disparity in the treatment of particular and general propositions ('observation statements' and 'laws').

7. On the F/I approach the body of 'evidence' from which the reasoning proceeds must be self-consistent. The coherence analysis has no need for this unrealistic supposition.

Thus a coherentist theory of 'inductive logic' has various substantial epistemological advantages over the standard, probabilistic (Carnapian) version of the discipline.

The diagram also brings to the fore one facet of coherentist method that merits special emphasis. Foundationalist inductivism adopts the basically *linear* systematization of reasoning typical of mathematics: here once a result is obtained one simply passes on to other matters—there is no need ever to return to the reappraisal or resubstantiation of something that has already been 'established'. But with coherentist inductivism the case is quite otherwise, as the feedback loop of the diagram illustrates graphically. Here there is a definite place for a dialectical process of cyclical structure, where one returns repeatedly to an item already 'established'. For the process of confirmation is now more complex, and a thesis might first appear on the status of a mere datum of low plausibility, later as one of higher plausibility, and ultimately even as a validated truth. The reader can readily discern that this repeated reappraisal of claims is in fact closer to the processes of thought one generally employs in the empirical sphere.

3. *Coherence and the Problem of Inductive Method*

What has come to be characterized by some writers as the 'problem of inductive method' may be posed in the following terms:[1]

1. A corpus of factual evidence e is given.
2. A series of hypotheses $h_1, h_2, \ldots, h_n$ is devised, to each of which e significantly lends some credence.
3. It is observed that $\{e, h_1, h_2, \ldots, h_n\}$ forms an inconsistent set of propositions.
4. *Problem*: To find a rationally warranted 'principle of acceptance and rejection' for deciding which of the h_i to accept and which to reject so that $\{e, h_1', h_2', \ldots, h_k'\}$ forms a consistent set, with every h_j' as an *accepted* h_i.

[1] The problem—characterized simply as 'the problem of induction'—is formulated in just these terms in R. Hilpinen, *Rules of Acceptance and Inductive Logic* (Amsterdam, 1968; *Acta Philosophica Fennica*, fasc. 22), pp. 39–49.

Approaching the issue of the method of inductive reasoning in these terms of a search for a mechanism of rational acceptance, it becomes clear that the coherence machinery is naturally suited for the resolution of questions of essentially this type. To have a concrete setting for the elaboration of the relevant ideas, consider the following example:

Evidence (e): (1) A certain urn contains exactly five balls, each of them either black or white.

(2) In two random drawings with replacement a white ball has been drawn each time.

Hypotheses (h_i, with $1 \leqslant i \leqslant 5$): The urn contains exactly i white balls.

In approaching the problem of hypothesis-acceptance through the mechanism of the coherence analysis, we begin by forming the set of 'truth-candidates' containing both the evidence and the various competing hypotheses:

$$\mathbf{S} = \{e, h_1, h_2, h_3, h_4, h_5\}.$$

In the present context the 'data' will of course include propositions that are not *presumed* to be true but are mere *candidates* for truth. The only *e*-containing m.c.s. of this (inconsistent) set will be:

$$\mathbf{S}_1 = \{e, h_1\}$$
$$\mathbf{S}_2 = \{e, h_2\}$$
$$\mathbf{S}_3 = \{e, h_3\}$$
$$\mathbf{S}_4 = \{e, h_4\}$$
$$\mathbf{S}_5 = \{e, h_5\}.$$

Let us assign plausibility values to the **S**-elements as follows:

1. *e* has plausibility 1
2. each h_i has a *plausibility* value determined by its conditional *probability* with respect to *e*, as per the following scheme:

Probability value (x)	Plausibility
$0.75 \leqslant x \leqslant 1$	2
$0.5 \leqslant x < 0.75$	3
$0.25 \leqslant x < 0.5$	4
$0 \leqslant x < 0.25$	5

We accordingly arrive at the following situation:

Hypothesis (h_i)	Probability ($Pr(h_i/e)$	Plausibility
h_1	$\frac{1}{55} = 0{\cdot}02$	5
h_2	$\frac{4}{55} = 0{\cdot}07$	5
h_3	$\frac{9}{55} = 0{\cdot}16$	5
h_4	$\frac{16}{55} = 0{\cdot}29$	4
h_5	$\frac{25}{55} = 0{\cdot}46$	4

The plausibilities for the several m.c.s. may now be tabulated:

m.c.s.	Plausibilities	Maximum	Average
S_1	(1, 5)	5	3
S_2	(1, 5)	5	3
S_3	(1, 5)	5	3
S_4	(1, 4)	4	2·5
S_5	(1, 4)	4	2·5

On this basis, given a probabilistic preferential criterion appropriate to the case, the $\mathscr{P}$-consequences of **S** would presumably be axiomatized by e & $(h_4 \vee h_5)$. Accordingly we should (subject to this probabilistic criterion) not 'accept' any one of the h_i individually, but should take 'the presumptive truth of the matter' to be given by the essentially disjunctive result: the urn contains four-or-five white balls. (Note, however, that adoption of this presently envisaged probabilistic preferential criterion $\mathscr{P}$ hinges upon our willingness to reject low-probability alternatives, and so requires us to construe *presumptive* truth as *probable* truth.[2])

The probabilistic procedure of the preceding analysis may seem problematic. If, as in the example, we want to apply a Baysian inversion of the probabilities—and accordingly consider the conditional probabilities $Pr(h_i/e)$ as somehow genuine likelihoods for the h_i—we are, in effect, committed to regarding e as a 'given truth'.[3] But does this not call for a prior application of a different standard of truth? Not really. As long as e is *consistent* (as it must be) and classified as *substantially more plausible* than the h_i (as it must also be), there is adequate justification for treating e as 'true for the purposes of the problem'. Just this consideration—that e should 'emerge as true'—motivated our earlier decision to accord e a high plausibility ranking.

---

[2] This key point will come up again in Section 7 below.

[3] And clearly it would not do to confine ourselves to the absolute, unconditionalized, *a priori* probability of the h_i. For then we should be proceeding by the distinctly non-inductive route of treating the evidence as irrelevant.

An alternative approach to the preceding example would be to proceed in terms of the conception of 'degrees of truth' as explicated in Appendix H. By use of probabilistic information regarding the h_i we should rank the m.c.s. as follows:

$$S_5 > S_4 > S_3 > S_2 > S_1.$$

One accordingly obtains the following sequence of the results of a coherence analysis—ordered by increasing 'degrees of truth'.

(1) e & (h_5) [there are 5 white balls]

(2) e & $(h_5 \lor h_4)$ [there are 4-or-5 white balls]

(3) e & $(h_5 \lor h_4 \lor h_3)$ [there are 3-or-4-or-5 white balls]

(4) e & $(h_5 \lor h_4 \lor h_3 \lor h_2)$ [there are 2-or-3-or-4-or-5 white balls]

(5) e & $(h_5 \lor h_4 \lor h_3 \lor h_2 \lor h_1)$ [there are 1-or-2-or-3-or-4-or-5 white balls].

How far we should insist on going down this list to reach an increasingly secure but decreasingly informative conclusion would, of course, depend upon a cost-benefit analysis as to how high a price in decreased assurance we are willing to pay for the benefit of increased definiteness. For as is usual in these cases the higher the 'degree of truth' of a result the less specific its assertive content. (If we were to determine an 'information-index' for each result as the product

informativeness of the result × probability of the result R

measuring informativeness by $1 - [R\text{'s } a \text{ priori probability}]$, we should obtain the following tabulation of outcomes:

Result No.	Informativeness	Probability	Information Index
(1)	$1 - \frac{1}{5} = 0.80$	0·55	0·44
(2)	$1 - \frac{2}{5} = 0.60$	0·75	0·45
(3)	$1 - \frac{3}{5} = 0.40$	0·91	0·36
(4)	$1 - \frac{4}{5} = 0.20$	0·98	0·20
(5)	$1 - 1 = 0.00$	1·00	0

This result, as above, suggests that e & $(h_4 \lor h_5)$ once again has a claim to being considered an optimal outcome.)

4. *Coherence and 'Duhem's Thesis'*

The example in the preceding section has been misleading in one crucial respect: the various m.c.s. of the inconsistent sets of data that have arisen contain only one single hypothesis. This envisages the situation of the 'crucial experiment' where the factual evidence *e* is so contrived as to effect a decisive ruling for one theory in contrast with all others. Many methodologists of science nowadays follow the lead of the eminent French historian and philosopher of science Pierre Duhem (1861–1916) in viewing this situation as not only atypical in science, but at bottom impossible. Hypotheses and theories—it is quite rightly argued —never enter into observational situations one at a time, but always in clustered groups. Thus when an incoherence develops it cannot be attributed to any one specific hypothesis, but must be located somewhere in the theoretical cluster. Duhem —followed among contemporaries by Adolf Grünbaum and W. V. O. Quine—insists that observation places theories and hypotheses at risk collectively as a system, never individually.[4] Hence when a conflict occurs between theory and data, this does not simply call for the substitution of one hypothesis for another, but demands a systematic revision of the whole structure of a body of theory that involves many hypotheses. Duhem puts the issue as follows:

> In sum, the physicist can never subject an isolated hypothesis to experimental test, but only a whole group of hypotheses; when the experiment is in disagreement with his predictions, what he learns is that at least one of the hypotheses constituting this group is unacceptable and ought to be modified; but the experiment does not designate which one should be changed. . . . Physics is not a machine which lets itself be taken apart; we cannot try each piece in isolation, and in order to adjust it, wait until its solidity has been carefully checked; physical science is a system that must be taken as a whole; it is an organism in which one part cannot be made to function without the parts that are most remote from it being called into play, some more so than others, but all to some degree. If something goes wrong, if some discomfort is felt in the functioning of the organism, the physicist will have to ferret out through its effect on the entire system which organ needs to be remedied or modified without the possibility of isolating this organ and examining it apart.[5]

In short, no factual hypothesis can be conclusively falsified: any

---

[4] For the definitive statement of Quine's position see his essay 'Two Dogmas of Empiricism', reprinted in *From a Logical Point of View* (2nd edn., Cambridge, Mass., 1961). Quine holds that 'Any statement can be held true come what may, if we make drastic enough adjustments elsewhere in the system'. For a recent exposition of A. Grünbaum's more qualified endorsement of a Duhemian point of view see his essay 'Can We Ascertain the Falsity of a Scientific Hypothesis?' in M. Mandelbaum (ed.), *Observation and Theory in Science* (Baltimore, Md., 1971).

[5] 'Physical Theory and Experiment', *Readings in the Philosophy of Science*, edited by H. Feigl and M. Brodbeck (New York, 1953), pp. 240–1. For a detailed exposition of Duhem's views see his classic work, *The Aims and Structure of Physical Theory*, r.by H. Q. Zilch (London, 1940).

scientific hypothesis can be held true in the face of apparently disconfirming evidence as long as we are prepared to make appropriate adjustments at other places in the over-all structure of our factual commitments.

Duhem encapsulated this view in the dictum that 'A "crucial experiment" is impossible in physics.'

The situation may be schematized by an illustrative example:

Old observational data: e = observed evidence, o = observed findings

New observational data: e' = observed evidence, o' = observed findings where e' = e+something; $o' = o$ +something.

Hypotheses comprising the theory at issue: $h_1, h_2, \ldots, h_n$. (Note: these are not competing alternatives but function in cooperative conjunction.)

Old situation as to deductive interrelationships:

$e, h_1, h_2, \ldots, h_n \vdash o$ (all the h_i are assumed necessary to the deduction).

New situation as to deductive interrelationships:

$e', h_1, h_2, \ldots, h_n \vdash \sim o'$ (all the h_i are assumed necessary to the deduction).

Accordingly the theoretically *predicted* outcome ($\sim o'$) now conflicts with the actually *observed* outcome (o').

Note here that the new epistemic situation confronts us with the inconsistent totality of data

$$S = \{e, e', h_1, h_2, \ldots, h_n, o, o'\}.$$

These data are inconsistent because the actual finding o' disagrees with what, given e', is to be expected on the basis of the hypotheses h_1–h_n. Given that the plausibilities of the situation are such that we must retain the observational data e' and o' (and e and o), it is clear that the 'new situation' requires us to drop one or more of the h_i, in general without in any way forcing us to alter any particular one of these hypotheses.

Of course, if the mechanisms for a plausibility analysis of the h_i were on hand, then one might well obtain the more specific guidance that is needed. In the absence of such machinery it will not be possible to tell which particular hypothesis needs to be revised in the face of the discovery of a 'discordant fact'. But if suitable assessments of plausibility are given, then a specific hypothesis may well be identifiable as the particular place at which the theory needs revision. A much oversimplified example will illustrate the processes at work:

Old observational data: e, o.
New observational data: e', o'.
Hypotheses: h_1, h_2, h_3.
Deductive relationships d_1: $e \& h_1 \& h_2 \& h_3 \vdash o$.
d_2: $e' \& h_1 \& h_2 \& h_3 \vdash {\sim}o'$.

Initial assessment of plausibilities:

Observational data and deductive relationships: all 1.
Hypotheses:
$$|h_1| = 2$$
$$|h_2| = 3$$
$$|h_3| = 2.$$

The totality of data is:

$$\{e, e', o, o', h_1, h_2, h_3, d_1, d_2\}.$$

The m.c.s. containing all 1-plausible propositions are:

$$\mathbf{S}_1 \{e, e', o, o', d_1, d_2\} \cup \{h_1, h_2\}$$
$$\mathbf{S}_2 \{e, e', o, o', d_1, d_2\} \cup \{h_1, h_3\}$$
$$\mathbf{S}_3 \{e, e', o, o', d_1, d_2\} \cup \{h_2, h_3\}.$$

According to this analysis, the preferred set is $\mathbf{S}_2$, and ${\sim}h_2$ is now a $\mathscr{P}$-consequence. As might have been expected from the plausibility assignments, h_2 has been identified as the 'trouble maker' that needs to be amended.

On the other hand, if the plausibility assignment differs from the preceding only in that $|h_1| = 3$, $|h_2| = 2$, $|h_3| = 3$, then *both* $\mathbf{S}_1$ and $\mathbf{S}_3$ are preferred. The $\mathscr{P}$-consequences of $\mathbf{S}$ thus include $h_2 \& (h_1 \lor h_3) \& {\sim}(h_1 \& h_3)$. While we can count on retaining h_2, the difficulty has now become ramified over the hypotheses h_1 and h_3 in such a way that while *some* fundamental revision is necessary, it is required in a place we are unable to locate and identify in any specific way.

As this example shows, the coherence analysis can provide a theoretical articulation and substantiation of the nature and implications of Duhem's thesis of the essential ambiguity of a discordant observational finding in the case of a complex confluence of hypotheses. In short, close attention to Duhem's thesis can provide a strong endorsement of the coherence approach. W. V. O. Quine puts the matter as follows:

The notion lingers [among empiricists] that to each statement, or each synthetic statement, there is associated a unique range of possible sensory events such that the occurrence of any one of them would add to the likelihood of truth of the statement, and that there is associated also another unique range of possible sensory events whose occurrence would detract from that likelihood. . . .

The dogma of reductionism survives in the supposition that each statement, taken in isolation from its fellows, can admit of confirmation or infirmation at all. My countersuggestion . . . is that our statements about the external world face the tribunal of sense experience not individually but only as a corporate body.[6]

The thesis that the correspondence concept of the confirmation of statements about the world through an item by item comparison with fact must be replaced by a somehow *systematic* assessment that verifies such statements 'not individually but only as a corporate body' is, of course, one of the key concepts of the traditional coherence theory.[7]

5. *Rival Hypotheses as 'Data'*

The workings of the coherence methodology in the context of a discordant group of rival hypotheses warrants closer scrutiny. Let us begin with the simplest case of just two alternative hypotheses, both explaining the same body of observations. The situation that arises here may be schematized in the following example:

Hypotheses: h_1, h_2; these are to be rival in that $\sim(h_1 \,\&\, h_2)$

Observational findings: o.

Initial Conditions: i_1, i_2.

---

[6] *From a Logical Point of View* (Cambridge, Mass., 1953), pp. 40–1. Quine's position is designed to counter the item-confirmationism of many writers on scientific method, a view clearly articulated in the following passage by H. Feigl: 'It is precisely for the sake of systematic examination through empirical testing that we must unravel the knowledge claims of a theory into a maximal number of independently confirmable postulates. . . . A view that maintains that the whole body of a scientific theory (if not of all science) confronts experience and that modifications may be required in *any* part of the system if it does not 'fit',—such a view obscures dangerously what is of the greatest importance for the progress of science: the successive testing and securing of parts of science—at least in the sense of an approximation. Naturally, no part can be considered as established with finality—but this insight which impresses the pure logician should not blind him to the recognition of the methods of successive confirmation' ('Conformability and Confirmation', in P. Wiener (ed.), *Readings in Philosophy of Science* (New York, 1953), p. 528). The Quinean position rejects the quest for 'independently confirmable postulates' as unworkable and Quixotic.

[7] While the coherentist agrees with Quine in this emphasis upon the systematic aspect, they differ in accounting for its root source. For Quine sees this to lie in the fact 'that in general the truth of statements does obviously depend both upon language and upon extralinguistic fact' (op. cit., p. 43)—so that the truth of a given statement can always be salvaged in the face of recalcitrant fact by linguistic manipulation. The coherentist, on the other hand, sees the systematic aspects of truth-determination to reside not so much in the interrelation of fact with language, but within the factual area itself, and specifically in the logico-epistemological relationships among the truth-candidates.

It is supposed that we have the (for the present incontestible) deductive relationships:

$$h_1 \mathrel{\&} i_1 \vdash o$$
$$h_2 \mathrel{\&} i_2 \vdash o$$
$$h_1 \vdash \sim h_2.$$

We begin, as usual, with the initial (inconsistent) set of all the data

$$S = \{h_1, h_2, o, i_1, i_2\}.$$

(Given the ordinary use of the term, it is virtually a contradiction in terms to speak of a *hypothesis* as a *datum*, but no anomaly is involved on our technical conception of data.) Here there will be just two m.c.s.:

S_1 consisting of h_1 plus all the rest save h_2

S_2 consisting of h_2 plus all the rest save h_1.

Now as regards preferability, just three possibilities exist:

(1) S_1 is preferred over S_2
(2) S_2 is preferred over S_1
(3) Neither S_1 nor S_2 is preferred over the other.

These will lead to the following results:

(1) yields h_1
(2) yields h_2
(3) yields $h_1 \vee h_2$.

The first two results are not surprising, the presence/absence of h_1 and h_2 being the only point of difference between S_1 and S_2. Result (3) is, however, significant. It means that $h_1 \vee h_2$ must obtain *in any case*. We began with the fact that h_1 and h_2 are mutually *exclusive*, but the coherence methodology now forces us to accept them as mutually *exhaustive*. This reflects a fundamental aspect of the way the coherence approach treats its 'data': the determination to accept as much as we consistently can. The classification of a proposition as a datum carries a substantial truth-oriented commitment, a commitment to take as true in so far as counterindications permit. The concept of datahood carries a firm alethic presumption. In so far as a 'hypothesis' can be a mere conjecture without having a firm epistemological basis (akin to that of the 'data of perception'), we can treat hypotheses as data only at the expense of comprehensiveness (i.e. exhaustiveness). It is thus crucial in these cases of applying the coherence analysis to rival hypotheses—all of which are genuinely 'in the running'—that the data be complete in that the hypotheses considered must exhaust the whole spectrum of the 'real possibilities'. Otherwise a coherence analysis of 'the truth' will yield a result that is more definite than the postulated epistemic situation warrants. In treating only certain rival hypotheses as the data input for the coherence process, we, in effect, assume the epistemic stance of regarding these as the only *genuine* possibilities. When this stance is not warranted, the procedure itself is inappropriate. It is readily seen from this standpoint that a Feyerabendian insistence upon a diversified search for (actually warranted) hypotheses in science is validated on a coherence approach in terms of its essential stress on the completeness (i.e. external maximality) of the data.[8]

Of course, we need only go to the length of canvassing enough data to exhaust 'the real possibilities'. In the special case of utter ignorance this, alas, includes all the logically possible alternatives: having no specific indication of where the truth lies, we only know it lies *somewhere* in the group. If we are going to use an utterly non-eliminative, scatter-shot approach, then we have to make sure of canvassing all the possibilities. But when the data *qua* set of data can be taken to have some cognitive bite (so that we are entitled on this basis to eliminate certain logically possible alternatives as not really feasible—as not being *genuinely* possible), then there is no need for the data to exhaust the whole spectrum of the logically possible.

In line with these considerations one aspect of the application of the coherence machinery to hypotheses must be re-emphasized. The 'data' of the problem will not include just a mass of conjectural 'hypotheses' alone, but also the various observational 'facts' of the matter. The coherence at issue is thus not just a matter of relations among various free-floating hypothetical theses, but involves an anchoring to the *terra firma* of more solidly based considerations. This presence of the (relatively) factual along with the (relatively) hypothetical—and on a different footing reflected by differential plausibility rankings —affords the whole procedure its qualifications to provide a warrant for claims of truth.

One qualifying amendment must be added. The preceding sections have spoken as if the difference between theoretical hypotheses and observational evidence-statements were somehow

---

[8] Such inclusiveness must, to be sure, be accompanied by careful attention to plausibility considerations—a point to which Feyerabend's epistemology of science does not give its due. For his position see especially Paul K. Feyerabend, 'Problems of Empiricism' in R. G. Colodny (ed.), *Beyond the Edge of Certainty* (Englewood Cliffs, N.J., 1965), pp. 145–260.

fixed, determinate, and absolute. This is misleading. Many recent philosophers of science have rightly questioned the absoluteness of this distinction, arguing that factual statements —however 'observational'—always have a theoretical element. Our discussion has no need to quarrel with this very sound contention. Its purposes are wholly served by conceding no more than that there is a distinction between 'relatively factual' and 'relatively hypothetical' which can be made operative within the context-relative setting of particular problem-situations.

6. *Inductive Support via a Coherence Analysis*

To see how the coherence analysis of a body of data can provide inductive support for a conclusion, let us consider the question of a 'forced choice' between P and $\sim P$ in the face of the (potentially inconsistent) evidential data **S** and with respect to a given preferential criterion $\mathscr{P}$. Such a forced choice is not as artificial as it might on first view seem to be: in cases of very incomplete information we might be in substantial doubt as to whether P or $\sim P$ obtains and so would 'go for safety' by treating both alternatives as truth-candidates for a coherence analysis. Assuming that we must make such a choice, ought we to favour P or $\sim P$? Adopting the approach of the preceding section we should use the coherence analysis as a means for answering this question by determining whether the set $\mathbf{S}' = \mathbf{S} \cup \{P, \sim P\}$ yields P or $\sim P$ as a $\mathscr{P}$-consequence. It is thus a natural step to offer the definition:

> The propositional set **S** is such that it $\mathscr{P}$-*favours* P
> (over $\sim P$) iff $\mathbf{S} \cup \{P, \sim P\} \vdash_{\mathscr{P}} P$.

Accordingly, a set **S** $\mathscr{P}$-favours P iff *all* the $\mathscr{P}$-preferred m.c.s. of $\mathbf{S} \cup \{P, \sim P\}$ entail P, and so:

> The propositional set **S** is such that it $\mathscr{P}$-favours P iff every $\mathscr{P}$-preferred m.c.s. of $\mathbf{S} \cup \{P, \sim P\}$ is P-entailing (and so P-containing).

For the sake of illustration, let us begin with the *consistent* set $\mathbf{S} = \{p \supset r, q \supset \sim r, q\}$ and let the proposition *sub judice* be $p \& q$, so that by adding this proposition and its negation to **S** we obtain $\qquad \mathbf{S}' = \{p \supset r, q \supset \sim r, q, p \& q, \sim(p \& q)\}$.

The m.c.s. of $\mathbf{S}'$ are:

$\qquad \mathbf{S}'_1 = \{p \& q, q \supset \sim r, q\}$
$\qquad\qquad$ which is axiomatized by $p \& q \& \sim r$

$S'_2 = \{p \ \& \ q, p \supset r, q\}$
which is axiomatized by $p \ \& \ q \ \& \ r$

$S'_3 = \{\sim(p \ \& \ q), p \supset r, q \supset \sim r, q\}$
which is axiomatized by $\sim p \ \& \ q \ \& \ \sim r$.

As long as $\mathscr{P}$ is such that S'_3 is effectively eliminated, then S will $\mathscr{P}$-favour $p \ \& \ q$. On the other hand, if S'_3 were alone preferred, then S would $\mathscr{P}$-favour $\sim(p \ \& \ q)$.

Again, consider the set $S = \{q, q \supset r, r \supset s, \sim s \ \& \ \sim p\}$. Letting r be the proposition *sub judice*, we may form

$$S' = S \cup \{r, \sim r\} = \{q, q \supset r, r \supset s, \sim s \ \& \ \sim p, r, \sim r\}.$$

The m.c.s. of S' are:

$S'_1 = \{r, q, q \supset r, r \supset s\}$
axiomatized by $q \ \& \ r \ \& \ s$

$S'_2 = \{r, q, q \supset r, \sim s \ \& \ \sim p\}$
axiomatized by $\sim p \ \& \ q \ \& \ r \ \& \ \sim s$

$S'_3 = \{\sim r, q, r \supset s, \sim s \ \& \ \sim p\}$
axiomatized by $\sim p \ \& \ q \ \& \ \sim r \ \& \ \sim s$

$S'_4 = \{\sim r, q \supset r, r \supset s, \sim s \ \& \ \sim p\}$
axiomatized by $\sim p \ \& \ \sim q \ \& \ \sim r \ \& \ \sim s$.

As long as we avoid evaluating S'_3 and S'_4 as preferred (say because of a disinclination to accept anything incompatible with $r \lor s$), then S will $\mathscr{P}$-favour $q \ \& \ r$.

A cognate approach replaces the all or nothing procedure of 'favouring' by one admitting of degrees. This approach is inherent in the definition:

> The propositional set S is such that it $\mathscr{P}$-*inclines to P* if more of the $\mathscr{P}$-preferred m.c.s. of $S \cup \{P, \sim P\}$ are compatible with P than with $\sim P$.

Consider again the set S' of the example just given whose m.c.s. are enumerated above. If S'_1 alone is eliminated by $\mathscr{P}$, then S will $\mathscr{P}$-incline to $\sim r$, though it will not go so far as to $\mathscr{P}$-favour $\sim r$.

It is useful to view this approach in terms of concepts discussed in the last chapter. We there introduced the idea that the 'degree of truth' (in one sense) of a proposition P relative to a set of data S is to be measured by:

$d'(P) =$ the proportion of m.c.s. of S with which P
is compatible.

Given this notion, we see that a set's *inclination* to a proposition (in the present sense) is bound up wtih this proposition's having a greater *degree of truth* with respect to this set than does its negation. From this standpoint, degrees of truth reappear in the form of a possible basis for the assessment of inductive support. (For this theme of degrees of truth see pp. 197–200 above, as well as Appendix H.)

7. *The Lottery Paradox*

One of the central issues of inductive logic is posed by the 'Lottery Paradox'. This paradox is the immediate result of a decision-policy for acceptance that is based upon a probabilistic threshold value. Thus let us suppose the threshold level to be 0·80, and consider the following series of statements:

> This (fair and normal) die will not come up 1 when tossed
>
> This (fair and normal) die will not come up 2 when tossed
>
> This (fair and normal) die will not come up 3 when tossed
>
> This (fair and normal) die will not come up 4 when tossed
>
> This (fair and normal) die will not come up 5 when tossed
>
> This (fair and normal) die will not come up 6 when tossed.

According to the specified standard, each and every one of these six statements must be accepted as true. Yet their conjunction results in a patent absurdity.[9] Moreover, the fact that the threshold was set as low as 0·80 instead of 0·90 or 0·9999 is wholly immaterial. To recreate the same problem with respect to a higher threshold we need simply assume a lottery wheel having enough (equal) divisions to exhaust the spectrum of possibilities with individual alternatives of sufficiently small probability. Then the probability that each specific result will *not* obtain is less than 1 minus the threshold value, and so can be brought as close to 1 as we please. Accordingly we should, by accepting each of these claims, be driven to the impossible conclusion that there is no result whatsoever.

This, then, is the Lottery Paradox.[10] It decisively rules out a

---

[9] The derivation of the paradox presupposes that 'acceptance' is acceptance *as true*, and that truths obey the standard conditions of mutual consistency, conjunction (i.e. that a conjunction of truths be a truth), and of closure (i.e. that the logical consequences of 2 truths be true).

[10] The lottery paradox was originally formulated by H. K. Kyburg, Jr., *Probability and the Logic of Rational Relief* (Middletown, Conn., 1961). For an analysis of its wider implications for inductive logic see R. Hilpinen, *Rules of Acceptances and Inductive Logic* (Amsterdam, 1968; *Acta Philosophica Fennica*, fasc. 22), pp. 39–49.

propositional acceptance rule that is based upon a probabilistic threshold.[11] Indeed, it is sometimes construed as ruling out the prospect of any rational acceptance procedure whatever—and sometimes as showing that acceptance strangely lacks the feature of being 'logically closed' in that one can be warranted in accepting both P and Q but not in accepting their conjunction P & Q.[12] Such doctrines re-enforce considerations of the sort which (already prior to any explicit formulation of the lottery paradox) had inclined Rudolf Carnap and his school to exile categorical acceptance processes from the sphere of inductive epistemology.[13] Carnap argues that the acceptance of hypotheses conflicts with the principle that one should always act so as to maximize one's expected utility. As long as the acceptance standard can rule favourably in the face of any possibility— however remote—of being wrong, it will always be possible to contrive a situation in which the prospect of maximizing expected utility will be foregone.[14] At any rate, the lottery paradox decisively shows that probability cannot of itself guide acceptance, since acceptance is conjunctive and probability is not. One must either give up an acceptance-oriented view of rational inquiry in science or else abandon the probabilistic theory of inductive reasoning.

The coherence analysis of truth is in fact well qualified as a means to treat the difficulties of rational acceptance procedures posed by the lottery paradox. Thus consider the following family of statements, each a truth or a 'likely truth':

a_0: When tossed, the die must come up with one of the series 1, 2, . . ., 6.

a_i: The die will not come up i when tossed ($i = 1, 2, . . ., 6$).

[11] Cf. also I. Levi, *Gambling With Truth* (New York, 1967), chs. II and VI.

[12] See H. K. Kyburg, Jr., 'The Rule of Detachment in Inductive Logic', in I. Lakatos (ed.), *The Problem of Inductive Logic* (Amsterdam, 1968), pp. 98–119 (see especially pp. 118–19). On such a view the real question becomes why one's epistemic stance towards the propositions in view should merit the label of 'acceptance'; and *idem*, 'Conjunctivitis' in M. Swain (ed.), *Induction, Acceptance, and Rational Belief* (Dordrecht, 1970), and also I. Levi, *Gambling With Truth* (New York, 1967), chs. II and IV. This entire problem-area is surveyed in R. Hilpinen (op. cit.).

[13] See R. Carnap, *Logical Foundations of Probability* (Chicago, Ill., 1950; 2nd edn., 1960), sect. 50, and P. A. Schilpp (ed.), *The Philosophy of Rudolf Carnap* (La Salle, Ill., 1963), pp. 972–3. Carnap's position is followed by R. Jeffrey. See his 'Valuation and Acceptance of Scientific Hypotheses', *Philosophy of Science*, 23 (1956), 237–46.

[14] However, one way of blunting the impact of this argument is to observe that *at a prespecified given level of risk* the acceptance of hypotheses can still be justified. This, of course, relativizes acceptance to specific levels of risk, and so to the context of the risk-situations at issue, but this does not of itself seem an untoward or un-acceptable result. Moreover, there remains the issue of the proper stance to take under the hypothesis that all *non-cognitive* risks (i.e. practical risks distinct from the theoretical risk of 'falling into error') are to be discounted altogether.

From the standpoint of the coherence analysis, we are now confronted with the following (inconsistent) set of data:

$$S = \{a_0, a_1, a_2, \ldots, a_6\}.$$

There will be seven m.c.s.:

$$S_0 = S - \{a_0\}$$
$$S_i = S - \{a_i\} \quad i = 1, 2, \ldots, 6.$$

Note that the axiom for S_i ($i = 1, 2, \ldots, 6$) is simply: 'The die will come up i when tossed.' The probabilities involved are:

$$\Pr(S_0) = 0$$
$$\Pr(S_1) = \Pr(S_2) = \ldots = \Pr(S_6) = \tfrac{1}{6}.$$

We can now proceed on what is a perfectly genuine probabilistic acceptance rule, but one not for eliminations among the propositions (a_i) at issue, but for eliminating m.c.s. (S_i). Adopting a probabilistic basis for S_i-preference (with a cut-off of, say, 0·10) we see that we can only eliminate S_0, and retain S_1-S_6. Accordingly, the truths are axiomatized by the quite innocuous (if highly uninformative): 'The die will come up 1 or 2 or . . . or 6.'

The coherence approach thus presents a way of reconciling a 'probabilistic acceptance rule' (for the m.c.s.) with the requirements of the logic of the case. A contradiction results when we apply a probabilistic acceptance rule for propositions applied to the a_i directly. For here the accepted results are to be treated *conjunctively*, and to 'accept all' the possibilities in conjunction is to accept a contradiction. But no difficulty arises when we apply a probabilistic acceptance rule for the m.c.s., i.e. one that is applied to the S_i. For here, accepted results are to be treated *disjunctively*, and to 'accept all' the possibilities in disjunction is to accept a harmless inevitability. Within the coherence framework a 'probabilistic rule of acceptance'—but now of m.c.s. and not of propositions—is perfectly viable and in no way paradoxical.

The lottery paradox does, however, have one important lesson for the coherence analysis itself. It will not in general do to adopt a probabilistic standard of truth-candidacy (datahood), that is, it will not do unless there are 'extraneous' reasons for eliminating the low probability cases. Thus let it be supposed that there are ten mutually exclusive and exhaustive alternatives, a_1-a_{10}, with probabilities as follows:

$$\Pr(a_1) = 0·2 - \epsilon$$
$$\Pr(a_2) = \Pr(a_3) = \ldots = \Pr(a_9) = 0·1$$
$$\Pr(a_{10}) = \epsilon \text{ (ϵ being a small quantity, significantly} < 0·1).$$

Let us now form the set **S** of data, assuming that we eliminate a_{10} on probabilistic grounds: $\mathbf{S} = \{a_1, a_2, \ldots, a_9\}$. In the absence of any preferential eliminations, the coherence analysis will now see the truths relative to **S** axiomatized by $a_1 \vee a_2 \vee \ldots \vee a_9$. Thus we shall have it as a truth that $\sim a_{10}$. But a_{10}, although unlikely, is not to be ruled out in this way: it is—or could well be counted as—a *candidate* for truth, albeit an unpromising one. The lesson of the lottery paradox for the coherence analysis of truth is thus both that a probabilistic threshold cannot be adopted for acceptance *as a truth*, and that it cannot serve automatically for acceptance *as a datum* (truth-candidate), except in circumstances where there is warrant for neglecting cases of low probability. Even an improbable alternative can be accepted as a *candidate* for truth, and have its candidacy recognized in the mechanisms of the coherence analysis.[15]

8. *Coherence and the Justification of Induction*

Coherence theorists and their allies have made large claims for their doctrine in relation to the 'Humean problem' of the justification of induction:

> The coherence principle provides the only rational justification for induction. The newer school of logicians admit that they have not succeeded in providing such a justification. . . . But, if we assume that in any given case the hypothesis which comes nearest to making experience a coherent system is the one which ought to be accepted, then we have a principle by which we may easily justify the inductive process in general and any subordinate principles which it may require. We have arrived at a single principle again and can dispense with a plurality of unjustified assumptions. For obviously any principle really necessary for induction must be *ipso facto* one without which it would be impossible to make any coherent system of our experience, and all such assumptions could therefore be deduced from the principle of coherence alone.[16]

It is a matter of obvious importance to arrive at a just assessment of the merits of these large claims.

A paradigm inductive argument proceeds by noting first that all the objects (of a certain type) observed to date, $a_1, a_2, \ldots, a_n$, have a certain (qualitative) property F and then maintaining on this ground that the next object a_{n+1} will also have F. The argument thus in effect moves from the premises $F(a_1), F(a_2), \ldots, F(a_n)$ to the (inductive) conclusion $F(a_{n+1})$.

---

[15] It is, however, clear that a probabilistic threshold for acceptance *can* be adopted routinely when the issue is one not of truth as such, but of *probable* truth. Compare the example of Section 3 above.

[16] A. C. Ewing, *Idealism: A Critical Survey* (London, 1934), pp. 247–8.

The central problem of 'the justification of induction' is to exhibit a rational warrant for this inferential procedure and its cognates. We are to grapple with Hume's puzzle: what could possibly assure that the future instance (a_{n+1}) will be like the past ones $(a_1, a_2, \ldots, a_n)$? Given that $F(a_1), F(a_2), \ldots, F(a_n)$, what justifies the conclusion $F(a_{n+1})$ rather than its contradictory $\sim F(a_{n+1})$?

In the context of our present concerns it is tempting to think of answering such a question in terms of a coherence analysis. And this can indeed be done—along lines now to be described.

Let it be that the evidential base $F(a_1), F(a_2), \ldots, F(a_n)$ is given and that we are to judge in this context between the truth-candidates $F(a_{n+1}), \sim F(a_{n+1})$. We thus begin with the set of data:

$$\mathbf{S} = \{F(a_1), F(a_2), \ldots, F(a_n), F(a_{n+1}), \sim F(a_{n+1})\}.$$

Here there will be but two m.c.s.

$$\mathbf{S}_1 = \{F(a_1), F(a_2), \ldots, F(a_n), F(a_{n+1})\}$$
$$\mathbf{S}_2 = \{F(a_1), F(a_2), \ldots, F(a_n), \sim F(a_{n+1})\}.$$

To justify deriving $F(a_{n+1})$ from our data—rather than $\sim F(a_{n+1})$ —comes down to showing that $\mathbf{S}_1$ is to be preferred over $\mathbf{S}_2$ by a suitable criterion of preference $\mathscr{P}$. Now this comes down to showing that $F(a_{n+1})$ is more plausible than $\sim F(a_{n+1})$.

The given evidence $F(a_1), F(a_2), \ldots, F(a_n)$ establishes a certain logical pattern: its items answer to the generic form $F(x)$. Plainly, from this standpoint $F(a_{n+1})$ appears as pattern-concordant while $\sim F(a_{n+1})$ is pattern-discordant. Let us suppose a plausibility-delimiting rule to the following effect:

> When the initial evidence exhibits a marked logical pattern, then pattern-concordant statements are—*ceteris paribus*—to be evaluated as more plausible than pattern-discordant ones.

Given such a rule—and a very natural rule it is—our inference of the pattern-conforming result $F(a_{n+1})$ obtains a rational warrant.

A further example may be helpful. Consider yet another paradigm of inductive reasoning, the 'argument by analogy':

> We have observed that the properties F and G have been conjoined in the case of objects $a_1, a_2, \ldots, a_n$. We now observe further that a_{n+1} has F. Hence we infer 'by analogy' that a_{n+1} will also have G. Thus we move from the premises $F(a_1)$ & $G(a_1), F(a_2)$ & $G(a_2), \ldots, F(a_n)$ & $G(a_n), F(a_{n+1})$ to the conclusion: $G(a_{n+1})$.

Again, contemplating the contrary result $\sim G(a_{n+1})$ as a truth-candidate, we arrive at the following set **S** of data:

$$\mathbf{S} = \{F(a_1) \text{ \& } G(a_1), F(a_2) \text{ \& } G(a_2), \ldots, F(a_n) \text{ \& } G(a_n),$$
$$F(a_{n+1}) \text{ \& } G(a_{n+1}), F(a_{n+1}) \text{ \& } \sim G(a_{n+1})\}.$$

Once more there are just two m.c.s., namely, conjoining the initial premisses with the two propositions $F(a_{n+1})$ & $G(a_{n+1})$ and $F(a_{n+1})$ & $\sim G(a_{n+1})$, respectively. The preference of one of these m.c.s. over the other is justifiable in terms of a differential judgement of the plausibility of these two propositions. Again, given that the initial evidence exhibits the generic pattern $F(x)$ & $G(x)$, it is clear that one of these propositions is pattern-concordant and the other pattern-discordant. Resort to the preferential rule formulated above thus suffices to underwrite drawing the inductively proper conclusion.

These illustrations show how the coherence theory would propose to handle the problem of justifying induction by a two-stage process:

1. to rely on pattern-conformity considerations to support a differential assessment of the *plausibilities* of the truth-candidates involved, and then
2. to use the general procedure of the coherence analysis to vindicate 'the inductively right conclusion' in the move from plausibility to acceptance as a presumptive truth.

Of course, in situations that do not fit the textbook patterns of inductive inference, but reflect more closely the more intricate realities of scientific practice, the workings of plausibility-considerations would have to be adapted to accommodate this complexity. (For example, when judging between hypotheses some of which explain a great deal more of the observed evidence than others, one would—other things being equal—definitely incline to consider the former as significantly more plausible than the latter.)

All this points to a central and crucial aspect of the coherence theory of truth: its striving towards systematization. The very rationale of the theory is such that not only does coherence *qua* consistency contribute to the potential for truth, but so does coherence *qua* orderliness, that is to say, system. If, as the coherence theory insists, truth is to be sought in maximal systematization, then the stress of inductive procedures upon pattern-conformity may be seen in the light of a special facet of the general approach. A coherence analysis that deploys pattern-conformity as a guide to plausibility is in strict accord

Q

with the spirit of the entire doctrine, as epitomized in Bradley's dictum: 'If by taking certain judgments of perception [for us, 'data'] as true, I can get more system into my world, then these "facts" are so far true. . . .'[17] The reliance upon pattern-conformity—an obvious facet of orderliness and system—as a guiding criterion to plausibility, and hence to alethic preferability, is clearly one way to 'get more system into my world'. And in so far as system is, as the coherence theory insists, a guide to truth, the reliance on pattern-conformity as a measure of plausibility simply implements a basic commitment of the whole approach.

But can such a procedure—with its 'division of labour' between plausibility and coherence—succeed in justifying induction? We must first become clear about just what 'to justify induction' could possibly mean. It may mean one of two things:

(1) to establish that the 'inductively proper' conclusion is *rationally warranted.*

(2) to establish that the 'inductively proper' conclusion is *correct* in that matters must in fact so eventuate as the inductive argument maintains.

Clearly the coherence analysis provides no justification in sense (2). Everything that we have said about the character of the coherence criterion as a potentially fallible standard makes this perfectly clear. Moreover, Hume has shown with all the lucidity of which philosophical conclusions admit that there simply can be no justification of induction in sense (2). Thus if we are willing to rest satisfied with a type (1) justification—as we *must* be—then the coherence approach does indeed yield the sort of justification we seek: it shows that the inductively proper conclusion is *rationally warranted*—though not that it is *correct* (*that* contention is not capable of demonstration).

But what sort of warrant is at issue here if this be not the warrant of guaranteed truth, which we have maintained to be in principle unavailable? To see what response is appropriate we must retrace the line of reasoning given in our justificatory support of induction. We have *not* attempted to argue directly that the future will be like the past—i.e. that statements about the future are true if they are past-conforming. We have not used the conformity to past patterns as a criterion of truth *per se* —but only as a guide to *plausibility*. The pivot of the coherence

[17] 'On Truth and Coherence', in *Essays on Truth and Reality* (Oxford, 1914), pp. 202–18; see p. 210.

approach is that it requires merely that statements about the future be viewed as *more plausible* when they conform to the past. The inductive application of the coherence analysis brings about a crucial division of labour. On the standard view, the 'justification of induction' requires us to make the drastic move from pattern-conformity to *truth*; but on the coherence approach, all that is asked is the more modest move from pattern-conformity to *plausibility*. The coherence analysis itself subsequently functions—in its characteristic way—to provide a vehicle for the move from plausibility to truth. The coherence theory enables us to shift the argument from the *truthfulness* of the pattern-conforming to its *plausibility*, and so lightens substantially the burden that pattern-conformity is asked to carry.

The analysis of inductive reasoning in the coherence framework thus effects an essential reduction of the problem of 'justifying induction'. Seemingly the task of justifying induction is the impossible one of arguing *directly* for the truth of certain propositions about the future on the basis of (clearly insufficient) evidence relating to the past. What the coherence approach does is to shift the requisite argument from an argument for truth to an argument for plausibility. It invokes pattern-conformity merely as a *basis of plausibility*, not as a *basis for truth*. The burden of the move from plausibility to presumptive truth is then borne by the generic mechanisms of the coherence analysis.

In sum, we are not prepared to claim with Ewing that the coherence analysis justifies induction by showing that we are somehow confronted with a choice between induction and chaos. Other non-deductive methods are no doubt *possible*—tea-leaves and the entrails of birds, among others. But if the coherence analysis does not solve the problem, it does at least effect a criterially important reduction in shifting a significant part of the burden from *truth* as such to mere *plausibility*.

In synoptic outline, the coherence justification of induction proceeds thus:

(1) Induction is but one alternative among others. There are indeed genuinely alternative methods for validating statements going beyond the area of known fact. There is not only the way of orthodox 'induction' (i.e. standard scientific practice), but also tea-leaf reading, astrology, palmistry, necromancy, etc.

(2) We could, of course, attempt to support the greater claim of induction inductively (in terms of its greater success in past applications), but this procedure would prove circular. In the first instance we must content ourselves with

arguing the thesis that there is no reason of general principle for regarding any of these other methods as superior to induction on *a priori* grounds.

(3) Since we are asking, *ex hypothesi*, for an argument to show that the use of induction is *rationally warranted*, we must judge induction by the standards of rational procedure as operative in *other* fact-oriented domains. Here we note:

(i) that a general criterion of rational acceptance-as-true can be articulated in terms of coherence considerations, and*

(ii) that the very use of inductive procedures can itself be viewed in the light of an instance of coherence methodology.

(4) Induction is therefore a process that, through its assimilation to the coherence approach, conforms to the general canons of rationality. The methodology of coherence underwrites a methodological uniformity across a wide domain, a domain in which inductive reasonings play only a part—albeit a large and important one.

This coherentist 'justification of induction' is achieved by the argument that the only thing that can reasonably be asked of such a justification is that it show inductive processes to be rationally warranted. That such warrant is indeed available can then be established through an assimilation of induction to the paradigm of rational procedure manifested in the coherence approach to truth. In induction we impute truth to a conclusion on an evidential basis that is deductively insufficient, so that other imputations are logically possible. How are we to justify this specific resolution given that distinct possibilities exist? The coherentist answer is that we do so in terms of coherence considerations by selecting that resolution which best fits the given evidential basis, so that the rational basis for the inductivist imputation of truth is provided in terms of the general rationalizing procedure of coherence considerations. From this standpoint, induction comes to be justified in terms of its being yet one more specific instance of the coherence approach.

But what justifies the coherence approach itself? Is its justification not inductive in nature, bringing us round a full circle?

9. *Is the Justification of the Coherence Analysis Itself Inductive?*

Coherence theorists themselves have sometime used the this-or-nothing argument that unless coherence is taken as our criterion, all knowledge of truth is impossible. A. C. Ewing states the case for this position as follows:

> . . . a fundamental principle [may be established] by showing that it is a necessary presupposition of any attainment of truth. . . . In both cases we are using the coherence test, only in the one we are working forward with it, so to speak, and in the other working·backward. . . . The proof of the coherence principle itself would lie in showing that it was presupposed in all our thinking, and if this could be shown it would be fair to maintain that it had been itself proved by its coherence with all other truths, the attainment of which truths it alone made possible. The circle involved is not vicious in the case of a principle which is necessary to all thought, for if it has really been shown that the coherence test provides the only possible test, it has been shown that the only alternative to its adoption is the impossible one of absolute scepticism. According to Bosanquet, the ultimate argument in proving anything is always the disjunction—this or nothing, the appeal to which is inseparable from the principle of coherence, or is even, we might say, the same as that principle viewed from a different angle.[18]

But such a *this-or-nothing* argument will not do; (1) because utter scepticism and the coherence approach to knowledge do not exhaust the range of possible alternatives, and (2) because even if they did it is at least theoretically possible that scepticism is the warranted view, and not coherentism, so that the argument leaves its justification unaccomplished.

The coherence approach itself certainly stands in need of justification. But what justifies the coherence analysis in its essentially ampliative move from a lesser to a wider body of truths? The old central question remains: why is it rational to maintain that what is coherent is true? A definitional approach will not help. No matter how we twist and turn we just cannot get 'true' to *mean* 'coherent'. Certainly there cannot be a theoretical proof that proceeds deductively from general principles to establish that the coherence procedure must be inevitably or predominantly successful in providing actual truths. In the very nature of things no such proof can be given *a priori* for any method of criteriological character. And it is a desperate and fruitless expedient to try to argue transcendentally that what coheres must accord with reality. Our very reason for going to a coherence criterion was, after all, the fact that one cannot get any direct and criterion-independent assessment of what 'accords with reality'.

Can this needed justification perhaps be provided along

---

[18] *Idealism: A Critical Survey* (London, 1934), p. 237.

inductive lines? One might argue in the negative by saying 'The coherence analysis is itself to be used in justifying induction. Hence one must not use induction to justify the coherence theory.' But this argument would carry no weight whatever with someone not minded to grant a coherence justification of induction. If the inductivist justification of a coherence approach is to be invalidated—as is, indeed, inevitable—then it becomes necessary to argue quite differently.

Any inductive argument to justify the coherence analysis of truths must take the general form: 'Coherence considerations have generally succeeded in providing truths in the past, and so may be presumed to provide truths in the future.' But the development of any such argument itself requires a prior criterion of truths (namely in the premiss: 'Coherence has generally succeeded in providing truths in the past'). Thus if coherence is to be validated as the standard of truth we must *already* possess this very standard in order to implement an inductive argument in its support. This last point is of substantial importance and deserves emphasis. It shows that a working criterion of truth cannot be justified inductively because the very structure of an inductive argument for the desired conclusion requires us to deploy a criterion of truth.[19] An inductive justification of the coherence analysis is thus in principle not feasible.

10. *The Pragmatic Justification of the Coherence Approach*

It follows from the preceding considerations that the justification of the coherence methodology itself can be neither deductive nor inductive in character. We shall argue that it must be pragmatic.

Viewed in its criteriological light, it is clear that the coherence theory of truth is fundamentally *methodological* in nature: it seeks to provide a *method*—a logico-epistemological procedure—for the validation of certain propositions as true. But now as regards any sort of machinery (methods, tools, instrumentalities, procedures, etc.) the characteristically natural and appropriate mode of validation is to show *that it works*. Working well—that is, manifesting effectiveness and efficiency in discharging the tasks

---

[19] B. Russell advanced essentially this same line of thought as an argument against the pragmatic theory of truth: 'since no *a priori* reason is shown why truth and utility should always go together, utility can only be shown to be a criterion at all by showing inductively that it accompanies truth in all known instances, which requires that we should already know in many instances what things are true' (*Philosophical Essays* [London, 1910], p. 149).

for which it is designed—is the key standard for the rational evaluation of methods. With respect to methodology, at any rate, the pragmatists were surely right: there just is no alternative way of justifying a method apart from showing that 'it works' with respect to the tasks held in view.

This general point applies with full weight to the criteriology of truths. Why do we seek to identify truths? Partly for epistemic (theoretical) and partly for action-guiding (practical) reasons. With respect to the former, our interest is in *systematization*, above all in explanation (i.e. rational co-ordination) and prediction. Here success is merely 'rational satisfaction'. With respect to the latter, our interest is in *success* proper, in guiding our actions along satisfactory lines. That truth-criterion, whose results 'work out' in suitably practical ways, receives the pragmatic support which is rational and appropriate to ask of a method of the sort at issue. (These somewhat sketchily presented ideas will be worked out in greater detail in the following chapter.)

Some writers have sought to support a coherence theory on the grounds that it represents the inherently *natural* method of truth-determination that is appropriate to our verification procedures in science and common life, and that answers the demands of common sense.[20] This approach is not adequate to the philosophical needs of the situation, for seemingly natural and common-sense procedures are not rationally justified by their possession of these features of naturalness. It is in their suitability to common-sense *aims*, not their conformity to common-sense *methods*, that we see the validation of the coherence methodology. And this points in the direction of pragmatic considerations. The justification of the coherence

---

[20] E. W. Hall represents perhaps the most clear-cut example of this tendency: 'We need not be too disturbed by the skeptic's challenge, "If truth be a relation between experience and something extra-experiential, how can coherence-patterns of experience have any bearing, even that of mild probability, upon it?" for every philosophical system rests on categorical assumptions which for it are beyond question, and in the strife of such systems the only really firm neutral ground is that found in the categories of everyday thought. The epistemological position outlined in these chapters is commonsensical . . . in its acceptance of coherence as regards verification. If it be asserted that common sense is involved in contradiction when it combines the categorial assumptions mentioned, I would reply with a flat denial: they may be independent but they do not conflict. However, I should like to qualify this last admission. Although an intentionalist theory of meaning and truth and a coherence theory of verification are independent logically, neither strictly implying the other, they do have an appropriateness to one another which adds to the plausibility of their combination. Take the principle of quantitative corroboration. If we accept the intentionalistic account of experience outlined earlier, it is reasonable to suppose that there can be a multiplicity of perceptions of the same external object. If so, when in agreement, they can bear one another out' (*Our Knowledge of Fact and Value* (Chapel Hill, N.C., 1960), pp. 110–11).

theory of truth as an essentially methodological instrument of truth-criteriology is best seen as ultimately pragmatic.

11. *Need Coherentist Metaphysics Enter In?*

This pragmatic justification of the coherence theory of truth severs its traditional idealist links with coherence metaphysics. Thus A. C. Ewing, for example, argues as follows:

> Even if coherence were not *the* criterion but *only one* criterion of truth, it is difficult to see how we could possibly be justified in supposing that because a proposition fulfilled the coherence test it was true unless we assumed that the real was coherent. If something might be real and yet incoherent, why should a coherent view be more worthy of acceptance, more likely to be true, than an incoherent?[21]

According to this line of thought, idealist coherentists have been inclined to argue as follows:

> Reality is a coherent whole
> Truth must agree with reality
> ∴ Truth must be a coherent whole.

The tendency among idealists has been to support a coherence theory of truth on the basis of a coherence metaphysic of reality. Our approach avoids this dependence altogether. The pragmatic justification of the coherence theory makes it unnecessary to justify this theory by recourse to a metaphysical doctrine regarding the coherence of reality.

But what of the reverse relationship? Coherentists of the idealist school have often argued along the lines of the following remarks by A. C. Ewing regarding B. Blanshard's *The Nature of Thought*: 'The author is right in insisting that the acceptance of coherence as the test [of truth] implies that reality itself is a coherent system and therefore leads to important consequences in metaphysics. For if reality were incoherent, an incoherent and not a coherent set of propositions would be true.'[22] Coherentists have thus also maintained that the coherence theory of truth validates a coherence concept of nature. But surely this asks of a coherence theory of truth a task it is ill fitted to accomplish. The 'coherence' of nature had best be argued directly, and neither through the theory of truth nor even on the basis of metaphysical considerations, but simply on grounds of mere logic.

What, after all, would an inconsistent world be like—one that violates the requisite of self-consistency in the strong (logical,

---

[21] *Idealism: A Critical Survey* (London, 1934), p. 237.
[22] Review of *The Nature of Thought, Mind,* 53 (1944), 75–85 (see p. 82).

Aristotelian) sense? Such a world would have to have the feature that in some perfectly definite way something both is and is not so. Definite, that is, in that *all* relevant respects would have to be identical. None of your subterfuges about something being both malleable and not malleable because malleable in one environment and not malleable in another. The focal idea and leading principle of this explanation of the 'Law of Contradiction' (or better *Non-contradiction*) as it is generally called is that something cannot both be and not be so unequivocally and in one and the selfsame respect. Of course, a substance can be hard by one standard of comparison and not hard by another; but, granted a definite and unequivocal specification of the respect at issue, only one outcome in point of a characterization as malleable or not malleable is possible.

But now let us assume that the worst has come to the worst and that we are confronted with the situation where there is an outright logical conflict in the characterization. Suppose, in short, that reality is inconsistent: suppose that once all the relevant issues about sameness of respect are settled something both is and is not so. What then?

Clearly, only one rationally viable upshot is now possible. We have no choice but to regard the very hypothesis we are making as self-destructive, as simply annihilating itself. That is, the demands of intelligibility constrain us to suppose that it is not *nature* that is self-contradictory (and ultimately unintelligible) but the very assumption that we are being asked to make about it.

On this point, the correct view is surely that of the essential Kantian insight. We must hold that consistency (or rational intelligibility) is not a *constitutive* feature of nature—not, that is, ultimately a properly descriptive characteristic of it—but a *regulative* feature, an aspect, that is, of our *concept* of nature; of the way in which we thinking beings do *and must* conceptualize it if the interests of minimal intelligibility (viz. logical viability) are to be achieved. On such a view consistency is not a constitutive and empirical (i.e. experientially discovered) feature of the world, but is, in the final analysis, a regulative and conceptual feature of our understanding of it, an aspect—to be blunt—not of *reality* as such but of our procedures for its conceptualization and accordingly of *our conception* of it. To say of reality *per se* that it is 'incoherent' would be to say of it something that, in the final analysis, is simply meaningless. The hypothesis that reality is incoherent is ultimately senseless because to ask of reality that it meet this condition is to ask of it something in principle impossible. At the metaphysical level the thesis that reality is coherent is essentially empty because no stable sense can possibly be made of its denial.

From this standpoint it becomes evident that the contention that nature is self-consistent is ultimately not really descriptive of *nature* at all, but inheres in the language-embedded conceptual machinery that we deploy for talking and thinking about it. This consistency-of-nature thesis is in effect a regulative principle for conceptualization. Its foundation is epistemologico-conceptual and not ontological, and the ultimate source of the putative non-contradictoriness of nature lies in 'the mind' rather than in 'reality' itself, because the mind and not objective reality is inescapably the *locus of meaning* and the very idea of a self-contradictory reality is meaningless.

Thus our present advocacy of a coherence criterion of truth breaks the chains that linked the traditional coherence theory of truth with idealistic metaphysics. The metaphysical roots of the classical idealist doctrine of coherence lay in the theory of internal relations and the organic view of reality. The version of a coherence theory presented here can waive the entire question of these ontological issues and still establish a useful and legitimate role for coherence considerations in such a way that their utility is by no means contingent on a prior favourable resolution of such metaphysical issues. It may well be that the coherence approach is somehow in spirit more congenial to a systematist/organicist concept of reality, but it certainly does not involve any metaphysical commitments along these lines.

The metaphysical route to a justification of the coherence theory of truth via the principle that the real is rational has here been rejected in favour of a pragmatist approach. Actually, this position does not depart as radically from idealist orthodoxy as it might seem to do at first sight. F. H. Bradley, that shrewdest of idealists, at any rate, did not disdain the pragmatic perspective:

And the view which I advocate takes them all [i.e. all 'judgments of perception'] as in principle fallible. On the other hand, that view denies that there is any necessity for absolute facts of sense. Facts for it are true, we may say, just so far as they work, just so far as they contribute to the order of experience. If by taking certain judgments of perception as true I can get more system into my world, then these facts are so far true. . . .[23]

It is exactly this principle, that truths are marked as such 'just

23 *Essays on Truth and Reality* (Oxford, 1914), p. 210.

in so far as they work, just so far as they contribute to the order of experience', that has provided our key guide-line in the justification of the coherence theory itself (although our pragmatism operates at the methodological rather than the substantive level).

X

THE PRIMACY OF PRACTICAL REASON

1. *The Task of Pragmatic Validation*

IT was argued in section 10 of the preceding chapter that the validation of the coherence criterion of truth is to be given along pragmatic lines. The task remains to explore in detail the grounds for this circumstance, and to make it clear just how such a pragmatic validation can be made to work. For the pragmatic validation of *a criterion of factual truth* obviously poses special difficulties, since, in particular, it would seem that such truths are already required as *inputs* into the pragmatically justificatory argument. Exactly how, then, can a pragmatic justification of a coherence theory of truth be developed?

2. *The Basic Argument*

Let *C* represent the criterion we actually propose to use in the determination of factual or empirical truth—whatever this criterion may be. Accordingly, one is to be committed to classing a fact-purporting proposition *p* as a truth if and only if $C(p)$, that is if and only if *p* meets the conditions specified in *C*.

It will make no difference to our argument what the nature of *C* is. Whether it is the standard processes of scientific methodology, the deliverances of immediate intuition, the indications of tea leaves, or the declarations of sacred sages, all this is totally indifferent for our immediate purposes. Nor need *C* be uniform and homogeneous: it can be as complex and composite as you please. If you choose to divide the real or potential fact up into a variety of themes or topics or subject matters, and apply an altogether different standard in each region, so be it. Then *C* is simply a complex composite of multiple subcriteria. Well and good. All that I ask is that we be *serious* about *C*; that *C* really and truly is the criterion we are actually to employ in practice for the determination of factual truth.

How are we to validate our employment of *C*? Can it be shown that we are rationally justified in using *C*? This had better be so, considering our very libertarian approach.

Now to all appearances the question of the appropriateness

of C is simply this: Does C yield truths? But how could one meaningfully implement the justificatory programme inherent in this question? Seemingly in only one way: by looking on the one hand at C-validated propositions and then checking on the other hand if they are in fact truths. But if C really and truly is our criterion for the determination of factual truth, then this exercise becomes wholly pointless. We cannot judge C by the seemingly natural standard of the question whether what it yields is indeed true because *ex hypothesi* we use C itself as the determinant of just this.

At this point it becomes altogether crucial that C really and truly is the criterion we actually use for truth-determinations. Clearly if someone proposed an alternative procedure C', the preceding methodology would work splendidly well. For we would then simply check whether the C'-validated propositions are indeed truths—that is, whether they are also validated by C. But with respect to C itself this exercise is patently useless.

It is difficult to exaggerate the epistemological decisiveness and the importance of this extremely simple argument. It shows in as clear a manner as philosophical argumentation admits of that our standard of factual truth cannot be validated by somehow showing that it does indeed accomplish properly its intended work of truth-determination.

So much, then, is a firm basis. But the problem of interpretation remains. In particular, the ominous question arises: Is the proper conclusion to be drawn from this argument the sceptical result that any and all rational justification of our standard of factual truth is in principle impossible? The remainder of the chapter seeks to develop a line of argument against this sceptical conclusion.

3. *The Pragmatic Turn*

Since a method is never a method pure and simple but always a method-for-the-realization-of-some-end, the instrumentally teleological question of its effectiveness in the realization of that purpose becomes altogether decisive. As already stated, with respect to *methodology*, at any rate, the pragmatists were in the right—there can be no better or more natural way of justifying a *method* than by establishing that 'it works' with respect to the specific tasks in view. The proper test for the correctness or appropriateness of a *method* is plainly and obviously posed by the question: does it work—that is, does it attain its intended purposes? Anything methodological—a tool, procedure, instrument, etc.—is best validated in terms of its ability to achieve the purposes prescribed for it; its success at accomplishing its appropriate work. The obvious standard of appraisal of any method (instrument, procedure) is framed by the paradigmatically pragmatic or instrumentalistic question: Does it deliver the goods?

The problem of a truth-criterion can be illuminated by viewing the issue from the perspective we obtain once we take the instrumentalistic turn. After all, a truth-criterion is at bottom methodological: it is naturally to be viewed as a means towards realizing those purposes for which the acceptance of truths is a requisite. But just what are the purposes of a truth-determination method; what is it we propose to do with the propositions that it validates for us as truths?

This deceptively simple-seeming question involves profound and far-reaching issues. In particular it forces us to give prominence to a recognition of man's amphibious nature as a creature of mind and body; intellect and will; reason and action; theory and practice.

To this fundamental duality there corresponds a duality in our acceptance of truths:

(1) On the one hand there is the *cognitive or theoretical* dimension of our concern for the intellectual aspect of information or knowledge. From the purely intellectual aspect of man as knower success is represented by our mastery of correct information about things and failure entails the natural sanction of error.

(2) On the other hand there is the *practical and affective* aspect of man as an agent cast *in medias res* within the blooming buzzing confusion of the goings-on of this world of ours. The critical element here is our welfare not as abstract intellects concerned solely to acquire information and avoid error but as embodied agents concerned for their welfare in situations where failure entails frustration, pain, or even catastrophe.

Our acceptance or non-acceptance of truths, of course, has profound involvements on both the cognitive and the affective sides of the theoretical/practical divide, since such acceptance is a guide both as to belief and as to action. Hence a truth-criterion comes to be endowed with a duality of objectives: truth on the one hand is a standard of belief in purely intellectual regards and on the other a guide for our practical life.

Now in the light of these considerations, it would appear that one way of drawing the moral of the argument of the preceding section is not as establishing scepticism, but rather as showing merely that we cannot apply the conception of success in the *theoretical* mode as the justificatory standard for our criterion of factual truth. One is accordingly led to the conclusion that the natural and appropriate step is to use success in the *practical* mode as the justificatory standard proper to a criterion of factual truth. But how is such an approach to be implemented?

4. *Pragmatic Validation of the Criterion of Truth*

The structure of the pragmatic justification of a method or procedure inevitably conforms to a certain generic pattern. We begin with two items, a specification of (1) the method M in question, and (2) the practical purposes μ at whose achievement the method M is directed. The pragmatic justification of M then takes the generic form of the following paradigmatically pragmatic reasoning:

(I) M works (as well as any envisaged alternative).
Therefore, M is to be adopted as the correct
(i.e. best or most appropriate) method.

Note this is a piece of practical reasoning in a sense approximating (though not coincident with) Aristotle's. The conclusion has to do with adopting a course of action rather than establishing a fact. Contrast the cognate reasoning

(II) M works (better than any possible alternative).
Therefore, M is the correct method.

This is not practical reasoning but demonstrative, and its conclusion does not indicate an action but a fact. (The establishment of the fact that the conclusion asserts of course has certain practical 'implications', but this is always and inevitably so.)

At this stage the focus of concern naturally is on the premiss of the argument. What can 'M works' mean in such a situation? Clearly, its meaning must be construed somewhat as follows:

(W_M) If a course of action instantiates M, then it will (certainly, probably, as probably as any other method) lead to the realization of the aims μ.

Thus the 'standard task' of a pragmatic justification—a task whose discharge is required for providing the premiss for an application of an inference pattern of type (I)—is to establish the *success* (in the sense just specified) of the method M at issue. Let us apply these general considerations to our special case of a criterion C of factual truth, now looking at C as a methodological instrument of truth-determination. Of course, we must begin by specifying the entire range of relevant purposes for having such a criterion, viz.

(1) the *cognitive* purpose of affording the knowledge of truths: the purely intellectual aspect of providing information.
(2) the *practical* purpose of providing a satisfactory guide to action—i.e. a guide to a satisfactory course of action.

As maintained in the preceding section, our initial argument may be construed to eliminate (1) as a usable standard of assessment. Accordingly, it seems that we are thrown back on an exclusive reliance upon (2), a circumstance that indicates the classically pragmatic test of a truth criterion as the natural recourse at the methodological level.

If we adopt this stance and restrict the purview of relevant purpose for a criterion of factual truth to the pragmatic domain of specifically *practical* purposes, then (W_M) comes to take the specific form:

(W_C) If we use the criterion C as basis for classing a thesis as true, then this thesis will provide a satisfactory guide to action.

But plainly, *if* the criterion C is itself simply that of practical success, of 'working out in the guidance of action', *then* the crucial premiss (W_C) comes to be altogether trivialized.

The pragmatic criterion of truth itself has therefore at least this merit, that its very nature is such that it will discharge the 'standard task' of a pragmatic justification. But it does so only too well. It provides a *logically tight* guarantee of validation for the essential premiss that the method in question works in terms of the relevant range of intended purpose. In adopting the pragmatic criterion we close the otherwise inevitable logical gap between the methodological instrument on the one hand and the realization of its correlative purposes on the other. Clearly, such an essentially tautological premiss cannot possibly provide the basis for drawing any useful and non-trivial conclusion.

The lesson of this line of thought must be construed as follows: that while the pragmatic validation of a criterion C of truth— at the methodological level—may well be a worthwhile venture when $C \neq$ (the pragmatic criterion of truth), the pragmatic approach cannot possibly be fruitful when we contemplate the specifically pragmatic criterion $C =$ (the pragmatic criterion of truth). Use of the pragmatic criterion at the methodological level *pre-empts* its use at the substantive level. And since there seem to be excellent and compelling grounds for its employment at the methodological level, we would be well advised on this ground alone (not to speak of others at all) to write off the pragmatic criterion as a substantive test of the truth of particular theses.

Accordingly, the appropriate policy is to give a pragmatic argument not at the particularistic level of justifying a specific propositional thesis, but at the generic level of a process for justifying theses-in-general. Thus (W_M) would take the form:

> (W_C') If we use the criterion C as basis for classing theses (in general) as true, then this generic process, this general strategy, will provide a satisfactory guide to action.

Our pragmatism thus proceeds at the wholesale level of a general procedure, not at the item-specific, retail level of justifying particular propositions.

The pragmatic theory of truth comes close to being the epistemological counterpart to ethical utilitarianism. Now it is well known that utilitarianism can take two forms:

(1) *Act utilitarianism* which asserts that an act is to be done (i.e. qualifies as morally right) if its performance is maximally benefit-producing.

(2) *Rule utilitarianism* which asserts that an act is morally right if it conforms to ethically warranted rules, and that a rule is warranted if its general adoption as a principle of action is maximally benefit-producing.

Analogously, pragmatism can take two forms:

(1) *Propositional pragmatism* which asserts that a proposition is to be accepted (i.e. qualifies as true) if its adoption is maximally success-promoting (= benefit-producing).

(2) *Criterial pragmatism* which asserts that a proposition is to be accepted (i.e. qualifies as true) if it conforms to an epistemically warranted criterion, and that a criterion is warranted if its adoption as a principle of acceptance is maximally success-promoting (= benefit-producing).

When one considers acceptance-as-true as an act and looks—as it is natural enough to do—upon classing a proposition as true as a type of action, then the result of applying the utilitarian approach (in one or another of its forms) just is pragmatism (in one or another of its forms). And even as one can in principle be an act utilitarian and not a rule utilitarian (or vice versa) so one can be a propositional pragmatist and not a criterial pragmatist (or vice versa).

But there is one crucial disanalogy. Our argument has shown that if one is a criterial pragmatist then it is altogether *pointless* to opt for a propositional pragmatism as one's specific criterion of acceptance because the process of criterial justification could not in principle succeed in this instance. On the other hand if one were a rule-utilitarian then it would be not pointless but (presumably) simply *wrong* to opt for an act-utilitarian rule of conduct because (presumably) this specific rule would be invalidated on rule-utilitarian grounds. Adoption of the utilitarian standard at the level of rules does not pre-empt but rather (presumably) invalidates its use at the substantive level of act-assessment.

5. *Three Strategies of Pragmatic Justification*

If we are to implement and apply the line of reasoning inherent in an argument of the form

> The method M works (in terms of its effective realization of the purposes μ)
> ———————————————————————————
> The method M is to be adopted (relative to a commitment to μ)

then we are, of course, immediately faced with the problem of obtaining its premiss. But how is one to show that a method M works?

Three possible alternatives come to mind:

(1) *Demonstrative justification*
   To establish that M works as a matter of logico-conceptual necessity (for example, a certain procedure for determining the roots of a cubic equation).

(2) *This-or-nothing justification*
   To establish that M works on grounds of principle as well as any method possibly can. It is thus to be shown that if any method works then this one does:

$$(\exists M)\ \text{works}\ (M) \to \text{works (this)}.$$

(An example would be Hans Reichenbach's celebrated pragmatic justification of induction.[1]) Note the equiva-

---

[1] For H. Reichenbach's justification of induction see his books *The Theory of Probability* (Berkeley, Calif., 1949) and especially *Experience and Prediction* (Chicago, Ill., 1938). For 'this or nothing' argumentation see ch. V of A. C. Ewing, *Idealism: A Critical Survey* (London, 1934), and B. Bosanquet, *Implication and Linear Inference* (London, 1920).

lence of this tactic with another—with 'if this does not work then nothing works'

$$\sim \text{works (this)} \to \sim(\exists M) \text{ works } (M)$$

or consequently 'this works or nothing does'

$$\text{works (this) } \mathbf{v} \sim(\exists M) \text{ works } (M).$$

This is exactly identical with the well-known this-or-nothing mode of justification used by certain of the English idealists for the justification of induction.

Both of these lines of reasoning represent a *theoretical* mode of justification, and call for arguments that proceed on matters of general principle. But a variant empirical rather than theoretical course is also open:

(3) *Experientially practical justification*

To show that M works as a matter of empirical experience as well as any other tried alternative, i.e. that it has proven itself in practice.

Let us now attempt to bring these abstractly possible alternative lines of approach to bear upon the specific problem in hand, viz. that of justifying a criterion of factual truth through its success in providing a basis for action. Unfortunately, it transpires that all three modes of pragmatic justification have their difficulties here.

6. The Prospects of a Pragmatic Justification of a Non-pragmatic Criterion of Factual Truth

Our approach to the validation of a criterion of truth regards this criterion from a methodological angle as affording a method of truth-determination. The structure of the problem is thus as follows: one begins with some proposed (non-pragmatic) criterion C of factual truth. The task is then that of showing that adoption of C is successful in practice. Note that success here is *not* truth-production (our earlier argument ruled this out). Here 'successful practice' excludes the purely *epistemic* practice of knowledge-acquisition and is confined to considerations of actual practice: action-guidance as assessed in the affective order of leading to physically and emotionally satisfying results (no pain, frustration of plans, unpleasant shocks, etc.).

But just how is this methodological metacriterion to be implemented? How is one to go about establishing that adoption of C

as basis for guidance of actions is successful; that if we use C then good results will ensue? Three procedures come to mind.

(A) *The Route of Necessity*

To give a logico-conceptual demonstration of the necessity that, if we use C, then we must necessarily have beneficial results (because action on C is *inherently* benefit-productive).

Such a necessitarian approach could succeed only if C were itself the pragmatic criterion. But this is not feasible for previously indicated reasons. And if C is not the pragmatic criterion but something else, then this necessitarian line of argument is not very hopeful. After all, we know that even if, instead of dealing with C-validated propositions, we dealt with *true* propositions purely and simply (never mind for the moment where we got them from) then even this cannot provide a guarantee of practical success.[2]

(B) *The This-or-Nothing Route*

This approach calls for establishing that, if anything can produce success, then this C will produce success. We are to show as a matter of principle that if any criterion whatsoever can deliver the goods, then this C will do so.

Here C is validated on the-only-game-in-town principle. This approach may hold promise in theory but in practice it seems methodologically over-ambitious. Its prospects are certainly not hopeful. How could one hope to show on grounds of general principle that C alone can prove benefit-providing?

(C) *The Dominance Route*

With this approach we are to establish on grounds of general principle that, whenever C' is any method other than C that has some promise of success, then C will do at least as well as C'. Thus C has the feature of intrinsic non-inferiority.

This dominance approach may be more promising than (B) because it is less ambitious; but it still seems over-ambitious. For it requires us to demonstrate a claim—viz. the predominance

---

[2] I have argued this point in the chapter 'Pragmatic Justification: A Cautionary Tale', in *Essays in Philosophical Analysis* (Pittsburgh, Pa., 1969).

of *C*—that we can scarcely hope to establish on theoretical grounds of general principle.

Accordingly it is well-advised to explore the prospects of an empirical and *a posteriori* justification. For (C) shares with the two preceding approaches the feature of representing an *a priori* demonstration that proceeds wholly in the theoretical terms of matters of general principle. And it is problematic (not to say, with Hume, illusory) to claim that an operative criterion of factual truth can be validated by strictly theoretical considerations. We are thus led to consider a quite different strategy:

(D) *The Route of Experience*

> This approach calls for an empirical justification of *C* on the basis of observed results. In effect we are to show that *C* has been tried and found to work out to satisfaction.

This line of attack suffers from various seemingly decisive impediments. In particular, three of these seem especially serious for this method of validating a criterion of factual truth:

(i) Any appeal to experience seemingly presupposes an established criterion of factual truth to tell us what experience has been.

(ii) Even if the employment of a criterion has been followed by good results, what guarantee is there that this success was actually produced by the criterion? *Post hoc* is not *propter hoc*.

(iii) Experience is past-oriented but the justification of a method must envisage its future applications as well. Even if the criterion has worked to good avail in the past what reason is there to think it will prove successful in general? (Hume's Problem).

The remainder of the chapter will for the most part be devoted to considering the ways and means by which these obstacles in the way of an empirical validation of a truth-criterion *can* be overcome.

7. *The Problem of Prior Truths: The Plausibility of Memory as a Minimal Requisite for an Appeal to Experience*

To begin with, one must face up to the critical point that any use of the pragmatic approach to methodological justification which invokes the record of actual experience will require some empirical facts as inputs. We inevitably have to talk about our own actions and subsequent developments. The pragmatic defence in terms of actual experience of the adoption of a certain method is given by fleshing out the following skeletal line of reasoning:

(1) We specify the method M at issue and specify the appropriate family μ of its intended practical objectives and purposes.

(2) We adopt the method M as basis of operation towards the realization of μ—that is, we apply M in practice.

(3) We note that none of the promising methods M', M'', etc. alternative to M, prove on balance as effective as M in conducing to the realization of μ.

Accordingly, we draw the conclusion that we are (relatively) justified in adopting M for the realization of μ.

Now it is clear that this line of argument is heavily laden with factual commitments since the premisses at issue in both items (2) and (3) represent a significant incursion into the realm of empirical fact. It is in principle impossible to attempt 'the appeal to experience' regarding the 'effectiveness in practice' or the 'success in employment' of a method if we lack any and all data regarding the actual occasions of use of this or similar methods and the occurrences that followed thereupon. The generic structure of a pragmatic justification of the experiential type requires us to recognize that we have adopted and implemented certain courses of action; to note that certain occurrences supervened upon these steps; and finally to evaluate these occurrences in terms of their relationship to our objective μ. Ignoring for the moment the evaluative issues of this final stage, we remark that the remaining points are entirely matters for a record relating to our own doings and observations. To implement the pragmatic programme of determining whether a certain procedural method works out we must inevitably have some informative data regarding what was done and what happened. It is self-evident that to apply any argument from experience we need factual records to tell us what experience has been.

We thus come to the crucial question: given that factually informative inputs are needed for any application of the pragmatic line of justification then whence are we to obtain these factually informative historical inputs when this justification relates to our very criterion of factual truth itself? Clearly if they are to come from the criterion C itself, then we move in the unhappy circle of invoking C to validate certain claims which claims are then in turn used for the validation of C.

If the pragmatic justification of a criterion C of factual truth is to succeed, this circle must be broken. But how are we to break it?

Only one way seems to be open to us. In so far as they function as premiss-inputs into the justificatory argument for C, the experiential data must be seen not as truths but merely as plausible presumptions. We must distinguish the claim of certainty (a truth is, after all, in principle not defeasible—otherwise it would not be a truth) from the claim of presumptiveness. To class a proposition as true is (as John Dewey was wont to insist) very different from characterizing it as of warranted acceptability. From an epistemic standpoint there is a whole world of difference between an established truth and a provisionally accepted supposition. There is a critical difference between characterizing a thesis as prima facie correct and acceptable in the first analysis (plausible or credible) and claiming it ultimately correct and acceptable in the final analysis (actually true). To limit our purview to truths is to ignore that vast and important class of theses that are *tentatively* acceptable but subject to correction by systematic considerations and so defeasible.[3]

I have re-emphasized this distinction between genuine truths and merely presumptive truth-candidates at some length because it is crucial for present purposes. Any *experiential* justification of a truth-criterion must pull itself up by its own bootstraps. It needs factual inputs, but yet these factual inputs cannot at this stage already qualify as truths. To meet this need it is natural to appeal to the concept of truth-candidates, data that are no more truths than candidate-presidents are presidents.

It is quite sufficient for our objectives to have it that retrospective records and memory yield informative yet infirm data, data of merely prima facie correctness that need not be ultimately true but are plausible truth-candidates. Not the outright truth but the mere plausibility of our retrospective records can provide the information-base needed for our pragmatic argument from experience. To be sure, it must be granted that only an argument from true premises can *demonstrate* its conclusion. But this undoubted fact does not entail the consequence that arguments from merely plausible premisses cannot carry substantial

---

[3] This conception of data not as truths as such but merely as truth-candidates is elaborated in considerable detail in Chapter III.

probative weight. Nothing untoward ensues from a recognition that our justificatory argument is presumptive rather than demonstrative.

8. Post Hoc Ergo Propter Hoc: *A Residual Circularity*

Yet another fundamental difficulty resides in the very nature of the premiss pivotal to any pragmatic validation, the premiss to the effect that M works; i.e. that employment of M is conducive to realization of the objective μ. From the moment that we take the experiential route to the establishment of this premiss, the only information we can obtain on the basis of the matters of historical record dealt with in the preceding section will take the form:

(1) The method M has been tried (as have its alternatives M', M'', etc.)

(2) The objectives μ were realized better (more efficiently, more effectively) by M than in those cases where its competitors (M', M'', etc.) were employed.

But this will not suffice to establish the necessary degree of intimacy between the method M and the correlative desideratum μ. What is clearly needed to warrant the 'is conducive' claim of the premiss is not just the *post hoc* information that M was adopted and the good result μ achieved, but the *propter hoc* information that μ was attained because of the adoption of M. If the realization of μ is to validate M, then its attributability to the use of M must be established. To (1) and (2) above we must add

(3) In all (most) instances i, attainment of μ in instance i is attributable—or at least presumptively attributable—to the use of M.

That is, the thesis that 'M works' must be regarded as a generalization of a host of specific cases of attribution to the use of M of instances of a successful realization of μ.

Now in general there is nothing in this state of affairs to create problems for a pragmatic validation. But in the specific case of a criterion of truth C a serious difficulty crops up with respect to (3). For if our argument is to have proper probative weight, then all its premisses must be established, and while the matters of fact at issue in (1)–(2) can be handled by the procedure in the preceding section, the patently factual premiss (3), which is clearly *not* just a matter of historical record, poses altogether new difficulties. For any attempt to show that (3) is true once again raises the spectre of circularity: its truth will obviously be a matter of fact, but it is a criterion of factual truth we are endeavouring to validate. We seem once more to be plunged into the patently circular position that our validation of a criterion of factual truth calls for our *already* being in the possession of a validated factual truth.

The best solution to this problem of validating the attributability-claim (3) is to see it as occupying in the over-all justificatory argument not the status of a *validated truth* (since this would be circular), but rather the status of a *warranted postulate*. Note that it does not even make sense to ask with respect to postulates (unlike theses, conjectures, assumptions, or hypotheses) whether they are true (*qua* postulates). With this approach we take the stance that when the *post hoc* facts are suitably adjusted, subject to all the controls and cautions of the theory of the design of experiments, then a certain postulation is warranted or justified.

Accordingly, we would adopt at the *regulative* (rather than the factual/constitutive) level the operative precept of the type (*P*): *to treat a certain postulation as warranted under suitable circumstances.* This is itself a practical/procedural principle rather than a cognitive/factual thesis whose validation is part and parcel of the over-all pragmatic validation programme we have taken in hand. Such a regulative policy enables us to move from the fact of a *post hoc* success that is sufficiently *systematic* in its attendance upon the use of a method, to the warranting of an imputation to this method of *propter hoc* efficacy in producing this success. Of course our willingness to assume this regulative stance is bound up with a certain 'realistic' metaphysical stance towards the 'stern realities' of this world: that practical success at the generic level of methodologies and systematic procedures will not (at this general level) be the product of a lucky accident and the unmerited cooperativeness of a benign nature (Bismarck's classic dictum regarding God's protection of fools notwithstanding).

It is worth noting, incidentally, that its treatment as a justified postulate within the pragmatic argument does not preclude the prospect of eventually classing an attributability thesis as a truth *ex post facto*, once the (duly justified) criterion *C* is itself applied. Nor indeed should we rule out the possibility that in a particular instance an attributability-contention of type (3) should be ultimately classed as false by *C* (that *C* should, so to speak, occasionally bite the hand that feeds it).

On this line of approach, then, we start with a validation of a (3)-type thesis that is regulative and affords us with needful factual input in the light of a warranted postulate rather than an established truth. Some such pre-justification-as-true warrant is clearly needed to avoid circularity in the justificatory argument. But nothing vicious ensues if it turns out from the post-justificatory standpoint—as indeed if all goes well it must, at least by-and-large—that the thesis whose *antecedent* status is a postulate should have the *consequent* status of a truth. And there is nothing fatal if some instances of this postulation turn out to be such that their consequent status is that of falsehood. A warranted postulate—unlike a truth—is defeasible and can in the final analysis turn out to be untrue without loss of its initial status. Its regulative acceptance does not render it incorrigible at the constitutive level.

9. *Hume's Problem*

We come, finally, to the third seeming—and seemingly decisive —obstacle in the way of an experientially pragmatic justification of a criterion of truth, namely Hume's problem of the validation of reasoning from past to future.

To begin with, it is obvious that if one attempts any *experiential* justification of a truth-criterion, then one obtains a line of argument whose direction of motion is as follows:

C has provided truths → C provides truths in general.

And accordingly this argument comprises *a fortiori* a sub-argument of the form

C has provided truths → C will provide truths.

It is clear by parity with our earlier reasoning that (quite apart from any special difficulties posed by Hume's problem) no justificatory reasoning of such a form can succeed with respect to a truth criterion (that is, to what really and truly in the final analysis is our truth criterion), because its essential premiss that C has provided truths is vacuous in having us judge the products of C by the circularly trivializing standard of C itself.

But, of course, no comparable difficulty will affect the cognate inductive argument that proceeds on the practical (rather than theoretical) side, and has the aspect:

C has provided useful results
→ C provides useful results in general.

It is evident, however, that this reasoning comprises *a fortiori* the sub-argument whose principle direction of motion is as follows:

C has provided useful results → C will provide useful results.

And such an argument, while evading the previous obstacle of circularity, at once encounters Humean difficulties. For it seems that what is at issue here is still an *argument*, though one of the *practical* form

works in the past → works in the future

rather than the factual/cognitive form

true in the past → true in the future.

Both lines of argument at once run into the roadblock erected by Hume to preclude inferences regarding the future from premises relating to the past.

But in fact any such discursive appearance is misleading. For our actual concern here is not with an argument to establish a thesis regarding the relationship of past and future occurrences —such as the regularity of nature—but with the validation of a practice: namely the implementation of the precept inherent in the following practical policy:

> To continue to use a method that has proven to be success-ful (i.e. more effective than alternatives) in those cases (of suitable numerousness and variety, etc.) where it has been tried.

The validation of this methodological precept lies deep in the nature of rationality itself. For it is quintessentially rational to continue to use for the attainment of specified objectives methods and procedures that have proven themselves effective in their realization.

An objector will complain: 'But you cannot vindicate a policy by just *saying* it is rational, you have to *show* that it is rational. That is, you must point to something about it that *makes* it rational.' So be it. The consideration that rationalizes the policy of continuing the use of a method (procedure) that has suc-ceeded is just this very fact itself. Of course, success in the past does not *guarantee* continued success. But the very fact that it has proved effective in certain cases is, after all, some reason—however inconclusive—for thinking that the procedure may work in general. And if there is no reason at all to think that any other method that lies to hand will do better, then we do, after all, have adequate warrant for continued use of the method. Our reasoning here conforms to the paradigm of this-or-nothing-better argumentation:

> There are some good grounds for thinking this method merits adoption.
>
> There are no grounds for thinking that any available alternative method will work better.
>
> ∴ We are warranted in adopting this method.

Accordingly our warrant does not reside on any demonstration of the thesis that applications of the method must prove successful in the attainment of its objectives. All we obtain and *all we need* is a more modest basis of appropriate rational justification for the use of a method. Precisely because an appropriate provision of rational warrant can take the practical rather than theoretical route, a pragmatic justification need not, at the methodological level, attempt the sort of theoretical guarantee of success inherent in arguments for the regularity of nature, or other tempting steps that collide outright with Hume's barrier.

The critical point is that we are not dealing with the establishment of a factual thesis at all—be it demonstrative or presumptive—but merely with the rational validation of a practical course of action. And the practical warrant that rationalizes the use of a method need not call for a guarantee of success (which is, in the circumstances of the case in view, altogether impossible) but merely for having as good reasons as, under the circumstances, we can reasonably hope to have.

So much, then, for the third seeming difficulty in the way of an experientially pragmatic justification of a criterion of factual truth.

10. *The Primacy of Practical Reason*

The discussion has to this point proceeded on an abstract and methodological plane. We have not yet attempted to validate any specific criterion of truth, but have dealt solely with meta-criteriological issues. All the same, some useful conclusions have, I think, emerged from these abstract deliberations.

Theoretical reason in the factual area moves towards a conclusion of the form '. . . is in fact the case regarding the world'. Practical reason moves towards a conclusion of the form '. . . is to be done'. With respect to the employment of a method it is clear that practical reason is the appropriate mode since the correctness of a method does not reside in its truth (methods and instrumentalities are by their very nature neither true nor false) but in its appropriateness (i.e. suitability to the task in view). And since the rational espousal of a factual truth must be governed by *some* appropriate criterion of acceptance, and any such criterion is in effect methodological, it follows that in the factual domain practical reason is basic to the theoretical.

But how can the practical justification of a criterion C of factual truth proceed? Plainly by showing that 'it works'. But 'it works' cannot here mean 'succeeds in the theoretical/cognitive task of providing truths', which would involve a blatant circularity. Accordingly 'it works' is best and most appropriately to be construed as 'works in terms of the practical purposes of action-guidance', purposes no less crucial for truth than the range of theoretical/cognitive purposes.

These considerations indicate that the ultimate metacriterial standard for weighing a criterion of truth-acceptance (in the factual area) is not *cognitive* at all, but rather *affective*, and the reasoning of the test-procedure of truth-determination represents in the final analysis an appeal not to knowledge but to feeling. The affective dimension of pain, frustration of hope, disappointment of expectation—and their opposites—becomes the court of appeal that stands in ultimate judgment over our procedures for deciding questions of truth and falsity. In a real sense cognition is ancillary to practice and *feeling* becomes the arbiter of *knowledge*.

It is worth while to set the whole line of reasoning out in detail. The components of a pragmatic validation of a truth criterion that takes the route of an appeal to experience are as follows:

(1) A practical principle of regulative import is invoked to afford the plausibility (not truth) of matters of record.

(2) We note (as matters of record) that employment of the truth-criterion C has provided the C-validated propositions $p_1, p_2 \ldots$

(3) We note (as matters of record) that in various cases we acted upon these C-validated propositions.

(4) We note (as matters of record) that affectively advantageous results obtained in these cases—at least by and large.

(5) We note (as matters of record) that comparably advantageous results did not obtain in those cases where we acted upon criteria C', C'', . . ., that are alternative to C.

(6) A practical principle of regulative import is invoked to afford the plausibility (not truth) of the claim that the advantageous results that ensued upon the use of C were obtained *because* we employed C. Accordingly we attribute these results to C, and so obtain the essential premiss that 'C works' in the pragmatic manner appropriate for its methodological validation.

(7) We then take the pragmatic step of inferring, from the premiss that 'C works' in this practical/affective sense, the

(methodological) correctness of C with the full range of wider implications that this carries with it.

Only with this last step—after invoking two practical principles and a great many presumptively factual claims—do we reach our final goal of experientially validating on pragmatic grounds the correctness of the truth-criterion C at issue.

This course of pragmatic validation is not in any direct way a pragmatic justification of the acceptance as true of some thesis or proposition. Rather it is a justification of a methodology and its bearing on propositions is altogether indirect. A two-layer process is envisaged: the acceptance of a thesis as true is validated not in pragmatic terms at all but in terms of the verdict of a criterion, but the appropriateness of this criterion is in its turn validated on pragmatic grounds.

But how is one to argue that a criterion of factual truth works (from this pragmatic/affective angle)? Either on theoretical grounds of general principle (which are not available in any promising way) or else on the basis of past experience. Now recourse to the lessons of experience calls for two inputs: (1) information of the matter-of-record type, and (2) information regarding the attribution of results to procedures. Here the matters-of-record in question must be seen not as *actual* (factual) truths, but as merely *presumptive* data. And the status of the attribution-theses must also be viewed as merely presumptive in that it represents a presumption based upon postulation. Finally, undergirding this whole process, is an appeal to certain practical precepts of procedural justification that serve to define and constitute the very essence of rationality of action.

11. *Application to the Coherence Theory*

The question now remains: How can the general considerations of this analysis be brought to bear specifically upon a validation of a coherence criterion of factual truth? How, that is, are we to show that an appeal to experience makes manifest the success of this criterion?

The answer to this question cannot be contained within the confines of one short chapter: it is, in effect, given in the discussion of applications which have to some extent occupied us in the preceding discussion and to which virtually the whole remainder of the book will be devoted. Our strategy is this: to show that a great part of scientific method, of information processing theory, and of the general theory of knowledge, can be successfully accommodated within the framework of the coherence criterion. Hence the successful record of these disciplines in their established routines can be invoked on behalf of the coherence theory itself. In so far as these cognitive disciplines have proved themselves successful in the guidance of our conduct of affairs and in so far as they can be incorporated within the province of the coherence criterion of factual truth, an appeal to successful experience can be made on behalf of our coherence theory itself. This justificatory strategy that holds that 'the proof of the pudding lies in the eating' renders it desirable and necessary to take detailed account of the various applications of our coherence theory.

But before turning to these substantiating considerations a preliminary review of the general situation that confronts us may be in order.

To begin with, it is crucial to note, however, that the pragmatic test is here applied not to *individual* propositions as a test of *truths* but to generic *criteria for truths*. A two-layer process is at issue: truth-claims are validated as such with reference to criteria, and only these criteria in turn are justified with reference to the pragmatic considerations of success in rational systematization and in practical action. Our pragmatism here is of the second order: *theses* are viewed as warranted non-pragmatically by *methods*, and methods in turn as warranted pragmatically by results. Two distinct justificatory stages are at issue, only the second of which is pragmatic in character. The case is analogous to that of act *v.* rule utilitarianism in ethics. The rule utilitarian wants to justify actions with reference to rules, these rules themselves alone being supported by utilitarian considerations. The distinction between the *proposition-pragmatism* of the Jamesian variety and our own *criterion-pragmatism* is exactly parallel to this. Of course this 'criterion pragmatism' descends to the specific details of the coherence analysis, for— as we have seen—both considerations of datahood eligibility and of preferential schemes (and, in particular, those for plausibility assessments) are to be validated in pragmatic terms.[4]

Indeed the father of the pragmatic justification of coherence theory is that arch-rationalist, G. W. Leibniz. I cannot forbear quoting at some length from his classic essay 'On the Method of Distinguishing Real from Imaginary Phenomena':

Let us now see by what criteria we may know which phenomena are real. We may judge this both from the phenomenon itself and from the phenomena which are antecedent and consequent to it as well.

---

[4] For a comparison between the approaches of the present theory of truth as based upon a *methodological* pragimatism and the pragmatic theory of W. V. O. Quine see Appendix I.

We conclude it from the phenomenon itself if it is vivid, complex, and internally coherent [*congruum*]. . . . A phenomenon will be coherent when it consists of many phenomena, for which a reason can be given either within themselves or by some sufficiently simple hypothesis common to them; next, it is coherent if it conforms to the customary nature of other phenomena which have repeatedly occurred to us, so that its parts have the same position, order, and outcome in relation to the phenomenon which similar phenomena have had. Otherwise phenomena will be suspect, for if we were to see men moving through the air astride the hippogryphs of Ariostus, it would, I believe, make us uncertain whether we were dreaming or awake. But this criterion can be referred back to another general class of tests drawn from preceding phenomena. The present phenomenon must be coherent with these if, namely, it preserves the same consistency or if a reason can be supplied for it from preceding phenomena or if all together are coherent with the same hypothesis, as if with a common cause. But certainly a most valid criterion is a consensus with the whole sequence of life, especially if many others affirm the same thing to be coherent with their phenomena also. . . . Yet the most powerful criterion of the reality of phenomena, sufficient even by itself, is success in predicting future phenomena from past and present ones, whether that prediction is based upon a reason, upon a hypothesis that was previously successful, or upon the customary consistency of things as observed previously. . . . We must admit it to be true that the criteria for real phenomena thus far offered, even when taken together, are not demonstrative, even though they have the greatest probability; or to speak popularly, that they provide a moral certainty but do not establish a metaphysical certainty, so that to affirm the contrary would involve a contradiction. Thus by no argument can it be demonstrated absolutely that bodies exist, nor is there anything to prevent certain well-ordered dreams from being the objects of our mind, which we judge to be true and which, because of their accord with each other, are equivalent to truth so far as practice is concerned. Nor is the argument which is popularly offered, that this makes God a deceiver, of great importance. . . . For what if our nature happened to be incapable of real phenomena? Then indeed God ought not so much to be blamed as to be thanked, for since these phenomena could not be real, God would, by causing them at least to be in agreement, be providing us with something equally as valuable in all the practice of life as would be real phenomena.[5]

Leibniz clearly makes the following points: (1) that the coherence of lawful orderliness is the proper test as between real and illusory phenomena, (2) that this test does not and cannot be

[5] From Leibniz's *De modo distinguendi phaenomena realia ab imaginariis* in C. I. Gerhardt (ed.), *G. W. Leibniz: Philosophische Schriften*, vol. 7 (Berlin, 1890), pp. 319–22, tr. by L. E. Loemker, *G. W. Leibniz: Philosophical Papers and Letters* (Dordrecht 1969), pp. 363–5 (see pp. 363–4).

certified as correct by any demonstrative proof (and certainly not by an appeal to a Cartesian *deus ex machina*), and (3) that accordingly support for a coherence approach in the final analysis comes from pragmatic considerations relating to success in prediction and the guidance of 'the practice of life'.

The 'success' of a criterion of truth cannot be construed as '*inevitably providing* the actual truth'. Putting aside its inherent circularity, this is in principle a goal no criteriological standard of factual truth can meet. What is to be asked for is not invariable success, but the provision of an adequate rational foundation that works out for the purposes in hand. As we have stressed from the very first, the aim of a criterion of factual truth is to provide not for infallibility but for a working approximation to truth. A viable criterion of factual truth need not (indeed cannot) provide an unfailing guarantee of *de facto* success, but at best a reasonable, rationally warranted promise of success. The justification provided by such a pragmatic line of support for a criteriological theory of truth cannot be of the this-or-nothing type (as criticized above). Nor does it guarantee that a correct result will invariably or even preponderantly be obtained (for no 'inductive'—i.e. ampliative—mode of reasoning can issue such a guarantee). Since it deploys the standard of 'what works out', the only upshot it can extract is that we shall do as well on this basis as on any other: its result is not 'this or *nothing*', but 'this or *nothing better*'.[6]

But what are 'the purposes' that define the success with reference to which the acceptability of a criterion of truth can be assessed? Clearly if the criterion purports to be a *global* standard of factual truth this cannot be construed as 'providing the actual truth', since this would require an independent prior criterion. So we must not here construe 'success' in theoretical terms at all—i.e. with reference to 'our knowledge of the truth'. Rather the pragmatic standard must—as the very name implies —relate to the *practical* dimension. Man is not only a theoretical being who aims at understanding but a practical being who acts in the world, and who acts with a view not simply to theoretical purposes (knowledge, systematization, etc.) but to the strictly practical purposes of affective life. Accordingly the propositions we accept in part serve theoretical purposes (with reference to our understanding of the truth and its systematization) but also

---

[6] It is worth observing that the self-corrective aspect of H. Reichenbach's classic 'pragmatic justification of induction' can also be deployed, *mutatis mutandis*, to a defence of the coherence analysis of truth. Cf. Reichenbach's *Experience and Prediction* (Chicago, Ill., 1962), as well as his *Theory of Probability* (Berkeley, Cal., 1949).

the strictly practical purposes of human welfare and the affective and hedonistic side of our lives. The propositions we accept are a *guide to life* and the success of any acceptance-procedure (a criteriological theory of truth included) can be appraised in terms of its success in this regard. 'Does it conduce to the interests of our control over nature?' is the eminently practical question, and it is in this sense of the objectives of man's action rather than his theorizing that the pragmatic test of a criterial theory of truth must be understood.

One amendment is needed. The coherence theory of truth is actually not a *single* well-defined specific method, but a family or cluster of structurally similar methods which in detail are diverse (there being different standards of datahood and different modes of alethic preference). In various sorts of logico-epistemological situations a context-relative choice among these is necessary. This choice is itself guided by pragmatic considerations. The pragmatic justification of the coherence theory of truth cannot be global and generic but will have to be particular and specific. It can do no more than invoke the fact that a particular version of the coherence procedure is effective in a particular type of application.

Above all, the mechanisms of plausibility-grading illustrate this pragmatic aspect. They do not in general reflect factual/descriptive information at all, but play a *regulative* role in guiding the inquiry, since they constitute inputs for the analysis of the given data rather than its results. On this view, the legitimation of plausibility considerations also calls for a pragmatic justification: they are neither forced upon us by the specific epistemic circumstances nor validated 'on general principles' by considerations of a purely logical or epistemological sort. They are not extracted from the problem by an inquiring mind but *supplied* by it, though not, of course, at haphazard or by wishful thinking but rather in a *controlled* manner subject to functional considerations regarding the aims of the cognitive enterprise at issue. And these controls are, as we have said, themselves provided by ultimately practical rather than purely cognitive factors.

Accordingly, we reject the metaphysician's path to the justification of a coherence methodology through the argument that the search for truth through coherence is warranted by the fact that reality is itself coherent. The question 'Why do our conceptual mechanisms fit "the real world" with which we interact intellectually?' is to be answered in basically the same way as 'Why do our bodily mechanisms fit the world with which we interact physically?' Both alike are to be resolved in essentially pragmatic/evolutionary terms.

Our categorical perspective upon things and the intellectual mechanisms by which we form our view of 'the way the world works' are built up by a historic, evolutionary process of 'trial and error'—exactly as are the bodily mechanisms by which we comport ourselves in the physical world. These conceptions accordingly develop subject to revision in terms of 'success and failure' as these are defined by the standards of the enterprise of rational inquiry. The concept of a 'governing purpose' here serves as a regulative guide exactly as in any other goal-oriented human activity.

The evolutionary development of intellectual methodologies proceeds by natural selection. It is a matter of 'survival of the fittest', with *fitness* assessed in terms of the practical objectives of the rational enterprise. Legitimation comes about through the fact of survival through historical vicissitudes. As changes come to be entertained (within the society) it transpires that one 'works out for the better' relative to another in terms of its fitness to survive because it answers better to the socially determined purposes of the group. Just what does 'better' mean here? This carries us back to the Darwinian perspective. A Darwinian legitimation requires a standard of 'fitness'. We want to argue here that this normative standard is provided by considerations of *practice*, and is inherent in the use to which conceptual instrumentalities are put in the rational conduct of our affairs. In the western intellectual tradition the ultimate norms of rationality are defined by a very basic concept of knowledge-wed-to-practice. The governing standards of the western tradition of human rationality are presented by the goals of *explanation*, *prediction*, and *control* (and thus not, for example, sentimental 'at-oneness with nature'. Think of magician *v.* the mystic *v.* sage as cultural ideal.) This line of thought delineates in skeletal outline the reasoning of an essentially pragmatic defence of coherentism.

The present approach to the problem of a truth-criterion has actually brought the three traditional theories of truth together in systematic coexistence. To see this, consider the fact that one must begin with a potential variety of diverse alternative criteria to indicate the truth-status of propositions:

C_1: it is true that P

C_2: it is false that P

C_3: it is true that P

etc.

The basic issue is one of a choice among such criteria. Now as regards the *meaning* of 'is true' our position is correspondentist —to claim '*P* is true' is tantamount to claiming that *P* is the case ('*P* is true' iff *P*, i.e. $|P| = T$ iff *P*). But our position is *pragmatist* as to the *nature* of the choice among alternative truth-criteria: a criterion is basically methodological, and here the question 'Does it work?' reigns supreme. Finally, our position is *coherentist* as to the *outcome* of this choice: the criterion superior to the rest is provided by the principle of coherence. The over-all theory has thus managed to bring the three classical principles together in a systematic unity.

XI

THE COHERENCE APPROACH TO COUNTERFACTUAL CONDITIONALS

1. *Belief-Contravening Hypotheses and Hypothetical Reasoning*

ITS applications to situations of hypothetical reasoning represent one of the most striking and valuable uses of the coherence analysis of truth. Coherence should afford not only a means for determining the actual truth, but also a mechanism for determining the *relative* truth with respect to hypothetical assumptions, including false ones. On the coherence approach the deliberate introduction of a false hypothesis must clearly have ramified implications: some true and some false propositions will certainly be incoherent with it; others, however, will cohere perfectly well with it.

Some coherence theorists have tended to take a negative view of inference from hypothetical suppositions. According to Bernard Bosanquet, for example, 'Hypothetical affirmation is a contradiction in terms, and so is hypothetical inference. The whole process apart from any categorical meaning it may make explicit is . . . mere make-believe. [A claim like] "if a donkey is Plato, it is a great philosopher" [is arrant nonsense because it] scatters underlying reality to the winds.'[1] Taken at face value this seems far too drastic a position. Coherentists need not dismiss the entire enterprise of hypothetical reasoning as unworkable and improper (and actually Bosanquet does not intend to do so). A false hypothesis is not simply incoherent *per se*, it is incoherent with *some* of the truth, but may perfectly well cohere with some of the rest. The operation of coherence considerations in the hypothetical realm is merely difficult, not impossible. The matter needs—and deserves—detailed examination.

---

[1] Quoted in J. Passmore, *A Hundred Years of Philosophy* (London, 1968), pp. 166–7. Compare the following passage from Bosanquet's *Logic* (London, 1911): 'But the purposes of supposition in argument are so various that the limits of legitimate supposal are exceedingly hard to define. Undoubtedly its use is one of the most fallacious if one of the most effective means of controversy. "If A.B. were to turn coward"—"But he could not"—"But I am only putting a case"—"But if you put such a case I may put any consequence I choose as equally likely", i.e., it is felt that the real basis on which judgment rests is annihilated' (pp. 273–4).

A hypothetical inference is, of course, an inference made from a 'hypothesis', that is, from a proposition whose truth-status is doubtful or undetermined, or from a proposition known or believed to be false. Thus, hypothetical inference is reasoning which derives a conclusion from premisses[2] one or more of which is *problematic* (of unknown truth-status) or *belief-contravening* (negating some accepted belief and thus taken to be false) or outright *counterfactual* (i.e. actually known to be false). Arguments whose essential premisses are all known or accepted to be true, and only these, are excluded from this conception of *hypothetical* inference; the premisses being (*ex hypothesi*) given as true, they can be asserted and need not be hypothesized. The conclusions of *such* arguments can be asserted categorically, without explicit relativization to 'iffy' premisses of questionable truth-status.

On this specific conception of the matter, an inference is 'hypothetical', not because of the character of the logical (deductive or inductive) *linkage* between the premisses and the conclusion, but solely because of the epistemic status of its premisses as propositions whose truth is considered as open to doubt or question. The hypothetical inference *par excellence* is thus the counterfactual argument, some of whose premisses are actually known to be false. Accordingly, an inference is *hypo-thetical* not because of its having a conditional 'if-then' form, but because of the 'iffy-ness' of its antecedent premisses. On this view of the matter, an argument of type 'if . . . then . . .', which reasons from an antecedent whose truth is recognized or acknowledged, is not strictly 'hypothetical'.

It is in the nature of the case that we are not in a position to class as true certain of the premisses of a hypothetical inference: the status of such a premiss within the framework of our know-ledge must be that of a *supposition*. This term will here be used in a very broad sense, to apply to any informative statement put forward within what may be called a *supposition-context* illus-trated by such qualifying phrases as:

> Let us suppose that . . .
> Let us assume that . . .
> Let it, for the sake of argument, be agreed that . . .
> Let it, for the sake of discussion, be accepted that . . .
> Let the hypothesis be made that . . .
> Let . . . be so.

[2] It is to be assumed, of course, that the premisses in question are actually required for the valid inference of the conclusion, and are not irrelevant and superfluous. In this sense, the 'premisses' at issue must be *essential* to the inference.

A supposition is not an accepted fact, but a thesis that is accepted 'provisionally' or laid down 'for the time being'; it must be uncertain to some extent.[3] A hypothesis is a statement which, rather than being put forward as an asserted truth, is nothing other than a suppositional premiss of this sort. On our present conception of the matter, it is the occurrence among the premisses of an argument of such a suppositional hypothesis that renders the argument 'hypothetical'.

Suppositions—and so also the hypothetical arguments that contain them as premisses—can be either *problematic*, or actually *counterfactual*, or merely *belief-contravening* in a weaker sense, according to whether they are of unknown truth-status, known to be false, or believed to be false. We can accordingly classify suppositions in order of an increasingly close liaison with falsehood by the tripartite scheme:

CLASSIFICATION OF SUPPOSITIONS

Type	*The proposer views the proposition as*
1. problematic	one that is possibly true and possibly false, no definite view being held
2. (weakly) belief-contravening	one he believes to be false
3. (strongly) belief-contravening = counterfactual	one that is certainly and definitely false

In the case of a valid *deductive* argument, the suppositional status of the conclusion cannot be weaker than that of the weakest premiss (though it could possibly be stronger). In the case of a (correct and appropriate) *inductive* argument no general relationship as to suppositional status can be claimed to obtain between the premisses and conclusion (e.g. in an inductive argument even a counterfactual conclusion might—in certain instances—be drawn, correctly and appropriately, from premisses known and claimed to be true).[4]

---

[3] 'What you say about knowledge having the existent or the hypothetical existent as its object is false of God's knowledge of the world's non-existence in eternity [i.e. prior to the creation], for the world did not exist then, nor could there have been a supposition thereof, because its supposition or any supposition on the part of the Creator would be ridiculous, for supposition implies doubt' (A. Guillaume (ed.), *The 'Summa Philosophiae' of Al-Shahrastānī* (Oxford, 1934), p. 62 of the translation).

[4] Indeed this very feature could be viewed as an essential characteristic of inductive in contrast to deductive inferences.

A hypothesis is to be characterized as 'belief-contravening' if it either:

(*a*) negates a believed proposition or otherwise stands in *logical* contradiction with such propositions, or

(*b*) conflicts with accepted beliefs upon grounds that are *inductive* or *probabilistic* rather than logico-deductive (though these grounds must qualify—from the inductive or probabilistic standpoint—as relatively strong).

An example of the former mode of belief-contravention is afforded by the supposition:

Assume that Lincoln had been defeated by Douglas in the Presidential election of 1860.

Since we believe, and indeed know, that Lincoln won in 1860, this hypothesis is in *logical* conflict with a proposition that is actually believed. The second (that is, inductive or probabilistic) mode of belief-contravention is illustrated by the hypothesis:

Assume that Methuselah died at the age of 969 years.

This assumption does not actually involve an explicit contradiction with our beliefs about the history of the early Semitic peoples. But it is plain, on the basis of everything that we do believe about human mortality, that the balance of probabilities goes heavily against the claim put forward with this hypothesis. Accordingly it is belief-contravening not in the rigidly logical, but in the inductive or probabilistic manner. Further examples of hypotheses which the generality of persons will surely regard as belief-contravening are the suppositions:

Assume that Napoleon had won at Waterloo.

Assume the State of Georgia to include New York City.

Assume that Newton had not discovered the principle of gravitation.

Assume that Washington's dedicated leadership of the revolutionary cause was prompted primarily by considerations of personal gain.

It deserves remark that while *fact-violating* assumptions are perfectly viable, the matter is quite otherwise with *logic-violating* assumptions. Such essentially self-contradictory assumptions must clearly be ruled out altogether, and so there will indeed be some conceivable suppositions that cannot rationally be made. An instance of such a logically *blocked* assumption is: 'Assume three were an even number.' Quite in general, if it is 'of the essence' of X to be ϕ (i.e. if ϕ is a logically or definitionally necessary feature of X), then one cannot rationally assume that X is a ψ where being a ψ is logically or definitionally incompatible with being a ϕ. Thus, to give another example, *if* (and this may well be a very big if) we regard Pegasus as being *by definition* a winged horse, then we cannot introduce the assumption:

Assume Pegasus had no wings.

In the circumstances, we are logically blocked from making this assumption. (This stance eliminates Meinong's square circles.)

Within the setting of a coherence analysis the need for such blockages readily becomes apparent. Consider the example regarding the number three. We know as matters of logico-definitional fact that:

No odd number can (by definition) be even.
The odd numbers are (by definition) those of the sequence $1, 3, 5, 7, \ldots, 2n+1, \ldots$

Now we cannot conjoin to these two definitional truths the assumption:

Three is an even number.

For the two logico-definitional truths must—in virtue of that fact—be accorded a maximally plausible indexing status (i.e. 0 or 1). And the assumption in question must also—in virtue of that fact—be given a high plausibility status (i.e. 1). But the basic ground-rule is that the set of all up-to-1 indexed propositions must be logically consistent, and this fundamental requirement is now clearly violated.

Thus it is clear that logic-contravening (though not merely fact-contravening) assumptions must be regarded as blocked within the framework of our analysis. On the present view also, *some* assumptions are rejected as not viable and ruled out as leading to logical chaos. But these blocked assumptions are confined—on our position—within the narrow logico-definitional sphere.

Hypothetical inferences, in the sense in which the term is being used here, thus arise over an enormously wide range of subject-matters, which includes:

1. Heuristic reasoning (both in discussion and theoretical inquiry).
2. *Reductio ad absurdum* reasoning and especially *per impossibile* proof (in logic and in mathematics).

3. Thought-experimentation in tracing through the consequences of a disbelieved proposition (this occurs both in common life and in technical contexts).
4. The didactic use of hypotheses in learning situations.
5. Contingency planning (in everyday life).
6. Games and make-believe of all kinds.
7. The hypothetico-inductive process of testing theories (in science and to some extent in everyday life).

Hypothetical inference thus plays a very widespread part in both scientific and in common-life reasonings, and occurs in an enormously wide spectrum of applications, ranging from the most serious to the most frivolous contexts.

If—as some coherentists have claimed—adoption of a coherence theory of truth were to countermand the legitimacy of such reasoning, this would constitute a grave defect of the theory itself, a defect one could not but score against it as a most serious drawback. A systematic examination of the logical theory of hypothetical inference from the coherence point of view is thus an enterprise of substantial significance.

2. *The Contextual Ambiguity of Belief-Contravening Hypotheses*

As observed above, the more strictly 'hypothetical' of the modes of hypothetical inference are based upon outrightly *belief-contravening* suppositions (the only type of hypotheses with which this is not the case being the purely *problematic* hypotheses). In the most typical and important classes of hypothetical inference, the hypotheses involved stand in deductive or inductive conflict with accepted beliefs. Because of the problems posed by such conflicts, special attention must be given to the logical theory of belief-contravening hypotheses.

It is clearly by no means necessary that a belief-contravening hypothesis should assume a falsehood. Whether it assumes something that is actually true or something that is actually false is wholly immaterial to the belief-contravening status of a hypothesis. What alone matters is that the hypothesis is *believed* to be false, or that it clashes with what is *believed* to be true. A hypothesis is not rendered belief-contravening through failure to square with the actual facts, but simply and solely through discord with other propositions that are believed.

It is necessary to recognize a distinctly disconcerting feature of hypothetical arguments of the belief-contravening type. It appears that certain very perplexing and paradoxical difficulties are inextricably inherent in this common and seemingly innocuous procedure. Take, as a concrete instance of a belief-contravening hypothesis, the supposition:

Assume that tigers were canines.

Of course this hypothesis arises in a context in which, patently, we know each of the following:

(1) Tigers are felines.
(2) Tigers are not canines.
(3) No felines are canines.

The assumption explicitly instructs us to drop item (2). But are we to alter the boundaries of the classification 'felines' (and so drop (1) as well), or to keep these boundaries the same and so countenance tigers as canines-cum-felines (thus dropping (3))? Obviously we must, in the interests of mere self-consistency, adopt one or the other of these procedures if logical paradox is to be avoided. Some of the environing beliefs must always be rejected in the wake of the hypothetical assumption; some of them must always be retained to provide structure and context to the reasoning.[5] But this can always be accomplished in alternative ways, and the assumption itself gives us no directions for effecting a choice.

As this example illustrates, every belief-contravening hypothesis is by nature ambiguous. Its specific assertive content is unclear in that its conflicts with cognate beliefs always require further adjudication. Within the wider environment of other accepted beliefs, a belief-contravening hypothesis must of necessity be contextually ambiguous. The removal of such ambiguity must be viewed as an urgent task for our inquiry.

Let us probe somewhat more deeply towards the root source of the contextual ambiguity that we have seen to infect belief-contravening hypotheses. Once more it seems best to begin with a concrete example. Let it be that we hold the following three statements to be true:

(1) Jones did the work, or he will lose the contract (symbolically: $W \vee L$).

---

[5] In *this* regard B. Bosanquet's position is perfectly correct: 'Some real basis can never be dispensed with in judgment. The nearest approach to dispensing with it is made when elements of reality which would conflict with the suggested case are wilfully kept out of account by an act of abstraction [in hypothetical reasoning]; which act of abstraction may be either borne in mind, or forgotten. . . . Thus judgments are subject to the reservation implied in the abstraction from reality which enables them to be made. Yet, in as far as they are judged at all, they must rest upon, and involve the affirmation of, properties of reality' (*Logic* (London, 1911), p. 274). Bosanquet errs, however, in his inclination that because *something* must remain, coherence requires that *everything* remains, with the result that the hypothesis is rendered without effect. We shall criticize his position in detail at the end of the chapter.

(2) If Jones was ill, he will lose the contract $(I \supset L)$.
(3) Jones did the work, or he was ill $(W \lor I)$.

The assumption is now submitted: assume that (1) is false, that is, assume that Jones will retain the contract although he failed to do the work $(\sim W \,\&\, \sim L)$. Note the consequences of this supposition. It is consistent with (2) singly, and it is consistent with (3) singly, but it is inconsistent with (2) and (3) taken conjointly.[6] Thus the supposition is such that, in making it, we must also revise our prima facie unaffected residual beliefs —that is, we must also reject either (2) or (3).

This example typifies a paradigm situation. To make a belief-contravening assumption, it does not suffice to reject only the particular belief that is directly and explicitly involved, but because of the logical *interconnections* between our beliefs (or our knowledge) we must also reject, change, or modify our other beliefs so that the ultimate residue is logically compatible with the supposition in question. This, of course, can be done in various *alternative* ways, and the supposition itself leaves us entirely in the dark as to the specific way in which it should be accomplished. This ambivalence with respect to its 'wider implications' for our relevant beliefs accounts for the contextual ambiguity inevitably present in belief-contravening hypotheses.

It is important to recognize that this paradigm effectively accommodates all examples of the kind considered above. It will perhaps suffice to show this in detail for a single case. Let us consider an example taken from W. V. O. Quine's *Methods of Logic* (New York, 1950):

Beliefs: (1) Bizet was French by nationality.
　　　　　 (2) Verdi was Italian by nationality.
　　　　　 (3) Compatriots are persons who share the same nationality.
Supposition: Assume Bizet and Verdi were compatriots.

Note that our supposition is entirely compatible with (1), (2), and (3) taken singly, and with (1) and (3), and (2) and (3), taken in pairs, but not with (1), (2), and (3) together. In making the assumption we must thus reject either (1) or (2)—the definitional

---

[6] Note that $\sim$(1) & (2) comes to

$$(a) \quad \sim W \,\&\, \sim L \,\&\, \sim I$$

and that $\sim$(1) & (3) comes to

$$(b) \quad \sim W \,\&\, \sim L \,\&\, I$$

but that the conjunction $\sim$(1) & (2) & (3), or equivalently (a) & (b), is patently inconsistent.

thesis (3) is scarcely a candidate—and it is a matter of complete indifference which of them we select for rejection.[7]

The situation illustrated by these examples is a general one. Each and every belief P_1 is a member of a family of related beliefs $P_1, P_2, P_3, \ldots, P_n$ of such a kind that, even when P_1 is dropped from explicit membership in the list, the remainder will collectively still yield P_1.[8] (The trio $P_1, P_2 = P_1 \vee Q, P_3 = \sim Q$ yields an example.) This circumstance reflects what might be called the *systematic constrictiveness* of truth: the fact that truths constitute a mutually determinative domain such that even if some element is hypothetically deleted it can immediately be restored from the rest. This is an aspect of the cohesiveness of truth upon which the traditional coherence theory has placed great weight, and it is worth dwelling upon.

Consider any counterfactual hypothesis, for example:

Suppose that this penny were a dime.

Such a hypothesis does not (and cannot) be made in a cognitive vacuum. It can only arise in a context where we know such facts as:

1. This coin is a penny.
2. This coin is not a dime.
3. Two coins like this one make two cents.
4. This coin will buy one (but only one) piece of candy.

The 'true facts' are invariably redundant in this way—even if we negate (1) and (2), as the hypothesis instructs, we must still make readjustments among the residual items of background knowledge of propositions within the 'epistemic neighbourhood' of those at issue. Every given truth is 'hemmed in' by other truths (for example, by its own 'consequences'—logical or otherwise) to the point where even if it is assumed to be abrogated

---

[7] To give a graphic illustration, consider a painting of some group scene including, say, B. Franklin. We are told: 'Assume Franklin were not in the picture.' The problem now confronts us: whom or what are we to put in his place? (Notice that it might on first thought seem to be plausible to 'remove' the surface ambiguity of the assumption that 'Bizet and Verdi were compatriots' by translating this into an explicit alternative in the form: 'Either Bizet and Verdi were both Frenchmen or Bizet and Verdi were both Italians.' But this attempt at eliminating overt ambiguity does not in the least affect the contextual ambiguity present in this hypothesis —as is readily seen by introducing the supposition in this reformulation into the analysis of the foregoing example. Although this revised assumption seems to be quite unambiguous by itself, we have not in the slightest mitigated what we have termed the *contextual* ambiguity that it generates when put alongside other beliefs. We still do not know how to undertake the necessary revision of our relevant beliefs so as to integrate the assumption with them; that is, we are still unable to say what the assumption is actually to 'mean for' our relevant beliefs.)

[8] See Sect. 2 of Chapter VII.

and removed the remainder will collectively redetermine and restore it.[9] Hence any truth—and any belief—is part of a *system* that collectively regenerates it even if it be surgically excised therefrom by means of a hypothesis. This systematic constrictiveness is a descriptive logico-epistemological thesis[10] about the cohesiveness of the domain of truth that represents one of the central doctrines of the traditional coherence theory.

The systematic constrictiveness of beliefs has implications of crucial importance for our present concern with belief-contravening suppositions and counterfactual assumptions. Since a belief P_1 is always one of a family $P_1, P_2, \ldots, P_n$ that restores P_1 even if it is deleted therefrom, it follows that our labours are only at a beginning when we replace P_1 by $\sim P_1$, as the hypothesis explicitly demands. For the sake of consistency, appropriate readjustments in the residual beliefs $P_2, \ldots, P_n$ must also be made: one or more of them must also be rejected in the interests of logical consistency if $\sim P_1$ is to be assumed. The belief-contravening assumption of $\sim P_1$ is thus *contextually ambiguous* in that the explicit instruction to reject P_1 leads to the consequence *that* the residual beliefs must also be revised, without telling us *how* this is to be done, i.e. which of the invariable plurality of alternative ways of achieving this result is to be adopted. In this way, a belief-contravening or counterfactual hypothesis is in general ambiguous as to the actual import and implications of the assumption in question—i.e. as to its intended 'meaning' with respect to the residual beliefs. This contextual ambiguity is, as we have seen, an inevitable consequence of the systematic constrictiveness of truths and beliefs.[11]

[9] Let $C(P)$ be the set of all logical consequences of a proposition P, and let $C^*(P)$ be the result of deleting from $C(P)$ all those elements equivalent with P itself. It is not difficult to show that given only $C^*(P)$ it is possible to obtain P itself by way of deductive inference.

[10] The thesis is *logical* as applied to truths *per se*, and *epistemological* as applied to our beliefs respecting the truth.

[11] It should be stressed that, although the previous examples here dealt with the 'stronger' case of a logical conflict between a belief-contravening hypothesis and the residual beliefs, our analysis also applies to cases in which the resulting conflict is not one of logical contradiction but of empirical incongruity. Consider the example:

Beliefs: (1) Napoleon lost the battle of Waterloo.
   (2) Napoleon attempted to flee France on an American ship a fortnight after the battle of Waterloo.
   (3) Napoleon was captured by the British and sent into imprisonment on St. Helena about a month after the battle of Waterloo.
   (4) Napoleon died in exile on St. Helena some six years after the battle of Waterloo.
Supposition: Assume Napoleon won the battle of Waterloo.

How are we to revise our beliefs in the face of this assumption? It is of course obvious that (1) must go; this again is a simple matter of logic. But what about (2)

We are thus confronted by what may be called the *problem of belief-contravening hypotheses*. Every such hypothesis, once adjoined to existing beliefs that lie in its epistemic neighbourhood, will render them collectively inconsistent: less bitingly, perhaps, but yet most unpleasantly, in the inductive cases, and downright viciously in the deductive ones. Somehow or other the totality of 'residual' beliefs with which we are left after the belief-contravening assumption in question has been made is paradoxical: it continues to conflict and to call for accommodation. The question of how to overcome its stultifying inconsistency so as to restore the harmony of mutual compatibility in the face of such hypotheses poses the central task of this problem-area.

3. *The Problem of Counterfactual Conditionals*

A conditional statement asserts a strictly consequential relationship between antecedent and consequent (if . . ., then . . .), without any reference to the specific nature of the antecedent. However, the epistemic status of this antecedent may be problematic (unknown), or known to be true, or known to be false. In these three cases we obtain—respectively—the *problematic* conditional (should it be the case that . . ., which it may or may not be, then . . .), the *factual* conditional (since . . ., so . . .), and the *counterfactual* conditional (if it were the case that . . ., which it is not, then . . .).

The familiar relationship of material implication—with $P \supset Q$ construed simply as the truth-functional 'not-P or Q'—is clearly not suited to the counterfactual case. For *any* such material conditional is true if the antecedent is false: when P is false, then both $P \supset Q$ and $P \supset \sim Q$ will be true, regardless of what we may choose to put in place of Q. Obviously this will not do to represent the counterfactually conditional relationships

and (3)? They plainly do not stand in any *logical* contradiction to the hypothesis we are asked to make, but they accord so poorly with this supposition that it is fairly obvious that they too must be jettisoned. And what of (4)? Here we can say little; it is altogether unclear just what ought to be done about its retention or rejection. The contextual ambiguity of our hypothesis is so pervasive that we have even less guidance in revising our beliefs than we have in cases of an actual *logical* conflict between a belief-contravening hypothesis and the residual beliefs. At any rate, the example makes vividly manifest the fact that in analysing the *modus operandi* of counterfactual hypotheses proper account must be taken not only of relationships of logical consistency and logical implication but also of relationships of factual 'consistency' (= empirical congruity) and of empirical 'implication' (= causal connections). The patterns of the causal interconnectedness of things, so dear to the coherence theorists of the idealist school, must—and can—be taken into appropriate account in elaborating the 'consequences' of a counterfactual hypothesis.

one actually maintains in real-life situations. We want to be able to maintain some counterfactual conditionals and to reject others as unacceptable.

Much of the initial impetus to discussions of 'The Problem of Counterfactual Conditionals' derived from Nelson Goodman's influential 1947 paper of the same title.[12] Goodman wrote:

> What, then, is the problem about counterfactual conditionals? Let us confine ourselves to those [conditionals] in which antecedent and consequent are inalterably false—as, for example, when I say of a piece of butter that was eaten yesterday, and that had never been heated:
>
> > If that piece of butter had been heated at 150 °F, it would have melted.
>
> Considered as truth-functional compounds [sic for 'implications'], all counterfactuals are of course true, since their antecedents are false. Hence
>
> > If that piece of butter had been heated at 150 °F, it would not have melted.
>
> would also hold. Obviously something different [from a truth-functional connection] is intended, and the problem is to define the circumstances under which a given counterfactual holds while the opposing counterfactual with the contradictory consequent fails to hold.[13]

In a somewhat ampler and yet more pessimistic statement of the problem, W. V. O. Quine has written:

> Whatever the proper analysis of the contrafactual [i.e. counterfactual] conditional may be, we may be sure in advance that it cannot be truth-functional; for, obviously ordinary usage demands that some contrafactual conditionals with false antecedents and false consequents be true and that other contrafactual conditionals with false antecedents and false consequents be false. Any adequate analysis of the contrafactual conditional must go beyond mere truth-values and consider causal connections, or kindred relationships, between matters spoken of in the antecedent of the conditional and matters spoken of in the consequent. It may be wondered, indeed, whether any really coherent theory of the contrafactual conditional

---

[12] *The Journal of Philosophy*, 44 (1947), 113–28; reprinted in L. Linsky (ed)., *Semantics and the Philosophy of Language* (Urbana, Ill., 1952), pp. 231–46. For a comprehensive survey of the recent literature on counterfactual conditionals see Jerzy Giedymin, 'Confirmation, Counterfactuals and Projectibility', in R. Klibansky (ed.), *Contemporary Philosophy*, vol. ii (Florence, 1968), pp. 70–87. The older discussions are inventoried in N. Rescher, *Hypothetical Reasoning* (Amsterdam, 1964).

[13] Op. cit., pp. 113–14 (pp. 231–2 in the Linsky volume).

of ordinary usage is possible at all, particularly when we imagine trying to adjudicate between such examples as these:

> If Bizet and Verdi had been compatriots, Bizet would have been Italian;
> If Bizet and Verdi had been compatriots, Verdi would have been French.
> The problem of contrafactual conditionals is in any case a perplexing one. . . .[14]

The 'Problem of Counterfactual Conditionals' thus turns on the question of providing an analysis which elucidates their logical characteristics, and does this in a way which makes palpable the fact that in some cases, such as Goodman's melting-butter example, one of opposed counterfactuals is 'right' and one is 'wrong', while in other cases, typified by Quine's Bizet–Verdi example, a genuine paradox arises in that the opposed counterfactuals seem equally acceptable.

Some writers have proposed a *deductive* approach to the analysis of counterfactual conditionals. On this approach, the conclusion (= the consequent of the counterfactual) is to be viewed as a deductive consequence of the assumption (= the antecedent of the counterfactual). Counterfactual conditionals are properly to be understood as metalinguistic, i.e. as making statements about statements. Specifically 'If A were so, then B would be so' is to be construed in the context of a given system of statements **S**, saying that when A is adjoined as supplemental premiss to **S**, then B follows. This approach was originally proposed by Henry Hiz;[15] it has been endorsed by Roderick Chisholm and has been put forward in one form or another by many recent writers, most of whom incline to take **S**, as above, to include all or part of the corpus of scientific laws.[16]

This explication warrants a closer scrutiny. On fuller analysis we face the following situation with a considerably enlarged group of auxiliary hypotheses:

Known facts: (1) This band is made of rubber.
(2) This band is not made of copper.
(3) This band does not conduct electricity.
(4) Things made of rubber do not conduct electricity.

---

[14] *Methods of Logic*, revised edition (New York, 1959), pp. 14–15.
[15] 'On The Inferential Sense of Contrary-to-Fact Conditionals', *The Journal of Philosophy*, 48 (1951), 586–7.
[16] For a helpful discussion of the issues see the article 'Contrary-to-Fact Conditional' by R. S. Walters in P. Edwards (ed.), *The Encyclopedia of Philosophy*, 2 (New York, 1967), 212–16.

(5) Things made of copper do conduct electricity.

Assumption: Not-(2), i.e.: This band is made of copper.

Now when we introduce this assumption within the framework of known facts, a contradiction obviously ensues. We do not in fact arrive at a workable system of statements **S** but at one that is mutually inconsistent. How can we repair this situation? Clearly we must begin by dropping items (1) and (2) and replacing them by their negation—the assumption itself instructs us to do just this. But a contradiction still remains. The following alternatives are open:

Alternative 1	*Alternative* 2
Retain: (3), (4)	Retain: (4), (5)
Reject: (1), (2), (5)	Reject: (1), (2), (3)

That is we actually have a choice between rejecting (3) in favour of (5) or (5) in favour of (3), resulting in the following conditionals:

1. If this rubber band were made of copper then it would conduct electricity (since copper conducts electricity).
2. If this rubber band were made of copper then copper would not (always) conduct electricity (since this band does not conduct electricity).

Thus *alternative* results are possible, and the deductive approach does not really resolve the basic indeterminacy inherent in counterfactual situations.

The nature of the difficulties encountered by counterfactual conditionals to which Goodman and Quine in particular have called attention can very easily be appreciated from our present point of view. A 'counterfactual conditional' is, in effect, nothing other than a conditional which elicits a consequence from an antecedent that is in fact a belief-contravening hypothesis. Any such conditional will therefore exhibit the same problems and difficulties found to be generally present in belief-contravening hypotheses. This is readily shown by analysing in terms of belief-contravening hypotheses the standard examples cited in the literature:

Example 1 (Goodman): Suppose Georgia included New York City.

Notice the drastic ambiguity of this assumption: are we to retain the location of New York City and change the boundaries of Georgia, or are we to retain the boundaries of Georgia and change the location of New York City? This ambiguity can be pin-pointed by raising the question whether the statement 'New York City lies south of Washington, D.C.' is to follow from our assumption or not.

Example 2 (Quine): Suppose that Bizet and Verdi had been compatriots.

Again there is a radical ambiguity. Are we to suppose that both men were Italians, or both Frenchmen? This ambiguity can be pin-pointed by raising the question whether the statement 'Bizet was Italian' is to follow from the supposition.

Example 3 (Reichenbach): Suppose Plato had lived during the Middle Ages.

Once again notice the ambiguity. Are we to transport the *person* Plato alone through the time barrier, or are we to shift his entire biography? That is to say, are we or are we not to accept the inference:

Plato lived during the Middle Ages (assumption).

Plato witnessed the trial of Socrates (believed fact).

∴ Socrates lived during the Middle Ages.

Such examples serve to illustrate forcibly the general point that counterfactual conditionals can be regarded as conditional statements that draw their conclusions from a belief-contravening hypothesis, and that they will thus exhibit exactly the same difficulties of conflict-generation that are universally inherent in such hypotheses. It is therefore natural that their logical analysis should be approached from this point of view.

On the line of approach being proposed, it is readily seen that the problem of a choice among divergent counterfactual conditionals arises because the antecedents of such conditionals are belief-contravening hypotheses. For as a result, the contextual ambiguity generically inherent in such hypotheses must thus also enter into counterfactual conditionals, and gives rise there to mutually discordant conditionals of the type we have witnessed. The antecedent of a counterfactual conditional must, in the nature of things, be a belief-contravening hypothesis that can be rendered consonant with the residual beliefs in various *alternative* ways. It would appear that the problem of discordant counterfactuals is but a specific manifestation of the generic phenomenon of the paradoxical character of belief-contravening hypotheses inherent in their contextual ambiguity.

Although the Problem of Counterfactual Conditionals—that is, the question of discriminating between the natural and acceptable counterfactuals, and those that are unnatural and unacceptable—still remains unresolved at this point of discussion, it is now possible to see whence the problem arises, and thus to identify the issues to which a solution of it must address itself. For it has become clear that a solution of the Problem of Counterfactual Conditionals lies in making and supporting a distinction, within the group of logically eligible alternatives, between 'natural' and 'unnatural' ways of effecting a reconciliation between a belief-contravening hypothesis on the one hand, and on the other the entire set of residual beliefs which continue to be collectively inconsistent with it. Once the problem of counterfactuals is seen in this light, its assimilation to our problem of a coherence analysis of inconsistent premisses is relatively straightforward.

4. The Need for a 'Principle of Rejection and Retention'

To see how a solution of the problem of discriminating between plausible and implausible counterfactual conditionals is to be provided within the framework of the foregoing discussion, an examination of some concrete cases is called for. Let us re-examine the puzzle-cases of counterfactuals adduced by Goodman and by Quine from our present standpoint by viewing counterfactual conditionals as statements that elicit a consequence from a belief-contravening hypothesis.

Case 1: Goodman's Example

Beliefs: (1) This piece of butter was not heated to 150 °F.
(2) This piece of butter did not melt.
(3) All pieces of butter melt when heated to 150 °F.
Hypothesis: Assume that this piece of butter was heated to 150 °F.

The hypothesis explicitly instructs us to give up Belief (1). But it is still inconsistent with the residual beliefs (2) and (3) taken together. Thus one of them must also be given up. In the instance of Goodman's first ('natural' or 'acceptable') counterfactual—namely, 'If this piece of butter had been heated to 150 °F, it would have melted'—we give up Belief (2). On the other hand, in the instance of the second ('unnatural' and 'unacceptable') counterfactual—'If this piece of butter had been heated to 150 °F, it would not have melted'—we give up Belief (3), which, being the more difficult feat, renders difficult the counterfactual itself.

This case contrasts interestingly with one of a rather different character:

Case 2: Quine's Example

Beliefs: (1) Bizet was of French nationality.
    (2) Verdi was of Italian nationality.
    (3) Compatriots are persons who share the same nationality.
Hypothesis: Assume Bizet and Verdi were compatriots.

Note that the hypothesis is entirely compatible with (1), (2), and (3) taken singly, and with (1) and (3), and (2) and (3) taken in pairs, but not with (1), (2), and (3) together. In making the assumption we must thus either reject (1) or (2)—(3) is scarcely a suitable candidate. It being a matter of complete indifference whether (1) or (2) is to be rejected (due to the symmetry of the cases) the paradoxical air of Quine's two mutually conflicting counterfactuals results.

The foregoing analysis of counterfactuals in terms of belief-contravening hypotheses shows that what is needed to solve the Problem of Counterfactual Conditionals is a mechanism for restoring consistency. The prime desideratum is a *principle of rejection and retention of beliefs* capable of providing adequate guidance for the reconciliation of the residual beliefs in the face of a belief-contravening hypothesis. Once such machinery for a choice of retention or rejection of believed statements is at hand, the question of a choice among competing counterfactuals is readily settled by its means.

At this point, an important distinction must be made: it becomes necessary to recognize that there are two significantly different types of counterfactual conditionals. The first type consists of what may be termed *nomological* counterfactuals. Such contrary-to-fact conditionals are simply counterfactual specifications of covering laws. Consider, for example, the conditionals:

Example 1: If Julius Caesar had been a lion, he would have had a tail.

Example 2: If Smith had eaten an ounce of arsenic, he would have died.

We have said virtually all that needs to be said about these counterfactuals when we are able to refer them to the appropriate covering laws:

All lions have tails.
All people who eat an ounce of arsenic die.

To be sure, even with these conditionals the now accustomed element of paradoxical ambiguity can be detected. For we could rebut the foregoing counterfactuals by:

Example 3: If Julius Caesar had been a lion, there would have been a tail-less lion (because Caesar had no tail).

Example 4: If Smith had eaten an ounce of arsenic, this dosage would not invariably have proved fatal (because Smith is still alive).

However, these rebutting counterfactuals are effectively to be ruled out in the cases under consideration. For we may analyse the nomological counterfactuals in terms of belief-contravening hypotheses as illustrated in the following example:

Example 5:

Beliefs: (1) Caesar was not a lion (known fact).
        (2) Caesar had no tail (known fact).
        (3) All lions have tails (accepted covering law).

Assumption: Caesar was a lion.

Notice now that Belief (1) must obviously be set aside in view of the assumption, but that we have an option between rejecting (2) and (3). In Example 1 we reject (2), and in Example 3 we reject (3). However, Example 1 is 'natural' and Example 3 is 'artificial' because the nomological use of counterfactuals represents a determination to retain the appropriate covering generalization—that is, (3)—at the cost of adapting all else to it.

Consider yet another example:

Example 6.1: If Saladin had not died, he would be alive today.

This counterfactual seems perfectly 'natural' and can be viewed as essentially unambiguous and trouble-free only because we construe it in the light of the covering law:

All real persons (that is, persons who have been born) who have not died are alive today.

Once we reject this law—for instance, by envisaging some way to join the non-living other than by dying (for example, bodily assumption)—the contextual ambiguity typical of belief-contravening suppositions also infects this counterfactual, since we can now construct the rebutting counterfactual:

> *Example 6.2*: If Saladin had not died, he would have 'gone yonder' by bodily assumption (since he is not alive today).

Thus in the case of nomological counterfactuals the situation is relatively simple and straightforward in that we *do* here have the necessary guidance needed for the reconstitution of our residual beliefs in the face of the belief-contravening hypothesis represented by the antecedent of the counterfactual. We have this guidance because we are, in effect, resolved to treat the covering law as immune to rejection. This resolution suffices to inform us how to restructure our relevant beliefs.[17]

Thus the nomological type of counterfactual condition is not drastically troublesome. The problems that do remain here are not logical problems, but problems revolving about the implementation of the concept of a law, that is, a generalization to which we (*inter alia*) so commit ourselves that we are willing to retain it at great cost, and to let it be a fixed point about which practically all else revolves when a belief-contravening supposition is made.[18] But this question of the nature of laws is an extralogical[19] problem of epistemology and the philosophy of science into which we shall not enter further here.[20]

One possible complication should be noted briefly, namely that which arises when the applicability of the law in question is subject to fulfilment of certain 'boundary-value conditions' whose satisfaction must be stipulated by auxiliary hypotheses. We may illustrate this complication by an example which has received much discussion in the literature, namely, the counterfactual 'If the match *M* had been struck, it would have lit'. Let

[17] Goodman discusses the puzzle of the 'law': 'All coins in my pocket are made of silver'. But it is precisely because this is a 'merely accidental generalization' and not a 'genuine law' (*inter alia* one that we are determined to yield up only in the face of 'actual evidence' and not in the face of a 'mere assumption') that this does not validate the counterfactual 'If this penny were in my pocket, then it would be made of silver'.

[18] The point is not that laws are more securely established (inductively) than facts—which is simply not the case—but rather that in certain contexts of discussion and reasoning we accord an epistemically superior status to those generalizations to which we are willing to accord the honorific characterization of 'being a law'.

[19] It is clear that 'logical' is here used in its narrower sense, and not in the wider sense of inductive logic, which includes such matters as the theory of scientific method.

[20] For an exposition of the author's views see his *Scientific Explanation* (New York, 1969) and the even fuller treatment of lawfulness in chs. III–IV of his *Conceptual Idealism* (Oxford, 1973).

us analyse this conditional from the standpoint of belief-contravening suppositions:

Example 7:

Beliefs: (1) All dry matches located in an oxygen-containing medium light when struck (covering law).
(2) M is a dry match (auxiliary hypothesis).
(3) M is located in an oxygen-containing medium (auxiliary hypothesis).
(4) M has not been struck.
(5) M has not lit.

Assumption: Assume M has been struck.

It is clear that this assumption directly requires that we reject (4), and that, since we are dealing with a nomological counterfactual, we are determined to retain (1). This appears to leave us with a choice among three alternatives, if we wish to settle for the minimum of a single additional rejection:

Alternative 1		Alternative 2		Alternative 3	
Retain	Reject	Retain	Reject	Retain	Reject
(1)	(4)	(1)	(4)	(1)	(4)
(3)	(2)	(2)	(3)	(2)	(5)
(5)		(5)		(3)	

If, however, we decide not only to regard our law (1) as sacred, but also the auxiliary assumptions which assure its applicability, namely (2) and (3), then it is clear that we are reduced to adopting Alternative 3. And in this way we can vindicate the 'plausible' counterfactual

If the match M had been struck, it would have lit.

over against its 'implausible' competitors:

If the match M had been struck, it would not have been dry.

If the match M had been struck, it would not have been located in an oxygen-containing medium.

This short discussion should suffice to show that, in the case of nomological or law-governed counterfactuals, the requisite *principle of rejection and retention* governing the residual beliefs is provided by the 'law' in question—that is, by our determination to treat the statement to which we accord the status of a law in such a way as to preserve it, and to maintain its applicability to the case in hand. [21]

Thus in all the cases of nomological counterfactuals that have been examined we in effect order our relevant beliefs into the three following groups, listed in order of our decreasing unwillingness to jettison these beliefs in the face of a belief-contravening hypothesis:

1. laws operative in the case at issue.
2. boundary-value facts needed for the applicability of the laws in the case at issue.
3. other matters of fact.

In harmonizing the residual beliefs we make the 'lower-order' beliefs give way to those 'higher-order' ones to which we have —under the circumstances—a more fundamental commitment.[22] This is our basis for determining one counterfactual as 'natural' and its (from a purely logical standpoint equally possible) competitors as 'unnatural'.

Of course, this analysis needs to be elaborated for application to more complex cases—e.g. hypothetical laws that conflict with accepted laws. But the basic steps of the analysis remain the same, *mutatis mutandis*. We class the relevant beliefs into distinct categories so as to indicate how fundamental they are in the scheme of our knowledge, and then let such an ordering be our guide in effecting the reconciliation demanded by a belief-contravening hypothesis. To be sure, these remarks illustrate only the general characteristics of the process involved, and do not specify in sufficient detail the logical and epistemological machinery for its workings. We shall have to return to that.

The remaining type of counterfactual conditionals, that is to say those that are not nomological, may be characterized as *purely speculative counterfactuals*. In addition to including the classic instance 'If wishes were horses, beggars would ride', this class is typified by such well-known mutually rebutting trouble-makers as:

Example 8.1: If Bizet and Verdi were compatriots, Bizet would be an Italian.

[21] For ramifications of this issue of the logical (i.e. inferential) ramifications of lawfulness see the writer's *Hypothetical Reasoning* (Amsterdam, 1964), pp. 34 and 78–86. The theoretical complexities of the position presented there are further clarified in *idem*, 'Counterfactual Hypotheses, Laws, and Dispositions', *Nous*, vol. 5 (1971), pp. 157–78.

[22] Just this is the foundation for the point made by many writers on the subject that counterfactual conditionals are such that 'although they do not actually describe the real, the nature of the real is such as to make them true' (A. C. Ewing, 'The Correspondence Theory of Truth', in *Non-Linguistic Philosophy* (London, 1968), pp. 193–204 (see p. 200)).

Example 8.2: If Bizet and Verdi were compatriots, Verdi would be a Frenchman.

Example 9.1: If Georgia included New York City, this city would lie south of the Mason–Dixon line.

Example 9.2: If Georgia included New York City, this state would extend north of the Mason–Dixon line.

It is clear that, in the case of the purely speculative counterfactuals, these essentially opposed results cannot be avoided. The contextual ambiguity of the antecedent supposition gives us no way of choosing among the various mutually rebutting counterfactuals. Perplexity is unavoidably upon us in these cases.

The point to be made here is by now doubtless anticipated by the reader. Purely speculative counterfactuals are also to be viewed as conditional statements based upon belief-contravening suppositions. So far as I have been able to determine, all of the really 'paradoxical' (that is, non-nomological) cases of contrary-to-fact conditionals are actually hypotheticals whose antecedents assert 'belief-' and indeed 'knowledge-contravening' suppositions. (Readers familiar with the literature on counterfactuals have doubtless noted that most of the examples of belief-contravening hypotheses have been drawn from this source.) All of the standard examples of problematical contrary-to-fact conditionals to be found in the literature are conditional or hypothetical statements whose antecedents put before us a palpably false (and thus belief-contravening) hypothesis and whose consequents assert a purported consequence of this supposition. Our analysis of belief-contravening suppositions is thus immediately applicable, and the difficulty arising from purely speculative counterfactuals is easily recognized as a manifestation of the underlying difficulty about belief-contravening hypotheses. All the difficulty vanishes as a logical problem once this fact is recognized. For as we have seen, the refractory nature of belief-contravening hypotheses is inherent in their fundamentally ambiguous character.

Belief-contravening suppositions can be pitfalls of paradox because—in the absence of due guidance—they covertly invite us to commit a fallacy of ambiguity. In making the corresponding counterfactually conditional statements we fall into the trap by accepting this invitation. A purely speculative counterfactual conditional leads to paradox not because it is meaningless, but because it means too much, being so ambiguous as to admit of contrary, or at least discordant, interpretations, and doing so in a setting where no machinery for resolving this conflict is to be found. It is clear from this point of view why purely speculative counterfactuals are genuinely paradoxical. We lack here the guidance of a sufficiently specific *principle of rejection and retention* of the sort available with nomological counterfactuals. It is the absence of all such guidance in the case of purely speculative counterfactuals that is responsible for their utterly perplexing character.

Now this requirement for a principle of retention and rejection posed by the problem of counterfactual conditionals points straightway towards the screening procedure of the coherence analysis. The prospects of solving the problem through coherence considerations are clearly worth exploring.

5. *The Resolution of the Problem of Counterfactual Conditionals as an Exercise in Coherence Analysis*

The process of the coherence-screening of truths from an incoherent (mutually incompatible) set of data is precisely suited as a means for the resolution of the problem of counterfactual conditionals. Consider a fact-contradicting hypothesis in the context of known facts, for example, the conditional 'If this rubber disc were made of copper, it would conduct electricity'. Here we are placed in the following cognitive situation:

Known items: (1) This disc is made of rubber.
(2) This disc is not made of copper.
(3) This disc does not conduct electricity.
(4) Copper conducts electricity.
Assume: not-(2): This disc is made of copper.

In making the assumption one must, of course, replace (2) by not-(2), in line with the instruction of the antecedent of the counterfactual; and this also requires immediately the sacrifice of (1). But the group of data we now have in hand—not-(1), not-(2), (3), (4)—clearly continues to form an inconsistent set, a set that needs to be diminished if consistency is to be restored. (Note that as the counterfactual conditional has it, this diminution is to be realized through the deletion of (3).) But such a consistency-restoring screening of an inconsistent set of data is paradigmatically the task to which the coherence theory of truth addresses itself.

The generic structure of a counterfactual conditional is as follows: 'If $\sim P$ were the case (which it is not), then Q_1 would be the case.' On an analysis of such conditionals in terms of belief-contravening—or indeed *knowledge*-contravening—hypotheses, a counterfactual conditional comes to be viewed as a summary representation of a situation whose logical structure is somewhat more complex than first meets the eye:

(1) We start out from a set S of 'accepted' propositions representing 'our knowledge' of what is in fact the case in the epistemic neighbourhood of the proposition P_1 that interests us: $S = \{P_1, P_2, \ldots, P_n\}$. This set S of the known facts intimately relevant to P_1 is, of course, mutually consistent.

(2) As the given conditional demands, we now transform this set by introducing the 'counterfactual' hypothesis $\sim P_1$ in place of P_1, thus forming the propositional set:

$$S' = (S - \{P_1\}) \cup \{\sim P_1\}.$$

(3) Because of the inevitable contextual ambiguity of belief-contravening hypotheses, this set S' still remains internally inconsistent—even after the requisite deletion of P_1—because the totality of the remaining propositions still yields P_1 as a consequence.

(4) The Problem of Counterfactual Conditionals arises from the fact that whenever some proposition Q_2 follows from some $\sim P_1$-containing m.c.s. of S', there will be other propositions Q_3, Q_4, etc., that likewise follow from such m.c.s., but are logically incompatible with Q_2.

(5) A 'solution' of the Problem of Counterfactual Conditionals is at hand when the particular W-consequence Q_1 of S' that is in question is also a consequence of all the $\mathscr{P}$-preferred $\sim P_1$-containing m.c.s. of S' (for some appropriate criterion of preference $\mathscr{P}$), with the result that Q_1—unlike its logically incompatible competitors Q_2, Q_3, etc.—is a 'natural' consequence of S' (with respect to the preferential criterion at issue). Note that Q_2, Q_3, ..., being incompatible with Q_1, cannot also be $\mathscr{P}$-consequences of S' when Q_1 is.

Thus a solution of any instance of the Problem of Counterfactual Conditionals can effectually be provided through the coherence machinery. By establishing a relevantly applicable preferential criterion $\mathscr{P}$, it becomes possible to vindicate some one among the alternative, mutually incompatible consequences of the hypothetical assumption posed by the antecedent of the counterfactual.

Some concrete examples will serve to clarify this approach to counterfactuals. Let us assume that the following set represents items of knowledge relevant to some proposition p that we know to be the case: $S = \{p, q \supset p, r \supset p, q, r\}$. Let it be that we are asked to examine the consequences of the counterfactual hypothesis $\sim p$.

Our first step is to form S' through the replacement of p by $\sim p$:

$$S' = \{\sim p, q \supset p, r \supset p, q, r\}.$$

As always in these cases, S' is inconsistent. Now there are three m.c.s. of S':

$S'_1 = \{\sim p, q, r\}$ axiomatized by $\sim p \ \& \ q \ \& \ r$

$S'_2 = \{\sim p, q \supset p, r \supset p\}$ axiomatized by $\sim p \ \& \ \sim q \ \& \ \sim r$

$S'_3 = \{q \supset p, r \supset p, q, r\}$ axiomatized by $p \ \& \ q \ \& \ r$.

Faced with the counterfactual hypothesis $\sim p$, we cannot but dismiss S'_3 as incompatible therewith. This is a central aspect of our preferential criterion. The invariably forthcoming inevitable consequences of the remaining m.c.s. are axiomatized by:

$\sim p \ \& \ [(q \ \& \ r) \ v \ (\sim q \ \& \ \sim r)]$ or equivalently $\sim p \ \& \ (q \equiv r)$.

We note at once that $\sim p$ is itself such a consequence (and that every $\mathscr{P}$-consequence has to be compatible with it). This result must, of course, obtain. Moreover, we see that we are still in a position to say something informative about q and r. Indeed we have established the counterfactual conditional:

'If $\sim p$ were the case, then q and r would be (i.e. would *still* be) materially equivalent.'

Going beyond this, let us suppose the availability of a preferential criterion $\mathscr{P}$ to introduce more definiteness, so as to result in a single one of these S'_i instead of a choice between two of them. Specifically, let us suppose a minimal plausibility indexing of S' along the following lines:

(1) $\sim p$ (and $\sim p$ alone) is to get an index value of 1, as is indicated by the conditions of the problem (this being the hypothesis we are explicitly instructed to make).

(2) Implications are to get a lower index value—and so be viewed as more plausible—than categorical propositions (atoms).

This would result in something like the following plausibility indexing of S':

$$|\sim p| = 1$$
$$|q \supset p| = 2$$
$$|r \supset p| = 2$$
$$|q| = 3$$
$$|r| = 3.$$

It can readily be verified that this is in fact a full-scale plausibility index. The index assignments to the $\sim p$-containing m.c.s. are as follows:

		Maximum	Average
$S_1' = \{\sim p, q, r\}$ gets $(1, 3, 3)$		3	$2\frac{1}{3}$
$S_2' = \{\sim p, q \supset p, r \supset p\}$ gets $(1, 2, 2)$		2	$1\frac{2}{3}$

Here S_2' is clearly the preferred m.c.s., and we would obtain the counterfactual:

'If $\sim p$ were the case, then $\sim q$ and $\sim r$ would be the case.'

By contrast, if we were to implement the principle that categorical propositions (atoms) were to get a lower index value than implications—and so be regarded as more plausible—then this would lead to a preferred status for S_1'. This would validate the counterfactual.

'If $\sim p$ were the case, then q and r would both (still) be the case.'

The preceding example, helpful though it is in illustrating the generic structure of the analysis, is still abstract and schematic. It is desirable to give some illustrations of a more concrete and content-laden sort. Consider the following set **S** of accepted beliefs assumed to correspond to what is in fact the case:

$p_1 = $ This coin is a penny.

$p_2 = $ This coin is not a dime.

$p_3 = $ This coin is made of[23] copper.

$p_4 = $ This coin is not made of silver.

$p_5 = $ All pennies are made of copper.[24]

$p_6 = $ All dimes are made of silver.

[23] Through this example, 'is made of' is to be construed as 'is made *predominantly* of' rather than 'is made *in part* of'.

[24] Through this example 'penny' is to be understood as 'penny *in current circulation*'. The fact that in some past periods pennies were made of other metals is thus immaterial.

We are now to introduce the counterfactual hypothesis $\sim p_2$:

Assume that this coin were a dime.

The propositional set **S'** that results from replacing p_2 by $\sim p_2$ is clearly inconsistent. It has two m.c.s. that are not incompatible with $\sim p_2$:[25]

$$S_1' = \{\sim p_2, p_3, p_4, p_5\}$$
$$S_2' = \{\sim p_2, p_5, p_6\}.$$

In the absence of any further preferential basis for choosing between S_1' and S_2', we arrive at the following axiomatization of the $\mathscr{P}$-consequences of the hypothesis:

$$\sim p_2 \;\&\; p_5 \;\&\; ([p_3 \;\&\; p_4] \lor p_6).$$

We would thus derive, *inter alia*, the result $P_3 \lor P_6$, and so, thanks to the incompatibility-relations at issue, we could, for example, obtain: $\sim p_3 \lor \sim p_6$. This leads to the counterfactual:

If this penny were a dime then *either* it would not be made of copper (since dimes are made of silver) *or* not all dimes would be made of silver (since this coin is made of copper, not silver).

However, if more specific preferential information were available, we could go beyond this result in definiteness. We might, for example, want to implement the standpoint of the preceding section by a differential treatment of laws and factual theses. In terms of plausibility indexing, two alternative policies offer themselves as to the relative position of facts (as presented in particular statements) and laws (as presented as universal generalizations):

Alternative 1: Particular statements are to be more plausible (and so receive a lower index value) than generalizations.

Alternative 2: Generalizations are to be more plausible (and so receive a lower index value) than particular statements.

On the first alternative we should obtain:

1-indexed propositions: $\sim p_2$
2-indexed propositions: p_3, p_4
3-indexed propositions: $p_5, p_6.$

[25] We suppose that p_1 is inconsistent with $\sim p_2$, so that p_1 will occur in no $\sim p_2$-containing m.c.s.

This plausibility indexing results in the preferential selection of S_1'. Correspondingly we should give up not only p_1 and p_2 (which follows as a matter of course), but also p_6. We should accordingly establish the counterfactual:

> If this penny were a dime, then all dimes would not be made of silver (since this penny is made of copper).

Note that—as our plausibility-assessing procedure insists—we have made a generalization give way to a particular statement.

By contrast, if we adopted Alternative 2, we should obtain:

$$1\text{-indexed propositions: } \sim p_2$$
$$2\text{-indexed propositions: } p_5, p_6$$
$$3\text{-indexed propositions: } p_3, p_4.$$

This plausibility-indexing results in the preferential selection of S_2'. Correspondingly p_1 and p_2 are joined in banishment by p_3 and p_4. We accordingly establish the counterfactual:

> If this penny were a dime, then it would be made of silver and not of copper (since dimes are made of silver).

Here—as expected—we have made particular statements give way to generalizations.

The fact that this last conditional seems less natural than the related variant considered above stems from the fact that, in the face of the counterfactual hypothesis at issue, the one asks us to sacrifice a particular fact (viz. that the band does not conduct electricity) in favour of a general law (viz. that copper conducts electricity), where the other counterfactual would have us sacrifice a law to a purely hypothetical fact. On this view, there is a fundamental epistemological difference between actual and hypothetical cases: when contradictions arise, we make the facts yield to laws in the latter but not the former circumstance. Indeed to *treat* a generalization as a law is exactly to accord to it an epistemological priority of this sort.[26]

In more complex cases, however, the fact/law distinction may not of itself remove all difficulties. For example, assume a group of three laws L_1, L_2, L_3 where $\sim L_1$ is inconsistent with the conjunction of L_2 and L_3. If asked to hypothesize the denial of L_1— so that the 'fact' we are going against is itself a law—then what remains before us is a choice between laws. In this case the distinction between facts and laws does not resolve the issue, and

---

[26] This view of the nature of lawfulness is set forth in detail in N. Rescher, *Scientific Explanation* (New York, 1970); see Pt. III.

some mechanism for a preferential choice among laws becomes necessary.

For the sake of a further example, consider the following set **S** of factual beliefs:

p_1 = All dry matches located in an oxygen-containing medium light when struck.

p_2 = M is a dry match.

p_3 = M is located in an oxygen-containing medium.

p_4 = M has not been struck.

p_5 = M has not lit.

Let us now investigate the consequences of the counterfactual hypothesis:

$\sim p_4$: Assume this match had been struck.

We thus replace p_4 of the preceding set **S** by its negation, and obtain a mutually incompatible set of premisses **S'**. What follows from this set?

The $\sim p_4$-containing m.c.s. of **S'** are obtained by the consideration that we must now either drop the 'law' p_1 or one of the 'facts' relating to its application ('boundary-value conditions'): p_2, p_3, p_5.

$$S'_1 = \{\sim p_4, p_1, p_2, p_3\}$$
$$S'_2 = \{\sim p_4, p_1, p_3, p_5\}$$
$$S'_3 = \{\sim p_4, p_1, p_2, p_5\}$$
$$S'_4 = \{\sim p_4, p_2, p_3, p_5\}.$$

Now the *natural* sort of plausibility-indexing to use in a case of counterfactual hypotheses of this sort is as follows:

(1) Lawful generalizations are to be taken as more plausible (i.e. receive a lower index value) than statements of particular fact.

(2) Among statements of particular fact some deal with invariable states (fixed circumstances) and present the *constants* of the problem, others with *activities* (manipulable responses) and present its *variables*. The former (fixed-state-presenting) statements are to count as more plausible (and so receive a lower index value) than the latter (manipulably variable ones).

(The 'naturalness' of this policy is maintained here in an *epistemological* sense, but the *psychological* facts of the matter also lend support to it.[27]) In applying these plausibility-indexing policies to our example, we obtain the following result:

Statement	Classification	Plausibility Index
p_1	lawful generalization	2
p_2	fixed-state presenting fact	3
p_3	fixed-state presenting fact	3
p_4	hypothesis (manipulable variable fact)	1
p_5	manipulable variable fact	4

We thus arrive at the following indexing of the m.c.s.

m.c.s	Index Values	Maximum	Average
S_1'	(1, 2, 3, 3)	3	$2\frac{1}{4}$
S_2'	(1, 2, 3, 4)	4	$2\frac{1}{2}$
S_3'	(1, 2, 3, 4)	4	$2\frac{1}{2}$
S_4'	(1, 3, 3, 4)	4	$2\frac{3}{4}$

The preferred m.c.s. is S_1', and we should accordingly retain p_1, p_2, and p_3, and reject p_5. This leads to the counterfactual conditional: 'If this match had been struck, it would have lit.' Such conceivable but more far-fetched and less palatable-seeming counterfactuals as 'If this match had been struck, it would not have been dry', which call for a rejection of a statement different from p_5 (specifically p_2), are ruled out—not by the 'logic' of the situation (S_2' is, after all, a perfectly good m.c.s.) —but by the policies adopted in implementing the natural plausibilities of the case.

Thus the programme of resolving the problems posed by counterfactual hypotheses by use of the coherence analysis may call for the assignment of differential plausibilities not only to the various *laws* that may be at issue, but to various *types of facts* as well.

Finally, let us return to Quine's Bizet–Verdi example. We begin with the premises:

$p_1 =$ Bizet was of French nationality.

$p_2 =$ Verdi was of Italian nationality.

---

[27] For an interesting empirical investigation of the inclination to accord preferential treatment to general laws over particular facts in purely hypothetical cases see R. Revlis, S. G. Lipkin, and J. R. Hayes, 'The Importance of Universal Quantifiers in a Hypothetical Reasoning Task', *Journal of Verbal Learning and Verbal Behavior*, **10** (Feb. 1971).

p_3 = Compatriots are persons who share the same nationality.

p_4 = Bizet and Verdi were not compatriots.

Let us investigate the consequence of the counterfactual hypothesis:

p_4: Assume Bizet and Verdi were compatriots.

Three m.c.s. are obtained for the resulting premiss set **S'**:

$$S_1' = \{\sim p_4, p_3, p_1\}$$
$$S_2' = \{\sim p_4, p_3, p_2\}$$
$$S_3' = \{\sim p_4, p_1, p_2\}.$$

The plausibilities of the case are clearly such that (1) the dropping of p_3 is not a live option, so that S_3' is to be ruled out, and (2) there is no possible basis for distinguishing between p_1 and p_2 in point of plausibility. The $\mathscr{P}$-consequences of **S'** are accordingly axiomatized by $\sim p_4$ & p_3 & $(p_1 \vee p_2)$.

We thus validate the counterfactual conditional: 'If Bizet and Verdi had been compatriots, then either both would have been French or both would have been Italian.' But in the face of the insufficient guidance we receive from the available plausibility assessments, we could not go so far as to justify either of the more particular (and conflicting) counterfactuals:

If Bizet and Verdi had been compatriots, then both would have been French (since Bizet was French).

If Bizet and Verdi had been compatriots, then both would have been Italian (since Verdi was Italian).

When counterfactual hypotheses resemble the Bizet–Verdi example in that some **S**-elements must be rejected in the interests of others, although the pertinent plausibility considerations do not afford specific guidance for a choice, then the resulting situation may be characterized as one of epistemic or alethic *indeterminacy*. Such hypotheses result in an inherent instability—they lead not to one definite and 'natural' counterfactual conditional, but equally to several that are competing and conflicting. Here the coherence methodology is in the very nature of the case unable to produce a more definite conclusion.

The analysis of examples has now been carried far enough to show with some clarity that the machinery of coherence analysis can be applied effectively to the exploration of the consequences of counterfactual hypotheses. We thus see that—and just how

—the coherence analysis (in its plausibilistic form) affords an instrument for resolving the Problem of Counterfactual Conditionals.

Several significant lessons have emerged. Foremost among these is that in tracing the consequences of a counterfactual hypothesis one must take careful and explicit account of the family of relevant knowledge in the epistemic neighbourhood of the belief-contravening assumption at issue. A false assumption does not 'scatter reality to the winds' (as Bosanquet has it); it always leaves a great deal intact, and we can use this unaffected part of the structure as the starting-point for reconstruction.

The task of drawing out the consequences of false assumptions invariably confronts us with a plurality of alternatives. If we are to get beyond the barren minimum of the inevitable alternative-invariant consequences to introduce any further specificity of detail, then we must be prepared to supplement the machinery of deductive logic by some suitable means for assessing the relative plausibilities of statements. It is thus another significant upshot of the analysis that such attempts to reason from falsehood to truth always require epistemic inputs (viz. plausibility assessments or some equivalent preferential machinery) that are not to be obtained from purely logical considerations alone. Its mechanisms for the treatment of counterfactual conditionals afford a vivid illustration of the significance and fruitfulness of plausibility analysis.

6. *Coherence and Counterfactual Assumptions*

Idealist adherents to the coherence theory of truth inclined to argue—on the very basis of coherence considerations!—against the propriety and viability of counterfactual hypotheses. They tended to reason in unison with Bernard Bosanquet in the following passage:

The idea on which we have been insisting—that of a system or unity which prescribes the relation between its parts or differences— is the idea of Ground, which includes the sphere of the Hypothetical Judgment, and indeed wherever it appears may be said to involve a Hypothetical element. . . . First, it is plain that when once a Ground is rightly stated, in conformity with the true nature of the system which it presupposes, and with which it is in fact identical, such a Ground is unalterable except by alteration of this system itself. With what justification, theoretically, we refuse to contemplate such alteration of the universe as a whole, or how far practically we permit ourselves to contemplate it in respect of subordinate systems, e.g., man's moral nature or the type of disease, are questions that must be reserved for a general discussion of the postulates of knowledge. Formally, we may say, the whole cannot alter, because any alteration must be included in the whole. But we shall see that so purely formal a postulate would not satisfy the purposes for which a postulate is required. . . .

It is a corollary from the idea of Ground as a relation purely relevant to a positive determinate system that the hypothetical judgment, when ideally complete, must be a reciprocal judgment. 'If A is B, it is C' must justify the inference 'If A is C, it is B'. We are of course in the habit of dealing with hypothetical judgments which will not admit of any such conversion, and the rules of logic accept this limitation as they accept the custom of ordinary speech as to the comparative range of subject and predication. Some cases of non-reciprocal sequence and their justification will be considered in the next section. But here we are only concerned to explain the principle upon which necessary sequence must ultimately rest; and according to that principle, the unity of a system in its determinations, it follows that if AB necessitates AC, then AC must also necessitate AB. We are not now speaking of causation, but simply of coherence in principle, and it is obvious that the idea of coherence in a system is reciprocal. A cannot cohere with B unless B coheres with A. If in actual fact this is found not to hold good, and AB is found to involve AC while AC does not involve AB, it is plain that what was relevant to AC was not really AB but some element $\alpha\beta$ within it.[28]

Here the procedure of from inference reality-contradicting hypotheses is linked, quite properly, to the maintenance of a reality-consonant ground to canalize the reasoning. But then an illegitimate step ensues. The unison and interlinkage of the propositions descriptive of reality is mistakenly seen as being so tight that due to this coherence any hypothetical disturbance whatsoever results in immediate wholesale destruction of the entire fabric.[29] The argument in view may be condensed into the following summary:

A coherence theory of truth must recognize, indeed stress the thoroughgoing interconnectedness of all truths. Hence an assumption that changes one truth affects indeed and abrogates all of the others. Counterfactual suppositions are consequently not viable, no rational line of thought can issue from them. Truths cohere so closely that the introduction of a discordant element into their midst results

---

[28] *Logic* (2nd edn., Oxford, 1911; reissued 1931), pp. 244–6.

[29] As G. F. Stout puts it: '[Coherence] rests on the principle that the Universe contains no *loose* elements. No partial feature entering into its constitution could be other than what it is without correlated difference in other features, which would again involve correlated differences in yet other features, and so on indefinitely. Thus, if anything in the universe is, had been, will be, or could be other than it is, has been, will be, could be, or could have been, the difference would penetrate the whole in its systematic Unity' (*Studies in Philosophy and Psychology* [London, 1930], p. 316).

in incoherence and conceptual chaos. Counterfactual hypotheses are consequently unworkable.

This line of thought takes up a good point, but carries it too far—and in the wrong direction. The argument rightly stresses the coherence and connectedness of truths. But the implications of these facts are exaggerated and distorted. The hypothetical change of a truth does indeed carry with it corresponding changes in *some* others, but certainly not in *all* others. There are certainly connections among truths, but they are not so close that if one truth is revised then *all* others are upset. Let it be true that there are *three* men in the room. Assume now the suppositional hypothesis that there are *four*. Many truths are now changed (e.g. that there are two fewer than five). But many 'old' truths are in the same *status quo ante*; for example, 'there are more than two' and 'there are fewer than six' will have their truth-status wholly unaffected. And this must *always* be so. For example, in changing any truth P to the divergent (and logically incompatible) alternative Q, we shall always leave still invariant the 'old truth' P-or-Q.

When counterfactual hypotheses are introduced we must indeed make revisions in the family of truths, but the scope of these revisions is limited and their character is rationally determinable. The essential fact is that the coherence relations among truths are not random and haphazard, they can (as we have seen) be articulated through rationally specifiable principles that operate in an environment of knowledge that remains in significant measure invariant.

The subtler minds among the idealists were keenly alive to this rooting of counterfactual conditionals in a soil of genuine fact that confines the course of reasoning within manageable limits. Bernard Bosanquet put the matter as follows:

Hypothetical Judgment, then, is Judgment that starts from a supposition. Every supposition is made upon a certain basis of Reality. Take as an extreme case, 'If you ask permission of A.B., he will refuse it.' This is a supposition and its result, on the basis of the known character, that, supposing you ask him for permission, etc. . . . Underlying them [hypothetical judgments] there is the implied Categorical Judgment, 'Reality has a character, such that, supposing so and so, the consequence will be so and so.' And if this implied assertion is true, then the Hypothetical Judgment is true, although its terms may be not only unreal, but impossible.[30]

On Bosanquet's view, as on ours, the effective operation of residual fact can prevent a counterfactual hypothesis from

[30] B. Bosanquet, *The Essentials of Logic* (London, 1897), pp. 122–3.

creating intellectual chaos. What Bosanquet did not recognize (as shown by the quotation at the start of the chapter) is the *pervasiveness* of this consequence-canalizing—and thus rationalizing—impact of 'reality' through a coherence mechanism, with the result that even so far-fetched a supposition as 'If a donkey were Plato . . .' is not outside the pale of rational consideration.

Actually, the argument that counterfactual hypotheses lead to chaos does not *implement* a coherence approach; it *fails to do justice* to the power of coherence considerations. Of course, the fact that truths cohere with each other means that non-truths must always to some extent fail to cohere with truths. Yet this lack of a comprehensive coherence *with truths* does not make counterfactual hypotheses incoherent *per se*. If, by hypothesis, we 'change' non-truths to truths then we must—and (as we have seen) *can*—reapply coherence mechanisms to 'restructure the realm of (presumptive) truth', so as to arrive at various new truths—and sundry old ones, too. With the introduction of a counterfactual hypothesis we do not reach what is incoherent *per se* but merely what is incoherent with the *status quo ante*; we arrive not at chaos, but at *a revised structure of coherence*.

These considerations have a significant upshot. In adopting a coherence theory of truth we need by no means gainsay the prospect of hypothetical reasoning from explicitly untrue assumptions as a rational resource. Quite the contrary: coherence itself can serve as our guide across this difficult terrain. Those coherence theorists who denied the viability of counterfactual assumptions have failed lamentably to recognize the power and utility of their own characteristic methods of inquiry.[31]

---

[31] Part of the material of this chapter has been drawn from the author's book *Hypothetical Reasoning* (Amsterdam, 1964), where this coherentist line of approach to counterfactual conditionals was initially developed in embryonic form.

XII

APPLICATIONS OF THE COHERENCE ANALYSIS IN INFORMATION PROCESSING

1. *The Processing of Reports*

THE preceding chapters have shown that, over and above whatever value and interest it may have in its own right as a theory of truth, the coherence approach possesses the added merit of significant applications to hypothetical and inductive reasoning. The aim of the present chapter is to extend this survey of applications outside the sphere of logical issues into the strictly empirical domain of information processing, specifically to the problem of the utilization of reports and estimates. We shall again proceed by way of examples (generally of a schematic type).

A. *Case (i): Text Restoration*

Suppose that one is trying to determine the actual text of a lost letter, the following basis of relevant information being available:

A: A fragment of a photocopy
B: A presumably quite accurate transcription by a copyist whose handwriting is often illegible
C: A transcription by a neat copyist known to be relatively inaccurate.

Clearly these sources can conflict: e.g. at a given place one of the documents might read 'shop', another 'shape', the third 'sheep'. It is clear that such discordant data regarding a portion of the text of the letter must be treated in accordance with the following schedule of plausibilities (or something closely approximating thereto).

Source	Evaluation	Plausibility Index
A	absolutely reliable	1
B	rather reliable	2
C	somewhat reliable	3

Thus whenever source A provides usable information, its declaration prevails; when A is silent, then B dominates over C. In ways analogous to this—though more complex—the standard procedures of text-restoration can be accommodated to the workings of the coherence analysis.

Note that in situations of this type one would proceed differently when compiling the reports of sources of roughly equal merit. For when the sources are appraised as essentially *uniform* in reliability, then one would presumably adopt a preference-evaluation based upon the majoritative principle described in Section 3 of Chapter V. When *equivalent* sources conflict, there is no reasonable alternative but to let the rule of the majority prevail and to assess the relative acceptability of the data on the basis of the *extent of agreement* among the sources.

B. Case (ii): Text Interpretation

Our coherence analysis can be applied in a closely similar form to problems of textual interpretation which arise when one is faced with a text that admits of distinctly different readings, due, say, to illegibilities of presentation or to ambiguity of formulation. For the sake of a concrete example, let us suppose that a document is at hand which makes four assertions as follows:

(1) p or q (one cannot make out which)

(2) $p \supset q$ or $p \vee q$ (one cannot make out which)

(3) $\sim p \vee \sim q$

(4) $q \supset p$.

The 'uncontested' assertions at issue in (3) and (4) may be accorded a plausibility ranking of 1; those at issue in (1) and (2) will get plausibility 2, due to the basic uncertainty involved. We form the over-all datum set:

$$S = \{p, q, p \supset q, p \vee q, \sim p \vee \sim q, q \supset p\}.$$

Its m.c.s. are as follows:

$S_1 =$ all of S except for $\sim p \vee \sim q$ (axiomatized by $p \& q$)

$S_2 =$ all of S except for $q, p \supset q$ (axiomatized by $p \& \sim q$)

$S_3 =$ all of S except for $p, q \supset p$ (axiomatized by $\sim p \& q$)

$S_4 =$ all of S except for $p, q, p \vee q$ (axiomatized by $\sim p \& \sim q$).

But note that S_1 and S_3 may be $\mathscr{P}$-eliminated because they sacrifice S-elements of plausibility 1. Thus S_2 and S_4 alone are left in the running. But S_4 can be eliminated because it involves dropping both members of a group of paired propositions (viz. p and q) representing alternative readings of the same item. Thus S_2 alone remains as an acceptable m.c.s. Accordingly we are led to the view that in the interests of preserving its viability as a series of truth-claims we must construe the initial document as reading: $p, p \vee q, \sim p \vee \sim q, q \supset p$. Of course the result of such an analysis need not, in general,. be as specifically determinative as this example in yielding a single result rather than a plurality of possible outcomes.

Again, consider the following case of ambiguity in the assertions of a text:

(1) $p \& q$ or $\sim p \& q$ (one cannot make out which)

(2) $p \& q$ or $p \& \sim q$ (one cannot make out which).

Note that in this case a strictly informal analysis of the situation will produce a decisive resolution. For—subject to our standard determination to 'save as much as possible' of the text (*sauve qu'on peut!*)—we know from (1) that q must have been intended either way, and from (2) that p must have been intended either way, so that $p \& q$ is the uniquely acceptable result.

Let us see how the coherence analysis produces the same upshot. We begin, as usual, with the set of all the data:

$$S = \{p \& q, \sim p \& q, p \& \sim q\}.$$

Its m.c.s. are:

$$S_1 = \{p \& q\}$$
$$S_2 = \{\sim p \& q\}$$
$$S_3 = \{p \& \sim q\}.$$

We should, of course, have to eliminate as 'non-preferred' any m.c.s. that does not render true at least one member of *each* of the two initially given pairs (1) and (2). And this at once reduces the field to S_1, so that $p \& q$ is the upshot, as desired.

C. *Case (iii): Reports From Multiple Sources*

What is perhaps the paradigm application of any coherence theory is its deployment to the exploitation of conflicting reports from one or more sources under circumstances where a 'direct' check is impossible.[1] We might, for example, be confronted by the different reports of different historical sources, or—to take another case—the different and potentially conflicting deliverances of distinct sensing devices, on analogy with the case when

---

[1] Or even if a direct check is possible, the checker may—if sufficiently diffident or self-distrustful (or realistic)—simply categorize himself as just another source (presumably with relatively high reliability).

a man's sight indicates that a stick held partially submerged under water is bent and touch indicates that it is straight. Quite apart from its illustrative use in relation to the coherence theory, the problem of conflicting reports clearly poses an epistemic issue of substantial interest in its own right. It represents a type of problem that recurs in many diversified information-processing situations apart from those already mentioned (historical reports, senses, and sensors): military intelligence, police investigation, courtroom hearings, etc. If it is to be really useful, then, a coherence criterion of truth must be able to prove itself as an efficient and effective instrument in such situations of conflicting reports.

The utilization of the reports of others as data for our knowledge has always been viewed as a key task of the coherence theory. As F. H. Bradley put it: 'To take memory [and perception] as in general truthworthy, where I have no special reason for doubt, and to take the testimony of those persons, whom I suppose to view the world as I view it, as being true, apart from special reason on the other side—these are the principles by which I construct my ordered world, such as it is.'[2] It is through such a *presumption* of truth that reports gain the status of data for our knowledge.

How would the coherence theory of truth as we have construed it address itself to the processing of reports? To see this in detail a certain amount of machinery must be introduced. We shall suppose there to be a multiplicity of sources $X_1, X_2, \ldots,$ X_k issuing reports about a variety of topics, $T_1, T_2, \ldots, T_m$. We may suppose further that the reliability of every source with respect to every topic has been specified in terms of some grading scheme for reliability (or for credibility), such as:

1: absolutely reliable[3]
2: highly reliable
3: fairly reliable
4: of doubtful reliability
5: highly unreliable.

We have a series of reports from each of these sources X_i:

$$\mathbf{R}_i = \{r_{i,1}, r_{i,2}, \ldots, r_{i,n}\}.$$

[2] 'On Truth and Coherence', in *Essays on Truth and Reality* (Oxford, 1914), pp. 202–18 (see p. 213).
[3] We may suppose without loss of generality that the reports obtained from all the sources we are prepared to class as 'absolutely reliable' are mutually compatible.

The total set of reports **R** is simply the compilation of the contents of all of these R_i. This set may be presumed to be inconsistent. The problem is: what conclusions may reasonably be drawn from the given data (i.e. inconsistent premises) in such a case? How are we to draw any reasonable inference here? The machinery developed for the coherence analysis of truth affords the means to a ready answer to these questions. The best way to show this is by working out some concrete examples.

Suppose that four sources (X_1-X_4) are at issue with respect to two topical areas (T_1-T_2). Let the reports themselves be as follows:

	T_1	T_2
X_1:	p & q, $q \vee s$	$r \supset s$
X_2:	$s \supset \sim p$	$\sim q$
X_3:	$\sim p$, q & r	s
X_4:	$\sim q$ & r	$\sim s$

Let us assume a reliability grading of the sources with respect to the topical area at issue:

	T_1	T_2
X_1	3	1
X_2	1	2
X_3	3	2
X_4	4	2

The upshot is the following group of propositions with the indicated minimal indexing:

(1) $\sim p$:   3 (goes to 2 by applying the index-revision rule)
(2) $\sim q$:   2
(3) s: 2
(4) $\sim s$:   2
(5) p & q: 3
(6) $\sim q$ & r: 4
(7) q & r: 3
(8) $q \vee s$:   3 (goes to 2 by applying the index-revision rule)
(9) $r \supset s$:   1
(10) $s \supset \sim p$:   1.

To obtain a full-scale plausibility index we must, as usual, take into account the implication-relations among the propositions at issue. These are as follows and lead to the indicated results (by the standard process explained in Chapter V):

(6) ⊢ (2)   4 ⊢ 2

(3) ⊢ (8)   2 ⊢ 3   ∴ (8) goes to 2

(4) ⊢ (10)   2 ⊢ 1

(7) ⊢ (8)   3 ⊢ 3 [2]

(3) ⊢ (9)   2 ⊢ 1

(1) ⊢ (10)   3 ⊢ 1

(8), (2), (10) ⊢ (1)   3 [2], 2, 1 ⊢ 3   ∴ (1) goes to 2[4]

(6), (9) ⊢ (3)   4, 1 ⊢ 2

(7), (9) ⊢ (3)   3, 1 ⊢ 2

(2), (8) ⊢ (3)   2, 3 [2] ⊢ 2

(3), (10) ⊢ (1)   2, 1 ⊢ 3 [2]

The indicated changes are the only ones necessary, and result in a full-scale plausibility indexing.

The m.c.s. of our initial set are:

$$S_1 = \{s, r \supset s, p \,\&\, q, q \vee s, q \,\&\, r\}$$
$$S_2 = \{s, r \supset s, \sim p, s \supset \sim p, q \vee s, q \,\&\, r\}$$
$$S_3 = \{s, r \supset s, \sim p, s \supset \sim p, q \vee s, \sim q, \sim q \,\&\, r\}$$
$$S_4 = \{\sim s, s \supset \sim p, p \,\&\, q, q \vee s, q \,\&\, r\}$$
$$S_5 = \{\sim s, s \supset \sim p, p \,\&\, q, q \vee s, r \supset s\}$$
$$S_6 = \{\sim s, s \supset \sim p, \sim p, q \vee s, r \,\&\, q\}$$
$$S_7 = \{\sim s, s \supset \sim p, \sim p, q \vee s, r \supset s\}$$
$$S_8 = \{\sim s, s \supset \sim p, \sim p, \sim q, \sim q \,\&\, r\}$$
$$S_9 = \{\sim s, s \supset \sim p, \sim p, \sim q, r \supset s\}.$$

Here S_1, S_4, S_6, and S_8 can be eliminated at once as conflicting with 1-obtaining reports, and therefore *ex hypothesi* with absolutely reliable information. We are left with S_2, S_3, S_5, S_7, and S_9, whose elements have the following plausibility values:

	Maximum	Average
S_2: 2, 1, 2, 1, 2, 3	3	$1\frac{5}{6}$
S_3: 2, 1, 2, 1, 2, 2, 4	4	2
S_5: 2, 1, 3, 2, 1	3	$1\frac{4}{5}$
S_7: 2, 1, 2, 2, 1	2	$1\frac{3}{5}$
S_9: 2, 1, 2, 2, 1	2	$1\frac{3}{5}$

[4] The preceding entry in the list now becomes 2 ⊢ 1 which calls for no further changes.

Accordingly, S_7 and S_9 could be considered as the 'preferred' m.c.s.

Note that

S_7 is axiomatized by: $\sim p$ & q & $\sim r$ & $\sim s$.

S_9 is axiomatized by: $\sim p$ & $\sim q$ & $\sim r$ & $\sim s$.

The consequences ($\mathcal{P}$-consequences) of the report-set will accordingly be axiomatized by:

$$\sim p \ \& \ \sim r \ \& \ \sim s.$$

This (surely far from intuitive) result illustrates the power of a coherence screening in eliciting the 'consequences' of inconsistent reports. It is worth observing that this analysis represents a sizeable advance from the starting position. For one thing, the initial data did not assure us of $\sim p$ in any obvious way.[5] Most surprising, however, is the result $\sim r$, which is maintained in no single one of our initial reports and flatly contradicted by two of them.

The application of the coherence analysis to reports illustrates an important aspect of the technique, namely how the requisite plausibility-considerations can arise very naturally out of the particular features of the case in hand. As has been stressed repeatedly, the yardstick for plausibility-grading is not something that can be settled once and for all on grounds of general principle, but represents a diversified factor that inheres in a context-relative way in the specific characteristics of particular problem-situations (and whose specific form results from a choice among alternatives that must be settled on ultimately pragmatic grounds). Another illustration in the present context of reports is this: whenever we have a report source that might have a 'change of mind' on grounds that deserve respect—for example because the reports come from an information-gathering mechanism whose reliability we have reason to think has been improved—then we should want to implement the precept that later data are more plausible than earlier ones.

D. Case (iv): Redundant Reports from a Homogeneous Source

Consider now the circumstance where a single source issues a series or *sequence* of reports that will for purposes of present discussion be presumed to be of uniform reliability.[6] Let it be

---

[5] Its *a priori* plausibility was 3 and it was flatly contradicted by one report.

[6] A restrictive assumption is clearly at issue here. A single source need not be homogeneous in its reliability—this could vary not only with subject-matter but with circumstances (fatigue, illness, etc.).

supposed, however, that the given sequence of such homo-geneous reports involves repetitions and redundancies, so that a repeated message is less likely to be in error. Thus a message gains further substantiation through repetitions. Here again an example can exhibit how the coherence analysis can be applied with good effect.

Let it be that a source of the specified kind issues the following sequence of specific reports:

$$p, p \supset q, \sim p, \sim q, \sim p \ \& \ q, p \ \& \ r, p, p \supset q, \sim p \ \& \ q, p, p \supset \sim r.$$

Note that here p is repeated in three reports and is a consequence of one other individual report, while $\sim p$ occurs but once by itself and is the consequence of two other individual reports. Accordingly, p should be classed as more plausible than $\sim p$. Moreover $p \supset q$ is the only repeated compound message (where a *relation* among propositions is involved) and hence it deserves to be classed as more plausible than the others. Let us proceed to assign index values to the propositions at issue by the rule:

> Every *non-tautologous* proposition—tautologies will, of course, automatically be assigned the value 0—reported m times is to have the index $N-m$. Here the fixed value N must be large enough to assure that no proposition gets an index value of 1. (Say that $N = m'+2$, m' being the maximal value of m.)

Correspondingly, we should obtain some such minimal indexing of the reports as:

(1) p 2
(2) $\sim p$ 3
(3) $\sim q$ 5
(4) $p \supset q$ 4 (goes to 3—see below)
(5) $p \ \& \ r$ 5
(6) $\sim p \ \& \ q$ 4
(7) $p \supset \sim r$ 5 (goes to 3—see below).

To obtain a full-scale plausibility index we must take account of the entailment relations:

(2) $\vdash$ (4)   3 $\vdash$ 4   hence (4) goes to 3
(2) $\vdash$ (7)   3 $\vdash$ 5   hence (7) goes to 3
(5) $\vdash$ (1)   5 $\vdash$ 2
(6) $\vdash$ (2)   4 $\vdash$ 3

(6) ⊢ (4)   4 ⊢ 4 [3]
(6) ⊢ (7)   4 ⊢ 5 [3].
(3), (4) ⊢ (7)   5, 4 [3] ⊢ 5 [3].

Now since the report-set in question is

$$\mathbf{S} = \{p, \sim p, \sim q, p \supset q, p \,\&\, r, \sim p \,\&\, q, p \supset \sim r\}$$

its m.c.s. will be:

$\mathbf{S}_1 = \{p, \sim q, p \,\&\, r\}$
    which is axiomatized by $p \,\&\, \sim q \,\&\, r$

$\mathbf{S}_2 = \{p, \sim q, p \supset \sim r\}$
    which is axiomatized by $p \,\&\, \sim q \,\&\, \sim r$

$\mathbf{S}_3 = \{p, p \supset q, p \,\&\, r\}$
    which is axiomatized by $p \,\&\, q \,\&\, r$

$\mathbf{S}_4 = \{p, p \supset q, p \supset \sim r\}$
    which is axiomatized by $p \,\&\, q \,\&\, \sim r$

$\mathbf{S}_5 = \{\sim p, \sim q, p \supset q, p \supset \sim r\}$
    which is axiomatized by $\sim p \,\&\, \sim q$

$\mathbf{S}_6 = \{\sim p, p \supset q, \sim p \,\&\, q, p \supset \sim r\}$
    which is axiomatized by $\sim p \,\&\, q.$

These m.c.s. have elements with the following series of plausibility values:

	Maximum	Average
$\mathbf{S}_1$: 2, 5, 5	5	4
$\mathbf{S}_2$: 2, 5, 3	5	$3\frac{1}{3}$
$\mathbf{S}_3$: 2, 3, 5	5	$3\frac{1}{3}$
$\mathbf{S}_4$: 2, 3, 3	3	$2\frac{2}{3}$
$\mathbf{S}_5$: 3, 5, 3, 3	5	$3\frac{1}{2}$
$\mathbf{S}_6$: 3, 3, 4, 3	4	$3\frac{1}{4}$.

Depending upon the extent to which we decide 'to play safe' we can either (i) retain only the single lowest-ranking m.c.s. $\mathbf{S}_4$ (and accordingly axiomatize the $\mathscr{P}$-consequences of $\mathbf{S}$ by $p \,\&\, q \,\&\, \sim r$), or (ii) retain only the two lowest-ranking group of m.c.s., $\mathbf{S}_4$ and $\mathbf{S}_6$ (and accordingly axiomatize the $\mathscr{P}$-consequences of $\mathbf{S}$ by $q \,\&\, [\sim p \lor (p \,\&\, \sim r)]$ or equivalently $q \,\&\, (\sim p \lor \sim r)$). Note that in either case q would count as a consequence of the initial report-set, despite the explicit presence of $\sim q$ among the reports.[7]

[7] We might, of course, play safer yet and retain all those m.c.s. whose average score is less than the average of the averages, viz. all the $\mathbf{S}_i$ except $\mathbf{S}_1$ and $\mathbf{S}_5$. The axiom of the $\mathscr{P}$-consequences then becomes $q \lor (p \,\&\, \sim r)$.

E. *Case (iv) continued: A Variant 'Statistical' Approach*

Cases of serial redundancy of the sort considered in the preceding section would seem to be handled more effectively and advantageously by a directly statistical approach. Each individual report, after all, amounts to a selection of certain 'favoured' state descriptions (possible worlds)—viz. those that are compatible with the report. The report indicates each of these with a certain probability. Examining the statistical pattern of such state-description selections, we can utilize the resultant information to reappraise the relative acceptability of the various m.c.s. Thus rather than determining relative acceptability by counting *propositional repetitions*, we determine this by probabilistic 'repetitions' in the indication of state-descriptions.

Accordingly, in the example considered in the preceding section one would begin with the tabulation:

State Description	A Priori Probability	Reports											Σ	Σ*
		p	$p\supset q$	$\sim p$	$\sim q$	$\sim p \& q$	$p \& r$	p	$p\supset q$	$\sim p \& q$	p	$p\supset \sim r$		
$p \& q \& r$	$\frac{1}{8}$	$\frac{1}{4}$	$\frac{1}{6}$				$\frac{1}{2}$	$\frac{1}{4}$	$\frac{1}{6}$		$\frac{1}{4}$		$\frac{19}{12}$	$\frac{19}{132}$
$p \& q \& \sim r$	$\frac{1}{8}$	$\frac{1}{4}$	$\frac{1}{6}$					$\frac{1}{4}$	$\frac{1}{6}$		$\frac{1}{4}$	$\frac{1}{6}$	$\frac{15}{12}$	$\frac{15}{132}$
$p \& \sim q \& r$	$\frac{1}{8}$	$\frac{1}{4}$			$\frac{1}{4}$		$\frac{1}{2}$	$\frac{1}{4}$			$\frac{1}{4}$		$\frac{18}{12}$	$\frac{18}{132}$
$p \& \sim q \& \sim r$	$\frac{1}{8}$	$\frac{1}{4}$			$\frac{1}{4}$			$\frac{1}{4}$			$\frac{1}{4}$	$\frac{1}{6}$	$\frac{14}{12}$	$\frac{14}{132}$
$\sim p \& q \& r$	$\frac{1}{8}$		$\frac{1}{6}$	$\frac{1}{4}$		$\frac{1}{2}$			$\frac{1}{6}$	$\frac{1}{2}$		$\frac{1}{6}$	$\frac{21}{12}$	$\frac{21}{132}$
$\sim p \& q \& \sim r$	$\frac{1}{8}$		$\frac{1}{6}$	$\frac{1}{4}$		$\frac{1}{2}$			$\frac{1}{6}$	$\frac{1}{2}$		$\frac{1}{6}$	$\frac{21}{12}$	$\frac{21}{132}$
$\sim p \& \sim q \& r$	$\frac{1}{8}$		$\frac{1}{6}$	$\frac{1}{4}$	$\frac{1}{4}$				$\frac{1}{6}$			$\frac{1}{6}$	$\frac{12}{12}$	$\frac{12}{132}$
$\sim p \& \sim q \& \sim r$	$\frac{1}{8}$		$\frac{1}{6}$	$\frac{1}{4}$	$\frac{1}{4}$				$\frac{1}{6}$			$\frac{1}{6}$	$\frac{12}{12}$	$\frac{12}{132}$

Here the value Σ is the sum across the rows, and Σ* is obtained by normalizing these Σ-values to 1 in order to obtain a distribution of *a posteriori* probabilities for the state descriptions. The column entries are to be accounted for as follows. Take the column for the first report. Given p, it is—under this supposition —certain (probability 1) that one of the first four possible worlds must obtain. In the (admittedly implausible) case that we know nothing further about the possible worlds in the way of *a priori* information provided by the context of the propositions at issue —so that all of these possible worlds have equal *a priori* probability—we should distribute the weight of 1 *equally* across these four cases, resulting in $\frac{1}{4}$ for each. (On the other hand, if differential weights of *a priori* probability were available for the possible worlds, we should arrange the distribution of probabilities in a proportionate manner.)

Let us now apply the Σ*-values of this table to a reexamination of the m.c.s.:

$S_1 = \{p, \sim q, p \,\&\, r\}$
  which is axiomatized by $p \,\&\, \sim q \,\&\, r$ with value $\frac{18}{132}$

$S_2 = \{p, \sim q, p \supset \sim r\}$
  which is axiomatized by $p \,\&\, \sim q \,\&\, \sim r$ with value $\frac{14}{132}$

$S_3 = \{p, p \supset q, p \,\&\, r\}$
  which is axiomatized by $p \,\&\, q \,\&\, r$ with value $\frac{19}{132}$

$S_4 = \{p, p \supset q, p \supset \sim r\}$
  which is axiomatized by $p \,\&\, q \,\&\, \sim r$ with value $\frac{15}{132}$

$S_5 = \{\sim p, \sim q, p \supset q, p \supset \sim r\}$
  which is axiomatized by $\sim p \,\&\, \sim q$ with value $\frac{24}{132}$

$S_6 = \{\sim p, p \supset q, \sim p \,\&\, q, p \supset \sim r\}$
  which is axiomatized by $\sim p \,\&\, q$ with value $\frac{42}{132}$.

This approach thus decisively favours S_6 as the only m.c.s. with above-average probability. The $\mathscr{P}$-consequences of S would accordingly be axiomatized by $\sim p \,\&\, q$.

But one further refinement is indicated. The above analysis creates a disproportion with respect to conjunctions. It seems warranted to take the position that in most cases of the relevant sort the preceding method of calculation will so operate that data given in a conjunctive form, such as $p \,\&\, q$, favour certain state descriptions too much in comparison with the same information presented serially as p, q. Let us therefore recalculate subject to the rule that *conjunctions must be broken up*:

State Descriptions	A Priori Probability	p (4)	q (2)	r (1)	$\sim p$ (3)	$\sim q$ (1)	$p \supset q$ (2)	$p \supset \sim r$ (1)	Σ	Σ^*
$p \,\&\, q \,\&\, r$	$\frac{1}{8}$	$\frac{1}{4}$	$\frac{1}{4}$	$\frac{1}{4}$			$\frac{1}{6}$		$\frac{25}{12}$	$\frac{25}{168}$
$p \,\&\, q \,\&\, \sim r$	$\frac{1}{8}$	$\frac{1}{4}$	$\frac{1}{4}$				$\frac{1}{6}$	$\frac{1}{6}$	$\frac{24}{12}$	$\frac{24}{168}$
$p \,\&\, \sim q \,\&\, r$	$\frac{1}{8}$	$\frac{1}{4}$		$\frac{1}{4}$		$\frac{1}{4}$			$\frac{18}{12}$	$\frac{18}{168}$
$p \,\&\, \sim q \,\&\, \sim r$	$\frac{1}{8}$	$\frac{1}{4}$				$\frac{1}{4}$		$\frac{1}{6}$	$\frac{17}{12}$	$\frac{17}{168}$
$\sim p \,\&\, q \,\&\, r$	$\frac{1}{8}$		$\frac{1}{4}$	$\frac{1}{4}$	$\frac{1}{4}$		$\frac{1}{6}$	$\frac{1}{6}$	$\frac{24}{12}$	$\frac{24}{168}$
$\sim p \,\&\, q \,\&\, \sim r$	$\frac{1}{8}$		$\frac{1}{4}$		$\frac{1}{4}$		$\frac{1}{6}$	$\frac{1}{6}$	$\frac{21}{12}$	$\frac{21}{168}$
$\sim p \,\&\, \sim q \,\&\, r$	$\frac{1}{8}$			$\frac{1}{4}$	$\frac{1}{4}$	$\frac{1}{4}$	$\frac{1}{6}$	$\frac{1}{6}$	$\frac{21}{12}$	$\frac{21}{168}$
$\sim p \,\&\, \sim q \,\&\, \sim r$	$\frac{1}{8}$				$\frac{1}{4}$	$\frac{1}{4}$	$\frac{1}{6}$	$\frac{1}{6}$	$\frac{18}{12}$	$\frac{18}{168}$

Here the numbers along the top of the list of report-units indicate how often each item occurs (once conjunctions are broken up), and are, of course, used as a weight in calculating the Σ-value. We now obtain:

$S_1 \cong p \ \& \ {\sim}q \ \& \ r$ gets the Σ^*-probability value $\frac{18}{168} = 0.11$

$S_2 \cong p \ \& \ {\sim}q \ \& \ {\sim}r$ gets the Σ^*-probability value $\frac{17}{168} = 0.10$

$S_3 \cong p \ \& \ q \ \& \ r$ gets the Σ^*-probability value $\frac{25}{168} = 0.15$

$S_4 \cong p \ \& \ q \ \& \ {\sim}r$ gets the Σ^*-probability value $\frac{24}{168} = 0.14$

$S_5 \cong {\sim}p \ \& \ {\sim}q$ gets the Σ^*-probability value $\frac{39}{168} = 0.23$

$S_6 \cong {\sim}p \ \& \ q$ gets the Σ^*-probability value $\frac{45}{168} = 0.27$.

This revised procedure once more places S_6 in a favoured position: again we obtain ${\sim}p \ \& \ q$ as axiom for the $\mathscr{P}$-consequences. (However, such a uniformity in the outcome of these two variant procedures is not a general and necessary feature.) For even here, as we should expect on the basis of the considerations canvassed in Chapter V, the result of our initial analysis in terms of plausibilities differs significantly from that of a directly probabilistic analysis:

m.c.s	*Average Plausibility of the elements*	A Posteriori *Probability*
S_1	4.0	0.11
S_2	3.3	0.10
S_3	3.3	0.15
S_4	2.7	0.14
S_5	3.5	0.23
S_6	3.3	0.27

Agreement on S_6 apart, the two standards diverge markedly.

At the outset of this chapter we concerned ourselves with the resolution of ambiguity in a text which one was prepared to credit with internal self-consistency. Let us now turn to the different but analogous problem of 'interpreting' the views of an author whose (unambiguous) assertions are—unhappily but all too realistically—not altogether self-consistent. Suppose our author makes all the statements of the following set:

$$S = \{p \lor r, p \supset q, {\sim}q, {\sim}r\}.$$

As usual, we begin by seeing 'how much we can possibly save', and accordingly calculate the various m.c.s.

$S_1 = \{p \lor r, p \supset q, {\sim}q\}$
     which is axiomatized by ${\sim}p \ \& \ {\sim}q \ \& \ r$

$S_2 = \{p \lor r, p \supset q, {\sim}r\}$
     which is axiomatized by $p \ \& \ q \ \& \ {\sim}r$

$S_3 = \{p \vee r, \sim q, \sim r\}$
    which is axiomatized by p & $\sim q$ & $\sim r$.
$S_4 = \{p \supset q, \sim q, \sim r\}$
    which is axiomatized by $\sim p$ & $\sim q$ & $\sim r$.

Proceeding in the now-familiar manner we derive possible-world probabilities from the distributions effected by the S_i over the possible worlds:

Possible Worlds	A Priori Probability	S-Elements				Σ	Σ^*
		$p \vee r$	$p \supset q$	$\sim q$	$\sim r$		
p & q & r	$\frac{1}{8}$	$\frac{1}{6}$	$\frac{1}{6}$			$\frac{4}{12}$	$\frac{4}{48}$
p & q & $\sim r$	$\frac{1}{8}$	$\frac{1}{6}$	$\frac{1}{6}$		$\frac{1}{4}$	$\frac{7}{12}$	$\frac{7}{48}$
p & $\sim q$ & r	$\frac{1}{8}$	$\frac{1}{6}$		$\frac{1}{4}$		$\frac{5}{12}$	$\frac{5}{48}$
p & $\sim q$ & $\sim r$	$\frac{1}{8}$	$\frac{1}{6}$		$\frac{1}{4}$	$\frac{1}{4}$	$\frac{8}{12}$	$\frac{8}{48}$
$\sim p$ & q & r	$\frac{1}{8}$	$\frac{1}{6}$	$\frac{1}{6}$			$\frac{4}{12}$	$\frac{4}{48}$
$\sim p$ & q & $\sim r$	$\frac{1}{8}$		$\frac{1}{6}$		$\frac{1}{4}$	$\frac{5}{12}$	$\frac{5}{48}$
$\sim p$ & $\sim q$ & r	$\frac{1}{8}$	$\frac{1}{6}$	$\frac{1}{6}$	$\frac{1}{4}$		$\frac{7}{12}$	$\frac{7}{48}$
$\sim p$ & $\sim q$ & $\sim r$	$\frac{1}{8}$		$\frac{1}{6}$	$\frac{1}{4}$	$\frac{1}{4}$	$\frac{8}{12}$	$\frac{8}{48}$

(In this calculation we have supposed equal prior probabilities for the possible worlds.) The four S_i accordingly obtain Σ^*-probabilities of $\frac{7}{48}, \frac{7}{48}, \frac{8}{48}, \frac{8}{48}$, respectively, so that S_3 and S_4 seem preferable on this basis. But note that we can go well beyond this point, for we can now calculate the probabilities of propositions (S-elements or not) with respect to S, for example that:

$$\mathrm{pr}(p) = \tfrac{24}{48}$$
$$\mathrm{pr}(p \, \& \, q) = \tfrac{11}{48}$$
$$\mathrm{pr}(p \vee \sim q) = \tfrac{39}{48}.$$

We are thus in a position to answer questions of the form 'How likely is it—given what he said—that our author would espouse the thesis that . . .?' even though the assertions he made are mutually inconsistent. Thus even if we do not choose to follow the path of the coherence analysis through to its indication of one definite and particular resolution, its methodology can also serve as basis for an approach to the probabilities of the case. As was observed above, serious difficulties lie in the way of determining on the basis of an orthodox, non-coherentist, probabilistic approach the probabilities of a proposition with respect to an inconsistent body of evidence. A coherence analysis along the indicated lines is thus able to extend the range of probabilistic techniques beyond their usual consistency-restricted sphere.

2. *Readjustments in Report Processing*

Suppose that just two reports are given by equally reliable sources regarding the number of participants at a certain gathering. Source No. 1 says that there were 500 people present, No. 2 says that there were 600. Application of the coherence methodology will yield:

(1) There were either 500 or 600 people present.

And as a logical consequence of (1) we shall also obtain:

(2) There were 500–600 people present.

So far so good. But unfortunately we shall also obtain:

(3) There were not 550 (or 490 or 530 or 580 or 610) people present.

In taking as our basic data only the two specified reports, we are committed to regarding these as the only relevant truth-candidates, and so must arrive at the disjunctive result:

(4) Either there were *exactly* 500 people present or there were *exactly* 600 people present.

This result hardly seems satisfactory in the case of reports dealing with the sort of estimates at issue in this example.

The realistically warranted procedure would undoubtedly be as follows. Let us introduce the abbreviation

$$[n] = \text{There were } n \text{ people present.}$$

On the basis of the two *explicit* reports of [500] and [600] we should open up the area of truth-candidacy to the whole series

$$[450], [451], \ldots, [500], \ldots, [600], \ldots, [649], [650].$$

We should now introduce differential plausibility rankings, presumably by some such procedure as ranking the plausibility of a given [n] in terms of (say) its average distances from the explicit reports (though more sophisticated procedures are certainly possible and probably superior). Then the plausibility of the implicit report [n] becomes a function of the quantity:

$$Q(n) = \tfrac{1}{2} \times (|[n]-500|+|[n]-600|)$$

where the vertical bars now represent the absolute value. Thus we might set the plausibility of [n] as follows:

Value of $Q(n)$	Plausibility of [n]
$Q(n) \leqslant 50$	2
$50 < Q(n) \leqslant 70$	3
$70 < Q(n)$	4.

Then the reports would obtain the following plausibilities:

[450]–[479] all rank 4 as rather implausible
[480]–[499] all rank 3 as fairly plausible
[500]–[600] all rank 2 as very plausible
[601]–[619] all rank 3 as fairly plausible
[620]–[650] all rank 4 as rather implausible.

On this basis we should obtain the result

(5) The number of participants present was somewhere in the range $c.$ 480–$c.$ 620.

This seems far more attractive than the initial result (4).

This example shows vividly that in cases of processing reports —especially reports of the sort involved in numerical estimation —it may well be appropriate to extend the range of the data beyond the explicit reports. Given certain overt or *explicit* reports one may well need—under the circumstances—to broaden one's information base to include also those '*tacit* reports' that lie in their logical neighbourhood, and to take the view that the explicit reports are—so to speak—only that part of an iceberg that projects above the water. Accordingly one would not hesitate in cases of the sort instanced above to expand the list of data in the sense of truth-candidates well beyond the explicit reports that come to hand. For example, if a man cannot distinguish between greens and blues (but can distinguish green–blue from other colours), then his report 'The object was green' must be transposed into the two truth-candidates: 'The object was green' and 'The object was blue'.

The move from reports to truth-candidates is not always automatic. In straightforward cases we can treat the reports as themselves the only truth-candidates. But in other, perhaps less standard, but for all that no less important cases, the reports *suggest* the realm of truth-candidacy rather than dictating it in being themselves exhaustive thereof. The overt reports can serve us as guides to the way in which the doors to truth-candidacy should be opened up to other propositions in the logical neighbourhood of what is explicit in the specific information they convey. The use of supplemental information about the nature of the case may be necessary and appropriate.

3. *Consensus Methodology*

The mechanisms of consensus analysis—of extracting a 'group position' from individual views—are virtually identical in their abstract, formal structure with those of the processing of reports.

We begin with a number of 'authorities' or 'experts'—or just 'sources'—who make affirmations regarding some issue placed before them. Their declarations may—alas generally do—stand in mutual conflict. Faced by this situation we should like to arrive at the supposition that best conveys 'the area of by-and-large agreement' among these conflicting views so as to represent a consensus position.

Here again, the coherence methodology is applicable in a manner essentially similar to its bearing upon the analysis of reports. That this is so is perhaps best and most vividly brought out by considering a concrete example.

Suppose we interrogate four sources X_1–X_4 with respect to two propositions that interest us (p and q) and find them to make the following declarations:

$$X_1: p \supset q$$
$$X_2: p \lor q$$
$$X_3: p \, \& \sim q$$
$$X_4: q.$$

The sources might, moreover, afford us a self-appraisal of their relative expertise in the topical area at issue, or perhaps we can ourselves obtain an independent evaluation. Let the results be as follows:

X_1 is very knowledgeable.

X_2 is very knowledgeable.

X_3 is reasonably knowledgeable.

X_4 is relatively uninformed.

To arrive at a consensus position we could apply the coherence machinery in the familiar way. We begin with the data:

$$S = \{p \supset q, p \lor q, p \, \& \sim q, q\}.$$

The m.c.s. of S are:

$$S_1 = \{p \supset q, p \lor q, q\} \text{ axiomatized by } q.$$
$$S_2 = \{p \lor q, p \, \& \sim q\} \text{ axiomatized by } p \, \& \sim q.$$

To develop a plausibility index we should begin with the correlation:

Expertise	Plausibility
highly expert	2
very knowledgeable	3
reasonably knowledgeable	4
relatively uninformed	5
utterly ignorant	6

Thus we obtain the indexing

$$|p \supset q| = 3$$
$$|p \vee q| = 3$$
$$|p \ \& \sim q| = 4$$
$$|q| = 5.$$

This indexing in fact provides a full-scale plausibility index. The plausibility situation for the m.c.s. is as follows:

		Maximum	Average
S_1	(3, 3, 5)	5	3.7
S_2	(3, 4)	4	3.5

Accordingly, the preferred m.c.s. is S_2 which is axiomatized by $p \ \& \sim q$. This proposition could thus serve us as the 'consensus result' of the initial declarations. (Note that the upshot is a preference for X_3's report to that of the more knowledgeable X_1.)

It should be observed that if we treated the sources of this example as of uniform knowledgeability then we should have no basis of preference among the m.c.s. In this case, one would arrive simply at the outcome $p \vee q$ to represent the (now substantially more meagre) consensus result—unless some other criterion of preference were adopted (e.g. the probabilistic, in which case—as the reader can readily verify for himself—$p \ \& \sim q$ would again result). Perhaps, however, one would in such a case prefer to apply the majority-rule criterion of Method II of Chapter V, and accordingly prefer those m.c.s. (viz. only S_1) which would render true the majority of the initial declarations. In this specific case we arrive at q as the consensus result.

This procedure for pooling diverse and discordant judgments into a composite result extends a standard resource from the sphere of numerical estimates into the propositional area. In numerous investigations, social psychologists have asked a group of individuals to make judgments about the temperature of a room, the number of beans in a jar, or the relative weights of a series of objects. Each individual in the group expresses his opinion without knowledge of the judgments of others. The arithmetic mean of the individual estimates is then viewed as constituting a group-consensus judgment. Various interesting results have been determined in this connection.[8] It has been

---

[8] See H. H. Kelley and J. W. Thibaut, 'Experimental Studies in Group Problem Solving and Process', in G. Lindzey (ed.), *Handbook of Social Psychology*, vol. 2 (Cam-

found, for example, that the mean value of the independent judgments is generally more accurate than the personal judgments of most of the individuals. Furthermore this mean tends to deviate less from the true value of the object being judged when it is based upon many individuals' responses than when it is based on the judgments of only a few persons. Such empirical studies cannot, however, move from the quantitative domain of numerical estimates to that of more qualitative propositional relationships unless a basic conceptual problem is first resolved. Before any such transfer can be attempted, some method must be found for determining a 'consensus of judgments' in the propositional case. Deployed in the way we have illustrated, the coherence analysis affords a means for solving this question of a propositional consensus.

It thus appears that the coherence methodology has significant applications in the empirical domain of information-processing, especially in the exploitation of reports and estimates. These applications render it a significant asset quite apart from any of its purely philosophical uses. The coherence approach is in this respect unique among the traditional theories of truth, all the others being confined to the role of purely philosophical instruments for answering purely philosophical questions. The coherence theory exemplifies a quite infrequent phenomenon: a philosophical theory capable of doing useful extra-philosophical work.

bridge, Mass., 1954); I. Lorge *et al.*, 'A Survey of Studies Contrasting the Quality of Group Performance and Individual Performance: 1920–1957', *Psychological Bulletin*, 55 (1958), 337–72; as well as a series of very important but yet unpublished studies carried out by a group under N. C. Dalkey at the RAND Corporation.

XIII

COHERENTIST EPISTEMOLOGY: KNOWLEDGE WITHOUT A FOUNDATION OF CERTAINTY

1. *Truth Without Foundations*

IT yet remains to consider the bearing of the coherence theory of truth on the larger issues of epistemology by posing the questions: What is the shape of a coherentist theory of knowledge? What epistemological consequences follow from the assumption that our assessments of truth are in practice arrived at by the coherence route?

A coherentist theory of knowledge views the founding of knowledge on its data in terms of the determination of truths relative to families of (not necessarily consistent) premises by means of a coherence analysis. It regards the coherence path to truth as paradigmatic of the rational path to knowledge. H. H. Joachim has sketched its approach as follows:

'My present knowledge as a whole', then, in spite of its manifest imperfection and instability, is the criterion and the measure of the truth of every constituent phase of itself. For me at least, as I make my present judgement, it is the sole and the sufficient criterion. There is nothing '*for*' me—nothing within my actual experience—on which I could base a reasoned doubt or criticism of 'my present knowledge as a whole'—however provisional and incomplete its 'wholeness' must (on the general principles of the 'idealist position') be admitted to be. Every judgement, therefore, which contributes essentially to constitute this relatively complete and relatively coherent system of judgements—to constitute (say) my present 'total' knowledge of English history, or of plane geometry—is, *for me as I judge*, true in proportion to the amount, the value or significance, and the indispensability (the irreplaceableness) of its contribution.[1]

To go from a coherence theory of truth to a coherence epistemology is to take a distinct and significant step. A coherentist epistemology adopts the coherence analysis of truth as its guide to route rational inquiry in the production of knowledge.[2] Its

---

[1] *Logical Studies* (London, 1948), pp. 273–4.

[2] One could well be a coherence theorist as to the criterion of truth and a non-coherentist in epistemology. In particular, this would be so if one believed in a

approach is fundamentally holistic, judging the acceptability of every purported item of information by its capacity to contribute towards a well-ordered whole. In this, its essentially Hegelian approach, coherentist epistemology stands in sharp contrast with the foundationalist approach of the mainstream tradition of western epistemology.

The idea of *immediate* or *basic* (or 'protocol') truths of fact has a long and distinguished philosophical history that goes back to Aristotle and beyond. Such truths—it is held—are to be apprehended in some direct and fundamental way, typified by the immediate sensory apprehension of phenomenal colours or odours. Within the epistemic structure of our knowledge of truth, such basic truths are to serve as a foundation; other truths are made to rest upon them, but they rest upon no others: like the axioms of a deductive system they provide the ultimate support for the entire structure. Many epistemologists have held that truths—even mere probabilities—can be maintained only on a basis of certainty. Thus one very influential recent philosopher writes: 'If anything is to be probable [let alone definitely true!] then something must be certain. The data which eventually support a genuine probability [or a warranted truth-claim!], must themselves be certainties. We do have such absolute certainties, in the sense data initiating belief. . . .'[3] This essentially *axiomatic* concept of truth finds its formal articulation in the foundationalist (or intuitionist) theory of truth with its invocation of a starter-set of foundational basic truths. This might be caricatured as an 'aristocratic' view of truth: truths as such are not equal; they are certain 'master' truths on which the other, 'client' truths depend.

The foundationalist programme of a quest for the evidential ultimates of factual knowledge has deep roots in antiquity and was decisively reasserted at the very outset of modern philosophy in the writings of Descartes. In the twentieth century apart from the main-line positivists, it finds its most devoted adherents in the school of Brentano.[4] However, the programme is not without

cognitive process (say 'intuition') that could provide a short cut to the truth as contrasted with the laborious process of coherence analysis. All the same it would seem somewhat incongruous to espouse a coherence theory of truth at the criterial level and then to shift to a fundamentally diverse position in epistemology.

³ C. I. Lewis, *An Analysis of Knowledge and Valuation* (La Salle, Ill., 1946), p. 186.

⁴ See F. Brentano, *Wahrheit und Evidenz* (ed. O. Kraus, Leipzig, 1930). The most influential present-day advocate of an epistemological position along Brentanoesque lines is R. M. Chisholm (see his *Theory of Knowledge* (Englewood Cliffs, N.J., 1966)). Compare also R. Firth, 'Ultimate Evidence', *The Journal of Philosophy*, 53 (1956), 732–9; reprinted in R. J. Swartz (ed.), *Perceiving, Sensing, and Knowing* (New York, 1965), pp. 486–96. For an informative general survey and critique of present-day foundationalism see Anthony Quinton, 'The Foundations of Knowledge' in

characteristic difficulties of its own. The quest for protocol statements as a foundation for empirical knowledge has always foundered on the inherent tension between the two incompatible objectives of indubitable certainty on the one hand and objective factual claims on the other. In so far as the statement provides information about the world (e.g. 'I now see a cat there' which entails, *inter alia*, that a cat is there) it is not invulnerable to a discovery of error; in so far as it is safeguarded (e.g. by some guarding-locution such as 'I take it that . . .', so that we have 'It now seems to me that I see a cat there' or 'I am under the impression that I see a cat there'), the statement relates to appearance not reality and becomes denuded of objective content. Egocentric appearance statements may have sense but are void of objective information; claims regarding impersonal reality are objectively informative but in principle vulnerable.[5]

In contrast to the foundationalist approach, the coherence theory dispenses with any appeal to basic, foundational truths of fact. A thoroughgoing coherentist epistemology opposes itself diametrically to just this thesis that knowledge of the actual, and even of the probable, requires a foundation of certainty. The coherence approach maintains that truth is accessible in the extralogical realm without any foundation of factual certainty. (The qualifier 'factual' occurs here because the need for the machinery of logic is, of course, conceded.) In this regard, the coherentist stands in firm alliance with those pragmatists who —since the days of Charles S. Peirce, the founding father of that

B. Williams and A. Montefiore (eds.), *British Analytical Philosophy* (London, 1971), pp. 55–86.

[5] Recognition of these and other weaknesses of foundationalism has in contemporary times not been spearheaded by coherentists—the idealistic advocates were ineffectual, the positivist advocates (i.e. Neurath and his sympathizers) were unsuccessful. The only effective opposition has centred about the refutationism of K. R. Popper's *Logik der Forschung* (Vienna, 1935; tr. as *The Logic of Scientific Discovery*, New York and London, 1959; 2nd edn. 1960) (I shall cite the book in the Harper Torchbook paperback reprint version, New York, 1965). Popper's position is too complex for treatment here. Suffice it to say that it is categorically decisive in its rejection of protocol statements as well as the entire programme of inductive logic in seeing scientific epistemology as a structure of inductively drawn conclusions from infallible premisses. However, Popper's own falsificationist theory has from our standpoint a decidedly negative tendency in that it calls, in the final analysis, for abandoning in the factual domain any and all application of the traditional conception of truth. Thus with respect to the claims of science Popper insists that 'we can never give positive reasons which justify the belief that a theory is true' (*Conjectures and Refutations* (3rd edn., London, 1969), p. 167). A technical concept of 'verisimilitude' is Popper's surrogate for the traditional concept of truth, but its ramifications are complex and require more space than the incidental discussion allows. For Popper, the whole idea of justifying or establishing the truth of empirical statements is anathema, and this view sets him apart from any position articulated along coherentist lines.

doctrine—have defended the fallibilist view that all of our claims to factual knowledge are potentially vulnerable.[6]

Negating the need for any axiomatic truths, the coherence theory sets out to implement a 'democratic' concept of treating all the truth-candidates as equal in the first analysis. The available data are treated with a complete 'equality of opportunity'; truthfulness is determined for some of them only through a process of interaction, that is, by considerations of a best fit in terms of *mutual* accord and attunement, rather than their falling captive to certain basic prior truths. In a way, the coherentist approach is exactly the inverse of the foundationalist. The foundationalist begins his epistemological work with a very small initial collection of absolutely certain truths from which he proceeds to work *outwards* by suitably *additive* procedures to arrive at a wider domain of truth; by contrast, the coherentist begins with a very large initial collection of insecure pretenders to truth from which he proceeds to work *inwards* by suitably *eliminative* procedures to arrive at a narrower domain of truth. The expansive procedure of the foundationalist is the very opposite of the contractive procedure of the coherentist. The foundationalist is forced to a starting-point of few but highly secure items, and immediately faces the dilemma of security *v.* content. The coherentist bypasses this difficulty altogether. He begins with too many items—far too many since they stand in a conflict of logical incompatibility—but proceeds to undo the damage of this embarrassment of riches by suitable hedging manœuvres. This approach avoids altogether the characteristic perplexity of foundationalist epistemology in finding appropriate candidates to supply the requisite foundation.

On the coherence theory, truth is not—as on the intuitionist theory—a tree-like structure supported by a firm-rooted trunk, but like a mass of objects (some tied to others) thrown into a liquid: some of them rise to the surface themselves or are dragged there by others, some of them sink to the bottom under their own weight or through the pull of others. For the coherentist, knowledge is not a Baconian brick wall with block supporting block upon a solid foundation, rather an item of knowledge is like a node of a spider's web which is linked to others by thin strands of connection, each alone weak but all together adequate for its support.

<hr>

[6] See Peirce's incisive essays, 'Questions Concerning Certain Faculties Claimed for Man', *Journal of Speculative Philosophy*, 2 (1868), 103–14 (reprinted in *Collected Papers of Charles Sanders Peirce*, ed. by C. Hartshorne and P. Weiss, vol. V [Cambridge, Mass., 1934], pp. 135–55), and 'Some Consequences of Four Incapacities', ibid. 140–57 (reprinted in *Collected Papers*, ibid., pp. 156–89).

The above description of coherentist methodology is, of course, figurative, but it is a figurative description that accurately characterizes a well-defined process that may be illustrated as follows: we begin with a set of inconsistent 'data', as in the now-familiar example: $S = \{\sim p, \sim q, p \vee q\}$. Treating all members of S precisely alike, we form its m.c.s.:

$$S_1 = \{\sim p, \sim q\} \quad \text{axiomatized by } \sim p \mathbin{\&} \sim q$$
$$S_2 = \{\sim p, p \vee q\} \quad \text{axiomatized by } \sim p \mathbin{\&} q$$
$$S_3 = \{\sim q, p \vee q\} \quad \text{axiomatized by } p \mathbin{\&} \sim q.$$

We may now apply some sort of preferential considerations to narrow the range of possibilities. For example, we might carry through a probabilistic analysis based on a 'principle of indifference', thus arriving—without having in any way prejudged the truthfulness of certain propositions—at the *emergent*, and definitely not *intrinsic*, alethic preference for a certain result (namely $\sim p \mathbin{\&} \sim q$). Accordingly, two S-elements would be classed as true and the third as false. This entire procedure goes wholly counter to the classical epistemologists' axiomatic quest for basic or foundational truths: nothing has been treated as basic to anything else (truths of logic excepted). The analysis implements a conception of *truth without true foundations*; it seeks to provide a procedure for arriving at output truths without requiring any input truths as an indispensable starting basis.

F. H. Bradley puts the matter as follows:

I agree that we depend vitally on the sense-world, that our material comes from it, and that apart from it knowledge could not begin. . . . We meet here a false doctrine largely due to a misleading metaphor. My known world is taken to be a construction built upon such and such foundations. It is argued, therefore, to be in principle a superstructure which rests on these supports. You can go on adding to it no doubt, but only as long as the supports remain; and, unless they remain, the whole building comes down. But the doctrine, I have to contend, is untenable, and the metaphor ruinously inapplicable. The foundation of truth is provisional merely. In order to begin the construction I take the foundations as absolute—so much certainly is true. . . . It does not follow that if these [foundations] are allowed to be fallible, the whole building collapses. . . . Some of these [foundational 'facts'] must be relegated, as they are, to the world of error. . . . And the view which I advocate takes them all as in principle fallible.[7]

Here we have a trenchant statement of the core idea of the coherence theory of factual knowledge as a basically 'non-Euclidean'—that is to say *non-axiomatic*—instrument of cognitive methodology.

[7] 'On Truth and Coherence', in *Essays on Truth and Reality* (Oxford, 1914), pp. 202–18; see pp. 207–10.

2. *The Epistemic Dualism of Contingent Knowledge*

An approach to knowledge by the coherence route creates a significant epistemic dualism on the side of contingent knowledge. There is knowledge-as-datum and knowledge-as-fact: we can claim to know something to be a *datum* and accordingly stop short of staking a claim to outright truth, or else we can claim to know it to be a *fact* and accordingly stake a claim to actual truth. The former is a qualified claim to knowledge, the latter a claim to knowledge pure and simple. This dualism extends across the whole epistemic domain. For example, verbs of perception are, for the coherentist, equivocal as between a strictly subjectivistic and experiential and an objectivistic and veridical sense: 'I saw Henry Smith' can be construed either as:

1. I had a visual experience of the Henry-Smith-seeing sort, but abstain from claiming more than that this was *presumptively* veridical; I do not flatly assert that Henry Smith was actually there, etc.
2. Not only did I have a visual experience of the Henry-Smith-seeing sort, but this experience was veridical; I claim that it was actually Henry Smith I saw.

In the manner of this example, a coherence-theory epistemology is basically dualistic throughout the contingent sphere. (That other aspect of epistemic dualism—the traditional division between knowledge of contingent matters and knowledge of the necessary truths of logic and pure mathematics—is beside the point here.) Its insistence upon the special role of data (to be sure data that may differ in plausibility) as contradistinguished from established truths is the basis of this fundamental dualism of a coherence epistemology. But with respect to the truths of fact themselves it is emphatically monistic: rejecting the foundationalists' distinction between elemental and derived truths, it sees the whole domain of factual truth as of a piece.

A coherentist epistemology accordingly sees two fundamental requisites for knowledge:

I. Sources of data (the senses, memory, etc.).
II. Mechanisms for implementing the coherentist extraction of truths from the data. These in particular include:
   1. the logical (or quasi-logical) machinery of consequence and compatibility.
   2. a mechanism for making assessments of alethic eligibility regarding the data (and especially a procedure for making judgments of plausibility).

Item I represents the empiricist side of coherence-theoretical epistemology, item II its rationalist side. The indispensable role of data—which marks the emphatically empiricist aspect of the coherentist approach—is by now too familiar to need further comment. At this stage, the second item has more interesting aspects. One of these resides in the thesis that to arrive at factual knowledge we must always to some extent *reason* about the data. In contradiction to those who maintain a faculty that provides for immediate, wholly non-discursive, protocol-like knowledge of truths, the coherentist regards *all* factual knowledge as discursive; for him, *some* reasoning is always needed to support claims to objective knowledge of truths (even if this goes no further than to recognize the lack of discordant data and apply this recognition). For the coherentist it is an essential aspect of all warranted truth-claims that unlike data-claims they will inevitably rest on at least a minimal measure of discursive reflection regarding their rational foundations. It is again instructive to see how F. H. Bradley formulates the point at issue:

> Why is it that this or that fact of observation is taken as practically certain? It is so taken just in so far as it is *not* taken in its own right. . . . [For to qualify as certain] the observed fact must agree with our world as already arranged, or at least must not upset this. If the fact is too much contrary to our arranged world we provisionally reject it. We eventually accept the fact only when after confirmation the hypothesis of its error becomes still more ruinous. . . . The question throughout is as to what is better or worse for our order as a whole.[8]

This analytical and discursive—and so inherently rational—aspect of knowledge is a central tenet of coherence epistemology.

Particular interest and significance relates to item II. 2. Here the rationalist tendency of the coherence theory comes sharply to the fore: its insistence on the *essential and substantive* contribution of the knower to knowledge. The abstract mechanisms of logical reasoning are not in themselves enough to erect a structure of knowledge out of the data; a scaffolding of considerations of alethic preferability—especially plausibility—is needed as well. Given a different appraisal of plausibilities, different results will be yielded by one and the same body of data. These are not (or at least not *in toto*) to be extracted from the data themselves, they will always have to be *added* to them to some extent through what the knower himself brings to the epistemic situation. The coherentist is thus committed to the rationalist doctrine of an active and constitutive contribution of the mind to the construc-

8 Op. cit., see p. 212.

tion of knowledge. The coherentist sees knowledge as a *system* and takes the view that the mind itself makes an essential and formative contribution to this systematization.

3. *The Spectre of Scepticism*

How can there be any genuine *knowledge* according to a view that insists on the insufficiency of the 'objective' data to underwrite the failproof extraction (or deductive determination) of the truth, requiring that they be supplemented by essentially ampliative processes (such as a coherence theory's 'subjective' assessments of plausibility or some similar mechanisms of alethic preference)? As a legitimate basis for *claims to knowledge*, a coherentist epistemology stands in need of a systematic vindication of its procedures. It must be shown that coherence-based claims to knowledge are not factitious and arbitrary, but appropriately justified. How is a coherentist approach to knowledge to be defended? In briefest outline the defence we envisage proceeds as follows: particular knowledge claims are supported through the application of a certain method, viz. the coherence analysis. The use of this method in the case at issue is then in turn justified in terms of pragmatic considerations.

The choice of a criterion of truth is a limited or circumscribed choice; only a handful of alternative possibilities are available: correspondence, coherence, pragmatism, etc. There is a *genuine* choice because there are alternatives; but this is a *limited* choice because its range is restricted. Now this plurality of alternatives is not the whole story, for the adoption of some one of these solutions is in this present case not a haphazard matter. The choice at issue is not only limited, it is guided—principally by the criteria of pragmatic success in the *practical* areas of prediction and control.

This line of thought indicates how findings of truth can be secured against the assault of traditional philosophic scepticism. The sceptic's argument goes as follows:

> The rational man must, of course, have a basis for his beliefs and opinions. Thus, asked *why* he accepts some proposition, he will adduce considerations that support it. But we can now ask him why he accepts these in turn, and this process can be continued as long as one likes. As a result, we shall either move in a circle—and so ultimately provide no justification at all—or become involved in an infinite regress, supporting the elephant on the back of a turtle on the back of an alligator, etc. The only way to terminate the regress is by a dogmatic acceptance, somewhere along the line, of an *ultimate*

unjustified (and presumably unjustifiable) truth that is used to justify others but is not itself justified. But any such unjustified acceptance is by its very nature arbitrary and irrational. Thus how can there ever be a secure standard of rational acceptance? How can we secure such a standard save by appealing to another standard— and then again onwards until ultimately some unjustified standard is irrationally accepted?

So reasons the philosophic sceptic. The best answer to this line of sceptical reasoning lies in recognizing that the things one rationally accepts are not of a piece. Specifically, it is necessary to give careful heed to the distinction between *theses* on the one hand and *methods* on the other. It is indeed ultimately unsatisfactory to justify theses in terms of further theses in terms of further theses, and thus onwards. But reflection on the rational justification of the rationale of truth-determination shows that this is not at all the issue here. Rather, we justify the acceptance of specific theses because (ultimately) they are validated by the employment of a certain method—on our view the scientific method as codified in the coherence approach. Accordingly, it becomes possible to break the cycle of justifying thesis by thesis —in that a thesis can be justified by application of a method whose use itself requires no conceded theses. And then in turn one justifies the adoption of this method by reference to certain *practical* criteria: success in prediction and efficacy in control.

Our dialectic of justification thus breaks out of the restrictive confines of the sceptic's circle, and does so without relapse into a dogmatism of unjustified ultimates. We justify the acceptance of theses by reference to the truth-criterion from which they derive, and we justify this criterion in terms of classically pragmatic considerations. The approach presently envisaged thus counters philosophical scepticism by a complex, two-stage manœuvre, combining the criterial justification of truth-determinations with a pragmatic justification of the criterion of truth. On this view, a particular, specific knowledge claim is supported with reference to a method, which is then in its turn supported on pragmatist lines.

The upshot of this line of thought is a rebuttal of a *wholesale* scepticism to the effect that knowledge-claims are in principle unjustifiable. There remains, of course, the question of a *retail* scepticism that calls into question the specific validity of a particular class of knowledge claims. This sort of scepticism of course cannot but be dealt with in an *ad hoc* scrutiny of the particular case. But an across-the-board scepticism regarding the prospects of knowledge in general can be countered by providing a justification of knowledge-claims in the manner indicated.

4. Truth and Certainty

The coherence approach needs in particular to be secured against possible shipwreck on the classical sceptics' challenge of the impossibility *in principle* of any actual knowledge of matters of fact. One of the few doctrines agreed upon by a broad consensus of writers on epistemological subjects is that one cannot (correctly) be said to *know* what is false. People argue as follows:

The proposition '*P* is true' is to be regarded as a logical consequence of the proposition 'I know (or *X* knows) that *P*'. To say 'I know that *P*' is to *claim* (*inter alia*) *that P*, and to say that '*X* knows that *P*' is to *concede* the correctness of this claim. And going beyond the implicit claim that *P*, the proposition '*X* knows that *P*' also claims (1) that *X* accepts *P* as certain, and (2) that *X* has adequate rational warrant for this acceptance. This second point in turn comes down to two subordinate items: (1) that adequate rational warrant *exists*, and (ii) that this fact (of the existence of a rational warrant for accepting *P* as certain) lies within *X*'s ken. These observations establish the close link between knowledge and certainty. A claim to knowledge is a claim to certainty. It would make no sense to say (of oneself or another) that '*X knows* that *P* but he regards it as in some way doubtful whether or not *P* is the case'. By their very nature knowledge-claims purport to be infallibly correct.

Is a coherentist approach to knowledge possible in the face of these considerations? Such an approach sees the foundation of knowledge-claims in the application of a coherence analysis. Accordingly, '*X* knows *P*' would presumably be interpreted as claiming at least two things among others:

(1) that *X* accepts *P* as true on a coherentist basis that *he* regards as sufficient, and moreover
(2) that is in fact sufficient.

But as we have seen, the coherence analysis of truth goes far in the direction of fallibilism. In dispensing with infallible data, it dispenses also with the requirement of a *certain* foundation for factual truth-claims, and maintains that other considerations (e.g. further data) could potentially reverse a verdict of truth.

Coherentist epistemology insists that claims to factual knowledge can never be made categorically and definitely, but only conditionally and provisionally. Surely this leads straightway to scepticism? Not so. In principle, one could—it may be supposed—be entitled to claim that all the relevant data (or all of the sufficiently plausible relevant data) are in. Or else we could determine 'on general principles' that all further highly plausible data will accord with the result we have obtained, and thus be warranted 'on general principles' in claiming that further data would not lead to a 'change of mind'. On a coherentist basis the finality requisite to genuine knowledge can be supported along these lines.

But is such an argument sound? As one recent critic has rightly observed, 'the Coherence Theory is irrevocably tied to the task of showing how truth can be known for certain'.[9] Thus an objector might reason as follows: in general, a coherence-based proposition could *possibly* be false, and so cannot be certain. How, then, can a coherentist ever be justified in being certain of P—as is necessary for genuine claims to knowledge? (It is worth noting, incidentally, that this sceptical standpoint will apply every bit as much to an *inductivist* as to a *coherentist* epistemology, both alike having the *ampliative* feature that the output of truth-claims can exceed the logical content of the input. Both approaches take the view that one can reasonably hold something to be certain on grounds that do not deductively guarantee this certainty, and so can rationally and warrantedly *claim to know* in cases where 'one might possibly be mistaken'.) We are thrown back to the problem of reconciling a fallibilist epistemology with the need for certainty in genuine knowledge.

The line of reasoning which underlies the objection in view is based upon use of the argument:

If—it is possible that P is false,

Then—no one is justified in being certain of P.

This inference, however, involves a fallacy. The possible falsehood of a proposition P constitutes grounds against one's being certain of P only for a person who has some information about this possible falsity, that is, is in actual possession of some indication of it. The missing factor which underlies this inference, whose absence vitiates its correctness, is the element of *information*. Only for a person *aware* of its reality can the possible falsehood of P serve as a ground for doubt.

This point can be brought out even more clearly by comparison with the analogous inference:

If—P is false,

Then—no one is justified in holding that P.

Here again, and quite obviously, information as to the falsity

9 D. W. Hamlyn, 'The Correspondence Theory of Truth', *The Philosophical Quarterly*, 12 (1962), 193–205 (see 198).

of *P* (or at least awareness of some evidence for it) is a necessary presupposition for the correctness of the inference. Only when evidence for the actual—or possible or probable—falsity of *P* is *recognized* by a person, can this presumptive falsity serve as a factor which militates against *his* accepting, believing, or being certain of *P* (given that all the indications at his disposal conspire to point emphatically in that direction).

Consider the pair of propositions:

P is justifiably held by *X* to be true.

P is true.

Does the first entail the second? Surely not. For the evidence at someone's command sufficient to justify him in holding something to be true need not provide a deductive guarantee of this something. An analogous situation obtains with the pair:

P is justifiably held by *X* to be certain.

P is certain.

Again, the first proposition does not entail the second. The standard gap between the epistemic issue of what someone justifiably holds to be and the ontological issue of what is again comes into the picture. It is no doubt correct to say that we cannot be said to *know* something to be that *is* not so. But we can certainly have an *adequate* rational basis for the claim to knowledge even in cases when that claim proves insufficient in the final analysis because 'we did not *really* know what we justifiably took ourselves to know'. A. J. Ayer has put this point in his characteristically trenchant way:

> But to allow that there are times when we may justifiably claim the right to be sure of the truth of . . . [a] statement is not to allow that . . . [we] are infallible. One is conceded the right to be sure when one is judged to have taken every reasonable step towards making sure: but this is still logically consistent with one's being in error. The discovery of the error refutes the claim to knowledge; but it does not prove that the claim was not, in the circumstances, legitimately made. The claim to know . . . [a] statement is satisfied only if the statement is true; but it is legitimate if it has the appropriate backing. . . .[10]

Any fallibilistic theory of factual knowledge (be it inductivistic, probabilistic, or coherentistic) faces the complaint that what it affords us is not 'real' knowledge because what is known must be certain and it can provide no guarantee of certainty. And indeed, philosophers have often felt driven to a conception of

[10] *The Problem of Knowledge* (London, 1956), pp. 43–4.

knowledge so rigoristic that in the event there is little of anything left that one can ever be said to know.[11] Against this tendency it is proper to insist that while what is known must certainly be true, a doctrine that sees our claims to knowledge as *in principle* defeasible can nevertheless quite properly insist that there are circumstances in which claims to certainty are perfectly legitimate and justified. And it can take this stance precisely because something's *being true in fact* just is not a necessary precondition for a justified claim that it is true.

Applying these considerations to the initial problem, we return to the pivotal fact that '*X* knows *P*' must be interpreted as claiming, among other things, that '*X* accepts *P* as true on grounds that are in fact sufficient'. Here an ambiguity is present, as indicated by the question: Sufficient for what? Two alternatives are open:

(1) sufficient to establish *P* with certainty
(2) sufficient to provide rational warrant for the claim that *P* is certain.

The coherentist approach must—in view of its fallibilism— reject claims of type (1) in the domain of contingent fact, and there is no reason why it cannot do so. In effect we trade upon the crucial difference between

1. a *deductive* argument moving from premises comprising grounds for *P* (themselves suitably established) to the conclusion *P*, with the result that we can claim that this conclusion, *P*, is certain
2. a *nondeductive* argument moving from premises comprising grounds for *P* to the conclusion '*P* is certain'.

For in cases of the second type we can obtain a 'warrant for claiming certainty' short of requiring a failproof demonstration that this is actually certain.

A coherentist theory of knowledge thus stresses and exploits the crucial distinction between what is certain as such, and what is justifiably and warrantedly held to be so. It stresses that a realization of fallibility-in-general, while precluding proofs or demonstrations of certainty as such, does not in appropriate special cases preclude a rationally warranted claim that something is certainly so.

[11] As, for example, in Carnapian inductivism no theses of any theoretical content can ever be known. For other, more recent, versions of scepticism see K. Lehrer, 'Why Not Scepticism?' *The Philosophical Forum*, vol. 2 (1971), pp. 283–98 and P. Unger, 'A Defense of Scepticism', *The Philosophical Review*, vol. 80 (1971), pp. 198–219.

It might, however, be argued that our evidence for any *sensory* proposition is always necessarily inadequate to afford the necessary warrant for 'being certain'. This argument must surely be rejected as doing gross injustice to the epistemic serviceability of our senses. It cannot, of course, be deductively *proved* that the data—e.g. those of sense perception—can in some cases provide adequate warrant for certainty, but our grounds of rational warrant for holding that they can do so are nevertheless very impressive.

Rather than adding to G. E. Moore's examples of specific instances of situations in which doubt of a sensory proposition would amount to virtually unintelligible folly, we shall content ourselves with presenting an argument—along essentially coherentist lines—which appears to qualify as entirely adequate to establish a warrant for certainty regarding sensory propositions:

1. Our perceptual faculties yield data (i.e. *presumptively* truthful information).
2. It can be shown that, in general, in simple cases of the ordinary employment of the senses under normal circumstances, these data are highly reliable.
3. There is no evidence whatever that this specific simple instance of sense perception now before me is either extraordinary or abnormal.
4. Despite a reasonable effort to elicit data discordant with this perception I determined none that conflict. The datum at issue coheres fully with all others at my disposal.
5. Therefore, I am justified in being certain with regard to this matter.

This argument-paradigm indicates that we are, in numerous instances, perfectly justified in being certain of the truth of sensory propositions, and in laying a claim to knowledge in such cases.

For the coherentist, egocentric data are definitely open to question, and indeed, coherence is the test applied even to firsthand information when I screen my own observations to separate the veridical from the illusory. Coherence becomes the test for distinguishing reality from 'mere appearance': in being the criterion of truth it becomes the criterion of reality as well.[12]

---

[12] An illuminating discussion of cognate issues is given in Leibniz's classic essay 'On the Method of Distinguishing Real From Imaginary Phenomena' (*Philosophische Schriften*, ed. C. I. Gerhardt, vol. 7, pp. 319–22; tr. in L. E. Loemker (ed.), *G. W. Leibniz: Philosophical Papers and Letters* (Dordrecht, 1969), pp. 363–6), and compare H. Reichenbach's discussion in *The Rise of Scientific Philosophy* (Berkeley, Calif., 1962), pp. 260–6.

For the coherentist the distinction between appearance and reality is one to be drawn *within* the domain of experience as between authentic and non-veridical perception, and does not represent a distinction between known reality and an unknowable reality *an Sich*. (This is why for the criterial perspective of the coherentist the claim that 'true propositions accord with reality' is not only true but trivially so.) The very fact that some such test as that of coherence is needed to authenticate the data of our own observation introduces the element of potential-error but the very fact of 'passing the test' constitutes a rational warrant for claiming knowledge. F. H. Bradley has formulated the fallibilist principle at issue with admirable clarity:

> To take [sensation and] memory as in general trustworthy, which I have no special reason for doubt, and to take the testimony of those persons, whom I suppose to view the world as I view it, as being true, apart from special reason on the other side—these are the principles by which I construct my ordered world, such as it is. And because by any other method the result is worse, therefore for me these principles are true. On the other hand to suppose that any 'fact' of perception or memory is so certain that no possible experience could justify me in taking it as error, seems to be injurious if not ruinous.[13]

The point is this: coherence considerations can *warrant* someone's claiming that he—or someone else—knows something. But the fact that someone is so warranted does not mean that he cannot possibly be mistaken. The claim or concession of *warrant* on our part—even so strong a warrant as that required to support rational claims to knowledge—does not commit us to an altogether unqualified insistence upon the fact. The fallibilist may be right in holding that in theory we may be wrong but—recognizing and conceding this—we may be equally right in insisting that *in this case* this theoretical prospect may 'for all practical purposes' be put aside. An espousal of fallibilism in principle at the generic level is compatible with an insistence in specific cases that a claim to certainty is rationally justified then and there, precisely because rational justification can—and in certain cases must—stop short of outright proof. Theoretical fallibilism at the generic and wholesale level of epistemological theory does not create a basis for doubt at the concrete level of particular situations. In suitable circumstances, case-specific considerations may well indicate that it would be quixotic to hold that there is still 'room for doubt'. For in cases where the evidential indications are strong enough, the burden of rationality

---

[13] 'On Truth and Coherence', op. cit., p. 213.

shifts against the side of sceptical disbelief, since the range of rational warrant outstrips that of demonstrative proof.[14]

A reply to the sceptic along these lines is not a refutation of scepticism concerning matters of observed fact, but a rebuttal of it. To rest discontent with this foundation of sensory knowledge on sceptical grounds because 'the theoretical possibility of error' cannot be excluded totally is not to be *irrational* (i.e. in conflict with the demands of logic) but it is utterly *unreasonable* by imposing upon observational knowledge a condition which —by the very nature of the thing at issue—it is in principle incapable of meeting.[15]

Actually, the coherentist theory of knowledge has much kinship with some parts of current-day epistemological scepticism. For one thing, it too rejects the foundationalists' realm of intuitively certain protocols. The coherentist is a Cartesian sceptic as regards factual knowledge: initially, when at the very beginning we confront a mass of data, we accept *nothing* as true in the first instance, since everything within the data is in principle vulnerable, and truth emerges only at the end of the analysis. And, indeed, the coherentist is a more thoroughgoing sceptic than Descartes himself. For he does not expect to find some starting-point of initial certainty, some utterly secure resting point for an Archimedean lever. A substantial part of current epistemological scepticism is motivated by a recognition of the inherent difficulties of the foundationalism so prominent in this day. And in *this* regard the coherentist's mind is wholly in accord with that of the sceptic.

5. *Cognitive Solipsism and the Quest for Certainty*

Yet another crucial facet of the coherentist approach arises in connection with this issue of the essential certainty of knowledge. As we have seen, a philosophical tradition going back to Plato, and most emphatically predominant since Descartes, never tires of insisting that knowledge must be indubitable and certain: it makes no sense to say '*X* knows that *p* but there is some possibility that *p* may not be so'. Any and all *reports*, however, are possibly erroneous, and thus uncertain. The reports of others,

---

[14] This section and the preceding include some material originally presented in the author's paper on 'The Legitimacy of Doubt', *The Review of Metaphysics*, 13 (1959), 226–34.

[15] For a lucid discussion of relevant issues see H. H. Price, *Truth and Corrigibility* (Oxford, 1936; An Inaugural Lecture held before the University of Oxford on 5 Mar. 1936).

however epistemically useful and valuable they may be, thus cannot afford knowledge. No knowledge through vicarious experience is possible; in so far as knowledge is possible at all, its sole foundation must be first-hand information. The architectonic view that certain knowledge must have certain foundations led the Cartesian tradition of intuitionist epistemologists into an ever narrowing spiral that converged inexorably upon the self. The search for an indubitably certain basis of knowledge unavoidably leads back to the self, to its cognitive states, as with Descartes, or to its sensations, as with phenomenalist constructionism. Either way, one arrives at the ineluctable primacy of first-person (i.e. self-referential) data. Accordingly, with a search for infallible foundations for knowledge we are well on the way towards the modern epistemologists' spectre of cognitive solipsism: the only properly usable data for knowledge are those that one produces oneself.[16]

A coherentist epistemology, however, escapes this insistence on the absolute primacy of the self. Its basic orientation is social rather than rigorously self-centred in approach. Dispensing with any insistence on certainty in its data, it proceeds on a far wider front. Coherence turns on considerations of system, and here the self is not the be-all and end-all; its deliverances are only one group of elements within the larger systematic structure. I myself am but one source of data among many: there is no need whatever to dispense with vicarious information, even if it be somewhat uncertain. (I might, of course, regard it as less plausible than my own contributions to the data base, but that is as may be.)

F. H. Bradley, for one, was perfectly explicit in his insistence that the vicarious information derived from the reports of other persons (of suitable qualification) are pretty much on all fours with the deliverances of a man's own memory in its contribution to the constitution of his knowledge: 'To take memory as in general trustworthy, where I have no special reason for doubt, and to take the testimony of those persons, whom I suppose to view the world as I see it, as being true, apart from special reason on the other side—these are principles by which I con-

---

[16] Just this is the line of objection urged by O. Neurath in his coherentist critique of the early Carnap's architectonic construction of science from truth-intuitions of the personal protocol type. (See Neurath's essay 'Protokollsätze', *Erkenntnis*, 3 (1932), 204–14; tr. in A. J. Ayer, *Logical Positivism* (Glencoe, Minn., 1959), pp. 199–208). Neurath argues that 'There is no way of taking conclusively established pure protocol sentences as the starting point of the sciences' (p. 201), and maintains that 'methodological solipsism . . . [does] not become any the more serviceable because of the addition of the word "methodological"' (p. 206).

struct my ordered world, such as it is.'[17] In the face of the Cartesian tradition in epistemology, with its strident insistence on the primacy of first-hand information, the idealistic coherentists tended to emphasize the fundamentally social nature of human knowledge. A coherentist perspective in epistemology views human knowledge as a collective, interpersonal structure, a position that foundationalist epistemology would render untenable. The coherence approach affords a theoretical rationale for the natural, albeit non-Cartesian, view of knowledge as a social product; in contrast to a Cartesian-style foundationalist approach that is driven ever more forcibly to an egocentric epistemology, it is fundamentally pluri-centric and other-involving. The coherence theory thus acquires the substantial merit of being able to avoid the disaster of cognitive solipsism implicit in the foundationalist approach. In short, it opens up the prospect of seeing the build-up of our knowledge as an essentially *interpersonal* enterprise.

[17] 'On Truth and Coherence', op. cit., p. 213.

POSTSCRIPT

DESPITE its length, this consideration of the coherence theory leaves much unsaid. Indeed, one of the salient features of the discussion is its incompleteness: our coherentism is not so much a finished theory as a programme for theory-construction. We have done no more there than scratch the surface of a fertile terrain, and the present considerations have often borne the aspect of a rather suggestive than definitive treatment. The full extent of the utility of the coherence theory cannot be determined until many further detailed inquiries have been carried out, and others have joined in accomplishing the great mass of needed investigations. The aims of this book will be amply realized if it persuades the reader of the substantial promise of this undeservedly neglected topic. Incomplete and imperfect though they are, the present considerations will hopefully convince its readers that the coherence theory of truth deserves a better fate than has fallen to its lot in recent times. For there is good reason to think that the coherence analysis affords a powerful and many-faceted resource that has prospects for fruitful applications in every department of epistemology. Its theoretical stance being wholly different from that of the principal epistemological doctrines currently in favour, there is reason to think that a thorough-going exploitation of the coherentist approach may produce a significant reorientation of ideas throughout the theory of knowledge, but above all in the philosophy of science and the methodology of inductive reasoning.

APPENDIX A

(CHAPTER II, SECTION 4)

EWING ON COHERENCE AND THE INDEPENDENCE OF PROPOSITIONAL SETS

I N defining the concept of *coherence* for propositional sets, A. C. Ewing stipulates that a coherent set must be such that 'No set of propositions within the whole set is logically independent of all the propositions in the remainder of the set.'[1] Clarifying the import of this requirement, Ewing defines 'logical independence' as follows:

> I call two sets of propositions logically independent where no proposition in one set either entails or excludes with logical necessity or belongs to a set of propositions, drawn from one or both of the sets, which conjointly entail or exclude in their own right any proposition in the other set. (I say A and B conjointly entail C where the compound proposition A & B entails C, but neither A nor B alone entails C.)[2]

Accordingly, Ewing's explication appears to require the following construction:

S_1 indep S_2 iff there is no pair of propositions $P \in S_1$, $Q \in S_2$ such that either one of the following two conditions obtains:

(1) $P \vdash Q \vee P \vdash \sim Q$

(2) $(\exists S)\{S \subseteq (S_1 \cup S_2) \;\& \; P \in S \; \& \; (S \vdash Q \vee S \vdash \sim Q)$
$\& \sim(\exists S')[S' \subset S \; \& \; (S' \vdash Q \vee S' \vdash \sim Q)]\}.$

The first of these conditions says, in effect, that P is *logically determinative* with respect to Q. The second that P belongs to a *minimal* set that is logically determinative with respect to Q (i.e. one such that no proper subset is logically determinative). Note that (1) entails (2), since if (1) obtains, the set $\{P\}$ containing P alone will play the role of the S required by (2). In view of this the stipulation that neither condition obtains can be simplified by dropping alternative (1) so as to obtain a more straightforward formulation:

S_1 indep S_2 iff there is no pair of propositions $P \in S_1$, $Q \in S_2$ such that:

$(\exists S)\{S \subseteq (S_1 \cup S_2) \; \& \; P \in S \; \& \; (S \vdash Q \vee S \vdash \sim Q) \;\&$
$\sim(\exists S')[S' \subset S \; \& \; (S' \vdash Q \vee S' \vdash \sim Q)]\}.$

---

[1] A. C. Ewing, *Idealism: A Critical Survey* (London, 1934), pp. 229–30.
[2] Ibid., p. 230.

Now if the over-all set $S_1 \cup S_2$ is a *consistent* set, then—since it will contain Q—there is no question of any subset of it yielding $\sim Q$. So in this special case the definition can be simplified further:

S_1 indep S_2 iff there is no pair of propositions $P \in S_1$, $Q \in S_2$ such that:

$$(\exists S)\{S \subseteq (S_1 \cup S_2) \ \& \ P \in S \ \& \ S \vdash Q \ \& \ \sim(\exists S')[S' \subset S \ \& \ S' \vdash Q]\}.$$

This has it that the sets S_1 and S_2 are independent if:

For every $Q \in S_2$ it must be the case that every minimal Q-yielding subset of the remaining total set (i.e. of the set $(S_1 \cup S_2) - \{Q\}$) will contain some $P \in S_1$.

Let us now return to Ewing's requirement upon a coherent (*a fortiori* consistent) set that 'no set of propositions (S') within the whole set (S) is logically independent of all propositions in the remainder of the set'. In the first instance this says simply

$$\sim(\exists S')[S' \subseteq S \ \& \ S' \text{ indep } (S-S')]$$

which amounts to saying that there is no way of splitting S into two logically independent sets S', S−S'. In view of Ewing's specified meaning of the condition of 'logical independence', this—in the special case of a *consistent* set—comes down to saying that a coherent set S cannot be partitioned into subsets S', S−S' in such a way that the derivation of every S'-element can be accomplished solely from the remainder within S' (without ever requiring the use of members of S−S' as premises).

Now clause (ii) of our own version of Ewing's definition of coherence as given above (see p. 36) requires that

For any $S' \subseteq S$ there will be a proposition $Q \in (S-S')$ such that the presence of *some* $P \in S'$ is required as member of *any* minimal Q-yielding subset of S.

It is thus evident that our version of Ewing's definition is equivalent with his own, though (hopefully) given in a somewhat simpler and more intelligible form.

APPENDIX B

(CHAPTER IV, SECTION 3)

MINIMAL INCONSISTENT SUBSETS

A SUBSET S^* of S is said to be a minimal inconsistent subset (m.i.s.) of S if S^* is an inconsistent subset of S, but the deletion of any arbitrary proposition from S^* will render it consistent. Thus given any propositional set S, a subset set S' of S will be a minimal inconsistent subset of S if

1. S' is a non-empty subset of S
2. S' is inconsistent
3. The deletion from S' of any one of its elements will render the resulting set consistent.

Thus the set
$$S = \{p, p \supset q, q \supset r, \sim q, \sim r\}$$

has two m.i.s.:
$$S_1^* = \{p, p \supset q, \sim q\}$$
$$S_2^* = \{p, p \supset q, q \supset r, \sim r\}.$$

Or again, let the initial set S be
$$\{p \vee q, r \supset q, p \vee r, \sim p, \sim q, s \ \& \ \sim s\}.$$

Then its m.i.s. are:
$$S_1^* = \{r \supset q, p \vee r, \sim p, \sim q\}; \ S_2^* = \{p \vee q, \sim p, \sim q\}; \ S_3^* = \{s \ \& \ \sim s\}.$$

It is easy to establish the theorem:

Let S be an inconsistent set of self-consistent propositions, then every culprit belongs to some m.i.s. of S.

The proof of this theorem lies in the fact that only innocent bystanders (i.b.) will fail to fall into the m.i.s. system.

In consequence of this theorem, every set of propositions can be built up as the union of (1) a set of i.b. and (2) a union of (possibly overlapping) minimal inconsistent subsets. Such a construction need not, however, be unique. Though helpful, therefore, this representation of a set as a union of one set of i.b. with various m.i.s. does not solve the problem of defining equivalence for inconsistent sets. This problem is resolved in the next Appendix.

APPENDIX C

EQUIVALENT PROPOSITIONAL SETS

THROUGHOUT the discussions of this chapter we have not put any restriction whatsoever on the initial set of propositions **S** that is to be allowed. Consider the following sets:

$$\mathbf{S} = \{p, q, \sim q\},$$
$$\mathbf{S}' = \{\sim\sim p, p \ \& \ q, \sim q \supset q, \sim q\},$$
$$\mathbf{S}'' = \{p, \sim\sim p, \sim\sim\sim\sim p, \ldots, q, \sim\sim q, \ldots, \sim q, \sim\sim\sim q, \ldots\}.$$

It seems strange to deal with each of these sets separately, for they clearly are m.c.s.-equivalent in the sense that their respective m.c.s. generate exactly the same consequence-sets. This leads to the following definition:

Let $\mathbf{S}_i$ be an m.c.s. of the set **S**. We say that the set

$$\{P_{i,1}, P_{i,2}, \ldots, P_{i,k}\}$$

of propositions is a *basis* of the consequence-set $C(\mathbf{S}_i)$ if:

1. $P_{i,j} \in C(\mathbf{S}_i)$ for all $1 \leqslant j \leqslant k$ (though not necessarily $P_{i,j} \in \mathbf{S}$).
2. For all $P \in C(\mathbf{S}_i)$, $P_{i,1} \ \& \ \ldots \ \& \ P_{i,k} \vdash P$.
3. There is no proper subset $\{Q_1, \ldots, Q_m\}$ of $\{P_{i,1}, \ldots, P_{i,k}\}$, when $m < k$, such that for all $P \in C(\mathbf{S}_i)$ one has $Q_1 \ \& \ \ldots \ \& \ Q_m \vdash P$.

We say that an m.c.s. $\mathbf{S}_i$ of the set **S** is B-*equivalent* (basis-equivalent) to an m.c.s. $\mathbf{S}_j$ of **S**' if there is a basis of $C(\mathbf{S}_i)$ which is also a basis for $C(\mathbf{S}_j)$—and so, of course, also conversely. (Clearly, the B-equivalence of two m.c.s. yields that they share *all* their bases.) Correspondingly, we shall say that the propositional sets are m.c.s.-equivalent iff for every m.c.s. of the one there is an m.c.s. of the other such that these two m.c.s. are B-equivalent, and conversely.

Note that addition of either tautologies or self-contradictory statements (or both) to a given set **S** yields a set **S'** which is m.c.s.-equivalent to **S**. Clearly, if **S** and **S'** are two m.c.s.-equivalent sets then they have the same I-consequences and the same W-consequences, while the converse obviously fails with respect to I but holds for W. This fact can be seen from the following theorem:

THEOREM 1

The propositional sets **S** and **S'** are m.c.s.-equivalent iff for every proposition P: $\mathbf{S} \vdash_w P$ iff $\mathbf{S'} \vdash_w P$ (that is, iff the W-consequences of **S** and **S'** coincide).

Proof of THEOREM 1

(i) Suppose **S** and **S'** are m.c.s.-equivalent. Assume **S** ⊢ $_w P$. Then there is an m.c.s. **S**$_i$ of **S** such that **S**$_i$ ⊢ P. Since **S** and **S'** are m.c.s.-equivalent, there is an m.c.s. **S**$'_j$ of **S'** such that **S**$'_j$ ⊢ P. But now by definition **S'** ⊢ $_w P$. Similarly we can prove that if **S'** ⊢ $_w P$, then **S** ⊢ $_w P$.

(ii)

(1) Suppose that for every proposition P, **S** ⊢ $_w P$ iff **S'** ⊢ $_w P$.

(2) Suppose for *reductio ad absurdum* that **S** and **S'** are *not* m.c.s.-equivalent, namely, there is an m.c.s. **S**$_1$ of **S** such that *for all* m.c.s. **S**$'_j$ of **S'**, **S**$_1$ is *not* B-equivalent to **S**$'_j$.

(3) Let $\{P_1, \ldots, P_k\}$ be a basis of **S**$_1$.

Then **S**$_1$ ⊢ P_1 & ... & P_k and by definition

$\quad$ **S** ⊢ $_w P_1$ & ... & P_k

which by assumption (1) yields

(4) **S'** ⊢ $_w P_1$ & ... & P_k.

Namely, there is an m.c.s. **S**$'_1$ of **S'** such that

(5) **S**$'_1$ ⊢ P_1 & ... & P_k.

By (2) $\{P_1, \ldots, P_k\}$ is not a basis of **S**$'_1$. This is possible (according to the definition of a basis) only if there is a proposition Q, such that

(6) **S**$'_1$ ⊢ Q

and

(7) Not: P_1 & ... & P_k ⊢ Q.

From (5) and (6) it follows that

(8) **S**$'_1$ ⊢ P_1 & ... & P_k & Q.

By definition this yields:

(9) **S'** ⊢ $_w P_1$ & ... & P_k & Q

and now by (1) we have

(10) **S** ⊢ $_w P_1$ & ... & P_k & Q.

Hence, there is an m.c.s. **S**$_2$ of **S** such that

(11) **S**$_2$ ⊢ P_1 & ... & P_k & Q

and, since $\{P_1, \ldots, P_k\}$ is a basis of **S**$_1$ and (7) holds, therefore

(12) **S**$_2$ ≠ **S**$_1$.

We have the following case: every proposition R in the m.c.s. **S**$_1$ is also in the m.c.s. **S**$_2$, for if $R \in$ **S**$_1$ then by definition of a basis P_1 & ... & P_k ⊢ R. And if $R \notin$ **S**$_2$ then by maximality **S**$_2$ ⊢ $\sim R$. But by (11) **S**$_2$ ⊢ P_1 & ... & P_k, i.e. **S**$_2$ ⊢ R & $\sim R$, in contradiction to the consistency of **S**$_2$. Hence **S**$_1$ is a proper subset of S_2, but this contradicts the maximality of the m.c.s. S_1. Hence, S and S' are m.c.s.-equivalent. Q.E.D.

The theorem is interesting in that it says that the set of weak consequences (W-consequences) of any propositional set S determines uniquely the consequence-sets $C(S_i)$ for all of its m.c.s. S_i, whether or not S is consistent.[1]

---

[1] This appendix is drawn from N. Rescher and R. Manor, 'On Inference From Inconsistent Premisses', *Theory and Decision*, vol. 1 (1970).

APPENDIX D

NORMAL FORM

1. *Preliminaries*

THIS Appendix seeks to define a *normal form* for propositional sets, so that for any given such set we can transform it to its normal form with the object that the original set and its normal form are m.c.s.-equivalent, and any two m.c.s.-equivalent sets have the same normal form. This will enable us to reduce the number of cases that must be dealt with, and also provide the needed procedure for determining whether or not two *inconsistent* propositional sets have the same 'content'.

We shall specify the procedure for transforming a given set to its normal form in two main steps. First, a procedure for consistent propositional sets is given, and then is extended to apply to arbitrary sets.

2. *Consistent Sets*

Let $S = \{P_1, P_2, \ldots\}$ be a consistent set of propositions, with only a finite number of atomic propositions occurring as well-formed (w.f.) parts of propositions in S. Let these atomic propositions be $X_1, X_2, \ldots, X_n$. (Note that the set S need *not* itself be finite.)

S^* is said to be the *normal form* of S if S^* is obtained from S as follows:

Step 1

Eliminate $P \in S$ whenever P is a tautology, to obtain S_1.

Step 2

Bring all remaining propositions $P \in S_1$ to (complete) conjunctive normal form, to obtain S_2.

Thus every $P \in S_2$ has the form

$$(X_{1,1} \vee \ldots \vee X_{1,n}) \,\&\, \ldots \,\&\, (X_{m,1} \vee \ldots \vee X_{m,n}),$$

and whenever $1 \leqslant i \leqslant m$ and $1 \leqslant j \leqslant n$ then $X_{i,j}$ is either the atom X_j or the negation of X_j, and for every $i \neq k$,

$$X_{i,1} \vee \ldots \vee X_{i,n} \neq X_{k,1} \vee \ldots \vee X_{k,n}.$$

Hence clearly $X_{i,1} \vee \ldots \vee X_{i,n}$ and $X_{k,1} \vee \ldots \vee X_{k,n}$ are non-equivalent, for $i \neq k$.

Step 3

Replace every proposition $P \in \mathbf{S}_2$ of the form

$$P = P_1 \,\&\, P_2 \,\&\, \ldots \,\&\, P_m, \quad m \geqslant 1$$

by the series $P_1, P_2, \ldots, P_m$. This yields $\mathbf{S}_3$.

Note that if $i \neq k$ and $P_i, P_k \in \mathbf{S}_3$ then $P_i \neq P_k$ since $\mathbf{S}_3$ is a *set* of propositions. Moreover, each proposition in $\mathbf{S}_3$ is a disjunction of n propositions $X_{i,j}$ each of which is the atom X or its negation.

Step 4

Replace every *pair* of propositions P, $Q \in \mathbf{S}_3$ such that

$$P = A \vee X \vee B \quad \text{and} \quad Q = A \vee {\sim}X \vee B,$$

where X is atomic (and possibly either A or B is empty) by the single proposition $A \vee B$. This yields $\mathbf{S}_4$.

This step is justified since it yields (logically) equivalent propositions as follows:

$$(P \,\&\, Q) \equiv [(A \vee X \vee B) \,\&\, (A \vee {\sim}X \vee B)] \equiv$$

$$[(X \,\&\, {\sim}X) \vee (A \vee B)] \equiv (A \vee B).$$

Step 5

If $P \in \mathbf{S}_4$ and $P \equiv (X \vee A)$ where X is an atom or its negation, and if also ${\sim}X \in \mathbf{S}_4$, then replace P by A and obtain $\mathbf{S}^*$. The process is now completed: $\mathbf{S}^*$ is the normal form of $\mathbf{S}$.

3. *Remarks Regarding Normal Form in the Consistent Case*

1. The normal form has thus far been defined only for propositional sets that are consistent, and moreover are such that the number of atomic propositions occurring as w.f. parts of their propositions is finite. This limitation does not constitute a defect in view of the purposes of this book. In any practical applications, the original propositional set will be, if not finite, at least of finite 'content', in that only a finite number of atomic propositions occur as w.f. parts of the propositions in the m.c.s. of the sets in question.

2. Clearly, $\mathbf{S}^*$ has been so constructed as to be (logically) equivalent to $\mathbf{S}$. All the steps towards normalization move only from one set to an equivalent set of propositions.

3. $\mathbf{S}^*$ has the form $\mathbf{S}^* = \{P_1, P_2, \ldots, P_m\}$. It is finite, and each $P_i \in \mathbf{S}^*$ is of the form $X_{i,1} \vee \ldots \vee X_{i,k}$ ($k \leqslant n$) where $X_{i,j}$ is an atom or its negation, and where an atom and its negation never both occur as disjuncts in one of the P_i. (This is insured by Step 2.) Moreover, if $i \neq j$ then $P_i \neq P_j$ and hence also P_i and P_j are not equivalent.

4. For no $P_i, P_j \in \mathbf{S}^*$ with $i \neq j$ do we have it that $\vdash P_i \supset P_j$.

Proof: Suppose $P_i = X_{i\,1} \vee \ldots \vee X_{i\,m}$ and $P_j = X_{j,1} \vee \ldots \vee X_{j,k}$

where $i \neq j$. And suppose—for *reductio ad absurdum*—that $\vdash (X_{i,1} \vee \ldots \vee X_{i,m}) \supset (X_{j,1} \vee \ldots \vee X_{j,k})$, then:

$$\{X_{i,1}, \ldots, X_{i,m}\} \subseteq \{X_{j,1}, \ldots, X_{j,k}\}.$$

Hence, there is an element in P_j which is not in P_i (for by Remark 3, if $i \neq j$ then $P_i \neq P_j$). Suppose now that $X_{j,1} \notin P_i$. Then by Remark 3 above, also $\sim X_{j,1} \notin P_i$. Consider now the construction of the normal form: the only place where an atom or its negation is eliminated from the propositions is in Step 4. This means that P_i was obtained from two propositions in S_3 which were (to within commutativity of disjuncts) of the form:

$$(X_{i,1} \vee \ldots \vee X_{i,m}) \vee X_{j,1} \quad \text{and} \quad (X_{i,1} \vee \ldots \vee X_{i,m}) \vee \sim X_{j,1}.$$

Now, if $X_{i,1} \vee \ldots \vee X_{i,m} \vee X_{j,1}$ is P_j itself, then in Step 4 of the construction only P_i is generated, while P_j is eliminated, in contradiction to the assumption that $P_j \in S^*$. And if $X_{i,1} \vee \ldots \vee X_{i,m} \vee X_{j,1}$ is not P_j itself (but is only part of the disjunction in P_j) then by the same considerations as above, suppose $X_{j,2}$ is the first disjunct different from $X_{j,1}$ in P_j and which is not in P_i. At each of these cases, only P_i is constructed while that disjunction which is a w.f. part of P_j is eliminated. Hence if $\vdash P_i \supset P_j$ then $\vdash P_i \equiv P_j$, in contradiction to the assumption that $i \neq j$ (and Remark 3).

5. Whenever **S** and **S'** are two consistent and logically equivalent sets, then **S** and **S'** have the same normal form.

Proof: If **S** and **S'** are logically equivalent then deleting the tautologous propositions from both sets yields two equivalent sets. Let S_1 and S_1' be the conjunction of all non-tautologous propositions of **S** and **S'** respectively, then S_1 and **S'** are logically equivalent. Hence, S_1 and S_1' as propositions have the same conjunctive normal form; and therefore all the other steps of the normalization will yield that **S** and **S'** have the same normal form.

4. Inconsistent Sets

Let **S** be any set of propositions (consistent or inconsistent), such that each m.c.s. of **S** has at most finitely many atomic propositions occurring as w.f. parts of its propositions. Then for each of the m.c.s. of **S** its normal form is defined by the above stipulations, since the m.c.s. are consistent. We now define the *normal form* **S*** of **S** itself as follows:

S* $= \mathbf{I} \cup \mathbf{C}$, where

$\mathbf{I} = \{P : P \in S_i^* \text{ for } all\ S_i^*\}$, where **S*** is the normal form of the m.c.s. S_i of **S**,

and

$P \in \mathbf{C}$ iff $P \notin \mathbf{I}$ and there is a set S_i^* such that P is the conjunction of all the propositions of **S*** *not* in **I**.

Example of the normal-form procedure:

Let $\qquad S = \{p, q, q \supset p, r, r \supset p, \sim p\}.$

Its m.c.s. are

$$S_1 = \{p, q, q \supset p, r, r \supset p\}$$
$$S_2 = \{\sim p, q, r\}$$
$$S_3 = \{\sim p, q, r \supset p\}$$
$$S_4 = \{\sim p, q \supset p, r\}$$
$$S_5 = \{\sim p, q \supset p, r \supset p\}.$$

The atoms of the m.c.s. are p, q, r. Hence the conjunctive normal form of the propositions in S will be:

$$p \equiv (p \lor q \lor r) \,\&\, (p \lor \sim q \lor r) \,\&\, (p \lor q \lor \sim r) \,\&\, (p \lor \sim q \lor \sim r)$$

$$q \equiv (p \lor q \lor r) \,\&\, (\sim p \lor q \lor r) \,\&\, (p \lor q \lor \sim r) \,\&\, (\sim p \lor q \lor \sim r)$$

$$q \supset p \equiv (\sim q \lor p) \equiv (p \lor \sim q \lor r) \,\&\, (p \lor \sim q \lor \sim r)$$

$$r \equiv (p \lor q \lor r) \,\&\, (\sim p \lor q \lor r) \,\&\, (p \lor \sim q \lor r) \,\&\, (\sim p \lor \sim q \lor r)$$

$$r \supset p \equiv p \lor \sim r \equiv (p \lor q \lor \sim r) \,\&\, (p \lor \sim q \lor \sim r)$$

$$\sim p \equiv (\sim p \lor q \lor r) \,\&\, (\sim p \lor \sim q \lor r) \,\&\, (\sim p \lor q \lor \sim r) \,\&$$
$$(\sim p \lor \sim q \lor \sim r).$$

In normalizing S we have first to consider the normal form S_i^* of each m.c.s. of S_i. Consider therefore S_1:

$$S_1 = \{p, q, q \supset p, r, r \supset p\}.$$

By Step 1 we obtain $S_1' = S_1$ (for S_1 has no tautologies). S_1' results in S_1^2, where

$$S_1^2 = \{[(p \lor q \lor r) \,\&\, (p \lor \sim q \lor r) \,\&\, (p \lor q \lor \sim r) \,\&\, (p \lor \sim q \lor \sim r)],$$
$$[(p \lor q \lor r) \,\&\, (\sim p \lor q \lor r) \,\&\, (p \lor q \lor \sim r) \,\&\, (\sim p \lor q \lor \sim r)],$$
$$[(p \lor \sim q \lor r) \,\&\, (p \lor \sim q \lor \sim r)], [(p \lor q \lor r) \,\&\, (\sim p \lor q \lor r) \,\&$$
$$(p \lor \sim q \lor r) \,\&\, (\sim p \lor \sim q \lor r)], [(p \lor q \lor \sim r) \,\&\, (p \lor \sim q \lor \sim r)]\}.$$

From S_1^2 we obtain S_1^3 by Step 3, i.e. eliminating the conjunction connective and all repetitions, thus:

$$S_1^3 = \{(p \lor q \lor r), (p \lor \sim q \lor r), (p \lor q \lor \sim r), (p \lor \sim q \lor \sim r),$$
$$(\sim p \lor q \lor r), (\sim p \lor q \lor \sim r), (\sim p \lor \sim q \lor r)\}.$$

Applying Step 4 to S_1^3 we first obtain the set:

$$\{(p \lor r), (p \lor \sim r), (\sim p \lor q), (\sim p \lor \sim q \lor r)\},$$

and by further applying the same step, we obtain S_1^4

$$S_1^4 = \{p, \sim p \lor q, \sim p \lor \sim q \lor r\},$$

and by applying Step 5 we obtain successively:

$$\{p, q, \sim p \vee \sim q \vee r\}$$
$$\{p, q, \sim q \vee r\}$$
$$\mathbf{S_1^*} = \{p, q, r\}.$$

Thus the normal form of $\mathbf{S_1}$ is $\mathbf{S_1^*} = \{p, q, r\}$.

Similarly, the normal form counterparts of the other m.c.s. of $\mathbf{S}$ are:

$$\mathbf{S_2^*} = \{\sim p, q, r\}$$
$$\mathbf{S_3^*} = \{\sim p, q, \sim r\}$$
$$\mathbf{S_4^*} = \{\sim p, \sim q, r\}$$
$$\mathbf{S_5^*} = \{\sim p, \sim q, \sim r\}.$$

Hence the normal form of the whole set $\mathbf{S}$ will be $\mathbf{S^*} = \mathbf{I} \cup \mathbf{C}$, where $\mathbf{I} = \varLambda$ so that

$$\mathbf{S^*} = \mathbf{C} = \{(p \,\&\, q \,\&\, r), (\sim p \,\&\, q \,\&\, r), (\sim p \,\&\, q \,\&\, \sim r),$$
$$(\sim p \,\&\, \sim q \,\&\, r), (\sim p \,\&\, \sim q \,\&\, \sim r)\}.$$

Remarks

1. The definition is consistent with the one given for consistent sets, for a consistent set has only one m.c.s., itself, and in this case $\mathbf{S^*}=\mathbf{I}$.

2. One may wonder why we do not define the normal form as simply $\mathbf{S^*} =$ the union of the $\mathbf{S_i^*}$. But such a definition will not yield the normal form as being m.c.s.-equivalent (in the sense of Appendix C) to the original set.

Example: Let $\mathbf{S} = \{p \,\&\, q, \sim q\}$; its m.c.s. are $\mathbf{S_1} = \{p \,\&\, q\}$, $\mathbf{S_2} = \{\sim q\}$; by the normalization we get $\mathbf{S_1^*} = \{p, q\}$, $\mathbf{S_2^*} = \{\sim q\}$. By defining $\mathbf{S^*}$ as the union of $\mathbf{S_1^*}$ and $\mathbf{S_2^*}$ we should have obtained $\mathbf{S^*} = \{p, q, \sim q\}$ and its m.c.s. are $\{p, q\}$ and $\{p, \sim q\}$ which are clearly not equivalent to $\mathbf{S_1}$ and $\mathbf{S_2}$. Moreover, $\{p \,\&\, \sim q\}$ is a W-consequence of $\mathbf{S^*}$ thus defined, but it is not a W-consequence of $\mathbf{S}$, hence $\mathbf{S}$ and $\mathbf{S^*}$ are not equivalent. For this same example, the specified definition for $\mathbf{S^*}$ as $\mathbf{I} \cup \mathbf{C}$ yields that $\mathbf{I}$ is empty (since $\mathbf{S_1^*}$, $\mathbf{S_2^*}$ do not share any propositions), and hence in this case $\mathbf{S^*} = \mathbf{C} = \{p \,\&\, q, \sim q\} = \mathbf{S}$.

3. It follows immediately from the construction that if $\mathbf{S_i}$ is an m.c.s. of $\mathbf{S}$ and $\mathbf{S_i^*}$ is its normal form, then $\mathbf{S_i^*}$ is an m.c.s. of the normal form $\mathbf{S^*}$ of $\mathbf{S}$.

Example:
$$\mathbf{S} = \{p, q \supset r, s \,\&\, q, \sim r\}.$$

Then the m.c.s. of $\mathbf{S}$ are:

$$\mathbf{S_1} = \{p, s \,\&\, q, \sim r\}; \qquad \mathbf{S_2} = \{p, q \supset r, s \,\&\, q\};$$
$$\mathbf{S_3} = \{p, q \supset r, \sim r\}.$$

The corresponding normal forms will be:

$$\mathbf{S_1^*} = \{p, s, q, \sim r\}; \quad \mathbf{S_2^*} = \{p, s, q, r\}; \quad \mathbf{S_3^*} = \{p, \sim q, \sim r\}.$$

Hence
$$\mathbf{I} = \{p\}$$
$$\mathbf{C} = \{s \,\&\, q \,\&\, \sim r, \, s \,\&\, q \,\&\, r, \, \sim q \,\&\, \sim r\}$$

and $\mathbf{S^*} = \{p, s \,\&\, q \,\&\, \sim r, \, s \,\&\, q \,\&\, r, \, \sim q \,\&\, \sim r\}.$

As can easily be seen, the m.c.s. of $\mathbf{S^*}$ are exactly the corresponding $\mathbf{S_i^*}$ when taken as the conjunction of their propositions.[1]

4. If $\mathbf{S}$ and $\mathbf{S}'$ are two m.c.s.-equivalent sets (i.e. for each m.c.s. of the one there is an equivalent m.c.s. of the other and conversely), then they have the same normal form. For it follows that for each m.c.s. of the one there is an equivalent m.c.s. of the other set which therefore has the same normal form. This amounts to the normal forms of the entire sets $\mathbf{S}$ and $\mathbf{S}'$ being the same, by definition.

[1] This appendix is drawn from N. Rescher and R. Manor, 'On Inference From Inconsistent Premisses', *Theory and Decision*, vol. 1 (1970). I acknowledge with gratitude the aid of Mrs. Manor in developing this treatment of the normal form problem.

APPENDIX E

PLAUSIBILITY INDEXING AND MODAL CATEGORIES

THE system of *modal categories* as explained by the author in a previous publication[1] is given by the following rules (where P, Q, R as usual range over propositions and M_0, M_1, . . ., M_n over propositional sets designated as 'modal categories'):

(C1) $\vdash P$ iff $P \in M_0$

(C2) If $i \leqslant j$, then $M_i \subseteq M_j$

(C3) M_1 is consistent (i.e. all the propositions of M_1 are mutually compatible)

(C4) If $P \vdash Q$ and $P \in M_i$, then $Q \in M_i$

(C5) $P \in M_k$ for some $0 \leqslant k \leqslant n$.

A system of modal categories is also *conjunctive* (or 'closed under conjunction' as it was put in *Hypothetical Reasoning*), when it satisfies the further condition

(C6) If $P \in M_i$ and $Q \in M_i$, then $(P \& Q) \in M_i$.

When this condition is also met, then it can be shown that the categorizing system is in effect a plausibility indexing. To show this, we adopt the rule that the plausibility index of any proposition P is to be obtained by the principle:

$|P| = k$ iff $P \in M_k$ and M_k is the minimally indexed modal category containing P.

Intuitively, we are to think of the M_i as a cumulatively expanding series of sets, where each one in the series includes all its predecessors, and where a proposition with the plausibility index value k makes its first appearance in the k-th member of this series.

Now, returning to the plausibility principles enumerated on p. 115 above, we observe as follows:

(1) (P1) is guaranteed by (C5)

(2) (P2) is guaranteed by (C1)

(3) (P3) is guaranteed by (C3)

(4) So we have only to show that (P4) holds in the system.

[1] N. Rescher, *Hypothetical Reasoning* (Amsterdam, 1964).

Suppose $P_1, \ldots, P_m \vdash Q$ where $P_1, \ldots, P_m$ are consistent. Then by (C5) each of the P_i, $1 \leqslant i \leqslant m$, is in some $\mathbf{M}_j$, $0 \leqslant j \leqslant n$, which by (C2) yields that there is a j, $0 \leqslant j \leqslant n$, such that for all the P_i, $1 \leqslant i \leqslant n$, $P_i \in \mathbf{M}_j$ and therefore $\max_{1 \leqslant i \leqslant m} |P_i| \geqslant j$. Hence by (C6)

$$P_1 \ \& \ \ldots \ \& \ P_m \in \mathbf{M}_j,$$

and since $P_1, \ldots, P_m \vdash Q$ this yields by (C4) that $Q \in \mathbf{M}_j$, which means that $|Q| \leqslant j$ which yields that $|Q| \leqslant \max_{1 \leqslant i \leqslant m} |P_i|$. Q.E.D.

Thus a conjunctive modal categorization yields a plausibility indexing. Conversely, it can also be shown that the preceding rule of correspondence leads to the upshot that any plausibility indexing generates a family of modal categories.

Proof: We adopt the rule that the modal category membership of any proposition P is to be obtained by the principle:

$$P \in \mathbf{M}_k \ \text{whenever} \ |P| \leqslant k.$$

Then clearly:

(1) (C1) is guaranteed by (P2)
(2) (C2) is guaranteed by the basic rule
(3) (C3) is guaranteed by (P3)
(4) (C4) is guaranteed by (P4)
(5) (C5) is guaranteed by (P1).
(6) (C6) is guaranteed by the rule:
$$|P \ \& \ Q| = \max[|P|, |Q|].$$

It follows that the procedure of plausibility indexing is essentially equivalent to that of modal categories in the special case of categories closed under conjunction.

For further elaboration of the concept of modal categories the reader may refer to *Hypothetical Reasoning* itself.

APPENDIX F

(CHAPTER V, SECTION 6)

HAMBLIN'S CONCEPT OF 'PLAUSIBILITY' AND SHACKLE'S 'POTENTIAL SURPRISE'

OUR specified concept of *plausibility* is different from—though not entirely unrelated to—another version of 'plausibility' proposed in an article by C. L. Hamblin.[1] Hamblin's plausibility measure is defined on the range from 0 to 1 (*this* difference from ours is immaterial) subject to three conditions:

(1) At least one state description (s.d.) obtains the maximal index value (i.e. 1).
(2) If P is 'known to be false', its index value must be the minimal index value (i.e. 0).
(3) The index value of a disjunction is the largest index value of its disjuncts.

Given these rules, the plausibility index of any proposition is determined as the maximum index value of the s.d. accordant with it. A proposition can be said to be plausible *per se* if its index value exceeds some predesignated threshold quantity. As expected, a conjunction of plausible alternatives need not itself be plausible—it may indeed be inconsistent.

Neither of Hamblin's conditions (1) or (3) need hold for our procedure for plausibility indexing. Nor need this be viewed as unfortunate. Why should one of the ultimate alternatives (i.e. s.d.) have to be 'maximally plausible' or any intuitive construction of this idea? On the other hand, on any intuitive view of the matter it can certainly happen for some proposition P, that *both P and* $\sim\!P$ should stand at only a fair-to-middling level as to 'plausibility'. (For example: 'On the next toss this die will come up $\leqslant 3$', 'On the next toss this die will come up > 3'.) But the proposition $P \vee \sim\!P$ will certainly and inevitably have to have maximal plausibility; and thus one (and by symmetry both) of the disjuncts P, $\sim\!P$ would by Hamblin's rule (3) have to be maximally plausible.

This last point can be transformed into a rather fundamental objection to the claims of Hamblin's concept to qualify as a conception of 'plausibility' in a sense consonant with any common understanding of this idea. On any natural interpretation of this conception, it should certainly be possible—at least in some cases—to divide the spectrum of possibilities into a family of alternatives $A_1, A_2, \ldots, A_n$

[1] 'The Modal "Probably"', *Mind*, 68 (1959), 234–40.

such that (1) all the A_i are alike in point of plausibility, and (2) the A_i are not all maximally plausible. In such a case all the alternatives, individually considered, are alike relatively implausible. It cannot but count as a flaw in Hamblin's conception that it excludes this possibility as a matter of principle. This flaw seems to me to render Hamblin's construction of 'plausibility' an implausible one. Hamblin rightly insists that each of several (mutually exclusive) alternatives might be plausible; he goes astray in ruling out the cognate possibility that each one of several (mutually exhaustive) alternatives be implausible.

Hamblin proposes to define a (non-standard) notion of probability —let $\Pi(P)$ mean 'P is H-probable' (probable in Hamblin's sense)— as follows: $\quad \Pi(P)$ iff P is more plausible than $\sim P$.

Hamblin rightly notes that—given his concept of plausibility—*this* (distinctly non-standard) concept of probability will be subject to the rule

$$(\Pi) \qquad \text{If } \Pi(P) \text{ and } \Pi(Q), \text{ then } \Pi(P \,\&\, Q)$$

unlike the situation in the case of the orthodox concept of probability. Now if we were to adopt Hamblin's definition for $\Pi(P)$ with respect to *our* concept of plausibility, then we should not be able to obtain the thesis (Π). For then we should have

$$\Pi(P) \text{ iff } |P| < |{\sim}P|.$$

Thus (Π) now becomes

$$(\Pi') \qquad \text{If } |P| < |{\sim}P| \text{ and } |Q| < |{\sim}Q|, \text{ then}$$

$$|P \,\&\, Q| < |{\sim}(P \,\&\, Q)| \quad \text{(or equivalently, } < |{\sim}P \vee {\sim}Q|).$$

But this is a plausibility-indexing principle that cannot be obtained from our rules without the substantial addition of further special and restrictive assumptions.

However, let us introduce a concept of 'improbability', analogous to Hamblin's 'probability' by the analogous definition:

$$\overline{\Pi}(P) \text{ iff } \Pi(\sim P) \text{ iff } \sim P \text{ is more plausible than } P.$$

Accordingly $\overline{\Pi}$ (P) iff $|\sim P| < |P|$. We can now establish—with respect to our own concept of plausibility—that the following (Π)-analogue obtains:

Proof: $\quad (\overline{\Pi}) \qquad \text{If } \overline{\Pi}(P) \text{ and } \overline{\Pi}(Q), \text{ then } \overline{\Pi}(P \,\&\, Q).$

1. $\|{\sim}P\| < \|P\|$	by hypothesis $\overline{\Pi}(P)$
2. $\|{\sim}Q\| < \|Q\|$	by hypothesis $\overline{\Pi}(Q)$
3. $\max[\|P\|, \|Q\|] \leqslant \|P \,\&\, Q\|$	by the entailments
4. $\max[\|{\sim}P\|, \|{\sim}Q\|] < \|P \,\&\, Q\|$	by (1)–(3)

5. $|{\sim}P \vee {\sim}Q| \leqslant \min[|{\sim}P|, |{\sim}Q|]$ by the entailments

6. $|{\sim}P \vee {\sim}Q| < |P \mathbin{\&} Q|$ by (3), (5)

7. $\Pi(P \mathbin{\&} Q)$ by (6).

Thus, interestingly enough, it is our concept of implausibility (rather than plausibility) that satisfies Hamblin's characteristic condition for H-probability.

Hamblin offers the intriguing suggestion that his (non-probabilistic) concept of plausibility can be used to explicate G. L. S. Shackle's idea of *potential surprise*.[2] The 'surprise' at issue arises when something 'improbable' turns out to be true. Shackle most emphatically stresses that the 'probability' here at issue is not the orthodox one, and Hamblin suggests that his concept of plausibility provides an adequate construction of Shackle's idea. But this is surely incorrect. There is nothing whatever in Shackle's discussion to warrant the Hamblinesque principle that one among mutually exclusive alternatives must be accorded a minimal value of potential surprise (= maximal plausibility). Indeed this seems quite counter to the whole tendency of Shackle's conception.

It would seem, however, that a concept defined in terms of our proposed style of plausibilities—via the stipulation that the potential surprise of a proposition is simply to stand in a reverse or inverse relationship to its plausibility—would answer quite well to the tendency of Shackle's ideas. Accordingly, the relative 'potential surprise' of a particular truth-finding with respect to a given plausibility assignment could be assessed in terms of the relative degree of plausibility of the proposition in question, so that we would be quite surprised to find an implausible proposition to be true and not surprised if a plausible one is. An example will serve to clarify this.

Let us begin with the following set of data:

$$\mathbf{S} = \{p, p \supset q, {\sim}q, q \supset r, r\}.$$

We may suppose the following plausibility indexing of $\mathbf{S}$:

$$|p| = 2$$
$$|p \supset q| = 3$$
$$|{\sim}q| = 4$$
$$|q \supset r| = 4$$
$$|r| = 4.$$

A plausibility survey of the m.c.s. yields the following results:

m.c.s.	plausibility	average plausibility
$\{p, p \supset q, q \supset r, r\}$	(2, 3, 4, 4)	$\frac{13}{4}$
$\{p, {\sim}q, q \supset r, r\}$	(2, 4, 4, 4)	$\frac{14}{4}$
$\{p \supset q, {\sim}q, q \supset r, r\}$	(3, 4, 4, 4)	$\frac{15}{4}$

[2] See Shackle's *Uncertainty in Economics* (Cambridge, 1955), especially Chapter II.

No matter how we resolve the issue of m.c.s. preference, we shall obtain as truths the I-consequences $q \supset r$ and r, despite the relatively high plausibility-index values of these propositions, indicative of their initial implausibility. And the 'potential surprise' of these findings is relatively high precisely because we were initially minded to regard them as relatively implausible.

As this example suggests, the plausibility-index value of a proposition may be regarded, from another angle, as a measure of the 'potential surprise' that ensues when we find it to be true. The lower its index value, the less the surprise potential; with propositions indexed at (say) less than 2 we should find no occasion for surprise at all: truth-finding 'would be only what we expect'. But the larger the index value, we (i.e. whoever provides the plausibility indexing) have increasing occasion for surprise; the more implausible we had deemed the proposition when setting up the preferential criterion $\mathscr{P}$, the more appropriate is 'surprise' at finding that the analysis based upon $\mathscr{P}$ yields this proposition as a truth. We would accordingly be motivated to adopt the rule that the plausibility-index value of a proposition is—from a variant point of view—simply identifiable with its potential for surprising us, should it eventuate as true. From this standpoint, our theory of plausibility might well provide the desideratum (stressed by Hamblin) of a formalization of Shackle's conception of 'potential surprise'.

APPENDIX G

THE UNIQUENESS OF A DERIVED FULL-SCALE PLAUSIBILITY INDEXING

GIVEN a finite propositional set S and a minimal plausibility indexing such that for every $P \in S$ there is a value $\|P\|$ conforming to the conditions for a minimal index, we can introduce the Index-Revision Rule:

When $P_1, \ldots, P_k \vdash Q$ where $P_1, \ldots, P_k, Q \in S$, and $P_1, \ldots, P_k$ are consistent, then reduce the index of Q to that of the maximal index of P_i, in the case that it exceeds it (where $1 \leqslant i \leqslant k$).

It must be shown that in any given case all of the various possible applications of this procedure will lead to a full-scale plausibility index, and to one that is unique.

The argument for this contention—viz. that a to-the-bitter-end application of the index-revision rule leads from a minimal index to a *uniquely determined* full-scale plausibility index—is as follows. Since S is finite, the number of sequences of propositions $P_{1,i}, \ldots, P_{k,i}$, Q_i within S such that $P_{1,i}, \ldots, P_{k,i}$ are consistent and $P_{1,i}, \ldots, P_{k,i} \vdash Q_i$ is also finite. Of these sequences, let us consider all those in which $\|Q_i\| > \max\limits_{1 \leqslant j \leqslant k_i} \|P_{j,i}\|$. Next we consider of these sequences one such in which the minimal index assigned to Q is maximal, i.e.

$$\|Q\| = \max\|Q_i\|.$$

Accordingly, we now have it that

$$P, \ldots, P_k, Q \in S, \text{ and } P, \ldots, P_k \text{ are consistent}$$
$$P_1, \ldots, P_k \vdash Q \text{ and } \|Q\| > \max\limits_{1 \leqslant i \leqslant k} \|P_j\|$$

and

for all $P_{1,i}, \ldots, P_{k,i}, Q_i \in S$, such that. $P_{1,i}, \ldots, P_{k,i}$ are consistent and

$$P_{1,i}, \ldots, P_{k,i} \vdash Q_i \text{ and } \|Q_i\| > \max\limits_{1 \leqslant i \leqslant k_i} \|P_{1\ i}\| \text{ we have:}$$
$$\|Q\| = \max\limits_{i} \|Q_i\|.$$

We now define a new index $\| \ \|_1$ for S as follows: for all propositions $P \in S$

$$\|R\|_1 = \|R\| \quad \text{if } R \neq Q$$

and otherwise $\|R\|_1 = \|Q\|_1 = \max\limits_{1 \leqslant j \leqslant k} \|P_j\|$.

Now it is clear that this index will satisfy (M1) and (M2). So to show that it is a minimal index, we have to show that (M3) the set $\{P: \|P\|_1 = 1\}$ is consistent.

By hypothesis, the original indexing is minimal, i.e. the set $\{P \mid \|P\| = 1\}$ is consistent. Hence if $\{P: \|P\| = 1\} = \{P: \|P\|_1 = 1\}$ we are home. If, on the other hand, these sets are not the same, this will be because there is a proposition, Q, which could, by construction only be such that $Q \in \{P: \|P\|_1 = 1\}$ and $Q \notin \{P: \|P\| = 1\}$. This means that we have some sequence such that $P_1, \ldots, P_k \vdash Q$ and $\max\limits_{1 \leqslant j \leqslant k} \|P_j\| = 1$ and $\|Q\| > 1$. But, if so, then $P_1, \ldots, P_k$ are consistent by assumption and $P_1, \ldots, P_k \vdash Q$; hence $P_1, \ldots, P_k, Q$ are consistent. Hence if $\{P \mid \|P\| = 1\}$ is consistent and for each j, $1 \leqslant j \leqslant k$, P_j is either a tautology (where $\|P_j\| = 0$) or

$$P_j \in \{P: \|P\| = 1\},$$

then also $\{Q\} \cup \{P: \|P\| = 1\}$ is consistent, i.e. $\{P \mid \|P\|_1 = 1\}$ is consistent. Hence the index $\| \ \|_1$ is a minimal index. We now consider $\mathbf{S}$ with this index and by the same procedure we construct a new minimal index $\| \ \|_2$—until, after a finite number of steps we arrive at a minimal index $\| \ \|_m$ for $\mathbf{S}$ such that the index-revision rule cannot be applied to it, and hence it is a plausibility index. Q.E.D.

One further result must be established. It must be shown that whenever the index-revision rule is applied according to the procedure above, then the plausibility index that results is unique. More specifically, since we may have two propositions R_1 and R_2 such that $\|R_1\| = \|R_2\| = \max\limits_{i} \|Q_i\|$ the resulting plausibility index does not depend on which of R_1 or R_2 we consider first to construct the next $\| \ \|_1$ minimal index.

Proof

Suppose the result is not unique. This means that there is a proposition $S \in \mathbf{S}$ such that the plausibility index resulting by applying the index-revision rule first to R_1 assigns S a value different from the plausibility index resulting by applying that rule first to R_2. In other words, we have two sequences of minimal indexings which assign to S the following values respectively:

$$\|S\|, \|S\|_{1,1}, \|S\|_{1,2}, \ldots, \|S\|_{1,m}$$
$$\|S\|, \|S\|_{2,1}, \|S\|_{2,2}, \ldots, \|S\|_{2,m}$$

and
$$\|S\|_{1,m} \neq \|S\|_{2,m}$$

where $\| \ \|_{1,m}$ and $\| \ \|_{2,m}$ are plausibility indexes.

Since we started from a certain given minimal index $\| \ \|$, there must be a first (minimal) i such that $1 \leqslant i$, $\|S\|_{1,i} \neq \|S\|_{2,i}$, and

$\|S\|_{1,\,j} = \|S\|_{2,\,j}$ for all $j < i$. This means that there are $P_1, \ldots, P_k$ $\in \mathbf{S}$ consistent such that $P_1, \ldots, P_k \vdash S$ and either

$$\|S\|_{1,\,i-1} > \max_{1 \leqslant j \leqslant k} \|P_j\|_{1,\,i-1}$$

or

$$\|S\|_{2,\,i-1} > \max_{1 \leqslant j \leqslant k} \|P_j\|_{2,\,i-1}$$

or both. (For otherwise, in both sequences the $i-1$ index will be the last one, for we shall not be able to apply the index-revision rule).

With loss of generality, we can assume that

$$\|S\|_{1,\,i-1} > \max_{1 \leqslant i \leqslant k} \|P_j\|_{1,\,i-1}.$$

If, in this case, $\max_{1 \leqslant j \leqslant k} \|P_j\|_{1,\,i-1} = \max_{1 \leqslant i \leqslant k} \|P_j\|_{2,\,i-1}$ then by construction

$$\|S\|_{1,\,i} = \max_j \|P_i\|_{1,\,i-1} = \max_j \|P_j\|_{2,\,i-1} = \|S\|$$

in contradiction to our assumption. If, on the other hand,

$$\max_{1 \leqslant j \leqslant k} \|P_j\|_{1,\,i-1} \neq \max_{1 \leqslant i \leqslant k} \|P_j\|_{2,\,i-1}$$

then we consider the minimal l, $1 \leqslant l \leqslant i-1$ such that

$$\max_{1 \leqslant j \leqslant k} \|P_j\|_{1\,l} \neq \max \|P_j\|_{2l}$$

and apply the same argument as above.

But, in each application of the argument above we reduce the number of the index. Hence, since we started from a given and the same minimal index $\|\ \|$, we shall after a finite number of steps arrive at the case where the propositions $T_1, \ldots, T_k \vdash U$ and $T_1, \ldots, T_k$ are consistent and $\|U\|_{1,\,s} \neq \|U\|_{2,\,s}$ but

$$\max_{1 \leqslant j \leqslant k} \|T_j\|_{1,\,s-1} = \max_{1 \leqslant j \leqslant k} \|T_j\|_{2,\,s-1}$$

which will involve a contradiction, as above. Q.E.D.

This argument establishes the well-definedness (uniqueness) of the full-scale plausibility index derived from a minimal indexing by systematic application of the index-revision rule.[1]

[1] This Appendix is drawn from N. Rescher and R. Manor, 'On Inference From Inconsistent Premisses', *Theory and Decision*, vol. 1 (1970), pp. 179–217.

APPENDIX H

DEGREES OF TRUTH

ONE essentially precriterial conception of 'degrees of truth' becomes available in the framework of the coherence analysis whenever we have an *ordinal* criterion $\mathscr{P}$ of alethic preference among the m.c.s. of an inconsistent propositional set **S**. In general we require of a criterion of alethic preference that it be merely *classificatory* and divide the m.c.s. of **S** into those which are eligible and those which are not. An ordinal criterion goes well beyond this. It provides for

(1) A preferential *ordering* of the m.c.s. $\mathbf{S}_i$

$$\mathbf{S}^1 > \mathbf{S}^2 > \ldots > \mathbf{S}^n$$

where $\mathbf{S}^j$ is one of the $\mathbf{S}_i$, and $\mathbf{S}^j > \mathbf{S}^h$ indicates that $\mathbf{S}^j$ is to be preferred to $\mathbf{S}^h$. (The case of $\mathbf{S}^j \geqslant \mathbf{S}^h$ as preferred or indifferent could also be contemplated.)

(2) A cut-off value m such that:

$\mathbf{S}^1, \mathbf{S}^2, \ldots, \mathbf{S}^m$ are (all) to be preferred (eligible) m.c.s.

$\mathbf{S}^{m+1}, \mathbf{S}^{m+2}, \ldots, \mathbf{S}^n$ are (all) to be non-preferred (ineligible) m.c.s.

Relative to such an ordinal criterion we may think in terms not simply of the *actually* preferred consequences, based on the specific cut-off value m, but can also consider the *potentially* preferred consequences depending upon where in the interval from 1 to n such a cut-off value is to be fixed. As this value k increases, we move from the consequences of $\mathbf{S}^1$ alone to those of both $\mathbf{S}^1$ and $\mathbf{S}^2$, and finally to those of *all* the $\mathbf{S}^i$. Accordingly, one may stipulate that 'the axiom of the truths of the k-th rank' is given by

$$A_k = \mathrm{Ax}(\mathbf{S}^1) \vee \mathrm{Ax}(\mathbf{S}^2) \vee \ldots \vee \mathrm{Ax}(\mathbf{S}^k)$$ where for any set **S** we have it that $\mathrm{Ax}(\mathbf{S})$ is an axiomatic basis for **S**.

Note that $k \leqslant n$, the total number of m.c.s., and that A_{n+1}, being 'the axiom of the truths of the $(n+1)$-th rank', is simply a *tautology*. We can extend this idea by stipulating that 'the truth-ranking of the potential $\mathscr{P}$-consequences of **S**'—the 'potential $\mathscr{P}$-consequences of **S**' being propositions which follow from some one of the A_i—is given by the rule

$$\mathrm{rank}(P) =_{\mathrm{DF}} \text{the } maximum \ k \text{ such that } P \text{ follows from } A_k \colon A_k \vdash P.$$

Finally we may define the 'degree of truth' of one of the potential $\mathscr{P}$-consequences of **S** to be determined in terms of the rank of P as follows:

$$\deg(P) = \frac{1}{(n+2)-\text{rank}(P)}.$$

It is an immediate consequence of this definition that:
1. all tautologies are of degree 1
2. the degree of any nontautologous I-consequence is $\frac{1}{2}$
3. the degree of $\text{Ax}(\mathbf{S}^1)$, the axiom of the single most preferred m.c.s., is $\dfrac{1}{(n+1)}$.

Intuitively considered, this measure would appear to accord well with the conception underlying the idea of 'degrees of truth'.

For the sake of illustration consider the set

$$\mathbf{S} = \{p \mathbin{\&} q, p \supset q, q \supset r, \sim r\}$$

and let us suppose the preferential criterion $\mathscr{P}$ to be probabilistic relative to **S** (via a principle of indifference). (Note that any possibilistic or plausibilistic criterion of preference is ordinal.) We thus obtain the following *a posteriori* probabilities for the possible worlds:

Possible World	A Priori Probability	S-elements $p \mathbin{\&} q$	$p \supset q$	$q \supset r$	$\sim r$	Σ	Σ^*
$p \mathbin{\&} q \mathbin{\&} r$	$\frac{1}{8}$	$\frac{1}{2}$	$\frac{1}{6}$	$\frac{1}{6}$		$\frac{10}{12}$	$\frac{10}{48}$
$p \mathbin{\&} q \mathbin{\&} \sim r$	$\frac{1}{8}$	$\frac{1}{2}$	$\frac{1}{6}$		$\frac{1}{4}$	$\frac{11}{12}$	$\frac{11}{48}$
$p \mathbin{\&} \sim q \mathbin{\&} r$	$\frac{1}{8}$			$\frac{1}{6}$		$\frac{2}{12}$	$\frac{2}{48}$
$p \mathbin{\&} \sim q \mathbin{\&} \sim r$	$\frac{1}{8}$			$\frac{1}{6}$	$\frac{1}{4}$	$\frac{5}{12}$	$\frac{5}{48}$
$\sim p \mathbin{\&} q \mathbin{\&} r$	$\frac{1}{8}$		$\frac{1}{6}$	$\frac{1}{6}$		$\frac{4}{12}$	$\frac{4}{48}$
$\sim p \mathbin{\&} q \mathbin{\&} \sim r$	$\frac{1}{8}$		$\frac{1}{6}$		$\frac{1}{4}$	$\frac{5}{12}$	$\frac{5}{48}$
$\sim p \mathbin{\&} \sim q \mathbin{\&} r$	$\frac{1}{8}$		$\frac{1}{6}$	$\frac{1}{6}$		$\frac{4}{12}$	$\frac{4}{48}$
$\sim p \mathbin{\&} \sim q \mathbin{\&} \sim r$	$\frac{1}{8}$		$\frac{1}{6}$	$\frac{1}{6}$	$\frac{1}{4}$	$\frac{7}{12}$	$\frac{7}{48}$

The m.c.s. of **S** are as follows:

$\mathbf{S}_1 = \{p \mathbin{\&} q, p \supset q, q \supset r\}$ which is axiomatized by $p \mathbin{\&} q \mathbin{\&} r$ and obtains probability $\frac{10}{48}$

$\mathbf{S}_2 = \{p \mathbin{\&} q, p \supset q, \sim r\}$ which is axiomatized by $p \mathbin{\&} q \mathbin{\&} \sim r$ and obtains probability $\frac{11}{48}$

$\mathbf{S}_3 = \{p \supset q, q \supset r, \sim r\}$ which is axiomatized by $\sim p \mathbin{\&} \sim q \mathbin{\&} \sim r$ and obtains probability $\frac{7}{48}$.

The axiom for the truths of the 1st rank is $A_1 = p \mathbin{\&} q \mathbin{\&} \sim r$ (for $\mathbf{S}_2$)

2nd rank is $A_2 = p \mathbin{\&} q$ (for $\mathbf{S}_1$-or-$\mathbf{S}_2$)

3rd rank is

$$A_3 = (p \mathbin{\&} q) \vee (\sim p \mathbin{\&} \sim q \mathbin{\&} \sim r) \text{ (for } \mathbf{S}_1\text{-or-}\mathbf{S}_2\text{-or-}\mathbf{S}_3)$$

4th rank is $A_4 = t$ (tautology).

A a 2

Some sample degree-of-truth calculations produce the following results:

The degree of truth of t is $\dfrac{1}{(5-4)} = 1$

The degree of truth of $(p \& q) \lor (\sim p \& \sim q \& \sim r)$ is $\dfrac{1}{(5-3)} = \frac{1}{2}$

The degree of truth of $p \& q$ is $\dfrac{1}{(5-2)} = \frac{1}{3}$

The degree of truth of $p \& q \& \sim r$ is $\dfrac{1}{(5-1)} = \frac{1}{4}$

And the degree of truth of $(p \& q) \lor r$, which follows from A_2 but

not A_3, is $\dfrac{1}{(5-2)} = \frac{1}{3}$.

This approach seems fitted to serve as yet another articulation of the concept of 'degrees of truth' within the framework of a coherence analysis.

Still another approach to the (precriterial) evaluation of the 'degree of truth' of a proposition is to establish the following measure for all of the W-consequences of S:

$d(P)$ = the *proportion* of m.c.s. from which P follows.

The larger such a d-value the larger the proposition at issue will be determined to be true by the criterion at issue. (Note that any self-consistent S-element must obtain a d-value > 0, and any self-inconsistent proposition whatsoever will obtain a d-value of 0.)[1]

Thus in the preceding example we obtain the following d-values for the several elements of S:

$$d(p) = \tfrac{2}{3}$$
$$d(q) = \tfrac{2}{3}$$
$$d(\sim p \lor \sim r) = \tfrac{2}{3}$$
$$d(r \supset p) = 1$$
$$d(q \& r) = \tfrac{1}{3}.$$

The fourth of these illustrates the fact that every I-consequence of a set S will obtain a d-value of 1, which thus becomes the mark of certain (relative) truth.

It is easy to see that the calculation of d-values has one very serious

---

[1] A closely related alternative is to take the measure

$d'(P)$ = the proportion of m.c.s. from which $\sim P$ fails to follow (i.e. the proposition of m.c.s. compatible with P).

Whenever $P \in S$, we must have it that $d'(P) = d(P)$, but for non-members of S the two values may differ.

shortcoming as a measure of degrees of truth, because in the case of degree 0 it completely fails to distinguish between

(i) Those propositions which fail to follow from an m.c.s. because they are *incompatible* with it.
(ii) Those propositions which fail to follow from an m.c.s. because they are *independent* of it.

Thus neither p & $\sim p$ nor s follow from any of the m.c.s. of the set **S** of our example, and both obtain a d-value of 0. The d-measure thus fails to catch a distinction crucial to an explication of degrees of truth, since p & $\sim p$ gets 0 because it *cannot possibly* obtain, whereas s gets 0 because on the basis at issue *we cannot tell whether* it obtains.

To obtain a measure that remedies this defect we can define:

$$\varDelta(P) = \mathrm{d}(P) - \mathrm{d}(\sim P).$$

By way of comparison with the d-measure we now obtain the following $\varDelta$-values for the preceding example:

$$\varDelta(p) = \tfrac{1}{3}$$

$$\varDelta(q) = \tfrac{1}{3}$$

$$\varDelta(\sim p \lor \sim r) = \tfrac{1}{3}$$

$$\varDelta(r \supset p) = 1$$

$$\varDelta(q \,\&\, r) = -\tfrac{1}{3}$$

$$\varDelta(p \,\&\, \sim p) = -1 \quad \text{(similarly for any contradiction)}$$

$$\varDelta(p \lor \sim p) = 1 \quad \text{(similarly for any tautology)}$$

$$\varDelta(s) = 0.$$

In general, the $\varDelta$-measure behaves in such a way that:

1. Any I-consequence of **S** will obtain a $\varDelta$-value of 1 (and thus every tautology will do so).
2. The negation of any innocent bystander will obtain a $\varDelta$-value of -1 (and thus every contradiction will do so).
3. Any 'irrelevant' proposition (such as s in the preceding example) will obtain a $\varDelta$-value of 0.
4. A proposition that 'holds more often than not' with respect to the m.c.s. at issue will obtain a positive $\varDelta$-value.
5. A proposition whose negation 'holds more often than not' with respect to the m.c.s. at issue will obtain a negative $\varDelta$-value.
6. In general $\varDelta(\sim P) = -\varDelta(P)$. This is so because, by definition $\varDelta(\sim P) = \mathrm{d}(\sim P) - \mathrm{d}(\sim \sim P)$ and so $\varDelta(\sim P) = \mathrm{d}(\sim P) - \mathrm{d}(P)$.
7. We know that whenever P is an **S**-element, then

$$\mathrm{d}(\sim P) = 1 - \mathrm{d}(P).$$

Hence, since in general

$$\varDelta(P) = \mathrm{d}(P) - \mathrm{d}(\sim P)$$

we know that in these cases

$$\Delta(P) = d(P) - [1 - d(P)]$$

and so

$$\Delta(P) = 2d(P) - 1.$$

In this special case the Δ-value is simply a linear transformation (based on $x \to 2x - 1$) of the d-value. However, this relationship will in general fail to obtain when P is not an S-element. Thus for s of the preceding example we have it that $d(s) = 0$, but also $\Delta(s) = 0$.

In view of such considerations, it seems that the Δ-measure also represents a plausible way of assessing the 'degree of truth' of propositions on our coherence approach, it being stipulated that this concept is now to be interpreted in its essentially *precriterial* sense.[2]

Finally, one further possible construction of degrees of truth is simply as a probability determined through relationships of the m.c.s. to the various possible worlds. Thus consider the set:

$$S = \{p \,\&\, q, \; q \supset \sim p\}.$$

This has two m.c.s.:

$$S_1 = \{p \,\&\, q\} \qquad S_2 = \{q \supset \sim p\}$$

We now proceed to the following calculation

| | m.c.s. | | | |
Possible World	S_1	S_2	Σ	Σ^*
$p \,\&\, q$	1	0	1	$\frac{1}{2}$
$p \,\&\, \sim q$	0	$\frac{1}{3}$	$\frac{1}{3}$	$\frac{1}{6}$
$\sim p \,\&\, q$	0	$\frac{1}{3}$	$\frac{1}{3}$	$\frac{1}{6}$
$\sim p \,\&\, \sim q$	0	$\frac{1}{3}$	$\frac{1}{3}$	$\frac{1}{6}$

The 'degree of truth' of various propositions is now readily calculable, for example, that of p is $\frac{2}{3}$ and that of $p \vee q$ is $\frac{5}{6}$, etc. The calculation is based on letting each m.c.s. as it were cast its (equi-weighted) vote for those possible worlds compatible with itself. (Note that this procedure could also be used to generate *a priori* probabilities for the possible worlds.)

[2] This Δ-measure is related to, but distinct from a measure of 'partial truth' treated by M. Bunge in Chapter 8 of *The Myth of Simplicity* (New Jersey, 1963). Bunge's measure V has the features (shared by Δ) that

$$-1 \leqslant V(p) \leqslant 1$$

If $\vdash p \equiv q$ then $V(p) = V(q)$

$$V(\text{tautology}) = 1$$

$$V(\text{contradiction}) = -1.$$

However, Bunge's V also has the feature

If $V(p) = V(q) = 0$, then $V(p \,\&\, q) = 0$.

This does not hold for Δ. Let there be four m.c.s., and let p hold in just the first two, and q in just the first and the last. Then $\Delta(p) = \Delta(q) = 0$. But

$$\Delta(p \,\&\, q) = 0 \cdot 25 - 0 \cdot 75 = -0 \cdot 50.$$

APPENDIX I

(CHAPTER IX, SECTION 10)

TRUTHS OF REASON AND TRUTHS OF FACT

IT may be useful to set out explicitly the contrast between the present pragmatic line of defence of a coherence theory of truth and the pragmatism of W. V. O. Quine's influential essay on 'Two Dogmas of Empiricism'. Quine vividly formulates his position in the following terms:

The totality of our so-called knowledge or beliefs, from the most casual matters of geography and history to the profoundest laws of atomic physics or even of pure mathematics and logic, is a man-made fabric which impinges on experience only along the edges. Or, to change the figure, total science is like a field of force whose boundary conditions are experience. A conflict with experience at the periphery occasions readjustments in the interior of the field. Truth values have to be redistributed over some of our statements. Re-evaluation of some statements entails re-evaluation of others, because of their logical interconnections—the logical laws being in turn simply certain further statements of the system, certain further elements of the field. Having re-evaluated one statement we must re-evaluate some others, which may be statements logically connected with the first or may be the statements of logical connections themselves. But the total field is so underdetermined by its boundary conditions, experience, that there is much latitude of choice as to what statements to re-evaluate in the light of any single contrary experience. No particular experiences are linked with any particular statements in the interior of the field, except indirectly through considerations of equilibrium affecting the field as a whole.[1]

This on-going reappraisal of 'the totality of our so-called knowledge or beliefs' is to be accomplished without any prior differentiation as between logical and factual truths, and is to be carried out in terms of pragmatic criteria of adequacy and effectiveness. Quine sees 'total science' as one vast, all-embracing allocation of truth-values to the propositions of the formal and the empirical disciplines alike, and proposes to judge the adequacy of this allocation by the pragmatic standard of practical satisfactions:

Carnap, Lewis, and others take a pragmatic stand on the question of choosing between language forms, scientific frameworks; but their pragmatism leaves off at the imagined boundary between the analytic and the synthetic. In repudiating such a boundary I espouse a more thorough pragmatism. Each man is given a scientific heritage plus a continuing barrage of sensory stimulation; and the considerations which guide him in warping his scientific heritage to fit his continuing sensory promptings are, where rational, pragmatic.[2]

[1] 'Two Dogmas of Empiricism', reprinted in *From a Logical Point of View* (Cambridge, Mass., 1961), pp. 42–6 (see pp. 42–3).   [2] Ibid., p. 46.

Accordingly, Quine (1) sees *all* statements—logical and factual alike —as coming up for critical evaluation *at one and the same time*, and (2) sees the evaluation test carried out in terms of 'considerations of equilibrium affecting the field *as a whole*'.

Our coherentist position differs from Quine's at both of these crucial points. First of all, it differs regarding the nature of the 'equilibrium' at issue. For Quine articulates this equilibrium analysis in essentially probabilistic terms:

> Certain statements, though *about* physical objects and not sense experience, seem peculiarly germane to sense experience—and in a selective way: some statements to some experiences, others to others. Such statements, especially germane to particular experiences, I picture as near the periphery. But in this relation of 'germaneness' I envisage nothing more than a loose association reflecting the relative likelihood, in practice, of our choosing one statement rather than another for revision in the event of recalcitrant experience.[3]

In contrast to this *probabilistic* model based on 'the relative likelihood, in practice, of our choosing one statement rather than another for revision', the coherentist validation for choosing one statement rather than another is fundamentally non-probabilistic, being based rather, in the final analysis, on *plausibilistic* considerations. Accordingly, the present position differs from Quine's in its espousal of an explicitly coherentist methodology for the requisite determination of a rational equilibrium.

Our second, and no less crucial difference from Quine lies in our refusal to combine logical with factual considerations so as to throw everything at one go into the melting-pot of simultaneous re-evaluation. We are prepared to retain the traditional distinction between logical and factual theses, and we see the issue of logical and factual truth as one to be resolved in a *separate* and *sequential* way. The validation of logical machinery—itself, to be sure, a pragmatic choice, as we see it[4]—is to be resolved first with primary reference to the non-empirical domain of mathematical, semantical, and logical considerations. The fundamental determination of logical truth is thus treated as a separable issue *prior* to the deployment of coherence considerations upon factual materials. Only *after* the mechanisms of logic are secured can we press on—guided in large measure by their means—to deploy coherence mechanisms in the factual domain. Here too, the process of legitimation is also seen as ultimately pragmatic, but pragmatic in a manner that invokes quite different objectives in another sphere.

This position differs from Quine's not as regards pragmatism, but as regards his deployment of it in a once-for-all evaluation. Instead, we see a two-phase, *sequential* process that—by giving priority to logic —leaves the situation in logic pretty much unaffected by subsequent developments in the factual area, and makes logic available as a *given* instrument for analysis in the factual sphere.

---

³ Op. cit., p. 43.
⁴ See N. Rescher, *Many-Valued Logic* (New York, 1970), pp. 213–35.

To be sure, even this break-up of the process of critical reappraisal and revalidation of our cognitive methodology into two stages—though more complex than the comprehensive, all-at-once inquiry envisaged by Quine in the initial passage—is still an oversimplification. For our division into two sequential stages has proceeded in the timeless present characteristic of most methodological discussion, and has left the aspect of historical process entirely out of account. But in fact at any given juncture we have both a logic for the conduct of our abstract reasoning and a scientific organon for the securing of empirical facts. And the process of rational validation and assessment is presumably of a cyclic structure. We may well test the capacity of our in-hand logic to systematize efficiently and effectively our total body of knowledge (in the formal and factual areas alike), with the result that this logic itself may be sharpened and revised—and this done in some measure with a view to 'the empirical facts'. (Note that this process itself will call for the use of logical machinery —be it the old one or, perhaps hypothetically, the new one to which we are conjecturally inclined.) And we will then presumably deploy this 'improved' logic in reappraising our methodological resources for empirical cognition. The result will then be the reaching of a new stage, parallel to the initial situation, with both a logic and a scientific organon as mechanism for the provision of factual know-ledge once more in hand as 'given' basis. And now a further iteration of the whole process can get under way. The over-all structure of this iterative process is not merely sequential but essentially cyclic. But the critical fact remains that a logic of some sort is indispensably requisite at each stage of the process, whereas the validation of a logic itself may or may not involve a reference to factual issues—since its basis of reference could in principle be limited to the domain of the formal sciences alone. Thus while the over-all structure of epistemic validation may well be cyclic, *at each stage* it remains sequential, with the issues of the logical machinery of inference and contradiction enjoying a certain priority of fundamentality.

There are very general and fundamental reasons for holding that some such sequential procedure to provide the normative standards of logic seems eminently desirable and even necessary. Think of the very structure of Quine's conception of a network of propositions structured in 'a loose association reflecting the relative likelihood, in practice, of our choosing one statement rather than another for revision in the event of recalcitrant experience'. Two considerations leap to mind:

(1) How in the absence of *given* logical standards, can one possibly even begin to determine what sorts of experiences are to count as 'recalcitrant'? What—other than logic—is to tell us that a *conflict* has come about with the result that 'revision' among various believed statements is in order?

(2) What of the 'relative likelihood in practice' of a choice between conflicting statements? Is this to be a purely *descriptive* matter

—a matter of the sociology of knowledge in various human communities of thinkers? Are we concerned merely descriptively with what people *will in fact* be disposed to choose or are we not rather concerned *normatively* with what—under the epistemic circumstances—they *ought* to be disposed to choose? For epistemological purposes, it is clearly the issue of normative appraisal that is crucial, and this imperatively calls for a deployment of logical machinery. Without logic to guide us we might conceivably be in a position to describe how people do reason, but we are muzzled on the topic of how they ought to reason so as to resolve belief-conflicts.

The point is that a pragmatic analysis regarding the internal adequacy of what Quine calls 'the totality of our so-called knowledge or beliefs' is in principle not feasible unless logical mechanisms already lie to hand for our guidance. And this is why an intrinsic advantage accrues quite as a matter of general principle to any multi-stage procedure of validation such as that envisaged here. By validating logical truths at the outset of the epistemological journey we assume their subsequent availability to provide the required guidance at later junctures.

Yet, while refusing to accept Quine's rejection of the distinction between truths of reason (i.e. logical truths) and truths of fact (i.e. empirical truths), we do endorse his comprehensive pragmatism. But we deploy this pragmatism at the methodological level rather than at the level of statements or classes of statements. And we resolve the problem of method in two phases, setting out first to validate the mechanisms of logic, and then to validate the coherence analysis as the standard of factual knowledge. And as we see it, two very different validation processes are at issue here, processes which—over-all conformity to the pragmatic strategy apart—actually have little or no immediate connection with one another.

To summarize: The pragmatism of Quine's 'Two Dogmas' differs from that of the present book in three crucial respects:

(1) Quine's pragmatism resembles its Jamesian predecessor in that it addresses itself directly to the allocation of truth-values to statements. It is accordingly a *propositional* pragmatism, rather than a *methodological* pragmatism like that of the present work, which applies the pragmatic standard to the validation of methods instead of the verification of propositions.

(2) Quine's programme envisages a *probabilistic* model by which the pragmatic 'germaneness' to sensation is determined through 'the relative likelihood, in practice, of our choosing [to accept statements]'. Our present approach sees the probabilistic model of statement-assessment as one possibility among alternatives which specially include the plausibilistically coherentist strategy.

(3) Quine treats the process of pragmatic analysis as a comprehensive evaluation of the *totality* of knowledge claims within the scope of one single all-comprising assessment, and specifically one which refuses to admit any differential status to the formal and the empirical sciences. Our own theory envisages a multistage process, within each phase of which the logical and the factual sectors are kept separate and treated differently, although, to be sure, there can be feed-back effects going across sector boundaries as one moves from one stage to the next.

BIBLIOGRAPHY

This bibliography concentrates its focus more or less directly upon the coherence theory of truth proper. For a fuller survey of references to the wider idealistic tradition within whose setting this theory was primarily developed, see the bibliography (prepared by J. Bayley and H. Heidelberger) appended to A. C. Ewing, *The Idealist Tradition* (Glencoe, Ill.; 1957).

I. *The German Originators of the Coherence Theory*

HEGEL, G. W. F. (1770–1831)

The Logic of Hegel, tr. by W. Wallace (2 vols., Oxford, 1892 2nd. edn. of vol. 2, 1894). [This is the so-called 'Shorter Logic' which forms the first part of the *Encyclopedia of the Philosophical Sciences*.]

The Science of Logic, tr. by W. H. Johnston and L. G. Struthers, 2 vols. (London, 1929).

LOTZE, R. H. (1817–81)

Logik (Leipzig, 1874), tr. by B. Bosanquet in his edition of *Lotze's System of Philosophy* (Oxford, 1884).

II. *Anglo-American Idealistic Exponents of the Coherence Theory*

GREEN, T. H. (1836–1882)

The Works of Thomas Hill Green, ed. by R. L. Nettleship (London, 1885–8, 3 vols.).

BRADLEY, F. H. (1846–1924)

Appearance and Reality (London, 1893; 2nd edn., Oxford, 1897; paperback edn. with an introduction by Wollheim, 1969). [See chs. 15 and 24.]

Collected Essays (2 vols., Oxford, 1935; reissue 1970).

Essays on Truth and Reality (Oxford, 1914). [See chs. 7 and 11.]

The Principles of Logic (2 vols., London, 1883; 2nd edn. 1922).

BOSANQUET, B. (1848–1923)

Knowledge and Reality (London, 1885).

Logic, or the Morphology of Knowledge (3 vols., London, 1888; 2nd edn., 1911).

'Contradiction and Reality', *Mind*, vol. 15 (1906).

Implication and Linear Inference (London, 1920).

The Principle of Individuality and Value (London, 1927).

ROYCE, J. (1855–1916)

The Religious Aspect of Philosophy (Boston, Mass., 1885). [See esp. ch. X, 'On the Possibility of Error'.]

The World and the Individual (2 vols., New York, 1901, 1902).

Logical Essays, ed. by D. S. Robinson (Dubuque, 1951).

JOACHIM, H. H. (1868–1938)

The Nature of Truth (London, 1906). [See esp. ch. III, 'Truth as Coherence'.]

Logical Studies (London, 1948).

BLANSHARD, B. (1892–)

The Nature of Thought (2 vols., London, 1939). [See vol. 2, chs. 25–7.]

Reason and Goodness (London, 1961; The Gifford Lectures for 1952–3).

MORRIS, C. R. (1898–)

Idealistic Logic: A Study of Its Aim, Method and Achievement (London, 1933). [See esp. ch. X, 'The Coherence Theory of Truth'.]

EWING, A. C. (1899–)

Idealism: A Critical Survey (London, 1934). [See esp. ch. 5.]

Review of Blanshard's 'The Nature of Thought', *Mind*, 53 (1944), 75–85.

'The Correspondence Theory of Truth' in idem, *Non-Linguistic Philosophy* (London, 1968), pp. 193–204.

III. *Earlier Critics of the Idealistic Coherentists*

BROAD, C. D.

'Mr. Bradley on Truth and Reality', *Mind*, 23 (1914), 349–70. [A review of Bradley's *Essays on Truth and Reality*.]

COOK WILSON, J.

Statement and Inference (2 vols., Oxford, 1926; reprinted 1969).

DEWEY, J.

Studies in Logical Theory (Chicago, Ill., 1903).

Logic: The Theory of Inquiry (New York, 1938).

JAMES, W.

Pragmatism: A New Name for Some Old Ways of Thinking (New York, 1907).

The Meaning of Truth: A Sequel to 'Pragmatism' (New York, 1909).

RUSSELL, B.

Philosophical Essays (London, 1910). [See ch. 6.]

The Problems of Philosophy (Oxford, 1912; 2nd edn. 1967).

'On Verification', *Proceedings of the Aristotelian Society*, 38 (1937–8), 1–20.

An Inquiry into Meaning and Truth (London, 1940). [See ch. 10.]

STOUT, G. F.

'Bradley on Truth and Falsity', *Mind*, 34 (1925), 39–54; reprinted in *Studies in Philosophy and Psychology* (London, 1930).

IV. *The Positivist Version of the Coherence Theory and its Critics*

AYER, A. J.

'The Criterion of Truth', *Analysis*, 3 (1935–6), 28–32; reprinted in M. Macdonald (ed.), *Philosophy and Analysis* (Oxford, 1954). [Attacks the positivist coherence theory.]

AYER, A. J. (*cont.*):

'Verification and Experience', *Proceedings of the Aristotelian Society*, 37 (1936–7), 137–56.

The Concept of a Person and Other Essays (London, 1963).

CARNAP, R.

'Über Protokollsätze', *Erkenntnis*, 3 (1932), 215–34.

HEMPEL, C. G.

'On the Logical Positivists' Theory of Truth', *Analysis*, 2 (1935), 49–59. [A historical survey of the controversy which espouses a form of the coherence theory.]

'Some Remarks on "Facts" and Propositions', *Analysis*, 2 (1935), 93–6. [A reply to Schlick's 1935 paper.]

JOERGENSEN, J.

The Development of Logical Empiricism (Chicago, Ill., 1951; *Encyclopedia of Unified Science*, vol. 2, no. 9).

NEURATH, O.

'Soziologie im Physikalismus', *Erkenntnis*, 2 (1931/2), 393–431; tr. in A. J. Ayer (ed.), *Logical Positivism* (Glencoe, Minn., 1959), 282–317.

'Protokollsätze', *Erkenntnis*, 3 (1932), 204–14; tr. as 'Protocol Sentences' in A. J. Ayer (ed.), *Logical Positivism* (Glencoe, Minn., 1959), 199–208. [Gives the initial statement of the positivist theory.]

'Radikaler Physikalismus und "wirkliche Welt"', *Erkenntnis*, 4 (1933), 346–62. [A reply to Schlick's 1933 paper.]

SCHEFFLER, I.

Science and Subjectivity (New York, 1967). [Ch. 5 on 'Epistemology and Objectivity' gives a detailed and interesting account of the Neurath/ Schlick controversy.]

SCHLICK, M.

'Ueber das Fundament der Erkenntnis', *Erkenntnis*, 4 (1934), 79 ff.; tr. as 'The Foundation of Knowledge' in A. J. Ayer (ed.), *Logical Positivism* (Glencoe, Minn., 1959), 209–27. [A critique of Neurath's 1932 paper.]

'Facts and Propositions', *Analysis*, 2 (1935), 65–70; reprinted in M. Mac-Donald (ed.), *Philosophy and Analysis* (Oxford, 1954). [A critique of the positivist coherence theory, addressed especially to Hempel's 1935 paper on the theory of truth.]

V. *Recent Expositions and Criticisms of the Coherence Theory*

ARMOUR, L.

The Concept of Truth (Assen, 1969). [See ch. 3, 'Coherence Theories'.]

KHATCHADOURIAN, H.

The Coherence Theory of Truth: A Critical Evaluation (Beirut, 1961). [A critical exposition and assessment of the Bradley–Bosanquet–Ewing–Blanshard tradition.]

LEWIS, C. I.

An Analysis of Knowledge and Valuation (La Salle, Ill., 1962). [See especially ch. 11.]

WHITE, A. R.

'Coherence Theory of Truth' in P. Edwards (ed.), *The Encyclopedia of Philosophy*, vol. 2 (New York, 1967), pp. 130–3. [An expository and evaluative article.] Reprinted in White's *Truth* (Garden City, Kans., 1970).

WOLLHEIM, R.

Bradley (London, 1959). [See ch. 4.]

WOOZLEY, A. D.

Theory of Knowledge (London, 1949). [See pp. 146–69.]

NAME INDEX

SUBJECT INDEX